GARLAND STUDIES IN

Entrepreneurship

Stuart Bruchey
University of Maine
General Editor

A Garland Series

Creating an American Institution
The Merchandising Genius of J.C. Penney

By Mary Elizabeth Curry

Garland Publishing, Inc.
New York & London
1993

Library of Congress Cataloging-in-Publication Data

Curry, Mary E. (Mary Elizabeth), 1947–
    Creating an American institution : the merchandising genius of J.C. Penney / Mary
Elizabeth Curry.
        p.   cm. — (Garland studies in entrepreneurship)
    "A Garland series."
    Includes bibliographical references and index.
    ISBN 0–8153–0991–0 (alk. paper)
    1. Penney, J. C. (James Cash), 1875–1971. 2. Merchants—United States—Biography.
3. Retail trade—United States—History. 4. Stores, Retail—United States—History.
5. J. C. Penney Co. I. Title. II. Series.
HF5465.U64P463 1993
381'.45'00092—dc20   92–42823
                                                                              CIP

Printed on acid-free, 250-year-life paper

Manufactured in the United States of America

TO MY PARENTS

". . . Genius deals with the possible, creates new combinations, discovers new laws, and acts from an insight into principles. . . ."

Selection from *A Manual of American Literature* by N.K. Royse, textbook used in Hamilton Public High School, 1892-1893

CONTENTS

Illustrations appear following page 158

PREFACE

My study of J.C. Penney's life was made in two stages. The first part was completed in 1980 as my doctoral dissertation; it started with Penney's ancestors in the 1700s and ended in 1935 when Penney was 60 years old. The second part, which covers the years 1935 to 1971, was completed at the publisher's request. The Epilogue contains information about Penney's legacy at the time of the J.C. Penney Company's 90th anniversary in 1992.

J.C. Penney continued working on the company's behalf and was active in philanthropic activities until his death at age 95 in February 1971. He served in an advisory position at the J.C. Penney Company as Chairman of the Board from 1917 to 1946, 1950 to 1958, and was a member of the Board of Directors from 1913 to 1971. Penney's interest in the company's progress after 1935 is documented in two chapters, "King of the Soft Goods" and "Main Street Merchant to Shopping Mall Anchor." The company Penney founded in 1902 had changed in many respects by the time he died in 1971. These changes and Penney's reaction to them, particularly the dramatic end of the company's cash only policy in 1958, are included in the new chapters.

Penney was "prodigiously active"; from age 60 to age 95, he wrote books, gave lectures and travelled hundreds of thousands of miles visiting stores, attending company conventions and participating in philanthropic related events. He enjoyed his work and hoped to live to be 100 years old. His life story inspired many people to try to accomplish more in their own lives; he believed in hard work and the Golden Rule. What set Penney apart from many other "merchant princes" was his belief in sharing profits with the people who helped produce them. It was Penney's one-third partnership plan that first made me curious about him 20 years ago.

J.C. Penney came to my attention in September 1972, one and a half years after he died. I was working at the National Portrait

Gallery, Smithsonian Institution, when it acquired a portrait of Penney. I completed the biographical research required to include him in the files of the Catalog of American Portraits. Of the hundreds of portrait subjects I had researched, Penney's life impressed me as being the most inspiring and instructive.

In 1975, as part of my course work at The American University, Washington, D.C., for a doctorate in American Intellectual History, I wrote a paper on Penney's business philosophy. That project increased my interest and raised several questions. The use of partnerships to expand the company, the important role of Penney's mentors, Thomas M. Callahan and William Guy Johnson, and the small town, western origins of the giant chain of dry goods stores made Penney's career worth investigating in greater detail, if materials documenting those years existed.

Locating Penney's personal and business papers was the first step. Obtaining permission from the J.C. Penney Company, Inc., in December 1975 to use their Historical File in New York City made the biography possible. The Company archivist, E. Virginia Mowry, a former history teacher and personnel administrator who had been Penney's executive secretary, had recently organized a vast amount of material saved by him. After removing papers from cartons, drawers and trunks in a storage room on the 45th floor of the New York Central Office, she catalogued Penney's records. The materials filled 23 file drawers and several cabinets. The collection's mixture of business artifacts, business and personal letters, published and unpublished company records was the basis of my study.

Additional information was obtained by extensive local history research and from interviews. With the encouragement of my dissertation committee, Dr. Thomas V. DiBacco, Dr. Albro Martin and Dr. C.C. Goen, I began part-time research in June 1976 and full-time research a year later. Between 1977 and 1979 my research took me from the rolling hills and rivers of Kentucky, Illinois and Missouri to small farming and mining towns in the Rocky Mountain states, to Salt Lake City and New York City, to Penney Farms, Florida, the site of his 1920s model farm community and a retirement home for ministers, and to the empty lot where Penney's elegant Miami Beach home once stood.

My visits, research and Penney's extraordinary records inspired me to try to recreate some of the excitement and adventure he experienced. I also corresponded with and met many people who gave me valuable information; their interest was equally inspiring.

Describing Penney's Baptist and Populist roots, the early Golden Rule Merchants' retailing system, and the step-by-step creation of what became an American institution and household word by the mid-1920s are the principal aims of the biography. Many people influenced Penney. His ability to grasp the essence of others' ideas, implement them and create new combinations explains much of his success. The creation of an influential company publication, *The Dynamo*, in 1917 and a complete business training correspondence course by 1921 are two examples of Penney's foresight and perception.

The solid foundation built in the World War I era led to rapid expansion during the 1920s. In late 1913 they had 48 stores; in 1930 there were 1,400 stores. By selling low-priced, good quality merchandise the Company created millions of loyal customers. A sophisticated, complex system enabled the chain to provide direct, simple service to its customers. How Penney used his personal fortune in the 1920s, survived financial disaster in the early 1930s, and continued to work on the company's behalf until his death in 1971 are important parts of the study.

All these events define Penney's particular form of genius and show how a young man raised in the small town of Hamilton, Missouri, and possessing few monetary resources, became one of America's six greatest merchants. The story of Penney's legendary career has been told before, but this study documents these events for the first time and adds valuable information to his story. Penney's accomplishments become more understandable. His story may also be useful to entrepreneurs in developing countries. Penney believed that effective systems of mass distribution could solve worldwide problems of poverty and unemployment.

ACKNOWLEDGMENTS

I wish to express my sincere appreciation to the many people who assisted me in preparing my biography of J.C. Penney in 1980 and in 1992. To complete the second part of the biography covering the years 1935 to 1971, I gratefully acknowledge the assistance of William M. Batten, former president, chief executive officer and chairman of the board of the J.C. Penney Company who gave me valuable information during two interviews in 1986. Mary Frances Penney Wagley and Carol Marie Penney Guyer graciously agreed to meet with me and discuss their father's life. Their great interest in the family's history encouraged me to continue my research. Clifford D. Anderson, a retired J.C. Penney Company executive who had travelled with J.C. Penney in the 1960s, also provided valuable information and encouragement during several meetings since 1986.

I also wish to thank Joan Gosnell, archivist and company historian at the JCPenney Archives, and her assistant Gary Long. They obtained photographs for me and answered many questions that arose during the final weeks of preparing the book. Helen Curran, who works for the Penney family, provided copies of news clippings saved by Mrs. J.C. Penney and answered many questions. Anne Romasco, managing director of the James C. Penney Foundation, provided information about the foundation's history and current activities. Jack Sheaffer, photographer, The Masonic Service Association and CBS News Archives also provided valuable information.

James Mintz, president of IGI (The Investigative Group, Inc.) allowed me to take time off from my investigative duties to complete the biography. His interest and encouragement and that of William D. Courtney and Larry Tell of IGI are greatly appreciated. Paul Walker, MIS Director at IGI, provided valuable assistance.

Martha Murphy's enthusiasm and word processing skills made the final weeks of manuscript preparation much easier. Her careful editing of the manuscript and many suggestions have been invaluable. Catherine Bishop's careful proofreading is greatly appreciated. Christopher Curry, Joseph Curry and Monica Curry have all made outstanding efforts to read, edit, and proofread the manuscript, and I will always be grateful for their help. Over the last ten years several friends have encouraged me to complete my biography of J.C. Penney. I want to thank JoAnna and Martin H. Levenglick, Nathaniel J. Bickford, Peggy Bastable, James R. Alexander and Diana and Donald Macsuga for their interest and persistence.

The original 1980 acknowledgments are included to express my continued appreciation for the help I received during the first stage of the biography. To complete my doctoral dissertation, I was helped by many kind, knowledgeable people from coast to coast. People in small towns, city professionals and retired J.C. Penney Company store managers were interested in helping me obtain information for my study of J.C. Penney.

First, I am grateful to The American University for allowing me to keep my original advisors, Dr. Thomas V. DiBacco, Dr. Albro Martin and Dr. C.C. Goen. Since Dr. Martin became the Editor of *Business History Review* at Harvard University's Graduate School of Business Administration and Dr. Goen was a member of Wesley Theological Seminary, I feel very fortunate that they were happy to serve on my committee. My deepest gratitude goes to Dr. DiBacco, Dean for Faculty Affairs and Professor of Business Administration, for assuming chairmanship of my dissertation and for encouraging me over several years. Dr. Martin's original support of my proposal and his constant interest have been inspiring. Dr. Goen's interest and careful proofreading of the first draft are most appreciated. Dr. Charles McLaughlin, my first advisor in the History Department, agreed to join my committee. His observations were, as usual, perceptive and helpful.

I am deeply grateful to the J.C. Penney Company, Inc., for allowing me to use their Historical File and other records that made my dissertation possible. I am especially grateful to E. Virginia Mowry, the Company's archivist and an expert researcher with B.A. and M.A. degrees in history and education. Miss Mowry provided materials and made many important suggestions. Ever since our first meeting in December 1975 her help has been invaluable.

I want to thank Alpha Chapter of Phi Delta Gamma at The American University for nominating me, and the national organization for awarding me their National Study Grant in July 1976. I am also very grateful to the Lincoln Educational Foundation of New York City for selecting me to receive a John E. Rovensky Fellowship in Business and Economic History in the spring of 1978.

Among the many people who provided information were retired Company store managers. Their enthusiasm and interest revealed how much they enjoyed working for the Company. I interviewed Harry J. Burns, Vern Crayne, Earl D. Faulkner, Charles Ferguson, Donald F. Foote, Harold G. Gross, Ray M. Jenkins, Phil Morgan, Paul Murphy, Ted Schmidt and Maurice J. Wright. With the exception of Mr. Murphy, they are located in the western states where the Company originated. They all made valuable observations besides answering my questions. Mr. Foote corresponded with me for several months before I met him in Colorado. His ties to the Company date to the World War I era. The managers and their wives extended gracious hospitality to me and my parents when we visited them. This was most thoughtful of them, and is deeply appreciated.

Relatives provided recollections and family history that clarified many details about Penney's early life and about the Golden Rule Merchants' story. My sincere appreciation goes to R.E. Penney, a nephew of J.C. Penney, for his detailed remembrances of life with Mr. Penney in the World War I era. His information and interest were very encouraging. Mr. Penney was also a retired Company manager, as was his younger brother, E.R. Penney, who was equally interested in my project.

Ina Ramsay Fox with her daughter, Betty Howlett, taped Mrs. Fox's recollections of the early Golden Rule Merchants in response to my questionnaire. Mr. and Mrs. C.H. Ramsay, Jr., and Greg Ramsay of Greeley, Colorado, were pleased to provide information and extended their hospitality when I visited their home. Mrs. George B. Miller is the daughter of C.E. Dimmitt who was active in both the Golden Rule Syndicate and J.C. Penney Company. She sent me valuable information, and piece by piece the history of the early merchants emerged. A.B. Peak, a niece of Berta Hess Penney, sent me information about the Hess family, and give me a tour of Penney family sites in Salt Lake City.

When I was in Chillicothe, Illinois, I received assistance from several people. Betty Uphoff and her entire family made my visit there pleasant and most useful. John Ford, managing editor of the *Chillicothe Bulletin*, allowed me to use their newspaper files. Thomas Hayden of Chillicothe, a relative of Thomas M. Callahan, and John Hood and Emmett Hood of New York City, relatives of Celia Callahan, supplied much of my information about the early years of Penney's most important mentor, Tom Callahan. The Hood family collection of photographs and business cards was most useful. Other people who helped me were Regina Armitage, librarian of the Chillicothe Township Free Public Library, and several long-time residents who tried to answer questions about the Callahan family and Celia Callahan's store.

Mary Ann Owens and her husband, Rick, made me feel at home in Humansville, Missouri. She answered many questions I had about the Barnetts and the small Ozark town. In Longmont, Colorado, I received information from many people. They included Mrs. Frank McDonough, Mrs. Donald Estes, Dorothy Large, Bea Malchow, Alberta M. Marlatt, and B.L. "Billy" Boyles. In Wyoming, I was assisted by Ida Wozny and Jim Donahue at the Archives and Public Records Division, and appreciated the interest shown by Katherine A. Halverson, Director of the Historical Research and Publications Department. In Kemmerer, Donald Kominsky, publisher of the *Kemmerer Gazette*, allowed me to use old newspaper files, and David L. Harvey, the J.C. Penney Company store manager, gave me a tour of the town. Evelyn Clark, librarian of the Lincoln County Library in Kemmerer, was interested in my work. In Evanston, Denice Wheeler was most helpful and provided background information about Evanston. In Ogden, Utah, at the Weber County Library, I received careful assistance from Jean Christensen. Librarians in Greeley and Fort Collins public libraries were of valuable assistance, too, as were the librarians I wrote to in Idaho.

In Hamilton, Missouri, Marguerite Overstreet was my guide to Penney's boyhood home and farms. Her long-time acquaintance with J.C. Penney was of great assistance. Mr. and Mrs. Dean Hales were most gracious to me and my parents. I also appreciate the interest shown by Colonel Leonard Orr, Dolores Humphry and Marion Ridings. In Lawrenceburg, Kentucky, Ann McWilliams of the Anderson County Public Library provided information on the Paxton and Penney families on very short notice. At Penney Farms, Florida, Dr. Paul P. Hagen discussed the history of Penney Retirement Community with me, and Maude Coker kindly loaned me some of her information.

At the State Historical Society of Missouri in Columbia, I was aided by Mrs. Oliver Howard, Librarian, and Alma Vaughan and Debra Duffen of the Newspaper Library. Dr. John A. Brennan, Cassandra Volpe and Laurie Simmons were most helpful when I did research at the Western Historical Collection of the University of Colorado at Boulder. I received valuable newspaper materials from The Western History Research Center of the University of Wyoming, courtesy of Dr. Gene M. Gressley. The Research Facilities Office and Stack and Reader Division of the Library of Congress allowed me to use materials in the library stacks on many occasions. Their courtesy is most appreciated. At the New York Public Library, I was assisted by librarians in the American History Division, the Map Division and the Local History & Genealogy Division. I especially appreciate receiving permission from the Research Libraries Administrative Office for working space in the Typing Room. Many old volumes I needed were located at the Annex, and I also received valuable assistance there.

I received assistance from Mrs. Nelson M. Vaughan of The Hill School, Pottstown, Pennsylvania, Sylvia Saltzman, of the Field Library, Inc. of Peekskill, New York, and Fran Bunce, of the Bryn Mawr Alumnae Office.

I met and corresponded with so many helpful people over four years that doubtless I have inadvertently overlooked some people who kindly assisted me, and I express my gratitude to them also. Finally, I am indebted for many reasons to my wonderful parents whose interest and financial support allowed me to work on my dissertation full time. I am especially grateful to Martha Murphy for her careful typing and enthusiasm while preparing the final copy of the biography.

Despite the help and support I have received in preparing the 1980 doctoral dissertation and 1992 book, I alone take responsibility for the interpretation of facts and their accuracy.

Creating an American Institution

PIONEER PREACHERS

Like narrow ribbons, farm-to-market roads divide northwestern Missouri's rolling countryside into a brown and green patchwork. In summer the windswept acres of Caldwell County, seventy miles from Kansas City, have an aura of tranquility: silos, barns and white frame houses sit clustered on hilltops; below, creeks wind zigzag paths through corn fields and pastures. Pink and blue wild flowers dot tangled grasses growing by roads and fences, and only the roar of an occasional truck, scattering gravel and dust in its wake, interrupts the murmur of crickets and cows.[1]

In contrast, a little over a century ago shrill whistles from daily freight and passenger trains pierced the countryside; farmers drove wagon teams over rutted roads to small towns to deliver their produce and do their shopping. However, many farm families became discouraged as they harvested less and less profitable crops from mortgaged fields. Over-expansion and declining prices caused severe problems, and a series of depressions from 1873 to 1896 hurt business, labor and agriculture.[2]

But intellectual, social and economic advances also occurred after 1870 as the nation was rapidly transformed by urbanization, industrialization and immigration. One development often taken for granted, the growth of mass distribution, made reasonably priced mass-produced items available to America's rapidly expanding population. As the industrial age emerged, mass distribution by perceptive entrepreneurs began improving the average American's standard of living.[3]

James Cash Penney, Jr., founder of the J.C. Penney Company, was born near Hamilton in rural Caldwell County in 1875.[4] He was the seventh of twelve children of James Cash Penney, Sr., and his wife, Mary Frances Paxton. Caldwell County, with its combination of farm and small town activities, was J.C. Penney's home for almost twenty-two years. His dream to be in business for himself originated

3

here. Penney's heritage of self-reliance, hard work and religious faith had a profound influence on him.[5] The family saga began in Virginia before the American Revolution.

John Penney, great-grandfather of J.C. Penney, was born November 10, 1759. The Penneys, originally from England, had been living in Virginia and North Carolina since the mid-1600s. In 1777 John Penney became a private in the 2nd Virginia State Regiment in Portsmouth. His regiment joined General Washington's Army at Valley Forge, Pennsylvania. In 1780, after fighting in the battles of Monmouth and Stony Point, Penney received an honorable discharge. With the North Carolina militia he then participated in the crucial battles of Camden and Guilford Courthouse. Fifty years later the federal government granted him an $80 a year pension for his war time service.[6]

Two years after the war Penney married Frances White, a daughter of Barrett White and Elizabeth Starke of Hanover County, Virginia.[7] That same year, 1785, he was one of sixty people converted to the Baptist faith at Chickahominy Church. The Hanover County church "refreshing" was conducted by Reuben Ford and William Webber, pioneer Baptist ministers, and under their guidance Penney became a minister.[8]

The disestablishment of the Virginia Anglican Church in 1785 was welcome news to Baptists, believers in complete separation of church and state. Membership in the new faith, however, had been growing ever since the American Revolution. Independent churches, adult baptism, receiving God's grace directly, salvation by grace and strict obedience to God's Word were their most important tenets. They believed preachers were called by God.[9]

The Penneys remained in Virginia for almost a decade. According to Hanover tax assessments, Penney owned four slaves, five horses and two "wheels" or carriages.[10] By 1792 he held title to 1,100 acres in Kentucky including a 100-acre land warrant from Virginia for military service. The young family started moving west in the mid-1790s, and in December 1796 Penney was a minister in Campbell County.[11]

From southwestern Virginia they followed the Wilderness Road through Cumberland Gap to north central Kentucky where they settled by Salt River.[12] The head waters of Salt River, near Harrodsburg, were one of the new state's three most populated areas.[13] The future Anderson County section Penney selected, though, was sixteen miles north of Harrodsburg in an unsettled area just west of the Kentucky River. Licking River property in northeastern Kentucky, which he had owned since the early 1780s, may have been sold or traded for this land.

Penney and brothers-in-law Philip White and Robert Blackwell created farms in the wooded, rolling countryside. With neighbors they formed a small community and established a church.[14] On February 3, 1798, John Penney helped found Salt River Baptist Church and was pastor of the congregation until his death.[15] Like many Baptist churches, Salt River had strict rules. Intoxication, attendance at parties where fiddles were played, working on crops on Sunday, wearing earrings and joining Masonic Lodges or other secret organizations were forbidden.[16] Under Penney's leadership, Salt River Church became the "Mother Church" for Baptists in that area. As the population grew he helped organize other small churches like Old Goshen, Fox Creek and Little Flock. In John Taylor's famous *History of Ten Baptist Churches*, published in 1826, Penney was described as a respectable minister from Virginia and was later considered one of the most active of the early preachers.[17]

Penney was host to an 1811 meeting of delegates from forty-one Baptist churches. Total membership in the "Long Run Association" of central Kentucky was 2,925.[18] By 1826 Salt River congregation alone had 185 members, and nearby congregations Penney had started also thrived. That year delegates from five local churches, representing almost 600 members, held their annual meeting at Glenn's Creek in adjacent Woodford County. Penney, sixty-seven, was convention moderator, gave the important Introductory Sermon and was selected to preach next year's sermon.[19] The farmer-minister, who delivered concise persuasive sermons, was a small man with keen blue eyes and a Roman nose. Penney's straight carriage and snuff-colored cloth coats styled in a military fashion were symbolic of his long, successful leadership of rural Kentucky Baptists.[20]

Anderson County was created in 1827 and Lawrenceburg, two miles north of Salt River Church, became the county seat and center of commerce for the hemp, tobacco and corn growing region.[21] John Penney, his sons and neighbors already owned town lots and buildings; they helped organize another Baptist Church.[22]

Ever since 1816, however, Baptists in England and America had engaged in heated arguments over scriptural interpretation.[23] Pamphlets, newsletters and magazines devoted to minute investigations of text meanings were published and controversy spread. Campbellism, Daniel Parker and Andrew Fuller were well-known names in the discussions.[24] Individual congregations in central Kentucky, though, did not divide until the mid-1830s.[25]

Penneys and Paxtons followed a "strict" scriptural interpretation and did not approve of missionary organizations ("purse-proud societies"), training or paying ministers, and teaching by Sunday Schools. Since they upheld early church traditions, they were known as Old School or Primitive Baptists. Calvinistic, independent, sincere but backward-looking, many Old School Baptist congregations flourished across the country through the nineteenth century.[26]

The Penney family lost their patriarch in a cholera epidemic in June 1833. John Penney's estate included farmland west of Lawrenceburg, a two-story brick house and a blacksmith shop. There were five surviving children; Frances Penney lived until 1839.[27] Eli Penney, born April 6, 1799, and one of John Penney's six sons, became a staunch Old School Baptist minister. Baptized by his father in 1811, he began preaching in 1833.[28] John Penney's contributions as a soldier, settler and renowned preacher inspired his children to make religion the focal point of their lives, and through education and leadership maintain the family's status.

Today, the once isolated pioneer settlement has vanished; a golf course, modern subdivisions and stores line roads near Lawrenceburg. Salt River Church, however, was recently restored by the community. Built in 1842 to replace the original log church and surrounded by row after row of thin, weather-beaten tombstones, the one-story rectangular building had three doors.[29] As was customary, one entrance was for men, one for women and one for slaves. Slavery had existed in Kentucky since its settlement and was accepted by many Anderson County farmers including Penneys and Paxtons. Penneys from the Lawrenceburg area fought and died for state's rights and the Confederacy.[30] The Civil War, however, caused a split among John Penney's descendants.

Unlike comfortable Kentucky society, life on the Missouri frontier was harsher and may have led to the family division. Eli Penney moved his family to Missouri during 1841. That October he paid $3,000 for 375 acres in western Caldwell County.[31] He may have heard about the property from an Anderson County neighbor, Richard H. Paxton, who had owned land in the northwest central Missouri county since 1839.[32]

Caldwell County, twenty-four by eighteen miles, was open for settlement due to a recent exodus of Mormon pioneers. Established in 1836, it became the center of a violent controversy when members of the new Church of Jesus Christ of Latter Day Saints moved northeast from Independence, Missouri, to build a community on its fertile land. By 1838 its population had grown from a few scattered pioneers to almost 5,000.[33]

The Mormons began building a Temple at Far West, the county seat. But the new settlers had to abandon their Temple, farms and houses after the tragic "Mormon War" in 1838. Forced to leave Missouri that winter, they moved east to Nauvoo, Illinois, and started another community. Caldwell's population dropped to about 1,000, but increased as word spread that vacant houses and farms were available.[34] During 1841, the journey of about 700 miles from central Kentucky to northern Missouri took several months.[35] The only way to reach landlocked Caldwell was by river and across open prairie after reaching Camden on the Missouri River.

Settled in his new home, Eli, forty-two years old, wrote to the *Signs of the Times,* an Old School Baptist publication sent around the country first from New Vernon and then Middletown, New York. He said, "I have left my birthplace, a place of refinement, for an unsettled, open, rich prairie county, in the general; yet I trust this forest will blossom as the rose."[36] He went on to state his life goal: "I am determined by the grace of God to be unlike the nations of the earth surrounding us, and to be religiously of a separate and distinct people."[37] As a pioneer settler, articulate preacher and writer, his life was strikingly similar to his father's.

Slowly but steadily Caldwell's population increased. Demand for flour, bacon, corn, horses and oxen during the California Gold Rush increased residents' wealth. By 1850 there were over 2,000 residents; in 1860 there were almost 5,000.[38] Farmers like Eli owned approximately 300 to 400 acres. Less than five percent, including Eli, also owned a slave family to help run their farms.[39]

Far West was abandoned and a new county seat named Kingston was created near the center of Caldwell. On a broad tree-covered hill above Shoal Creek, Kingston with its imposing court house and brick townhouses embodied the founders' hopes for a prosperous future.[40]

Eli, an experienced and respected preacher, joined nearby Log Creek Church, an Old School Baptist Church started in 1840.[41] A few miles south of his home, the meetinghouse was nestled among Caldwell's rolling hills where thick grass and colorful wild flowers grew during spring and summer; in winter ice and snow froze the land. His arrival strengthened the fledgling congregation, and by 1847 he was their sole minister. Similar to Kentucky Old School Baptist churches, strict rules prevailed.[42] Since contact with other churches was limited, Eli stayed in touch with distant friends by subscribing and writing letters to religious magazines like *Signs of the Times*. In well-written, elaborately phrased articles he discussed predestination and God's redeeming power. Both he and Polly enjoyed reading letters, sermons and editorials in the small publication.[43]

He had married Polly Burris in 1821 in Lawrenceburg, and their ninth child, James Cash Penney, was born December 29, 1841, in Caldwell.[44] The infant's middle name was in honor of Warren Cash, an Old School Baptist preacher and close friend. Cash, baptized by John Penney in 1799, was a highly respected traveling preacher and pastor in Hardin County, Kentucky.[45]

By 1850 Eli's real estate was valued at $10,000 and he owned eight slaves.[46] He told the census taker his occupation was "Old School Baptist Minister." In 1860 the total value of his real and personal estate, including six slaves, was $11,851.[47] His substantial estate was able to provide education and money for their children.

When James Cash Penney was an adolescent, Caldwell's rural character began changing. A railroad was to be built from Hannibal on the Mississippi River to St. Joseph, fifty miles west of Caldwell on the Missouri River. This farthest westward extension of the pre-Civil War "transportation revolution" would cross the upper portion of Caldwell and became a source of local speculation.[48] The Hannibal & St. Joseph Railroad Company received a generous 600,000 acres from Missouri to help pay for the expensive venture. It consisted of alternate square miles, 640 acre sections, for fifteen miles on both sides of the direct east-west route.[49] Enterprising Caldwell residents purchased 40 acres of cheaper federal land along the route in 1855 and platted a new town named Hamilton.[50] Albert Gallatin Davis, one of Eli's sons-in-law, was a town founder and the first resident. Eli also purchased several town lots at an auction. Unfortunately the railroad did not arrive until 1859 and town lots had little value until the mid-1860s.[51]

While county land speculation and national issues simmered, James attended Pleasant Ridge Academy in Platte County, forty-five miles southwest of Caldwell. Pleasant Ridge Male and Female College was founded in 1853 by Professor Brice W. Vineyard, son of a wealthy Platte County family.[52] When incorporated by the Missouri General Assembly in 1855, it was described as "an academy of the highest order for the education of minor males and females . . . with a library and valuable collection of philosophical, astronomical and chemical apparatus and other necessary appendages."[53]

A two-story brick building housed up to fifty female students while male students boarded with nearby families. Three miles from Weston, which was on the Missouri River and surrounded by woodland pastures, one of its features was its freedom from the "alluring distractions and frivolities of town."[54] Classes were co-ed, and tuition for a full term of forty weeks of collegiate studies was $30. The cost for primary and preparatory courses was $20 and $24. English literature and classical studies diplomas were granted and courses in natural sciences were offered.[55]

Graduation from an academy like Pleasant Ridge was for the few whose parents could afford it and who believed education was beneficial. Eli wanted his son to have more academic training than was obtainable in rural Caldwell. James C. Penney thus joined the very small percentage of mid-nineteenth-century Americans who received an advanced education.[56]

At school Penney joined the "Union Literary and Padeusian Societies." His graduation oration in June 1859 was published with other students' essays in the July issue of the school paper. The literary club's motto was "Know Thyself," and Penney's oration, titled "Earth's Benefactors," combined religion and science. His opening declaration was pure Calvinism, an important aspect of Old School Baptist beliefs: "Man, by nature is a fallen being, and inclined to evil rather than that which is good." He developed his theme by explaining, "but there have been, in every age of the world, bright exceptions who heeding the monitions of the heavenly monitor within, have, as Earth's Benefactors, toiled assiduously in endeavoring to radiate intellectual and moral light. . . ."[57] In effect, mankind's progress over the centuries was due to God's grace acting upon such luminaries as Galileo, Newton, Franklin, Luther, Calvin, Wesley, and Fulton. He concluded by proclaiming Jesus Christ to be man's greatest benefactor.[58]

In the same paper another student stated "a mere automaton" can never emerge from Pleasant Ridge with the faculty's sanction. The school's motto—"arduous labor conquers all things," the students' motto—"where there is a will there is a way," and that of the Padeusian Society, were practiced daily and guaranteed this result.[59]

James's religious character had been molded by a strict father, but self-knowledge and independent thinking increased during his academy studies. The scholarly training was agreeable to him; throughout his life he maintained an intellectual, questioning approach to problems. Penney was also exposed to many new people and new ideas. For example, in 1859 Pleasant Ridge College was directed by Dr. J.F. Bruner who, a few years later, became a Captain in the Union Army.[60]

Two years after Penney graduated the nation was torn apart by Civil War. In 1861 Missouri Governor Claiborne F. Jackson attempted secession but failed. Nonetheless he divided the state into military encampments for raising militia. In response to this call, a Caldwell secessionist force was organized in late April 1861.[61] The "Caldwell Minute Men" trained in front of the Court House at Kingston and in mid-June marched south to Lexington. The group of sixty-five, including nineteen-year-old Penney, joined the Missouri State Guard, became Company D of Colonel John T. Hughes' Regiment and participated in the battles of Carthage, Wilson's Creek and Lexington. Several men were wounded. David Thompson, Penney's brother-in-law, then became Captain of the Caldwell Company.[62]

After their six-month term of service most Caldwell men enlisted in the regular Confederate Army.[63] Penney, however, did not conform to his neighbors' and relatives' actions. He returned home, took an oath of allegiance to the Union and spent the remainder of the war teaching school in Kentucky.[64]

Kentucky was the family's ancestral home, and he also had a personal reason for moving there. Penney had recently fallen in love with an attractive first cousin from Anderson County. He escorted Mary Frances Paxton home when her visit to Caldwell was cut short by the war.[65] Among the many characteristics they shared were light brown hair and blue-gray eyes; after their marriage on September 28, 1862, the newlyweds lived near her family. Mary Frances, called Fanny, was the fifth child of Richard H. Paxton and Mildred Burris, who had a farm below Salt River. Born October 26, 1842, and raised as an Old School Baptist, she was educated at female seminaries in Bardstown and Lawrenceburg.[66]

James Paxton and Nancy Biggerhead, J.C. Penney's great-grandparents on his mother's side, had moved to central Kentucky in the early 1800s from Rockbridge, Virginia.[67] Of Scotch-Irish descent from Pennsylvania, they were farmers and a number of descendants became merchants.[68] The two Burris sisters, Polly and Mildred, grew up in adjacent Mercer County where their parents, Edmund and Frances Burris, owned a substantial farm. When the controversy over missionary societies arose they became Old School Baptist believers. Mildred married Colonel Richard Paxton in 1833, twelve years after her sister Polly had married Eli Penney.[69]

During James C. Penney's Kentucky sojourn, Penneys who died fighting on the Confederate side were hailed as heroes.[70] Confederate loyalists may have resented the Missouri newcomer, but Penney continued teaching. He involved himself in church activities, was baptized and wrote to *Signs of the Times*.[71] In a long essay, written in a language and style similar to Eli's letters, James described his rebirth as a Christian. The correspondence was featured on page one of the November 15, 1863, issue.[72]

After 1862 Union troops, using the convenient newly completed railroad, arrived in Caldwell and were stationed near Breckinridge, Hamilton and Kidder.[73] Raiding parties and bushwackers made the rolling countryside dangerous. Eli, age 64, complained to the editor of *Signs of the Times* of "this dismal war" and of indebtedness. He said he suffered from neuralgia, bronchitis and dyspepsia.[74]

In Kentucky James and Fanny began raising the first of their twelve children. Mittie and Elie were born in 1863 and 1865, but in February 1867 an infant boy died the day he was born.[75] The young couple then decided to return to Caldwell and settle near Hamilton.

By 1867 Hamilton was booming as northerners and easterners came in response to newspaper advertisements and pamphlets issued by the railroad. The response was remarkable. Caldwell's population more than doubled between 1860 and 1870, with nearly all the increase occurring after 1865. In these same years Missouri became the nation's fifth largest state in population, and the railroad network brought many changes in social and economic life.[76]

Northwestern Missouri was enthusiastically described as "well-wooded, rolling, healthy and extremely well-watered."[77] In fact, the county soil was a fertile sandy loam where corn, wheat, oats, rye, barley and other grain crops grew well. Melons, apples, peaches, plums and cherries could be cultivated and wild berries were abundant. It was known as excellent pasturage land, "equal to the famed blue grass region of Kentucky."[78]

The railroad may have renewed an earlier offer to sell "ready made cottages" that only required four or five days to erect.[79] Stations existed every five or ten miles but Hamilton's depot outgrew others in significance. With 120 residents in 1867 it was already considered a "brisk new town with fair prospects."[80] Incorporated one year later, Hamilton's population grew to 1,200 by 1876 when Caldwell County's population was an estimated 12,200. The town had three churches, a high school and fifty business houses ranging from one-person millinery stores to successful hardware firms.[81] The bank, "John F. Spratt & Co.," and "Stone & Menefee's Hardware Store" had the highest valuation—$20,000 to $35,000.[82] Shoemakers, blacksmiths, bakeries, livery and saddlers, druggists, jewelers, grocers and a newspaper appeared. Grain and produce dealers, a miller, carpenters, builders and a lumber company, general stores, a clothing house and furniture store thrived while saloons and two hotels were kept busy. The existence of the prosperous hardware store, lumber company, carpenters and builders indicated a continuing boom.[83]

Hamilton quickly became Caldwell's leading town, out-distancing Kingston. Frame houses, some with elaborate gingerbread trim, were built on sloping side streets joined at right angles to the business district on Davis Street. Both sides of the wide unpaved thoroughfare were lined with frame stores until a disastrous fire in 1886.[84]

Cattle and grain were shipped to eastern and western markets via the Hannibal & St. Joseph Railroad. In 1870 the Kansas City and Cameron route, a few miles west of Hamilton, was completed giving rail access to the large market and livestock center.[85] Farm products sold in town in 1878 received almost as high a price as products sold in Chicago and St. Louis.[86] After 1882 the line was acquired by the Chicago, Burlington and Quincy system; six east and six west bound trains stopped daily in Hamilton.[87]

The trains that cut across Davis Street were Hamilton's lifeline to the nation in more ways than one. For example, "Campbells Great New York and Philadelphia Zoological and Equestrian Institute" arrived in August 1878, bringing with it gymnasts, acrobats and a museum of marine monsters.[88] Famous politicians, traveling salesmen and future settlers arrived via the railroad, and the town named for both Alexander Hamilton and Joseph Hamilton, a western lawyer and soldier, flourished.[89]

In August 1878 *The Hamiltonian*, a new weekly publication that was Republican Party oriented, proudly stated:

> The prosperity of Hamilton is remarked by all visitors whose good fortune it is to come into our little city. . . . It is a notable fact that while banks and business houses throughout the country were suspending or going into bankruptcy during the late stringent period, the banks and business houses of Hamilton successfully resisted the shock.[90]

The newspaper praised the judicious, fair and honest methods of the town's businessmen, but also promoted its usefulness by adding that prosperity was caused "partly by persistent advertising."[91]

In some ways it was a prosperous time for businessmen and wage earners because the dollar's purchasing power increased in eras of deflation.[92] But declining real prices had an adverse impact on the mainstay of Caldwell—its farmers.[93] A political and economic split developed between town and county.[94] While most new Hamilton businessmen were northerners who supported Republican Party policies, many farmers, natives of Missouri, resented declining crop prices, high interest rates and relatively high railroad shipping rates.[95] Farmers believed the gold standard, promoted by Republican administrations and bankers, prevented price inflation needed to raise produce prices. Without higher produce prices their debts steadily increased.[96]

In the early 1870s the Grange, or Patrons of Husbandry, became popular in Caldwell and Missouri. A severe business depression in Spring 1873 plus an eighteen-month drought starting that summer caused land values in Caldwell to drop approximately in half from a high of $40 to $50 per improved acre.[97] Granges were established in every township as farmers tried to cope with economic disaster.[98]

Although membership began to drop after 1875, the experience in joint action interested farmers in politics.[99] Grange concerns included railroad long and short haul rate legislation, and co-operative producing and buying associations.[100] In fact, Montgomery Ward, the mail order catalog firm started in 1872, was committed to helping Grange members buy goods cheaply.[101] Many Grange aims became goals of later reform groups. James C. Penney, a Caldwell farmer, was familiar with, if not active in, the Grange.

When the young Penneys returned to Missouri in 1867 they managed Eli's farm in western Caldwell.[102] Eli and Polly, both ailing, were living in Hamilton with their daughter Elizabeth and son-in-law William Partin.[103] The next year, James Penney used loans from relatives to purchase 480 acres of Gomer township a few miles east of Hamilton.[104] Previous owners included Thomas P. Caldwell and his wife Temperance Rebecca of Shelby County, Kentucky, E.B. Ewing and Elizabeth A. Ewing of St. Louis County, and John W. Paxton. The total cost of $4,880 was financed through Deeds of Trust made out first to William Partin then to an older brother, John R. Penney. In 1878 through a refinancing arranged with John R. Penney the farm was reduced to 390 acres, but James had to pay seven percent interest on his remaining debts.[105]

The farm had two buildings: a tiny one-story square frame house and a wooden barn. Water came from a well and there was a pond for cattle and fish. Railroad tracks crossed the farm's southern boundary and a small bituminous coal mine was opened nearby. A branch of Little Otter Creek ran through the blue grass covered rolling fields where Penney raised stock cattle, hogs, sheep, horses and food.[106] In 1870, before land values fell, the farm was worth $14,400, and the young couple had five children and a personal estate worth $2,460.[107]

After Eli's death in summer 1871, James was licensed to preach at Log Creek Church and next year was ordained a minister.[108]

He continued writing to *Signs of the Times* and gave lengthy expositions on God's saving power and hope in the face of death. When a daughter, Mollie, died, he said resignedly, "Death has made another inroad in our family," but finished by declaring, "But, glory to God in the highest, she is now with the blessed Jesus, whom she most earnestly and piteously implored to have mercy on her. . . . Yours in hope, J.C. Penney."[109]

Every Sunday Penney and his family traveled by horse and buggy twelve miles southwest to Log Creek Meeting House where the Old School Baptists continued their austere ceremonies.[110] Services included hymns like "How Firm a Foundation," "Onward Christian Soldiers" and "Singing Sands," praying and a sermon.[111] Their routine of farming and preaching continued for over a decade.

On September 16, 1875, the middle year of a turbulent decade, Fanny gave birth to a healthy infant boy who was named James Cash Penney, Jr.[112] Jimmie, as he was nicknamed, became the center of attention. He was six to twelve years younger than the other children and the baby of the family until 1879.[113] At age two he appeared contented and rather solemn; a few years later he looked unflappable sitting on the arm of a chair, straw hat cocked, above sister Pearl.[114] Unfortunately, due to illness, there was much uncertainty in their young lives. Death had already claimed two Penney children and claimed four more by 1884.[115]

Although the farm was only two and a half miles from Hamilton, the Penneys moved into town so their older children could more easily attend high school in the often sub-zero winter weather.[116] After renting a house, perhaps since 1878, they purchased one in late November 1880. They paid $1,400 for a residence and three lots owned by Anthony Rohrbough on the corner of Bird and Burris Streets.[117] Located between Davis Street and the high school, Penney's boyhood home had an average size yard and fairly spacious, bright interior. Inside the front porch entrance was a combined living room and parlor; behind were the kitchen, dining room and back porch. Between the master bedroom and study a steep staircase led to two smaller bedrooms. The one-and-a-half-story white frame house, decorated with shutters and narrow gingerbread trim, was plain but sufficient for the family's needs as they settled into Hamilton, where J.C. Penney grew from a boy to a young man.[118]

NOTES

1.   June 1978 visit to Caldwell County, Mo., by the author.

2.   Richard B. Morris, ed., *Encyclopedia of American History* (New York: Harper & Row, 1956), pp. 248, 257, 508, 539; John D. Hicks, *The Populist Revolt* (University of Nebraska Press, 1961 ed.), Ch. 3 "The Grievances."

3.   Daniel J. Boorstin, *The Americans: The Democratic Experience* (New York: Random House, 1973), pp. 109-10 for chain stores, pp. 121-29 for mail-order catalogs, and pp. 98-99 for ready-made clothing; Claudia B. Kidwell and Margaret C. Christman, *Suiting Everyone: The Democratization of Clothing in America* (Washington, D.C.: The Smithsonian Institution, National Museum of History and Technology, 1974), pp. 17, 164, 165. Note: None of the above discusses the rise of the dry goods or apparel chain store of which J.C. Penney Company, Inc., is the outstanding example. Godfrey M. Lebhar, *Chain Stores in America 1859-1950* (New York: Chain Store Publishing Corp., 1952), Ch. 3 "The Movement Gains Momentum."

4.   *Penney and Allied Families, Genealogical and Biographical* (New York: National Americana Publications, 1963), p. 54.

5.   Daniel J. Levinson, *The Seasons of a Man's Life* (New York: Ballantine Books, 1978), pp. 90-93; Dr. Bertha Booth, "Brief Sketch of the Life of J.C. Penney," *Hamilton Advocate-Hamiltonian*, 7 April 1938. Dr. Booth was a classmate of J.C. Penney; C.P. Dorsey, "Missourians Abroad-No. 5, James Cash Penney," *Missouri Historical Review* 21 (1926-27): 547.

6.   *Revolutionary War Pension Records* (#W8512) (National Archives, Washington, D.C.).

7.   *Penney and Allied Families*, p. 8.

8.   Robert B. Semple, *A History of the Rise and Progress of the Baptists in Virginia* (Richmond: John O'Lynch, 1810), p. 110; John B. Taylor, *Lives of Virginia Baptist Ministers* (Richmond, 1838), p. 53.

9.   William Warren Sweet, *Religion on the American Frontier. The Baptists, 1783-1830. A Collection of Source Material* (New York: Cooper Square, 1964), pp. 14-17.

10.   William R. Cocke III, *Hanover County Taxpayers, Saint Paul's Parish, 1782-1815* (1956), p. 99.

11.   William Rouse Jillson, *Old Kentucky Entries and Deeds—Jefferson Entries* (Louisville: Filson Club Publications: No. 34, 1926; reprinted Baltimore: Genealogical Publishing Co., 1978), pp. 269, 354; *The Edward Pleasants Valentine Papers* (Richmond, Va.: Valentine Museum), I:469, 502.

12.   J. Russell, *Map of the State of Kentucky with the Adjoining Territories 1794* (New York Public Library, Map Division).

13.   W.R. Jillson, *A Transylvanian Trilogy* (Reprint of Harry Toulmin: 1792 "History of Kentucky" and Russell's 1794 Map) (Frankfort: Kentucky State Historical Society, 1932), p. 136.

14.   Lewis W. McKee and Lydia K. Bond, *A History of Anderson County 1780-1936* (Frankfort: Roberts Printing Co., c. 1936), p. 38; *Kentucky 1810 Census*, R.V. Jackson, G.R. Teeple, D. Schaeferneyer, eds. (Bountiful, Utah: Accelerated Indexing Systems, 1975), pp. 66, 608, 840.

15. *Signs of the Times* (Middletown, N.Y.) 50, No. 1 (January 1, 1882): 8.

16. Forest Wyatt Shely, *This Is Goshen 1812-1962* (Lawrenceburg, Ky.: By the Author, 1961), p. 6.

17. Sweet, p. 163; McKee and Bond, p. 85.

18. Shely, p. 26.

19. J.C. Penney Company Historical File (hereafter PHF; see note in Selected Bibliography) I, A-2 "Minutes of a Convention of Delegates from Baptist Churches, Glenn's Creek Meeting House in Woodford County on the First Saturday in October 1826" (Frankfort, Ky., 1826), p. 1.

20. J.H. Spencer, *A History of Kentucky Baptists from 1769 to 1885*, 2 vols. (Cincinnati, 1886), I: 372-73. (Description was given by a granddaughter.)

21. *Penney and Allied Families*, p. 10; McKee and Bond, pp. 25, 27, 10.

22. *Penney and Allied Families*, pp. 9-10.

23. Jesse L. Boyd, *A History of Baptists in America Prior to 1845* (New York: American Press, 1957), pp. 131-33. Note: In 1844 there were 1,600 Old School Baptist churches and 61,000 members.

24. Robert G. Torbet, *A History of the Baptists* (London: Carey Kingsgate Press, 1966), p. 79. (Andrew Fuller was pro-missionary.)

25. Spencer, II: 290.

26. Boyd, p. 133; *Signs of the Times*, an Old School Baptist paper, continued publication for over fifty years.

27. *Penney and Allied Families*, p. 12; *Pension Records* (#W8512).

28. *Signs of the Times* 10, No. 6 (March 15, 1842): 45; 39, No. 14 (July 15, 1871): 167.

29. Visit to Lawrenceburg, Ky., in June 1978 by the author; *The Anderson News*, 8 August 1977, p. 1; 1 September 1977, p. 18; and 3 November 1977, p. 26.

30. Shely, "Our Heritage," *Anderson News*, 31 May 1962 in PHF I, A-2.

31. Recorder of Deeds, Caldwell County, Mo. (Kingston, Mo.) *Book A*, 601 (October 25, 1841); also *Book A*, 613 (December 9, 1842) for additional purchase of 217 acres.

32. Ibid., *Book E*, 193 (November 16, 1839), 336 acres.

33. Crosby Johnson, "History of Caldwell County," *An Illustrated Historical Atlas of Caldwell County, Missouri* (Philadelphia: Edwards Brothers, 1876), p. 10.

34. Ibid.

35. *Map of Tennessee and Kentucky* (Exxon Road Map) and *Map of Missouri* (Texaco Road Map). This is the approximate distance via Salt River, Ohio River, the Mississippi and Missouri Rivers to Camden and Camden to Far West. Time required is an estimate.

36. *Signs of the Times* 10, No. 6 (March 15, 1842): 45.

37. Ibid.

38. Crosby Johnson, p. 10.

39. David D. March, *The History of Missouri*, Vol. I (New York: Lewis Historical Publishing Co., 1967), p. 811, illus. 41e.

40. Visit to Kingston, Mo. in June 1978 by the author. (Court House standing today was built in the 1890s; it was the third one to be built.)

41. Shely, *This Is Goshen*, p. 8; *Log Creek Church. One Hundredth Anniversary* (typewritten copy), pp. 1, 6, PHF I, A-1.

42. *Log Creek*, pp. 1, 7-9.

43.   *Penney and Allied Families*, p. 20.

44.   Ibid., p. 39. Note: Eli Penney and family are listed in the 1840 Anderson County, Ky., Census and are not included in the 1840 Caldwell County Census, so the 1841 date is correct.

45.   PHF I, A-1, 1958 newspaper clipping from Iowa; Spencer, I: 328 for Warren Cash.

46.   *1850 Census*, Caldwell County, Mo., Free Inhabitants, p. 182; Slave Inhabitants, Caldwell County, I: 169 (total number of slaves was 142). Note: In 1840 Eli Penney also owned eight slaves, 1840 Anderson County Census, p. 105.

47.   *1860 Census*, Caldwell County, Mo., Free Inhabitants, p. 71; Slave Inhabitants of Missouri, Caldwell County, I: 81 (total number of slaves was 223).

48.   Crosby Johnson, p. 10; George Rogers Taylor and Irene D. Neu, *The American Railroad Network, 1861-1890* (Cambridge: Harvard University Press, 1956), p. 35.

49.   *600,000 Acres of Hannibal & St. Joseph Railroad Lands in North Missouri* (Hannibal, Mo.: Hannibal & St. Joseph RR Office, 1860), p. 6; Charles W. Morse and Charles Colby, *Morse's General Atlas of the World* (New York: D. Appleton & Co., 1856), "Missouri."

50.   Crosby Johnson, p. 10; "Hamilton Centennial to Open Sunday—A Big Parade Monday," *Kansas City Times*, 8/25/55 clipping in PHF I, B-2.

51.   Crosby Johnson, p. 10.

52.   *Laws of the State of Missouri*, Passed at the First Session of the Eighteenth General Assembly . . . (Jefferson City: James Luck, Public Printer, 1855), pp. 438-40. W.M. Paxton, *Annals of Platte County, Missouri* (Kansas City, Mo.: Hudson-Kimberly, 1897), p. 337.

53.   *Laws*, pp. 438-40.

54.   "Pleasant Ridge Pearl" (Pleasant Ridge, Mo.: July 1859) II, No. 10, 1.

55.   Ibid.

56.   *Historical Statistics of the United States, Colonial Times to 1957* (Washington, D.C.: U.S. Department of Commerce, Bureau of the Census, 1960), p. 207 (no pre-1870 education statistics).

57.   "Pleasant Ridge Pearl," pp. 1-7.

58.   Ibid., p. 7.

59.   Ibid., p. 1.

60.   Paxton, *Annals of Platte County*, pp. 139-40.

61.   *History of Caldwell and Livingston Counties, Missouri* (National Historical Co., 1886), pp. 175-76.

62.   Ibid.; *Penney and Allied Families*, p. 42; *Index to Compiled Service Records of Confederate Soldiers Who Served in Organizations from Missouri*, "James Penny Co. C 1 Regiment Cavalry. 1 Division, Missouri State Guard. Private."

63.   *History of Caldwell*, pp. 175-76.

64.   *The Hamiltonian*, 22 October 1886, p. 4, col. 2.

65.   *History of Caldwell*, p. 334 (James D. Paxton, brother of R.H. Paxton, moved to Caldwell in 1850); *Penney and Allied Families*, p. 50; W.M. Paxton, *The Paxtons, We Are One!* (Platte City, Mo.: Landmark Print., 1903), p. 368.

66.   *The Paxtons*, p. 368.

67.   *History of Caldwell*, p. 334.

68.   *The Paxtons*, p. 361.

69. *Penney and Allied Families*, p. 23; *The Paxtons*, p. 367.

70. Shely, "Our Heritage"; McKee and Bond, pp. 79-81. Both federal and confederate troops passed near Lawrenceburg, p. 76.

71. *Signs of the Times* 31, No. 22 (November 15, 1863): 169-70; "Circular Letter of Licking Association" in PHF I, A-2 (Penney was Assistant Clerk).

72. *Signs of the Times* (1863).

73. *History of Caldwell*, p. 177; Dr. Bertha Booth, "A Short History of Caldwell County" (Hamilton, Mo.: Hamilton Public Schools, 1936, 1964), p. 10.

74. Kingston Road Plaque, erected by the State Historical Society of Missouri and State Highway Commission in 1957. In summer 1864, 300 Confederate soldiers under Thrailkill attacked Kingston. *Signs of the Times* 31, No. 2 (January 15, 1863), 10. Letter from Eli Penney to Mirabile, Mo., dated December 10, 1862.

75. *Penney and Allied Families*, p. 54; Paxton Cemetery Record, Anderson County Public Library Records.

76. Paul W. Gates, "The Railroads of Missouri, 1850-1870," *Missouri Historical Review* 26 (January 1932): 134; *History of Caldwell*, p. 247.

77. *600,000 Acres*, pp. 9-11.

78. Crosby Johnson, p. 10.

79. *600,000 Acres*, p. 17.

80. Nathan H. Parker, *Missouri As It Is in 1867* (Philadelphia: J.B. Lippincott, 1867), p. 202.

81. Dun, Barlow & Co., *The Mercantile Agency Reference Book* (New York) September 1873, Hamilton, Mo.

82. *Switzler's Illustrated History of Missouri from 1541 to 1877* (St. Louis: C.R. Burnes, ed. & publ., 1879), p. 493.

83. Dun, Barlow & Co. (1873).

84. Crosby Johnson, p. 10; Visit to Hamilton in June 1978 by the author; *The Hamiltonian*, 1 October 1886, p. 1, col. 1.

85. Crosby Johnson, p. 10.

86. *Report of the Directors of the Hannibal & St. Joseph Railroad Co.* (New York: John Polhemus Printer, 1878), p. 23.

87. Library of Congress Card Catalog for Hannibal & St. Joseph Railroad; *The Hamiltonian*, 5 November 1886, p. 1, col. 1 (time table), also *Hamilton News-Graphic*, 11 May 1893, p. 5.

88. *The Hamiltonian*, 1 August 1878, p. 4, cols. 5-6.

89. *The Kansas City Times* (8/25/55 clipping).

90. *The Hamiltonian*, 2 August 1878, p. 5, col. 4.

91. Ibid.

92. Ibid., p. 5, col. 3; *Encyclopedia of American History*, p. 539. 1873 to 1896 are referred to as a "long-wave" depression interspersed with "vigorous business upswings."

93. *History of Caldwell*, pp. 241-43, 229.

94. Ibid., p. 249.

95. Crosby Johnson, p. 10; Solon Justus Buck, *The Granger Movement* (Cambridge: Harvard University Press, 1913), pp. 308-9.

96. *Encyclopedia of American History*, pp. 248, 257.

97. Perry S. Rader, *Civil Government and History of Missouri* (Columbia, Mo.: E.W. Stephens, 1898), p. 380; *History of Caldwell*, p. 249.

98.   *History of Caldwell*, p. 229.

99.   Ibid.; Buck, p. 97.

100.   Buck, pp. 308-9.

101.   *Encyclopedia of American History*, p. 518; Boorstin, *The Democratic Experience*, pp. 122-23.

102.   Dorsey, "Missourians Abroad," p. 546.

103.   Ibid.

104.   Recorder of Deeds, Caldwell County, Mo. (Kingston, Mo.) *Book K*, p. 204 (January 3, 1868), *Book M*, p. 219 (May 6, 1868) and *Book M*, p. 221 (May 13, 1868).

105.   Ibid.: Book 11, p. 2 (May 14, 1878); Book 1, p. 108 (January 14, 1874).

106.   *Illustrated Historical Atlas of Caldwell County*, p. 20, map of Gomer township; visit to the Home Place Farm by author in June 1978; J.C. Penney, *J.C. Penney, The Man with a Thousand Partners* (New York: Harper & Brothers, 1931), pp. 13-14.

107.   *1870 Census*, Caldwell County, Mo., Gomer Township, p. 12.

108.   *Penney and Allied Families*, p. 21; *Log Creek Church*, pp. 2-3; *Signs of the Times* 39, No. 14 (July 15, 1871): 167.

109.   *Signs of the Times* 39, No. 15 (August 1, 1871): 177; 40, No. 4 (March 1, 1872): 59; 50, No. 4 (February 15, 1882): 47.

110.   Penney, *Man with a Thousand Partners*, pp. 4-5.

111.   JCP to Mrs. R.B. Aten, May 18, 1962, in PHF I, A-1.

112.   *Penney and Allied Families*, p. 54.

113.   Ibid.

114.   Photograph between pages six and seven in Penney, *Man with a Thousand Partners*; *J.C. Penney Memorial Library and Museum*, Hamilton, Missouri . . . September 16, 1975 (privately printed, 12 pages), pp. 2-3.

115.   *Penney and Allied Families*, p. 54.

116.   Penney, *Man with a Thousand Partners*, p. 6.

117.   Recorder of Deeds, Caldwell County, Mo. (Kingston, Mo.) *Warranty Deed Book 11*, p. 351, and *Mortgage Book O*, pp. 392-93 (November 29, 1880).

118.   Visit to Penney town house in June 1978 by the author.

THE POPULIST FAMILY

In Hamilton the Penneys became active in political and temperance movements. However, family finances remained a primary concern. With farm and house mortgages to pay the parents could provide few luxuries for their family. Graduates of private academies, they wanted all their children to graduate from high school. In poor health and forced to adapt to diminishing returns, Reverend Penney assessed his family's future and then made a significant request of his young son.[1]

Jim was called to his father's study and told he must begin earning money to pay for his shoes and clothes. This occurred between 1883 and 1885, a time when farm produce wholesale prices were dropping precipitously.[2] The few cents he could earn by running errands or selling lemonade would not be sufficient so Jim decided to imitate his father. By raising and selling pigs he earned $60, a substantial amount. He had heard of banks failing and to protect his savings he put $30 in each of Hamilton's two banks.[3]

Besides having the satisfaction of completing a task, Penney, almost ten years old, received a lesson in business ethics. He fattened twelve pigs in the Penney backyard with slops gathered from neighbors. Although he could have sold them for more money later, neighbors complained about the squealing pigs and his father ordered him to sell them immediately. Disappointed but obedient, Penney learned consideration for neighbors was more important than the extra money.[4]

A strict but sensitive father, Reverend Penney cared about the example he set and examples his children saw in town. As befitted a minister and educated person, his standards were high. Jim had to quit a part-time job as a grocery delivery boy when he told his father, quite innocently, the owner had put inexpensive coffee beans in the canister of a higher priced brand.[5]

Once he tried selling watermelons outside the county fair, an event held every August near Hamilton. When his father arrived and angrily ordered him home, Jim was surprised and hurt. At home Reverend Penney explained he had been taking advantage of people selling items inside the fair grounds. They had paid a concession fee; by selling outside the entrance Jim benefited from the crowds of fair visitors without paying his dues.[6]

Penney later wrote about these and other episodes from the vantage point of a successful career; he gave them credit for developing his self-reliance and business ethics, particularly "The Golden Rule" precept. At the time, however, he took new tasks in stride, pursuing them with imagination and enthusiasm. A remarkable autobiographical sketch makes this clear.

In 1891 he wrote:

"Life of J.C. Penney Jr. at 16 yrs of age"

James Penney Jr. was born Sept 16th 1875 at a farm two & ½ miles east of Hamilton. He was a son of James Penney the distinguished farmer, preacher & politician. We find him employed from his early days in one of these occupations. James lived on the farm till he was one year & a half old, then he removed to town where he was there reared. At the age of six he was sent to school until the present time at 16 yrs. At the age of 10 he felt that he must make some money. He purchased one pig for $2.50 & from that time he has dealt in horses and hogs. At the age of 12 or 13 he purchased a filly of Geo. Hopson for $50. He kept that filly and at the present day she is going on 5 yrs. old. She raised one & two colts. The mare was called Cora C. The others were Letha P. & J.C.P. the III. James has 4 brothers & 7 sisters of which the two brothers & 3 sisters still survive. My present teachers are Miss Fannie Gentry and Mr. D.T. Gentry. At the age of 15 he assumed a position in Anderson Bros. & stayed there for 1 year of Saturdays only. In his early days about 7 yrs old he edited a paper called the News. And several times we find him as a storekeeper. His nickname was Erastus & I dont guess there is a boy a living that they tell more stories than on him.[7]

Obviously a proud and energetic young person, he initiated work and games. But the short classroom exercise reveals he did not take himself too seriously. In the Penneys' strict and busy household Jim, the middle child, was left on his own more than the older or younger children—once school work and chores were completed.

On hot, humid days Caldwell boys explored creeks and swam at "Tony's Hole" on Lick Fork Creek.[8] In winter bobsled parties were popular. As farmers the Penneys grew most of their food, and meals were plain but ample. Lemon chiffon or mincemeat pies were served on special occasions. However, buttermilk and fried catfish were Jim's favorite foods.[9] In the evening families gathered around an organ to sing; Bible readings and prayers ended the day.[10]

Farming, however, demanded long hours, up to sixteen hours a day in July, and countless chores.[11] A farmer's son learned to feed, herd and milk cows, care for horses, hogs, and chickens and to plant, hoe and harvest crops.[12] But the drudgery and isolation so often associated with rural America were offset by Hamilton town life and the Penneys' involvement in civic and political issues.[13] Jim Penney's character was shaped by the latter two experiences, by his high school education and by the family's constant need for money. The most important years of his life were those between age ten and twenty.[14]

The same year as the Chicago Haymarket Massacre, 1886, there was drought in Missouri. Seeing crops wither helped mobilize Caldwell farmers. In August James C. Penney, Sr., chairman of the Hamilton Democratic Party organization, was selected by county Democrats to run for the Missouri General Assembly.[15] Midwestern farmers, laborers and some businessmen became increasingly discouraged when hard work had not brought financial rewards. Intermittent depressions and drought led to liens on crops, foreclosed mortgages and hungry families. Farmers, in fact, were slowly losing their independence. Hard work, the time-honored American ideal, was no longer a guarantee of prosperity. Farmers organized and their spokesmen claimed the nation's laws, particularly its financial system, were the source of their problems.

Reverend Penney had enough self-confidence to try to improve his fellow farmers' economic condition. By accepting the nomination, he demonstrated civic responsibility, an increasing social consciousness, and a belief that group action could solve their problems. The split between farm and city had continued with Republican candidates winning handily in places like Hamilton, but losing in rural townships. In 1884 Grover Cleveland, a Democrat, lost Caldwell County by 500 votes.[16] But Republicans were not assured of winning every election. Sometimes third party candidates attracted many votes or could deliver votes to one of the major parties.[17]

Penney led the county Democratic ticket. The Republican oriented *Hamiltonian* summed up their candidates' competition in a manner complimentary to Penney when they stated:

> The head and tail of the ticket are composed of good material, while the body contains streaks of fat and lean, . . . but on the whole it is, perhaps, the best ticket ever presented by the democracy, therefore it will be all the more honor to the republicans to lay it out handsomely at the polls.[18]

While reporting Republicans had an easy majority of 200, the editor reminded readers Democrats counted on apathy and hoped to elect at least half their ticket. Penney was one Democrat who had a fair chance to defeat his opponent, David R.B. Harlan.[19] On October 8th the opposition press praised Penney again:

> J.C. Penney, the democratic nominee for representative, is an excellent citizen, cautious, prudent and conservative. His character is unstained. Of his ability to discharge creditably the duties of a legislator there is no shadow of a doubt. But for whom will he vote for United States senator? Caldwell County cannot afford to send a man to the legislature who will vote for Cockrell.[20]

Education and public speaking skills were valuable campaign tools, but Penney was challenged on two issues that no doubt cost him needed votes: his stand during the Civil War and his alleged support of Governor Marmaduke, the current Democratic Governor of Missouri. Besides being an ex-Confederate Major General, Marmaduke was reputedly opposed to temperance legislation. Penney denied being a rebel soldier and declared he neither worked for nor voted for Marmaduke.[21]

The Greenback Party of Caldwell endorsed Penney; unfortunately, it was weak and divided. Penney's reputation as a strong temperance supporter, though, was helpful. However, when he lost the election by a heartbreaking nine votes November 2nd, his reaction was philosophical:

When remedies are past, the griefs are ended by seeing the
worst, which late on hopes depended. To mourn a mischief that
is past and gone is the next way to draw new mischief on.[22]

The winner had a more colorful but less profound reaction: "I ran
like a scared wolf but didn't manage to cut my throat with the toe
of my hind foot."[23]

Republicans were proud of the nation's economic growth; they
claimed Democrats were not for the common man and would return
the country to pre-Civil War financial instability.[24] On both local
and national levels the issues were complex and emotional. Penney's
leadership and organizational skills were now in greater demand but
he only joined idealistic causes. For example, a temperance revival
started by outside ministers in July had taken hold in Hamilton.
Penney was involved in organizing the township's "Red Ribbon"
Club. He then became president of the 1,000 member society.[25]

The active family sat for a portrait about 1888. At T.H. Hare's
photographic studio they posed carefully, but small gestures such as
touching and holding hands revealed loving ties. In the middle
between his parents stood Jim. With light blue-gray eyes and
blondish hair, his direct gaze is confident and perceptive. Mittie and
Reverend Penney look stern and uncompromising while Herbert,
born in 1886, sat on his mother's lap eating an apple. Pearl, six, and
Elle, twenty-three, completed the family circle.[26]

The forty-six-year-old mother of eleven children had retained
her youthful beauty. Mrs. Penney was also efficient and thrifty. She
never complained about running a large household on little money
and was devoted to her religion. With the exception of Mittie's and
Pearl's fancy outfits, the family was dressed plainly. Dark clothes
were the fashion; they might have been an average midwestern
family, except for the determination marking their faces.[27]

By 1888 Hamilton had stopped expanding. Two-story brick
buildings with painted iron columns and shiny showcase windows
faced Davis Street. Pigs and cows no longer rambled down wooden
sidewalks or along its pleasant tree-shaded streets. Frequent freight
and passenger train service dominated business activities in the
prosperous town. Of course, the "metropolis" of Caldwell County
was quite small compared to Kansas City, St. Louis or Chicago. Out
of a population of 1,800 to 2,000, though, almost 100 businessmen

and businesswomen were rated in *Bradstreet's Commercial Reports* for 1888.[28]

Among the largest firms were Houston, Spratt & Menefee, one of Hamilton's three banks, and W.W. Anderson & Brother's Dry Goods Store, F.D. George & Co.'s General Store, Frank Clark's Grist Mill and Anderson Brothers' Cattle Dealers who had valuations of $35,000 to $50,000. Twenty-two businesses had the lowest rating possible: a "pecuniary strength" of less than $500.[29] Needed staples and services were thus readily available. Prosperity for some merchants depended upon prices farmers received for crops and livestock. To buy necessities, however, farmers assumed increasingly larger debts.

Local newspapers kept readers informed of neighbors' activities and county, state and national events. Accidents from runaway horses and train mishaps occurred regularly; cures promised relief from ailments such as rheumatism and "that tired feeling," and dry goods advertisements, with stock and sales policies fully explained, appeared weekly.

"Public credit can only be maintained by good faith—by a punctual performance of contracts," a quote from Alexander Hamilton, was *The Hamiltonian*'s proud motto.[30] Published since 1878 it continued to promote business interests and Republican party candidates. The *News-Graphic*, one year older, favored the Democratic party. A third paper called the *Farmers' Advocate*, started in 1890, carried news and ads but had a different point of view than its rivals.

While Reverend Penney's political interests were evolving, he took a stand against Old School Baptist beliefs. In church he spoke in favor of Sunday Schools, education and salaries for ministers. Penney believed a more modern approach to religion was needed. Although he had willingly served as pastor for over thirteen years with no salary, his new views provoked many members.

In September 1889 he and Fanny resigned from Log Creek Church to avoid a divisive argument within the congregation.[31] Jim was present and later recalled, "I remember it as well as if it were yesterday—of going with father and mother to Church and all the charges made against my father." To him, his mother's loyalty and father's lack of bitterness were most remarkable.[32]

Now, political action aimed at solving community and national problems replaced Reverend Penney's church duties. He joined the People's Party of Caldwell, a Populist Party organization that grew out of earlier Grange and Greenback parties. In 1890 he was their candidate for county representative. With the family farm, a town house, a new baby girl, Letha Mae, and another campaign, their household was hectic. Elie and Jim, small for his fifteen years, were the oldest children at home after Mittie married Roswell F. Whitman, a local jeweler, in 1889.[33]

As a third party candidate Penney faced a campaign that was much more challenging than in 1886. This time he had to persuade voters to break with traditional party ties. The People's Party, nonetheless, believed they had a winning combination due to the depressed economy and numbers of farmers.

The *Farmers' Advocate*, as expected, praised Penney:

> PEOPLE'S CONVENTION. THEY MEET AT KINGSTON
> AND PUT A FULL TICKET OUT. A STRONG TICKET. IT
> IS HEADED BY A STRAIGHT MAN WHO WILL BE A
> WINNER. A FARMER'S MAN.[34]

Penney had been nominated by acclamation after first refusing the honor.[35]

The convention had debated whether or not to endorse candidates on Republican and Democratic tickets, but decided to present a ticket of "Farmers' and Laborers' Union" members. Their platform was identical to the December 1889 one created by the Farmers' Alliance and Industrial Union and Knights of Labor at St. Louis.[36] Two weeks later, though, the Caldwell Farmers' and Laborers' Union met again to draw up resolutions reflecting their interest in ballot laws, a mutual insurance company, debtors, prohibition and suffrage. For example, debtors should be allowed to deduct the amount of their indebtedness from tax assessments, and regarding prohibition they resolved, "We regard the liquor traffic as one of the greatest evils in our nation, and we hereby request our legislators to work for its suppression." They also requested lawmakers to amend the suffrage law "as to give equal right to all, regardless of sex."[37]

Penney promised if elected to do all in his power to ease the tax burdened farmer of Missouri. He was questioned on his

Democratic party ties; in late October the *Farmers' Advocate* carried the Populist candidate's eloquent rebuttal of some political gossip. Penney announced:

> That by my consent my name was used in the democratic convention is a base falsehood. That I am pledged to vote for or against George G. Vest for United States Senator is also untrue, but am pledged to vote for the man whom I believe will best guard the interest of the farmer and laborer of the State of Missouri. If it devolves on me to represent Caldwell County in the next general assembly I will wear no brass collar, will not be subservient to any party boss or caucus, but will affiliate with men elected by the toiling masses, and use my utmost endeavors to promote the general welfare of the whole people.[38]

"I will wear no brass collar," was typical of his independent thinking and impatience with the regular party system. However, Democrats, struggling to regain national power, appealed to party loyalty and tried to appease possible defectors. When election day in 1890 was over all of Caldwell's People's Party candidates had lost. Penney polled 564 votes compared to 1,391 for the Republican and 1,543 for the Democratic candidate. An angry *Hamiltonian* editor accused Penney of helping defeat the Republican. Certain liberal Republicans evidently supported him while Democratic voters followed party leadership.[39]

Penney's political coloring was neither Bourbon Democratic, nor radical reformer, nor reactionary farmer.[40] While trying to maintain farmers' independence, the well-educated former teacher knew the value of progress. He tried to shape the direction of new social and economic changes by promoting reforms to increase the money supply. He assumed it could be done and was ahead of his time.

As in 1886, losing this election was taken in stride; work and social routines continued. The Penneys were "royal entertainers." One evening a club of young people called the 3 B's met at their home to recite poems of John Greenleaf Whittier.[41] The "Gay Nineties" may have arrived, but life in northwest Missouri changed very little.

Jim raised and sold livestock, and he started an account book. In 1891 he made a $40 profit selling hogs he had purchased from Elie. In 1892, though, he only made $17.60. Elie received $10.50 for three months' use of a pasture, and he owed his father $24.61 for cash, clothing, overshoes, collars and a necktie.[42] He was also kept busy with school work.

In fall 1892 Penney and his son-in-law, Whitman, shipped "108 head of fat steers to Chicago," and they sold millet seed in town.[43] During these years, instead of planting corn, Penney kept his rolling fields of blue grass. This meant he had to buy corn to fatten cattle and lost some profit, but he was stubbornly proud of the lush green fields. Finally he consented to plant 225 acres of corn.[44]

Election year 1892 passed without Penney being a county candidate. However, he was one of six members elected to the Hamilton Public Schools' Board of Education.[45] Besides attending meetings once a month and approving curricula, he occasionally sat in on classes.

Hamilton public schools were benefiting from the services of Professor David Tillman Gentry and his niece, Miss Fannie Gentry. When he became Hamilton's first Superintendent of Schools in 1891, he revised the high school curriculum and combined some classes. Because of Gentry's high standards, diplomas now qualified recipients for immediate entrance into the freshman class of the state university at Columbia.[46] Students had to maintain a 90 or above average to graduate; if it fell below 85 for any one month they were reported to the School Board for suspension. School days consisted of six hours of classes for eighteen weeks each fall and spring. The atmosphere was disciplined, but in turn the Gentrys provided excellent teaching. They encouraged intellectual curiosity by deep questioning and possessed extensive knowledge of literature and science. Gentry taught math and science; his niece taught Latin, literature, history and elocution.[47]

In September 1892 Jim Penney was seventeen and started his final year of high school. In this era about five percent of America's seventeen-year-olds received high school diplomas; according to its curriculum, a diploma from Hamilton's high school was a significant achievement.[48]

The curriculum for eleventh grade, which was the graduating class of 1893 due to combined classes, consisted of Algebra, Geometry, American Literature, Rhetoric and an optional course in Latin. Tenth graders studied Algebra, Etymology, Civil Government and Physics with Zoology and Latin as optional subjects first term; Bookkeeping and Latin were optional second term. In ninth grade

Arithmetic, Grammar, United States History, Physical Geography and Physiology were studied; Elocution and Botany replaced the latter two subjects during second term.[49]

Although Gentry's choice of high school books did not include McGuffey's advanced Readers, patriotism and progress themes prevailed in the textbooks. Perhaps due to lack of time no British history or literature courses were offered.[50] Practical knowledge of math and science was valued as highly as history and language skills. Their algebra and geometry books belonged to a successful textbook series prepared by George A. Wentworth, Chairman of the Mathematics Department of Phillips Academy at Exeter, New Hampshire. Joseph Ray's *Practical Arithmetic* included a section on such useful subjects as bank discounts, interest rates, taxes, marking store goods, bankruptcy, partnerships and import duties. Asa Gray of Harvard was the author of *Gray's School and Field Book of Botany*, a detailed, complex study used by Gentry. Joel Dorman Steele's physiology books spelled out the evils of alcohol, opium and tobacco. One edition, published in 1884, had been edited and endorsed by the W.C.T.U. of the United States. A.S. Barnes & Company also published Steele's popular series of science and history books.[51]

Steele's *A Brief History of the United States*, revised in 1885 to include a "Manufactures and Mechanic Arts" section, was used in tenth grade. A prolific textbook author, Steele hoped students would learn to "prize their birthright more highly, and treasure it more carefully."[52] He emphasized American inventiveness and linked it to America's independence by declaring, "With freedom came such a marvelous development of the mechanic arts and manufactures as to make the word Yankee a synonym for ingenuity."[53]

Another school text was Townsend's *A Shorter Course in Civil Government*. The author linked education and good government; his political maxims presented a clear message. They included: "Schoolhouses and schoolmasters are forts and garrisons to a republic," and "In the United States the ballots of ignorant voters are more to be dreaded than the muskets of foreign soldiers."[54]

Noble Kilby Royse, author of the eleventh grade text *A Manual of American Literature Designed for the Use of Schools of Advanced Grades*, stated American literature had been born with the

Revolution. It was a political literature both "original and national."[55] Brief biographies included men and women of letters with such contrasting styles as Longfellow, Bryant, Poe, Hawthorne, Webster, Calhoun, Bancroft, Stowe and Emerson, along with some lesser known figures.[56]

The educators presented an age of unity and progress; New England "Yankee" values were promoted. Jim Penney's school essays and debates reflected many of his textbook authors' views on education, intelligence, ingenuity and the value of patriotism, honesty and healthy living habits. Penney also expressed the ideals and problems of a politically aware and chronically in debt family. One classmate recalled, "He shone in oratory."[57] Otherwise he was seen as reserved and shy. Actually he was more dependent on family ties than on outside friendships.

Throughout the nineteenth century oratory and debating skills were admired. Politicians crossed the country by train making "whistle stops" in small towns like Hamilton. William McKinley, then Governor of Ohio, arrived in 1892 and made a "short and eloquent speech"; during the 1894 campaign 2,000 people greeted Vice President Adlai E. Stevenson who spoke on a platform near the Hamilton depot.[58] For years the articulate elder Penney, always Jim's ideal, had spoken before groups in town and church halls, at conventions and picnics. By observing the campaigns and local literary contests, Jim learned how to convince debate judges and refute opponents.[59] He employed both personal experiences and historical events. With these skills a career in law or politics was possible; Jim considered attending college and becoming a lawyer.[60]

The somewhat surprising subject of Penney's first debate was the affirmative side of "Wealth is More Desirable than Wisdom." In 1890 the Populist's son praised wealth but sidestepped the question of how wealth is created. He said, "If a man or woman has money they are respected by everyone. While on the other hand the poor man is noticed by no one. . . ."[61]

"Money is the lever that moves the world" was proven by the fact that "all the important places of our government are occupied by the wealthy men. Most of whom have millions of dollars." Using an argument that aptly described his father's political experience, he continued, "They never elect a poor man to these offices. The rich men are no better than the poor and why is it, if it is not the money." He cleverly turned an old argument around by saying, "We will admit that wealth is the source of all evil but those that have and know how to keep it think it more desirable than wisdom."[62]

The Penneys, even though not wealthy, were well respected. Nonetheless years of seeing his parents worry about debts and his father's futile political efforts made him aware of the advantages of wealth.

An essay on wisdom reveals he could combine his family's idealism with practicality. He wrote:

> It is not like money, you have $25,000 one day and the next day lose it. But this is not the case of wisdom. It is about the only thing nobody can take from us. There is no occupation that does not require mental strength, even the farmer thinks what to put his money into to make a profit.[63]

With the wisdom education provided there would not be "so many ignorant voters." He had noticed "some men vote just as others tell them. Every man ought to be well enough educated to endorse his principles and not have other fellows to bulldoze them."[64]

In other school debates he argued that country life was far superior to city life. One defense involved sheer numbers—"Most of the inhabitants of the United States are farmers, the bone & sinew of this country . . . this shows conclusively that the farm life is far more desirable than city life." Even though "we all know that the cities are the ruination of boys," his favorite argument against the city was the healthfulness of country life. "What is not possible to the ambitious boy or girl to those that have a strong & vigorous health," he proclaimed.[65]

Penney debated the timely issues of immigration and intemperance. He favored continued immigration for many reasons. One was it was beneficial to the newcomers: "they are thrown among intellectual, prosperous, thriving people. They partake also of our inventive genius, they soon imbibe our morals, hence they are Americanized."[66] As could be expected, he argued convincingly that the evils of intemperance were worse than the evils of war.[67]

After graduation he participated in debates supporting his father's 1894 campaign views on free trade, free coinage of silver and organized labor. Explaining why farmers opposed strikes by organized labor, he said:

> It is supposed they strike to bring organized capital to tone, but
> my dear friends, they fall short of this. Where ever these men
> strike, it paralyzes trade, it injures the farmer because men out
> of work can not buy our pork, cattle, etc. It hurts the trade of
> the merchant, for if the laborers have no money they can not
> buy. Every strike is a death blow to the country.[68]

In these years violent and mostly unsuccessful strikes occurred as
workers tried to ameliorate oppressive working conditions. But the
heart of the matter was the harsh fact that labor was more
dependent on capital than vice versa.[69]

Although aware of America's economic problems, with youthful
optimism Jim believed in the country's future and analyzed it three
times. Of these the most significant was his high school graduation
oration. It elaborated several ideas he used in a short 1892 essay; in
1894 he discussed the coming century predicting "air ships" and
other marvels. "I will admit we have had hard times, but we will
soon be all right again" was his only acknowledgement of the Panic
of 1893.[70]

The Ninth Annual Commencement of Hamilton Public High
School was held in Anderson's "Opera House" Friday evening
May 19, 1893. The largest graduating class in Hamilton's history had
selected ten of its twenty-two members to deliver essays, talks and
orations. Flowers, cards and presents covered the stage, the school
chorus sang and the hall overflowed with proud families and friends.
Penney's oration on "American Progress" was presented just before
the diploma ceremony.[71]

Man's genius and ingenuity, America's vast natural wealth and
the spread of public education were his major themes. He proudly
declared, "No land in the world has made such material and
intellectual progress as that which has characterized the U.S. during
the century that is now nearing its end." Sentimental rhetoric was
combined with substantive facts about railroad mileage, telegraph
lines and especially electrical inventions like the telegraph, electric
light, telephone and new electric motor. "It is the American mind
that has given zest and impetus to these electrical inventions,
leading to the most brilliant success in scientific appliances," he
said.[72]

Freedom had bred progress: "the modern machinery used in
cotton and woolen factories of this country, paper mills, iron and
steel works, flouring mills, and on the farms, mowing, reaping and

threshing devices that have revolutionized agricultural pursuits, have been invented by American brains. We have the machinery and raw materials and are able, therefore, to compete with any nation on the globe." Penney praised the public school system: "in no land in the world is education so lavishly placed at the disposal of the people." He concluded by earnestly calling on supernatural powers: "God keep thee the purest, the noblest, the best, while all thy domain with a people he fills as free as the winds and as firm as the hills."[73]

Religion's power seen, for example, in his father's graduation oration was now overshadowed by man's intelligence. In expressing man's complete dependence on God, the senior Penney in 1859 had perceived an ordered universe. But in the progressively secularized era religion was being transformed into ethical behavior, hard work and sobriety.[74]

Both evolution's impact and a great emphasis on American progress were obvious in the son's 1893 oration. The assurance of a benevolent, ordered world had vanished in a struggle for markets, raw materials and sea power. Pride in America's ability to compete was a modern theme. However, Jim's oration also reflected many of Steele's views. Steele, in turn, may have been influenced by Lester Frank Ward, an important sociologist who emphasized man's intelligence and ability to cooperate to create progress.[75]

Writers of popular books and sermons were stressing the role of the individual, at a time when individuals were being submerged in an increasingly impersonal, industrialized society. Russell Conwell's *Acres of Diamonds* and Horatio Alger's books reinforced the traditional American belief in the individual. Self-made man stories and success cult magazines also entwined money and morality. The message of the Gilded Age was: one attained success, usually meaning money, through one's own efforts. Hard work was the ideal means, but luck and personality were helpful.[76]

Penney upheld the individualistic theme by stressing the role of inventors like Franklin, Morse, Edison and Bell. He saw how individuals could change and improve society. But he had also witnessed group endeavors by county residents on political and temperance issues.

That evening Professor Gentry in a "touching and earnest address" told the class of six boys and sixteen girls that their future was in their hands.[77] This, he explained, was the meaning of the class motto—"Qua Rivus et Amnis Obeunt," or "Where the brook and river meet." Gentry said they were the most satisfactory class he had in fifteen years of teaching.[78] The Gentrys had succeeded in inspiring the young people and wanted them to lead worthwhile lives. Penney saw himself as only an average high school student. It is true he did not win the scholarship to the state university or have one of the highest grade averages, but his intellectual curiosity had been awakened.[79] Like his father, he possessed a love of learning and belief in education. Although he never became a lawyer or politician, the skills developed in debate and essay exercises proved extremely useful.

Charles Dickens' famous description, "It was the best of times, it was the worst of times," could have described America in 1893. The World's Columbian Exposition had just opened its doors in Chicago. The "White City," beside Lake Michigan, celebrating the 400th anniversary of Columbus' discovery of America, was a showplace of man's progress and inventions.

Throughout the summer Caldwell residents traveled to the popular event. $14.40 round trip excursion fares were offered by the railroad to encourage sightseers.[80] The Penneys, however, did not have the time or money to attend. Jim began working full time on the family farm. Although he had hoped to attend college, his parents had no money to spare and a wealthy relative would not lend the needed funds.[81]

Farmers' problems worsened that spring when the most severe economic depression since the 1870s began. The New York Stock Exchange crashed on June 27, 1893, and America's gold reserve fell below $100 million, causing a national fiscal crisis.[82] Concern over free trade, monopolies and the silver issue as well as declining farm product prices and fears of foreclosed mortgages gave the next few years a grim aspect.

With a panic and widespread dissension in old party ranks, the Populists' dream of sweeping the country and electing legislators to enact reforms stirred once again. When the 1894 election was eight months away, Missouri Populists began organizing. James C. Penney, Sr., and several friends attended the state convention of the People's Party held March 27, 1894, at Kansas City.[83]

The *Farmers' Advocate*, claiming the largest circulation in the county, had been presenting a barrage of facts and some fiction to support Populist aims. On the same page as an advertisement for the Great Rock Island Route there was a reminder that railroad companies owned "211,000,000 acres or enough land to make six states as large as Iowa." Private estates and foreigners owned another 28 million acres. "What will our children own? A right to pay rent" was the editor's reply to his own question. They also quoted Edward Bellamy, author of the utopian novel *Looking Backward*, on the evils of "old parties."[84]

After repeal of the Sherman Silver Purchase Act in November 1893, urged by Democratic President Cleveland, Populist battle lines had been drawn. In addition, drought and high temperatures would plague central and northern Missouri in summer 1894. By August much of the valuable corn crop was beyond recovery.[85]

On July 27th the county Populist party held its convention in Kingston. Penney, Chairman of the County Central Committee, was among six delegates elected to represent Caldwell at the Populist congressional convention one week later at Gallatin, twenty miles north of Hamilton in Daviess County.[86] At Kingston, county Populists pledged support for the Omaha Platform and State Platform adopted earlier that year.[87] In special resolutions they refused to support any member of the two major parties and endorsed the free and unlimited coinage of silver at a ratio of 16 to 1. This "would set the wheels of industry and labor in motion, obviate the cause of striking, insurrections and riots."[88]

In Gallatin the congressional convention nominated Penney for the United States House of Representatives from the Third District (ten counties).[89] Six names were placed before the convention, thus Penney's selection was an honor for Caldwell Populists and the family.

The opposition press greeted him with both praise and cavalier remarks. *The Hamiltonian* said Penney was "a good selection of a man who is heart and soul in the work and able to fill the position in Congress."[90] They may have also hoped he would take votes away from the Democrat incumbent, Alexander M. Dockery, whom they liked to describe as "an oily tongued old pretender."[91]

According to the *Gallatin Democrat*, however, "The populist convention stopped talking long enough to nominate J.C. Penny of

Hamilton for congress. A penny is rather a small coin, but it is all the populists could afford to risk on the congressional fight in this district. . . ."[92] Political insults like this used to upset Jim. Once when he was younger, he was ready "to thrash" an insulting speaker.[93]

Penney ran against Dockery and Republican Judge H.G. Orton. Dockery had served in Congress for twelve years and eventually became Governor of Missouri. Aware of farmers' strong feelings in the Third District, Dockery endorsed portions of the Populist platform at a major speech in Hamilton that October. He supported an income tax, direct election of U.S. senators and he promised to vote, although reluctantly, for a free coinage bill.[94] Thus he kept mutinous Caldwell and other Third District Democrats in line, despite appeals by Populists to attract voters.

The *Farmers' Advocate* promoted their cause with political slogans: "If you are dissatisfied with the hard times vote for Penney"; "If you want better prices for labor and the products of labor vote for James C. Penney."[95] The newspaper believed Penney's chances for winning were "elegant"—"James C. Penney will receive such a large vote next Tuesday that it will surprise the old parties so that they will never rally from the effects thereof," and claimed his campaign was spreading consternation among the Democrats.[96]

Election day was a bitter disappointment. Dockery won in a close race and Penney did not carry Caldwell. The *News-Graphic*, however, saw Penney's campaign as helping Republican Orton. In their opinion, "Mr. Penney can now retire and take a rest from his long and tedious spell of calamity howling."[97] Penney ran ahead of his ticket in Hamilton but he caught a cold during the exhausting ten-county campaign.[98] He should have rested before working on another civic project. Within a month, though, he was elected to the Caldwell County Mutual Fire Insurance Company nine-member Board of Directors and became president of the new organization. Created by county farmers to provide "good safe insurance at the very lowest possible rate," it was another example of Penney's leadership skill and the farmers' cooperation.[99]

Between Christmas and March his health continued to deteriorate. As he rested trying to regain strength, Penney had time to think about the future. What lessons could be learned from his latest political defeat? What future did farmers, the majority of

America's population, have if they were always in debt? Perhaps it was no longer possible to be an independent farmer as he had tried to be and as his ancestors were. His faith in progress and hopes for his children's future were fading.[100]

In late January, he acted on an idea he had recently discussed with Jim. He visited John M. Hale, senior partner of J.M. Hale & Bro.'s dry goods store in Hamilton, and asked him to hire his son and teach him the dry goods business.[101] Hale, whose store opened in 1886, catered to farmers during the depression. His ads in the *Farmers' Advocate* said they were making a "superhuman effort to meet the peoples' wants," and were "offering goods lower than ever heard of before."[102] The successful merchant was happy to do a favor for the ailing civic leader, but said he could not pay the inexperienced helper a regular salary. He offered to pay Jim $25 for the remainder of the year—only $2.27 a month.[103]

Although this was less than he could earn by raising livestock, it was an opportunity to learn business skills from a respected merchant. The long-range goal outweighed the immediate rewards. Several Paxton cousins were merchants or managers of dry goods stores in Kansas; with experience Penney might be able to join them.[104] He was entering an increasingly popular and, therefore, competitive middle-class profession. But the white-collar job of salesman was more respected in small towns than in large cities.[105]

Jim Penney was nineteen when he reported for work on February 4, 1895, a cold clear Monday morning, at the two-story brick store on the corner of Davis and Bird Streets.[106] Without his father's initiative he most likely would have remained a farmer. However, with little to show for two years of farm work, but possessing a "trader's instinct," he was quite willing to try a salaried position. *The Hamiltonian* editor made a prophetic remark when he informed readers of Penney's job:

> J.C. Penney, Jr. will be found in J.M. Hale & Bro.'s store where he is learning the business. Jim is a good boy and we believe he will succeed.[107]

Earning the lowest salary of any of Hale's clerks, however, made Penney the object of jokes by experienced employees who also took sales away from him. Penney became very discouraged. He decided to do general chores around the store and try to learn the stock. He rarely saw Hale.[108]

Even though James C. Penney, Sr., had been confined to bed for the previous six weeks, his death on the evening of March 22 was a shock to family and friends.[109] He was fifty-three when tuberculosis combined with a heart ailment overcame his weakened condition.[110] Penney's life had been filled with worthwhile activities and his untimely death was ironic. One newspaper editor noted, "For some reason he has been stricken when many men are nearing the zenith of achievement."[111]

The silver haired leader was "one of the town's and county's most highly respected and esteemed citizens . . . by his honesty and uprightness and many kind acts towards his neighbors and those with whom he came in contact in a business or social way, he won many warm and lasting friends," said one admirer, M.C. Martin, editor of the *Farmers' Advocate*.[112] *The Hamiltonian* praised his political career:

> While he has been identified with more than one political party he was conscientious and strictly honest in all his moves and never resorted to any trickery to secure an election or secure advantage over his opponents. He was a true and good citizen, ever doing what he believed to be right in all matters, both public and private.[113]

Penney certainly fit the criteria of a leader. He tried to give a certain direction and character to the small community, took risks to achieve his ideals and exercised critical judgment on social problems.[114] His values were not centered on money or power. In fact, Populists had succeeded in lowering state officials' salaries, and if Penney had stayed within the Democratic Party, he might have won one of his last two campaigns.[115] Moral leadership and independent thinking were his strengths, but cooperation and organization were vital to his goals. It was not surprising the community felt bereaved.

The funeral was held at home, but many waited outside to pay their last respects because the small house was filled. Almost the entire town joined the procession to the cemetery that Sunday afternoon. His death left a sad void in the close-knit family, but they could try to live up to his high standards.

Family members reacted to their loss in different ways. Fanny Penney refused to sell the farm and assumed the difficult task of paying off the mortgages. She succeeded fourteen years later. Mittie and Elie helped her but had their own families and farms to look after; Pearl and Herbert were in school and Letha was only five. Jim was in a new job. Although low paying, he had obtained it through his father's efforts. He was determined to live up to his father's last words to him, "Jim will make it, I like the way he has started out."[116]

To Jim his father was "one of the finest men who ever lived"; he later said, "I have always set him up as my ideal."[117] By 1895 Jim's character had evolved into a blend of high ideals and practical sense. He shared his father's ideals, but out of necessity he had been thrifty and practical about money from early childhood.

The family's immediate need was money. John R. Penney helped Mrs. Penney refinance the mortgages. A large corn crop that summer also eliminated $6,000 of the $17,000 debt, and the Whitmans purchased 145 acres of the farm. Fanny saved money by remaking clothes and growing some food.[118]

At Hale's Jim studied merchandise and did general chores. By sweeping floors and dusting stock he learned the importance of "clean workmanship." One day, however, as he recalled, "Inside me a voice seemed to say, 'You're not making your way here, Jim. At the end of the year Mr. Hale will surely let you go.' In one illuminating flash I vowed that should not happen to me. I would not be confused, intimidated by the jibes of others, prevented by fear from what I had the capacity to do."[119]

The self-confidence and initiative he possessed from childhood returned. Penney practiced selling with a sympathetic saleswoman, Maria Austin Young, who also answered questions about materials and other merchandise. She saw him as "a very ordinary boy—except for his industry and determination. He was a tireless worker."[120]

In a polite, low-key fashion he used logic and persuasion to sell merchandise. The former debater had a distinctive low-pitched voice and an amazing memory. Next year he was paid $200, and starting in 1897 he received $25 a month.[121] Hale was obviously pleased, and Penney, now one of the store's top salesmen, was encouraged to work even harder. He loved the work; a dream of owning a store formed and he saved his money.[122] His hard-earned savings of about $300, however, were small compared to Hale's large establishment. During the 1890s J.M. Hale & Bro.'s rating with R.G. Dun & Company was a consistent $10,000 to $20,000 in value with good credit.[123] The two Hale brothers had strong competitors such as W.W. Anderson & Bro's and McDonald and Clarkson's stores, but some advertisements show how Hale's thrived.

At different seasons the store held special sales. One Christmas they had 150 overcoats for sale "CHEAP"; in August at inventory time the store was cleared of all remnants and summer goods. Stock included "Tiger" brand hats, Selz, Schwab & Co. shoes, "Pride of the West" shirts, and various kinds of suits, valises, silk handkerchiefs, neckties, etc. Twenty-five thousand yards of new dress goods were on sale in late October 1894, and they confidently predicted, "Seeing will simply be to buy, they are too stylish, too good, too cheap to ever resist."[124]

One April an intriguing notice appeared:

RED SHOES
RED SLIPPERS and
RED STOCKINGS
RED DRESSES and
RED TIES,

LADIES AND CHILDREN
MUST DRESS IN RED[125]

Certain to catch readers' attention and curiosity, the special promotion attracted customers. Hale studied the community, its wants and needs, and gained residents' respect and confidence.[126]

The new clerk was learning more every day, but he worked too hard. In early June 1897 Dr. Van Note, the family physician, noticed Jim was physically worn down and said he could become consumptive. He advised him to leave Missouri's humid climate and move to Colorado, world famous for its healthy, dry atmosphere.[127] Consumption or tuberculosis was a dreaded disease, and his mother insisted he must go. Although reluctant to leave family and friends as well as his job at Hale's, Penney followed Van Note's advice. Within a few days, he obtained letters of recommendation and packed his valise for the unexpected move.[128] On June 7th he boarded a train in Hamilton that would take him to Kansas City and the Rocky Mountains.[129] Twenty-one and a half years old, Jim Penney was five feet eight inches tall and a slim 135 pounds. He was just one of thousands journeying west in 1897.

Beyond a doubt it was a fortunate twist of fate that he left home. In Hamilton he would have remained the hard-working son of the late distinguished civic leader.[130] Now he had to establish an identity among people who knew nothing of his family and auspicious heritage. To inspire him were three generations of community leaders and the recent example of his father's idealism and social conscience in action. Penney was knowledgeable, observant and hard working, but his dream required money.

The rolling green acres surrounding Hamilton lay far behind as the train sped across Kansas for Colorado. A new world filled with opportunity lay before him, but the old one filled with triumphs and defeats, beauty and heartbreak, was not forgotten.

NOTES

1.   Penney, *Man with a Thousand Partners*, p. 6; *Log Creek*, p. 3.
2.   *Encyclopedia of American History*, pp. 257, 508.
3.   Penney, *Man with a Thousand Partners*, pp. 8-9.
4.   Ibid.
5.   JCP to Mr. J. Rosin, 27 April 1966, PHF I, A-5.
6.   Penney, *Man with a Thousand Partners*, pp. 11-12.
7.   Autobiography of JCP, PHF I, A-3. It was apparently written as a school assignment. He saved his essays and debates for almost eighty years.
8.   JCP to C.F. Ridings, 3 March 1937, PHF I, A-3.
9.   JCP to Mrs. B.H. Sullivan, 9 January 1969, p. 1, PHF, EVM Files; Author's interview with Mrs. Overstreet, resident of Hamilton and long time acquaintance of JCP, June 1978. Penney's love of buttermilk and catfish lasted his entire life.
10.   Eben Fine, "Autobiography of Eben Fine—Memories of My Childhood and Youth," Eben Fine Collection, I-2. Western Historical Collections, University of Colorado at Boulder, Colo. Fine was born in 1865 in Daviess County between Hamilton and Gallatin into a family of twelve. He became a lecturer and naturalist. Written c. 1956.
11.   *News-Graphic*, 21 July 1892, p. 1, col. 2.
12.   Eben Fine Collection, I-3 (another "Autobiography").
13.   Louis Hacker, *The World of Andrew Carnegie 1865-1901* (Philadelphia: J.B. Lippincott, 1968), pp. 166-71.
14.   J.C. Penney, *Fifty Years with the Golden Rule* (New York: Harper & Brothers, 1950), p. 245.
15.   *Encyclopedia of American History*, pp. 551-52; *The Hamiltonian*, 30 July 1886, p. 1, cols. 2-3; 1 October 1886, p. 1, col. 3.
16.   *History of Caldwell*, p. 246.
17.   Ibid., p. 243; *Atlas of Caldwell County, Missouri* (Kingston, Mo.: W.H.S. McGlumphy, 1907), p. 6.
18.   *The Hamiltonian*, 1 October 1886, p. 1, col. 3.
19.   Ibid., 8 October 1886, p. 4, col. 1.
20.   Ibid., p. 4, col. 2.
21.   Ibid., 22 October 1886, p. 4, col. 2.
22.   Ibid., 5 November 1886, p. 1, cols. 2-3; p. 1, col. 4.
23.   Ibid., p. 1, col. 4.
24.   Ibid., 22 October 1886, p. 4, cols. 1 and 4.
25.   Ibid., 12 November 1886, p. 1, col. 4; 26 November 1886, p. 1, col. 3.
26.   Original photograph is on display at the J.C. Penney Hall library, 4-H National Headquarters, Chevy Chase, Md.
27.   J.C. Penney, "How Women Have Influenced My Life," pamphlet reprint c. 1950 in PHF.
28.   *Bradstreet's Commercial Reports* (New York City) 83 (October 1888), Hamilton, Missouri.
29.   Ibid.

30.   *The Hamiltonian*, 12 November 1886, p. 1, top.

31.   *Log Creek*, p. 4.

32.   JCP to Mr. and Mrs. L.E. Thompson, 7 May 1923, PHF I, A-1.

33.   *Penney and Allied Families*, p. 54.

34.   *Farmers' Advocate*, 24 September 1890, p. 8, col. 1.

35.   Ibid., p. 8, col. 2.

36.   Ibid., p. 8, col. 1.

37.   Ibid., 8 October 1890, p. 8, cols. 2-3.

38.   Ibid., 29 October 1890, p. 1, col. 4.

39.   Ibid., 12 November 1890, p. 5, col. 4; *The Hamiltonian*, 14 November 1890, p. 5, col. 4.

40.   Populist interpretations are controversial as seen in Richard Hofstadter's *The Age of Reform* (1955), Louis Hacker's *World of Andrew Carnegie* (1968). Lawrence Goodwyn's *Democratic Promise* (1976) stresses the "cooperative" nature of the Populists as opposed to the "corporate" power then emerging.

41.   *Farmers' Advocate*, 12 November 1890, p. 1, col. 3.

42.   Account Book pages, PHF I, A-3.

43.   *News-Graphic*, 15 September 1892, p. 1, col. 1; *Farmers' Advocate*, 7 June 1893, p. 1, col. 2.

44.   Penney, *Man with a Thousand Partners*, pp. 13-14; Mittie Penney Whitman to JCP, 25 June 1930, PHF I, A-3.

45.   *Rules and Regulations and Course of Study of the Hamilton Public Schools 1892-1893*, By Order of the Board of Education (Hamilton, Mo.: Advocate Book and Job Print., 1892), p. 2. Note: located in the local history collection of the Missouri State Historical Society at Columbia, Mo.; *Farmers' Advocate*, 5 April 1893, p. 8, col. 1—school board members were elected when Hamilton's mayor and town council elections were held.

46.   *Rules and Regulations*, p. 20; Bertha Booth, "A Tribute to Prof. D.T. Gentry," *Hamilton High School 50th Reunion, Class of 1893, May 16 to May 19, 1943*, booklet in PHF I, A-4.

47.   *Rules and Regulations*, pp. 2-6; Bertha Booth, "A Tribute to Prof. D.T. Gentry," p. 10; Maud Mehaffie Wendorff, "A Tribute to Miss Fannie Gentry," p. 9; Edith Bunch Scoville, "History of the Class of 1893—The South Side Part," *Hamilton High School 50th Reunion* (1943).

48.   *Historical Statistics of the United States* (1960), p. 207.

49.   *Rules and Regulations*, pp. 12-13.

50.   Ibid.

51.   John F. Ohles, ed., *Biographical Dictionary of American Educators*, 3 vols. (Westport, Conn.: Greenwood Press, 1978), 3: 1373, George Albert Wentworth; 2: 541-42, Asa Gray; 3: 1229, Joel Dorman Steele; 3: 1074, Joseph Ray; Joseph Ray, *Practical Arithmetic by Induction and Analysis* (Cincinnati: Sargent, Wilson & Hinkle and New York: Clark & Maynard, 1857), pp. 212-57; Joel Dorman Steele, *Hygienic Physiology with special reference to the use of Alcoholic Drinks and Narcotics*, adapted from the *Fourteen Weeks in Human Physiology* (New York: A.S. Barnes, 1884); John Barnes Pratt, *Seventy Five Years of Book Publishing 1838-1913* (New York: A.S. Barnes, 1913), pp. 17-18.

52.   Joel Dorman Steele, *A Brief History of the United States* (New York: A.S. Barnes, 1885), p. 2. Note: the 1880 edition had no special section on inventions.

53. Ibid., p. 306.

54. Calvin Townsend, *A Shorter Course in Civil Government* (New York: American Book Company, 1892), p. 11. Also included a section on Missouri state and county government.

55. Noble Kilby Royse, *A Manual of American Literature Designed for the Use of Schools of Advanced Grades*, Revised Edition (Philadelphia: Cowperthwait, c. 1883), p. 15.

56. Ibid.

57. Booth, "Brief Sketch," Part II.

58. *The Hamiltonian*, 28 October 1892, p. 1, col. 5; *News-Graphic*, 18 October 1894, p. 1, cols. 4-5.

59. Debate: negative side of "Literary Exercises Are of No Benefit to the Schools," September 20, 1892, p. 2, PHF I, A-4.

60. Penncy, *Fifty Years*, p. 26.

61. Debate: affirmative side of "Wealth is More Desirable than Wisdom," 1891, PHF I, A-4.

62. Ibid.

63. Essay: "Wisdom," no date, PHF I, A-4.

64. Ibid.; Note: term "bulldoze" was a political slang term in the 1890s, according to definition in Funk & Wagnalls' *New Standard Dictionary of the English Language* (New York: Funk & Wagnalls, 1951; 1st ed. 1913).

65. Debate: negative side of "City Life is More Desirable than Country Life" (1891), PHF I, A-4.

66. Debate: negative side of "Foreign Emmigration Should be Abolished" (January 20, 1893), PHF I, A-4.

67. Debate: affirmative side of "The Evils of Intemperance are Greater than the Evils of War" (November 21, 1892), PHF I, A-4.

68. Debate: affirmative side of "Organization of Labor Is a Detriment" (November 20, 1894), PHF I, A-4.

69. Ibid.

70. Debate: negative side of "The Signs of the Times Indicate the Downfall of the Nation" (1894), PHF I, A-4.

71. *Farmers' Advocate*, 24 May 1893, p. 1, col. 5, "Our Pride, Our Public Schools."

72. Oration: "American Progress" (May 19, 1893), PHF I, A-4.

73. Ibid.

74. Gerald N. Grob and Robert N. Beck, eds., *American Ideas. Source Readings in Intellectual History of the United States* (New York: Free Press of Glencoe, 1963), 2 vols. in one. Vol. 2, Part I "American Thought in an Industrial Age" Introduction, pp. 2-7; Daniel T. Rodgers, *The Work Ethic in Industrial America 1850-1920* (Chicago: The University of Chicago Press, 1974, 1978), pp. 9-12.

75. Steele, *A Brief History*, p. 307; Grob and Beck, *American Ideas*, 2: 5.

76. Irving Wylie, *Myth of Rags to Riches* (New York: Free Press, 1954); Rodgers, *Work Ethic*, p. 38; J.C. Furnas, *The Americans: A Social History of the United States 1587-1914* (New York: Putnam's Sons, 1969), pp. 654-55. Note: Not all individualism can be attributed to Social Darwinism, or competition.

77. *News-Graphic*, 25 May 1893, p. 7, cols. 2-3.

78. Ibid.

79.   Penney, *Fifty Years*, p. 26.
80.   *News-Graphic*, 17 August 1893, p. 1, col. 3.
81.   Penney, *Fifty Years*, p. 26; Booth, "Brief Sketch," Part II.
82.   *Encyclopedia of American History*, p. 263.
83.   *Farmers' Advocate*, 28 March 1894, p. 8, col. 1.
84.   Ibid., 26 April 1893, p. 2, col. 2.
85.   Ibid., 15 August 1894, p. 4, col. 2.
86.   *News-Graphic*, 2 August 1894, p. 8, col. 3.
87.   *Farmers' Advocate*, 1 August 1894, p. 5, cols. 3-4.
88.   Ibid.
89.   Perry S. Rader, *Civil Government*, p. 11, Map of state districts.
90.   *The Hamiltonian*, 3 August 1894, p. 1, col. 5.
91.   Ibid., p. 4, col. 2.
92.   *News-Graphic*, 16 August 1894, p. 4, col. 4. Note: They reprinted the *Gallatin Democrat*'s article on the convention.
93.   Mittie Penney Whitman to JCP, 25 June 1930, PHF I, A-3.
94.   *Biographical Directory of the American Congress 1794-1961* (Washington, D.C.: G.P.O., 1961), p. 817; *Farmers' Advocate*, 10 October 1894, p. 1, cols. 5-6.
95.   Ibid., 31 October 1894, p. 2, col. 1.
96.   Ibid., p. 2, col. 2.
97.   *News-Graphic*, 8 November 1894, p. 1, cols. 4-6.
98.   JCP to Mr. R. Corkern, January 12, 1967, PHF I, A-1.
99.   *Farmers' Advocate*, 12 December 1894, p. 6, cols. 1-3.
100.   Dorsey, "Missourians Abroad," p. 548.
101.   Penney, *Man with a Thousand Partners*, pp. 12-13; Penney, *Fifty Years*, p. 27.
102.   *Farmers' Advocate*, 29 August 1894, p. 1, col. 5.
103.   William Bushnell, "J.C. Penney," *The Dynamo* 2 (April 1918): 4; Note: *The Dynamo* was the "house organ" of the J.C. Penney Company; Penney, *Fifty Years*, p. 28.
104.   *The Paxtons*, pp. 361, 367, 369. Also note: Daniel Paxton, Mrs. Penney's brother, had been manager of Hale's dry goods department from 1888 to 1890.
105.   Rodgers, *Work Ethic*, pp. 38-39; *Shoe and Leather Gazette* 30 (September 29, 1898), p. 15.
106.   Bushnell, "J.C. Penney," p. 4.
107.   *The Hamiltonian*, 15 February 1895, p. 8, col. 1.
108.   Bushnell, "J.C. Penney," p. 4; Penney, *Man with a Thousand Partners*, pp. 15-16.
109.   *Farmers' Advocate*, 27 March 1895, p. 1, col. 6.
110.   Ibid.; *The Hamiltonian*, 29 March 1895, p. 1, col. 6.
111.   *Farmers' Advocate*, 27 March 1895, p. 1, col. 6.
112.   Ibid.
113.   *The Hamiltonian*, 29 March 1895, p. 1, col. 6.
114.   Eugene E. Jennings, *An Anatomy of Leadership* (New York: McGraw-Hill, 1972; 1st pub. 1960), p. 8; Dorsey, "Missourians Abroad," p. 547.
115.   Homer Clevenger, "The Farmers' Alliance in Missouri," *Missouri Historical Review* 39 (October 1944): 42.
116.   Penney, *Man with a Thousand Partners*, p. 13.

117. JCP to Mr. and Mrs. L.E. Thompson, 7 May 1923, PHF I, A-1.

118. Dorsey, "Missourians Abroad," pp. 549-50.

119. Penney, *Fifty Years*, p. 29.

120. Dorsey, "Missourians Abroad," p. 551.

121. Bushnell, "J.C. Penney," p. 4.

122. Penney, *Fifty Years*, pp. 29, 40.

123. R.G. Dun & Company, *The Mercantile Agency Reference Book* (New York), Hamilton, Missouri, 1890-1895.

124. *The Hamiltonian*, 1 December 1893, p. 4, cols. 5-6; ibid., 4 August 1893, p. 2, cols. 5-6.

125. *Farmers' Advocate*, 26 April 1893, p. 2, cols. 4-5.

126. Penney, *Man with a Thousand Partners*, p. 19.

127. Ibid., pp. 17, 18.

128. Ibid., p. 18.

129. *News-Graphic*, 10 June 1897, p. 8, col. 1.

130. Levinson, *Seasons of a Man's Life*, pp. 72-73. He says leaving one's pre-adult home is part of the "early Adult transition."

COLORADO VENTURES AND MENTORS

Hometown reports had Penney moving to Colorado Springs, but information from cousins in Kansas City made Jim change his destination to Denver.[1] Happily his journey occurred at a propitious time: western commerce and population were expanding hand-in-hand. Economic troubles hindered Colorado's progress from the early 1890s to 1896, but by 1897 the future looked brighter. Despite the "frontier's" reported closing in 1890, during the decade Colorado's population increased by thirty percent and was over one-half million by 1900.[2]

Silver and gold mines like Leadville and Cripple Creek and the bonanzas they brought men had given the state international fame. In particular, silver mines discovered in the 1870s and 1880s attracted adventurers and businessmen.[3] Denver, founded in 1858, emerged as the region's manufacturing and supply center. Denver outdistanced nearby rival cities by gaining access to superior railroad transportation. Using newspaper promotions and bond sales, citizens financed a one hundred mile route north to Cheyenne to meet the Union Pacific Railroad crossing Wyoming. The same year, 1870, Denver boosters were pleased by the sight of the Kansas Pacific Railroad entering Denver from the east.[4]

The Queen City of the Plains, also named the Mile High City, became a mecca for thousands who sought new homes, economic opportunities, improved health and nearby dramatic mountain, canyon and river views.[5] Its proximity to the Rocky Mountain foothills presented a striking contrast to over six hundred miles of flat prairies and farm land lying eastward. Strategically located between the Mississippi River and California, Canada and Mexico, Denver was the West's geographic and commercial center.[6] The city's population tripled in the 1880s to become 100,000; in 1895 it had 115,000 residents.[7] By 1897 twelve railroads served Denver. The Atchison, Topeka & Santa Fe, Chicago, Burlington & Quincy,

Union Pacific and Denver & Rio Grande Railroads were among the largest.[8] Union Depot handled one hundred passenger train arrivals and departures daily.[9]

Jim arrived at Union Depot after a hot, dusty day-and-a-half ride from Kansas City.[10] Denver's weather was unusually warm (in the 80's) and cloudy, and distant peaks were barely visible on the horizon. He just missed being greeted by dangerous flooding and track washouts due to heavy thunderstorms.[11]

Denver began revealing its size and wealth to him at the depot, described as the finest west of Chicago. Of modern Gothic architecture, it was a fitting introduction to a city railroads helped create. The two-story structure, over 500 feet long with a 165-foot tower, was surrounded by ten acres of lush landscaped grounds. Outside, horse-drawn carriages filled wide gravel and asphalt streets, and four streetcar systems served the city. Tall shade trees bordered flagstone sidewalks.[12]

Although the tourist trade and health care business were substantial, manufacturing and retail and wholesale distribution were Denver's main industries. Evidence of prosperity was everywhere. Large retail and wholesale clothing stores, steel smelting and mining machinery plants, mills, packing houses, canning factories and breweries employed thousands. Small shops of all kinds thrived in the city and environs. At least five national banks catered to finance and trade.[13] Denver businessmen were deeply involved in their town's economic health. The Chamber of Commerce and Board of Trade met every Thursday evening and thirty standing committees reported on problems and prospects facing the city.[14]

Temporary visitors and new residents had a wide choice of lodging. Room and board by the week were usually offered. The Brown Palace Hotel was the newest and most celebrated lodging. Costing $1.2 million to construct in 1893, it was renowned for a ten-story marble and onyx center hall.[15]

Tabor's Grand Opera House and millionaires' mansions vied with the hotel for attention before completion of the state capitol building with its outstanding gold leaf dome. New colonial style residences, villas and modern business blocks and buildings stood out against the distant background of Pike's Peak, Long's Peak and Gray's Peak, Colorado's highest mountains.[16] The city had a fresh new aspect—buildings constructed before 1880 were considered old.

Culture palaces, academies, colleges, public libraries, over one hundred churches and its nine parks were the pride of Denver citizens.[17] Denver was very impressive, especially to someone like Penney from a small midwestern town.

Jim was on his own. Home was 700 miles east; neither relatives nor family friends were available to help him adjust to the new environment. He had no time to be lonely, however, for he had to find work and a place to live. Compared to Missouri, the dry clear air was invigorating. Convinced his health had already improved, Penney went job hunting the day he arrived.[18] Realizing hometown letters might not be too helpful in a strange town, he had asked a cousin in Kansas City, William T. Kemper of the Kemper Grain Company, to provide letters of introduction to business associates in Colorado Springs. Penney could present them in the smaller city if he failed to find work in Denver. Kemper described Jim as "energetic, steady, bright and active." He added, "We can recommend him highly as a young man of good family."[19] Kemper, born in 1866 to Sallie Paxton and James M. Kemper of St. Joseph, Missouri, had known him since childhood.[20]

Penney's letters from Hamilton were from John M. Hale, W.J. Wyatt and Seth M. Young, both leading attorneys, and Crosby Johnson and Dan Booth, the Hamilton Savings Bank president and cashier. Their remarks were proof of Penney's character, good habits and the family's reputation. Many young men had equally good references, but Penney's sponsors stressed the sincerity of their comments and strangers reading them would note this.

Jim's former employer said he was a "young man of more than ordinary ability" in his job as general salesman.[21] He added, "This coupled with his good moral character and honest disposition, I can with all candor truly recommend him to the public as a most worthy young man, and the only reason assigned for leaving my employ is failure of health."[22]

Crosby Johnson, the bank president, described his late friend's son:

> In point of morals and integrity, he may have equals, but no superiors. We never have heard the least question made over his truthfulness, his candor, nor his honesty. Full and complete reliance may be placed on his statements and promises. In his attention to business he was like clockwork, always attentive,

always polite, until every one was his friend and all now wish him success.[23]

Although Doctor Van Note had recommended outdoor work Penney was fascinated by Denver's large department stores and hoped to obtain a position in one. Walking to the main business district, he asked to meet store managers and requested a salesman's job. Quite proud of his references, he received a shock when one cynical manager told him, "I haven't any time to read letters! Besides, they don't mean a thing. In this store you couldn't steal anything if you wanted to!"[24]

Penney finally secured a job at Joslin Dry Goods Company on the corner of 16th SW and Curtis.[25] J. Jay and Frank A. Joslin were the prosperous owners of the highly rated department store.[26] Orem Newcomb, their manager, hired Penney and took an interest in him. Jim began attending church services with the Newcomb family.[27]

Living in Denver was an important experience for the twenty-one year old. Away from home for the first time, he was making decisions that changed his life. He selected friends, jobs and met financial obligations. He worked in large department stores, noticed with dismay gray-haired sales clerks toiling in positions they held twenty years earlier, and saw the outward trappings of culture and wealth. Of course he could only sample part of the large city during these months.

Denver's largest dry goods and clothing stores were ten and twenty times greater in monetary value than Hale's. Daniels and Fisher department store was worth over one million dollars.[28] Others like the May Shoe & Clothing Company, Golden Eagle Department Store, Denver Dry Goods Company, Appel's Big Store and Joslin's were rated from $200,000 to $500,000.[29] They had uniformed attendants to check customers' bicycles, and huge store-wide sales. While observing all that was new and exciting, Jim would have seen elaborate advertisements appearing in the *Rocky Mountain News*, Denver's largest circulation newspaper. Six column ads on June 13th included many items required for comfortable living in the 1890s. For example, ladies' parasols, white goods, silks and dress goods, fancy combs and ribbons, muslin underwear, high and low cut green and red button shoes, organdie dresses, broadcloth suits with embroidery and fully lined with taffeta silk, as well as shirt waists of percale, lawn, dimity and madras cloth were reduced for quick sale at the Denver Dry Goods Company.[30] Ice boxes, ice cream makers, lace curtains, baby carriages, clocks and stationery were also part of their "mammoth stocks."[31]

Penney had applied here but was not hired.[32] Circumstances behind the early sale may have caused clerks' jobs to be scarce. Owners would try to cut overhead expenses as well as inventories if sales were down.

May Shoe and Clothing Company, one of Colorado's oldest firms and of mining town origin, advertised "First Choice of the House in Men's Finest Spring and Summer Suits" worth from $18 to $30 for sale at $13.75. These "masterpieces of artistic tailoring" included selections from the "quietest effects to the most pronounced patterns." "Prices Gone To Smash—The Greatest Clothing Carnival of the Age" was their headline. In explanation they stated:

> This means that the times are out of joint—that the backward Spring, the lateness of the season, and the enormous stock we have on hand have decided us to part company with profits and seek the society of loss, mark you. . . . We've had such a sale as this before but never in the height of the season—never in the month of June and you know that we've lived up to every promise we ever made; therefore, we have the strongest claims on your confidence now. To the absolute truth of every line of this announcement we pledge our personal honor and business integrity, neither of which has ever been questioned.[33]

The Golden Eagle department store said they had to cut prices because stocks were double and treble what they should be. They promised, "To-morrow will be a day for bargains long to be remembered." Many items were sold at almost half price: ladies' $1.50 oxford shoes of genuine India kid in brown, black and oxblood were 79¢; $10 organdie dresses with lace and ribbon trimming were now $3.75, and five-piece ladies' bicycle suits in all colors were reduced from $6.50 to $3.45. Appels and Joslin's offered similar goods. While Joslin's did not admit they were overstocked, they said, "dollars never bought so much merchandise."[34]

Jim's position paid $6.00 a week, one dollar above the starting salary for Denver salesmen.[35] From that he paid $4.50 for room and board at a nearby lodging house.[36] Weekly salaries for experienced sales clerks were as high as $25, but sales people worked from nine to thirteen hours a day, six days a week.[37] Few expected to work less. Clerks' unions were being organized to lower hours, especially evening hours, but a minimum sixty-hour work week was average.[38]

How long Penney stayed at Joslin's is uncertain, but soon after arriving he was upset by an incident with a senior salesman. The clerk intervened and took a sale away.[39] This annoying practice, which he had encountered in Hamilton, was difficult to handle. The alternative to surrendering the sale was a quarrel before the customer—a reaction that could cause more problems. After the customer left, however, an angry Penney told the clerk never to do that again, or else he would "thrash" him. Despite Penney's smaller size, the salesman was more careful. Nonetheless, the unfriendly working atmosphere prompted him to change jobs.[40]

At a new sales job in a Larimer Street dry goods firm, Jim discovered they used a double pricing system. Hale had not followed this practice, which in effect was "let the buyer beware." Some customers could unknowingly pay much more for identical goods than other customers. Although the "one price" system where all items were clearly marked was in increasing use across the country, the old policy lingered in some stores for many decades.[41]

One day, thinking some socks may have been marked wrong, Penney questioned the proprietor about the price. He was informed, "You're here to sell things, not mark them. Do as the price mark says. Sell the socks for twenty-five cents a pair if you can. If you can't, sell them two pairs for a quarter." Recalling his father's standards as well as Hale's, Jim knew the policy was wrong and quit the job.[42]

After these unhappy episodes, an advertisement for part ownership of a butcher and bakery shop in a farming community north of Denver attracted him. With first-hand experience to back up earlier views on the desirability of rural life, he was eager to return to a small town. And after several months as an anonymous salesman, it would be satisfying to be in business for himself.[43] This partnership was a step in the right direction, or so he believed.

After writing home for his $300 savings, Jim moved thirty-five miles northwest of Denver to Longmont and began working in the small market located on the town's busy main street in late 1897 or early 1898.[44] On the surface the town had many similarities to

Hamilton. Social events included masquerade balls, lectures, and visits from traveling phrenologists. Chautauqua was held in nearby Boulder. However, Penney's move to Longmont was the historic turning point of his life.

By the middle of March 1898 Jim had purchased his partner's interest and was sole owner of the "Combination Store."[45] Family members were curious. Elie arrived for a brief visit in March and then Pearl moved from Hamilton to attend school in Longmont. Large gold letters saying "JAMES C. PENNEY" appeared on the window of the small brick store; a faded photograph shows Penney, Pearl, Glen Woods, the baker, and Berta Hess, who later became Jim's wife, standing in the doorway.[46]

The young ladies were dressed in fashionable white puffed sleeve dresses and had flat straw hats perched on upswept hair styles. The quartet looked pleased but store business gave them enough time to pose for pictures. Penney, Pearl and Woods boarded in a small house on Kimbark Street near one of Longmont's depots. Berta owned or rented the house and may have worked in the store as well.[47]

Jim's experience raising and trading livestock gave him a reasonably good background for the meat market venture. The new and quite proud businessman confidently introduced himself to the community with advertisements in the *Longmont Ledger*. On April 1st he said:

> To the people of Longmont and vicinity: Having purchased the whole interest of the Longmont Meat Market and Bakery, we are prepared to furnish you a choice line of meats and bakery goods. A revision has taken place, and everything will be conducted in an entirely different manner. We solicit a share of your patronage. Rest assured it will be appreciated, and confidence reposed in me shall not be misplaced. Leave your name at our shop, that our order man may call at your door every morning.
>
> JAMES C. PENNEY.[48]

At the end of April he ran a direct appeal for business by saying, "Well, have you heard? Heard what? That James C. Penney is running a first class MEAT MARKET and BAKERY? Everything neat and clean. Always a full and complete line. Men are gentlemanly and accommodating. GIVE HIM A TRIAL."[49] The

Longmont Ledger also carried ads for other meat shops and bakeries and for various stores. Penney was learning the hard way that owning a business involved many risks.

The town's growth and its numerous small enterprises, like Penney's, in fact, were proof of how rapidly the once empty west was being settled. Prior to 1870, for example, there was no Longmont, only dry high prairies and the winding St. Vrain River. After 1869 the Union Pacific transcontinental railroad and several branch lines such as the Denver to Cheyenne route had opened northern Colorado to easterners. New Colorado towns were created practically overnight. Greeley, founded in 1869 thirty miles northeast of the site of Longmont, became a model for groups of would-be westerners. Named in honor of the famous newspaper owner and reformer Horace Greeley, the town was also a temperance town.[50]

Longmont was founded in 1871 by the newly-formed Chicago-Colorado Colony.[51] Long's Peak, directly west of the site, provided a name, and mountain river water was available for irrigation and other needs. Burlington, a recent nearby settlement, quickly joined the well-organized Longmont colony.[52] Fifty advance members arrived in March 1871. Hundreds more were on the way and all had paid a $155 membership fee. The site was surveyed, city lots drawn and sold to members. Within four months churches, a school, stores and farms were thriving. By the end of July almost 500 people were in residence. Lumber, farm implements, garden seeds and fruit trees had arrived with the first members by train, and irrigation ditches were constructed as a community effort.[53]

A branch line of the Union Pacific, the Colorado Central, connected Denver, Golden—an older town in the steep foothills—and Longmont. Later the Burlington & Missouri River Railroad from Denver to Lyons served Longmont.[54] Many people came in hope of improving their health in the 5,000-foot elevation; others sought new business opportunities, cheaper land or simply a fresh start in the western state.

The region was scenic and, with proper irrigation, fertile. The town's energetic settlers who transformed the empty acres hoped for many prosperous years in the pleasant community. During the 1870s and 1880s Longmont's population grew slowly.[55] In 1886 it had 1,500 residents and by 1888 there were about 2,000.[56] Throughout the 1890s the population remained between 1,500 and 2,000.[57] Other nearby towns besides Greeley and Golden were Boulder and Fort Collins. Their populations ranged from 3,000 to 6,000.[58]

In summer 1890 R.G. Dun & Company's *Mercantile Agency Reference Book* rated sixty-seven business firms, including banks and mills, in Longmont. Ten were dry goods, notions, shoe and clothing stores. One was the Golden Rule Store.[59] The owners, Alice and Tom Callahan, moved from Humansville, Missouri, in October 1889 and opened the small notions store on Main Street with a capital of $300. They lived behind the store, worked long hours and gradually expanded into selling shoes, dry goods and other apparel.[60]

By 1899 their store was valued at $50,000 to $75,000, and they lived two blocks away in one of Longmont's finest homes. Built of red sandstone, it had balconies, porches and ornate Victorian style woodwork. The young couple had a son, traveled extensively and frequently entertained friends and relatives.[61]

In spring 1898 ads for the Golden Rule Store and information on what was called the Golden Rule "Syndicate" appeared on the same page as Penney's ads.[62] The ex-dry goods salesman became familiar with the store, only seven doors north of his market. Reports of the Callahans' continuing success contrasted with Jim's increasing difficulties.

His small market had stiff competition from larger, longer established firms such as Mrs. Jennie McKeirnan's grocery and bakery. The McKeirnans expanded their bakery at this time and at least two other meat markets existed in Longmont.[63] Jim added to his problems by losing his largest customer, the Imperial Hotel, soon after he became proprietor.[64]

Located just east of him on the corner of Main and Terry, it was Longmont's largest hotel and could accommodate one hundred guests.[65] Naturally, large supplies of food were required. Every week the hotel cook had been receiving whiskey from prior owners of Jim's market as an inducement to continue his regular large orders. In the middle of March he was angered at not receiving some and threatened to end the hotel orders. When Jim learned what was expected, he gave him a bottle of whiskey.[66]

Conscience-stricken afterwards, when he realized his father would never have acceded to the threat, he considered his plight. It was a question of business ethics and temperance beliefs. He was bribing the cook for business if he continued to supply the whiskey. On the other hand, it was difficult enough to survive in business without losing his best customer. Already intransigent in his ideals, he followed his upbringing and refused to give more liquor. In turn, the meat orders went to other markets.[67]

Jim's capital was small and, without new customers to replace the hotel, business dwindled and bills were hard to pay. In late summer when the Callahans were east buying fall and winter merchandise, Penney knew his venture was failing. He sold the bakery to two businessmen, Walter B. Jones and Harry Knoblock; in December they purchased the meat market.[68] A few months later they went out of business for lack of customers.[69] By early December, however, Penney was free of the store and, while not bankrupt, he had lost his savings and needed a job.

In town almost a year, Jim was well acquainted with nearby business firms. The Golden Rule Store was particularly attractive for it reminded him somewhat of Hale's store.[70] Moreover, it was always filled with customers. Callahan was connected with other dry goods stores through a buying arrangement and might be able to use Penney elsewhere. Thus, the popular store was Jim's first choice.[71]

Callahan, however, had already hired extra sales clerks for the holiday season and did not need him. One of his regular salesmen, Charles B. Smith, was on the "sick list," though, and the former meat market owner became Smith's replacement.[72] His previous job made Callahan a bit skeptical, and Penney had to persist to obtain the position, according to some accounts. Penney liked to recall this version of how he was hired:

> Mr. Callahan said, with a slight, friendly smile, "Young man, we sell dry goods—we don't have much use for a butcher in our store." He was having a bit of fun with me, at the same time putting me at ease; being a man with heart, he saw that what had happened was a big disappointment to me.[73]

Knowing the job was temporary, Penney was anxious to impress Callahan with his hard work and sales ability. He arrived early, asked questions and showed enthusiasm.[74] Jim's efforts were appreciated: three weeks later when Smith returned, Callahan asked Penney to work in the Golden Rule Store at Evanston, a busy railroad and mining town in southwestern Wyoming. Penney was so pleased at the offer, he did not hesitate to accept or even ask how much he would be paid.[75] Jim remained in the Longmont store until the end of March and learned first-hand his employer's policies, store merchandise and many of the Golden Rule Stores' success-proven methods.[76] Advertisements and other newspaper descriptions provide a clear image of the prosperous firm.

Beneath Main Street's arching cottonwood trees and close to the Second National Bank, its bright yellow-orange front and crowded showcase windows attracted both residents and farmers. A brick addition, being completed that winter, was needed to handle increasing business.[77] Opened to the public in May, it was enticingly described:

> Our new building is now complete. For beauty of the finish of this new storeroom and to equal the eloquence and elaborate fixtures, consisting of show cases, hat cases, counter, clothing tables and shoe fixtures, with which it is fitted, one will have to go to Broadway, New York City, to [see] the equal of this outfit. Our stock of goods is new, direct from the manufacturer, consisting of everything in wearing apparel for Men and Boys of all ages, from the cheapest to the finest to be found in Eastern markets. To display the extreme good qualities of our goods, we have built one of the best lighted store rooms in the state. All goods are seen beneath large sky lights, it being the best light to examine the qualities of goods.[78]

Located on one floor and much smaller than the Denver emporiums, Callahan's store was nonetheless considered one of the finest stores in agricultural northern Colorado. Penney discovered Golden Rule Stores located in Fort Collins, Boulder and Greeley, as well as the one in Evanston, were also popular and successful.[79] The stores had expensive new cash registers and other modern equipment. Business property was so valuable that family members often slept in the stores to protect them from theft. Iron shutters or bars were sometimes used to protect display windows at night. But this was not true of the Longmont store.

Two days before Christmas 1898 a front window was broken and three coats stolen. William Barnett, a young brother of Alice, was awakened by the crash but could not stop the robbery. Callahan offered a $50 reward; his window cost $150 to replace and the stolen coats were valued at $3 to $12.[80]

Although robberies occurred occasionally, the usual routine was fixed. Stores opened six days a week at 7:30 A.M. and closed about 6:00 P.M. except on Saturdays when they were open until 9:00 or 10:00 P.M. to serve farmers.[81] Sales clerks, however, enjoyed some variety. They could transfer from one nearby Golden Rule Store to another.[82] Prices were low, and in odd-cent prices that had been their trademark since the early 1890s. Golden Rule Stores were also cash-only stores—rare in farming communities that usually relied on credit until harvest time.[83]

Callahan, once established, believed in advertising constantly and aggressively. Comparing his weekly advertisements with those of Longmont competitors helps explain the store's success. Pictures and prices were always included. Each week a different item was featured. One week it was hats, then shoes, muslin underwear and dress goods followed, then ready-to-wear for men and boys was promoted. School supplies and winter coat sales began in the fall. There was a pre-Fourth of July summer sale and special spring and fall millinery displays. One spring opening was promoted with give-aways, and 800 bunches of artificial violets were handed to visitors in two days. Two-line mentions in the business notes section served to remind customers of various Golden Rule Store staple goods currently available.

Callahan benefited from "syndicate" purchases originally featured in St. Louis, New York and Boston trade journals and reprinted at his request in the *Longmont Ledger* for local information. For example, a $57,000 shoe purchase by the Golden Rule Syndicate from the Peters Shoe Company in St. Louis was described in a full-page two-column article reprinted from the *Boston Boot and Shoe Recorder*. Pictures of shoes and descriptions of their fine leather and workmanship were detailed.[84] Accompanying this feature was the shoe company factory picture.[85] Throughout 1898 *Longmont Ledger* articles and advertisements mentioned large syndicate purchases made by Golden Rule Store owners. No other local stores presented similar ads.

Although Callahan was a hard act to follow, Solomon Schey, owner of The Clothier, was equal to the task. He used humor to attract attention to his smaller ads. Once he said, "It's a Chinese Puzzle to us how some merchants expect the intelligent 19th

Century public to believe some of the fairy tales that occupy valuable space in our home town paper."[86] Besides weekly ads in May 1898 he invested in a small book for free distribution. It contained pictures of twenty-nine United States war vessels and other Spanish-American war information.[87]

Schey had been in the clothing business in Longmont since 1886, and during the 1890s he increased his wealth almost as much as Callahan did. In 1900 he was in the $35,000 to $50,000 category.[88] Twice a year Schey traveled to New York City to buy clothing stock. On his summer 1898 trip he left town July 12th and returned August 9th. On Schey's return the newspaper editor commented, "It is getting to be quite the thing now for our merchants to go east in person to lay in their stock. They have the advantage of knowing what goods are up-to-date, and can better judge what the demand will be."[89]

Next week Miss A.F. Lincoln headed east to select fall millinery goods for her shop and to study new styles in hats. She went to Chicago, St. Louis and Omaha.[90] Evidently Callahan's trips east and Golden Rule Syndicate articles reprinted by the *Longmont Ledger* were affecting local business methods. Certainly the outstanding success of the Callahans in ten years, from a net worth of less than $500 to over $50,000, was an inspiration and model for Longmont's businessmen, businesswomen and for the Callahans' new salesman. While working for Tom Callahan, Jim eagerly listened to him talk about early business ventures and the difficult time he had getting started.[91]

Callahan's experiences, a true life story that could have appeared in the popular magazine, *Success*, were an added inspiration to Penney as he looked forward to meeting his employer's partner, William Guy Johnson, and working in the Evanston Golden Rule Store.[92]

NOTES

1.   *News-Graphic*, 10 June 1897, p. 8, col. 1; Bushnell, "J.C. Penney," p. 4.
2.   *Ballenger & Richards Twenty-Fourth Annual Denver City Directory* (Denver: Ballenger & Richards, 1896), p. 5; Henry Gannett, *A Gazetteer of Colorado* (Washington, D.C.: G.P.O., 1906), p. 8.
3.   Harry Hansen, ed., *Colorado, A Guide to the Highest State* (New York: Hastings House, 1970 ed.), p. 131 (1941 ed., pp. 128-29 for founding of Denver).
4.   Ibid., p. 130.
5.   Ibid., p. 122.
6.   *Encyclopedia Americana* (1940 ed.), s.v. "Denver."
7.   Hansen, p. 131; *Bradstreet's Commercial Reports* (1896), Denver.
8.   *Lippincott's Gazetteer of the World, New Revised Edition* (Philadelphia: J.B. Lippincott, 1895), p. 930; Rand, McNally & Co.'s New Business Atlas Map of Colorado in *Rand, McNally & Co.'s New Enlarged Business Atlas* (Rand, McNally & Co., 1895, 1898), p. 327.
9.   Arthur Cooper, *Visitors' Pocket Guide to Denver* (Denver: A.J. Ludditt, 1896), p. 56.
10.   Geo. A. Crofutt, *Crofutt's Grip-Sack Guide to Colorado, A Complete Encyclopedia of the State*, II (Omaha: Overland Publishing, 1885), p. 33; *Rocky Mountain News* (Denver), 9, 10 June 1897, p. 2, col. 1.
11.   *Rocky Mountain News*, 11 June 1897, p. 1, cols. 3-7.
12.   Crofutt (1885), pp. 31-32; Cooper (1896), pp. 23-24, 56.
13.   *Lippincott's* (1895), p. 1026.
14.   *Ballenger & Richards Twenty-Fifth Annual Denver City Directory* (Denver: Ballenger & Richards, 1897), pp. 34-35.
15.   Cooper (1896), p. 53.
16.   Hansen, pp. 131-32; *Rocky Mountain News*, 10 June 1897, p. 1.
17.   *Lippincott's* (1895), p. 1026.
18.   Penney, *Fifty Years*, p. 37.
19.   Kemper Letters of Recommendation, 7 June 1897, PHF I, A-10.
20.   Ibid.; *The Paxtons*, p. 366.
21.   J.M. Hale Letter of Recommendation, 5 June 1897, PHF I, A-10.
22.   Ibid.
23.   Crosby Johnson Letter of Recommendation, 5 June 1897, PHF I, A-10.
24.   Penney, *Fifty Years*, p. 38.
25.   *Ballenger & Richards 24th Annual Denver City Directory*, p. 590.
26.   Ibid.
27.   Penney, *Fifty Years*, p. 43; *Ballenger & Richards 25th Annual Denver City Directory*, p. 809.
28.   *Bradstreet's Commercial Reports* (January 1896), Denver.
29.   Ibid.
30.   *Rocky Mountain News*, 13 June 1897, p. 13.
31.   Ibid.
32.   Penney, *Fifty Years*, p. 38.
33.   *Rocky Mountain News*, 13 June 1897, p. 8.

34. Ibid., pp. 3, 5.
35. Penney, *Fifty Years*, p. 38; *The Resources and Attractions of Colorado for the Home Seeker, Capitalist and Tourist* . . . (St. Louis: Woodward & Tiernan, 1893), p. 40 (salary tables).
36. Penney, *Fifty Years*, p. 38.
37. *The Resources and Attractions of Colorado* (1893), p. 40.
38. Ibid.; *Longmont Ledger*, 18 March 1898, p. 2, col. 6; *The Weekly Pocatello Tribune* (Pocatello, Idaho), 30 August 1902, p. 5, col. 6.
39. Penney, *Fifty Years*, p. 38.
40. Penney, *Man with a Thousand Partners*, p. 21.
41. Ibid., pp. 21-22; Boorstin, *The Democratic Experience*, p. 108.
42. Penney, *Fifty Years*, pp. 39-40.
43. Ibid., p. 40.
44. Penney, *Man with a Thousand Partners*, p. 22.
45. *Longmont Ledger* (Longmont, Colo.), 11 March 1898, p. 3, col. 3.
46. Photograph, PHF I, C-2.
47. *Boulder County Directory* (Denver: Inter-State Advertising and Investment, May 1898), pp. 92, 101.
48. *Longmont Ledger*, 1 April 1898, p. 4, cols. 7-8.
49. Ibid., 29 April 1898, p. 2, col. 7-8.
50. Hansen, pp. 163-64.
51. Ibid., p. 372; Crofutt's (1885), p. 116.
52. *Colorado Prospector* (Denver) Historical Highlights from Early Day Newspapers, 5, No. 8, p. 1, col. 1 (reprint from *The Boulder News* 3/18/1871).
53. Ibid., p. 1, cols. 1-2.
54. Crofutt's (1885), p. 116; *Bradstreet's Commercial Reports* 88 (January 1890), Longmont; James Steele, *Colorado via the Burlington Route* (Chicago: Passenger Department, Chicago, Burlington & Quincy Railroad Co., 1900), railroad map.
55. St. Vrain Valley Historical Association, *They Came to Stay, Longmont, Colorado 1858-1920. Centennial Edition* (Longmont: Longmont Printing Company, 6/1/1971), p. 1.
56. R.G. Dun & Co. 71 (January 1886), Longmont; Ibid., 82 (September 1888), Longmont. Note: There is a difference of several hundred in the population as reported by R.G. Dun & Co. and *Bradstreet's Commercial Reports*, i.e., Bradstreet's 83 (October 1888), for Longmont says it has 1,800 residents.
57. R.G. Dun & Co. and *Bradstreet's Commercial Reports*, 1890 to 1900, Longmont.
58. *Under the Turquoise Sky in Colorado* (Chicago: Passenger Department, Rock Island System, 1905), p. 74.
59. R.G. Dun & Co. 89 (July 1890), Longmont.
60. *Longmont Ledger*, 18 October 1889, p. 3, col. 2; taped interview with Mrs. Ina Fox of Montecito, Calif., January 1978, for the author. Mrs. Fox is a daughter of Hattie Barnett Ramsay of Greeley and Humansville, Mo., and a niece of Alice Barnett Callahan.
61. *They Came to Stay* (1971), p. 48; visit to the Callahan House, Longmont, Colo., by the author in September 1978; *Bradstreet's Commercial Reports* 127 (October 1899), Longmont; also R.G. Dun & Co. (September 1899), Longmont.

62.   *Longmont Ledger*, 29 April 1898, p. 2, cols. 4-5 & 7-8.

63.   *Boulder County Directory* (May 1898), Longmont section; *Longmont Ledger*, 5 August 1898, p. 3, col. 3.

64.   Penney, *Man with a Thousand Partners*, p. 23.

65.   *Under the Turquoise Sky*, p. 75, "Colorado Hotels and Boarding Houses," Longmont.

66.   Penney, *Man with a Thousand Partners*, p. 23.

67.   Ibid.; J.C. Penney, *View from the Ninth Decade, Jottings from a Merchant's Daybook* (New York: Thomas Nelson & Sons, 1960), pp. 44-45.

68.   *Longmont Ledger*, 9 December 1898.

69.   Ibid., 31 March 1899, p. 3, col. 4.

70.   Penney, *Fifty Years*, p. 41.

71.   Penney, *Man with a Thousand Partners*, p. 24.

72.   Ibid.; *Longmont Ledger*, 18 November 1898, p. 3, col. 4, and 16 December 1898, p. 5, col. 4.

73.   Penney, *View from the Ninth Decade*, p. 46.

74.   T.M. Callahan, "Mr. Penney's Commencement Exercises," *The Dynamo* 15 (April 1931): 6-8.

75.   Penney, *View from the Ninth Decade*, p. 47.

76.   Penney, *Man with a Thousand Partners*, p. 25; *Longmont Ledger*, 31 March 1899, p. 3, col. 3.

77.   *Longmont Ledger*, 10 June 1898, p. 3, col. 3, and 2 September 1898, p. 3, col. 4.

78.   Ibid., 12 May 1898, p. 3, cols. 4-8.

79.   *Bradstreet's Commercial Reports* 124 (October 1899), Boulder, Fort Collins, Greeley. Note: Callahan's store was the most successful to date.

80.   *Longmont Ledger*, 23 December 1898, p. 5, col. 4.

81.   Author's Files, Mrs. Donald J. Estes of Longmont to author, October 11, 1977.

82.   *Longmont Ledger*, 2 September 1898, p. 3, col. 4, and 15 September 1899, p. 2, col. 4.

83.   Mrs. Ina Fox Interview; *Souvenir Industrial Edition of the Daily Camera, Descriptive of Boulder County and the Achievements of the Year 1902* (Boulder, Colo.: December 15, 1902), p. 45.

84.   *Longmont Ledger*, 29 April 1898, p. 2, cols. 4-5.

85.   Ibid., p. 3, cols. 4-8.

86.   Ibid., 27 May 1898, p. 3.

87.   Ibid., 20 May 1898, p. 3, col. 2.

88.   R.G. Dun & Co. 127 (January 1900), Longmont.

89.   *Longmont Ledger*, 12 August 1898, p. 3, col. 4.

90.   Ibid., 19 August 1898, p. 3, col. 2.

91.   JCP to T.M. Callahan, 11 February 1926, PHF II, F-2.

92.   *Longmont Ledger*, 10 December 1897, p. 6, cols. 5-7, Advertisement for *Success* magazine. Dr. Orison S. Marden was the magazine's editor-in-chief; three feature articles were: "How a Young Farmer Became a Millionaire," "How Change of Business Brought Change of Fortune," and "Shall I Risk My Salary and Go Into Business for Myself?"; JCP to T.M. Callahan, 11 February 1926, PHF II, F-2.

THE GOLDEN RULE MERCHANTS

Tom Callahan was born June 16, 1858, in north central Illinois to Celia Hood and Thomas M. Callahan, Sr., immigrants from Galway, Ireland. The Callahans met and married in Peoria in the early 1850s soon after arriving in America. By 1858 they were living eighteen miles north of Peoria along the Illinois River on a small farm near the town of Chillicothe.[1] Wheat and corn crops planted on fertile, rolling fields, milling, and shipping by river barge and railroad formed the area's economy.[2]

Young Tom helped his father sell vegetables from a push-cart, and later his mother opened a grocery store in town.[3] Filled with ambition, the five Callahan children grew up to be teachers, physicians and merchants. After a slow start, Tom found his niche as a dry goods merchant.

Small town stores using ruinous credit systems existed across the country, but Tom, perceptive and innovative, discovered more efficient ways of buying and selling. Victorian family ties and small town friendships made his success possible. According to family tradition, Tom Callahan, a short thin man with deep set blue eyes, was teaching school on the outskirts of Chillicothe in the late 1870s. Wanting to change careers, but still undecided, he headed south to Mason City to visit his Hood relatives. On the way he met a traveling photographer and stayed with him to learn the popular profession.[4]

By 1884 "Thomas M. Callahan's Travelling Gallery" was operating in the Ozark region of southwestern Missouri.[5] He came by horse-drawn wagon to the town of Humansville, unfolded painted canvas backdrops, set up benches and pillars and advertised for customers. Cartes-de-visite, small cardboard-backed portrait photographs, were popular. In towns with no resident photographer an itinerant expert was a welcome addition. Business was good and

Humansville had certain other attractions so Callahan decided to stay.

A young sister, Julia, moved from Chillicothe to join him.[6] In 1885, Tom became the partner of an equally ambitious young man, Charles H. Ramsay, a telegrapher from Springfield and native of Indiana. Together, they opened a furniture and undertaker's store.[7] Tom continued to operate his gallery part time.

On the northwestern edge of Polk County, south of Osceola and north of Bolivar, Humansville was seventy miles north of the large commercial center of Springfield. Although secluded, Callahan's new home was an attractive town with enterprising citizens. In the 1830s James G. Human, an explorer and pioneer settler, came to a grassy valley on the edge of the Ozark hills and discovered a crystal clear bubbling spring. He built his home beside the "Big Spring" and gradually more people arrived. As farms were built on rolling hills, a town grew in the valley.[8]

In 1861 John Briggs Barnett, a seventeen-year-old from Bowling Green, Kentucky, arrived in Polk County. He served in the Union Army and in 1865 married Susan Tillery, whose parents were farmers near the village of Humansville. The young couple started a farm and lived in a log cabin. Five daughters and three sons were eventually born to them.[9]

With a neighbor, Barnett opened a general store that stocked stoves, tin and hardware. He was then elected county judge, a very responsible position in the community. Barnett's business prospered and in partnership with Oliver Williams Fisher, a grist and saw mill owner, he opened the town's first bank in 1881.[10] Humansville had almost 400 residents.[11] Its narrow main street was filled with wood and brick stores; Victorian residences of various sizes and shapes began to line haphazardly placed streets. In a few years, owing to a railroad connection, Humansville was transformed into a bustling town of 1,500 residents with a busy train depot, mills, small factories, many stores and a large shale brick manufacturing plant.[12]

Today Humansville has about 1,000 residents, but memories and remnants of the past remain. Weather-beaten mill stones rest in an empty field beside the once sparkling "Big Spring"; the train depot and prosperous industries have vanished, but a few brick buildings on Ohio Street recall the town's thriving commerce.[13] One housed Fisher's and Barnett's "Farmers' & Merchants' Bank." In the 1880s directly across from the bank, there was a small frame millinery shop owned by one of Barnett's industrious daughters.[14]

Among his gallery customers Tom Callahan photographed the Barnetts. A serious romance developed with Alice Eliza, the second oldest. Alice, a pretty, dark-eyed brunette, a little taller than Tom, had a wardrobe of fashionable clothes as did her sisters. One picture shows her in a lovely fur coat with a hairdo of upswept ringlets; popular rosettes decorate her dress. Another captured a carefree summer day in 1886. It was unusually informal: nineteen-year-old Alice and eighteen-year-old Hattie were carefully eating a large watermelon.[15] Other portraits by Callahan show the daughters' trimmed and pleated dresses, lace-edged parasols, gold chains, cameos and ostrich plumed hats—tangible evidence of their good taste and the family's wealth.

Tom and Alice were married February 28, 1886, and his partner Charles Ramsay married Hattie in November 1887.[16] Emma, the eldest and a milliner like Hattie, had married Andy Murphy by 1884.[17] Murphy, a popular young man, became town assessor after operating a boot and shoe shop for several years with a friend, Charles E. Dimmitt.[18] Carrie and Jennie, the two youngest daughters, were married in 1890 and 1893 to Drury G. Keirsey and Burr Fisher, respectively.[19] Their marriages to local businessmen were not surprising, but the fact that the five couples would soon be living in Colorado was.

In 1888, before the western move, a family portrait was taken. It shows the proud father with his five talented daughters—two ran profitable millinery shops and one was attending Baird College in Clinton, Missouri—and three small sons, William, Harry and Charles. Mrs. Barnett's attractive but tired-looking face shows she patiently endured her family's demands.[20] The Barnetts' polished appearance demonstrated that well-to-do residents of a remote Ozark town were as comfortable and as well dressed as their counterparts in much larger cities. Befitting their position, they lived in a large frame house near the center of town.[21]

Ever since the early 1870s Barnett had been considered a good credit risk by credit rating agencies.[22] Now, the bank's pecuniary value, his main source of income, was a substantial $20,000 to $40,000.[23] In the mid-1880s Barnett, Fisher and a new partner named H.H. Smalley entered the railroad building and repair business. Two years later Fisher and Barnett became partners in a lumber company in Shannon County, Missouri. This lucrative venture, called "Cordz & Fisher," brought the families increased wealth. Barnett was the principal capitalist, Fisher was sales manager and the Cordz family continued to cut and process the large stands of yellow pine.[24] At this time Barnett's sons-in-law and daughters decided to follow Horace Greeley's advice—they decided to seek their fortunes and futures in the West.[25]

Guide books described towns in detail, but Judge Barnett insisted on additional proof before giving his approval and financial support. Tom Callahan, experienced in selecting towns with good business possibilities, was elected to travel west and judge the situation in person.[26] First, he returned to Chillicothe to visit relatives.[27] Tom's home town had been growing and contained almost 1,000 residents.[28]

In March 1885 Celia Callahan invested her small capital in a dry goods and notions store on Chillicothe's main street, South Second Street, two blocks west of the Illinois River.[29] She had been separated from Tom's father for a number of years and had practically raised her large family by herself. A tiny but determined person, Mrs. Callahan worked hard in the highly competitive business. Her children inherited her determination. Celia's oldest daughter was now a physician in California; a son was finishing medical school at University of Oregon and another son had just completed his teaching course.[30] Her youngest daughter and namesake helped run the new store.

She promised to sell goods "very cheap" and catered to the farm trade by accepting chickens and eggs in exchange for merchandise.[31] Even before 1887, when the Atchison, Topeka & Santa Fe Railroad came to north Chillicothe, her store thrived.[32] But the addition of this railroad to the Chicago, Rock Island & Pacific Railroad, which had run through town for many years, naturally increased the amount of local workers and payroll, to the benefit of business. Her motto continued to be low prices and quick sales.[33] In April 1887, for example, she advertised she had just received "a large line of dry goods, ladies' and children's shoes, which she will offer to the trade at prices that cannot be beat."[34] "Extremely low prices" and "bottom prices" were two other examples of Celia's style of advertising.[35] That December she sold silk handkerchiefs for 15¢ and mufflers for 25¢.[36]

On the small capital invested, good profits were being made; Tom was impressed by her success. He left Chillicothe October 7, 1888, for San Francisco, carrying with him memories of his mother's popular store.[37] His observations would bring him the success that had so far eluded him. He began the journey, however, with very little money and only relatives' and friends' best wishes to cheer him on.

Not finding what he wanted in California, he traveled to Denver, possibly visiting a brother. In the rapidly growing region surrounding Denver he noticed a lack of small notions stores. He also noted the efficient railroad system, sound agricultural economy based on irrigation and decided to propose this area over all others. He returned to Humansville and made his report.[38] Family members listened eagerly to details of the towns and type of stores they might open. Judge Barnett was impressed by Tom's conservative approach. Tom was not proposing taking Alice to a tumultuous mining town where money might be made rapidly and lost just as quickly, but rather to an area of wheat and vegetable farms and small towns. Tom, in fact, wanted to earn Judge Barnett's respect. Barnett was a model for Callahan, who would enter banking after having been a successful merchant.

Barnett decided to give each daughter $300, a substantial amount, for the store venture. According to family tradition, Mrs. Barnett suggested the "Golden Rule Store" name. The popular Biblical precept, meaning "Do unto others as you would have them do unto you," was an integral part of Victorian moral teachings. The Barnetts were members of the local Baptist church and their religious background may have influenced her suggestion. The name was actually used by various manufacturing, retailing and other organizations at the time, but the young couples' use of it was intended to proclaim their fair business policy and disapproval of "buyer beware" practices.[39] It was quite appropriate to the family nature of the venture.

Alice and Tom were the first to move to Colorado. If they were successful, the rest would follow. Their store's capital was not more than $500, including Alice's $300.[40] No amount could guarantee success, so it was a test of business acumen and thrift.

In early fall 1889, Alice and Tom traveled from Missouri to Longmont; upon arriving they walked up a short hill from the train depot to the main business district. Cottonwood trees, stone sidewalks and painted store fronts with swaying signs lined both sides of Main Street.[41] On the western horizon were the Rocky Mountain foothills. The windswept dusty road was filled with tethered horse-drawn carriages and farm wagons.

They rented a building on the busy street and prepared for opening day. On October 18th the weekly newspaper reported:

> A very cozy little store has been opened on Main Street, second door south of First National Bank, by T.M. Callahan, who carries a carefully selected stock of notions and gents' and ladies' furnishing goods. Mr. and Mrs. Callahan are constantly on hand to welcome their customers.[42]

Overhead was kept to a minimum; they lived behind the store and some furniture was made from old packing cases.[43] Tom put into practice the good advice he had received and successful methods he had observed. They were careful not to overstock the store, but it remained a highly competitive undertaking. In January they began advertising in the *Longmont Ledger*.

Under the title "Convincing Arguments from the Golden Rule Store," they listed numerous items and quoted prices such as "ladies fleece lined arctic gloves for 18¢ and 20¢, worth 40¢ and 50¢."[44] Other items included: children's all wool ribbed hose, 3 pairs for 25¢; boys' 75¢ oil tan wool lined gloves for 40¢; and heavy all wool berege veiling, double width, going for 14¢ a yard.[45] In their first ad they said they were the cheapest place on earth; later they claimed to sell merchandise for wholesale prices.[46] Only one restriction existed: customers had to pay cash.[47] Callahan decided he could not risk extending credit even though this was customary in farming communities.[48] The cash was used to obtain suppliers' discounts for prompt payments. A good reputation with suppliers, bankers and the business community was thus quickly established. The store's very low prices were an inducement for customers to pay cash.

Initially they sold small items—notions and accessories like linen torchon lace, silk handkerchiefs, blouses, corset covers, overalls, jean pants and dress pants. They may have bought them in job lots at greatly reduced prices from suppliers. Gradually they increased stock to a full line of clothing and shoes. This cautious policy gave them time to study Longmont's needs. Attractive displays of carefully selected items kept customers returning. The resulting rapid turnover produced a small but constant profit over the months.

Encouraged by reports of a successful first year, Andy Murphy visited Longmont in early 1891. In May he and Emma opened a Golden Rule Store in Boulder, the county seat of Boulder County and thirteen miles southwest of Longmont.[49] In October they advertised, "Don't buy until you have seen our stock." They were giving a 25 percent to 50 percent discount on ladies', gents' and children's woolen hosiery and underwear, on ladies' mittens of wool and silk, and on ladies' hats, tips and wings.[50]

Next year the Callahans received their first recognition in a trade journal, and Golden Rule Stores were opened in several more Colorado towns. The March issue of the New York City *Dry Goods Chronicle and Fancy Goods Review* noted:

> T.M. Callahan, Longmont, Col. is in the market, accompanied by his wife, making a selection of all the latest and most desirable spring novelties. Mr. Callahan acts wisely in bringing his wife with him, as no one knows the wants of the trade better than a lady, especially in such lines as laces, gloves, millinery and fancy goods.[51]

Alice's good taste in fashion and accessories had already been helpful. Female customers appreciated her suggestions and regarded her as an expert on the latest styles.

In April of the same year Callahan opened a branch Golden Rule Store in Fort Collins, a town thirty miles north of Longmont. Dr. George Mitchell and his wife, Ella, of Humansville were managing the store. They were friends of Callahan who had become interested in the store venture.[52] Mitchell was called a genial and practical businessman who gave excellent bargains. "There is scarcely anything under the sun that cannot be found somewhere in his well selected stock of goods," was a visitor's impression of the new store.[53]

In November 1892 Callahan moved the Longmont store to a larger site on Main Street and installed glass-covered cabinets and counters of polished oak. The newspaper noted customers no longer had to be afraid of crowding each other out—a fine tribute to the store's popularity.[54] That same fall Hattie and Charles Ramsay moved to nearby Greeley and opened their Golden Rule Store.[55]

By 1892 Greeley was a prosperous town of approximately 2500 residents, and the Ramsays had stiff competition. At Christmas they sold notions such as albums, dolls, fancy Christmas cards, silk throws and felt scarfs. Hattie was the store's milliner, and her creations were quite popular. She also ordered and sold merchandise.[56] Although family and business responsibilities had to be balanced—she would have five children—Hattie was a dedicated entrepreneur and preferred store work to house work. The husband-wife team was a great success. Within a decade the Ramsays were listed among the wealthiest families in Colorado.[57]

Humansville and Chillicothe received glowing reports of their native sons' and daughters' western success. Mrs. Barnett took a respite from Missouri's hot, humid June weather and visited Emma and Alice in northern Colorado in 1891.[58] Mrs. Callahan and her sister, Mrs. Agnes Blumle, traveled from Chillicothe to Denver and Longmont in August 1892. After returning to Illinois, Celia started advertising under the name "Golden Rule Store."[59]

The last two daughters of Judge Barnett and their husbands joined the store venture in spring 1893.[60] Carrie and Drury Keirsey moved to Canon City in southern Colorado to open a Golden Rule Store. Burr Fisher had worked in the Longmont store in 1892, and now married to Jennie, he and brother William Peter Fisher became partners with the Murphys in Boulder. Will had opened stores in Alamosa and Salida, Colorado, in 1891 or 1892, but both were closed by 1893.[61] More neighbors and relatives were seriously considering joining the successful young merchants.

In some ways Golden Rule Stores were identical to other small town stores whose owners' names filled the thick credit books issued by R.G. Dun & Company and Bradstreet Company. Notions and dry goods were necessities of life, and ready-to-wear clothing for men, women and children as well as factory-made shoes were becoming increasingly popular.[62] Like others who could afford to, the Golden Rule Store merchants traveled east twice a year to buy merchandise. They also used the well-known firm of Charles "Broadway" Rouss of New York City as a middleman between trips.[63]

However, their merchandise was sold at unusually low prices and for cash only, thus attracting attention. They established a strong identity by using the Golden Rule name on all the stores, and brightly painted yellow-orange store fronts emphasized their name. Due to the low odd-cent prices, local banks often had to order supplies of pennies for the first time after a Golden Rule Store opened in town.[64]

Most significant, besides their rapid success in northern Colorado, was their increasing cooperation. Enlightened self-interest made them unite instead of compete with one another. Their grasp on the ladder of success, though, was seemingly threatened by economic forces beyond their control when 1893 arrived. The nationwide financial panic of June 1893 was followed by an economic depression lasting several years. But instead of collapsing or retrenching, as did many business firms, Golden Rule Stores flourished and expanded.

The *Greeley Tribune* gave northern Colorado readers a grim warning in early July:

> No man can tell where the swiftly culminating events may land us, or what the end may be; but meantime let no farmer, or stockgrower, or banker or business man, for a moment comfort his soul with the lame conclusion that his interests are not at stake, or bound up with the interests of silver and the mines. All that has hitherto made the difference to the farmer of Colorado between his profits and those of his unfortunate brethren of Kansas and Nebraska must be placed to the credit of the mining industry, . . . for years to come, every industry of the state must be closely associated with and largely dependent on our silver mines.[65]

This, at least, was how contemporaries interpreted the future.

Starting in late June 1893 and throughout July, many Denver banks closed. Confidence was at low ebb as the depression deepened. Colorado businessmen blamed New York bankers for the financial disaster while New Yorkers blamed the silver interests of the West for the nation's unsound money.[66] Large Denver department stores were vulnerable in the hard times. With banks closed money was scarce and cash customers were few. Early fall merchandise had already been ordered and this increased owners' worries. As stores became overstocked owners were hard pressed to pay suppliers. Many merchants would be ruined unless business conditions drastically improved.

Golden Eagle Department Store owner, Leopold H. Guldman, took steps to protect himself. On July 1st he stopped all selling on credit, countermanded fall orders by one-third to one-half, and delayed his August buying trip to New York City.[67]

In late July Guldman wrote to his New York agent:

> From what I understand, none of the merchants have gone East yet, Daniels' and Fisher's people are not going East until the very last of next month, and all the merchants have countermanded all they could, just as I did.[68]

He added, "The town looks busted," and said eleven banks and two dry goods houses were closed.[69] In letters to suppliers he asked for November 1st and even December 1st dating on remaining fall orders. As he explained, "The season will be late, if any . . . it will require double the time to dispose of goods."[70]

The Callahans, despite the hard times, proceeded with their eastern buying trip with great confidence. On the way home, they visited the World's Fair at Chicago and were in Longmont by the middle of September. When questioned about business conditions, Tom said he "expected a good run of trade whether the times are hard or easy."[71]

New fall and winter goods were already arriving and a prominent advertisement showed the Golden Rule Stores owners' response to the depression in practical terms. "Hard Times Made Easy at the Golden Rule Store" was their banner and they promised to sell merchandise "at prices to suit the times."[72] Confidence was high in Boulder as well. The Murphys and Fishers proceeded with a move to larger quarters. The *Boulder Daily Camera* noted they had long needed more room.[73]

Success in satisfying customers with low cost items, and the established one-price, cash-only policies were vital to their survival. But there was an additional factor to buoy their confidence: group buying by the five stores. In early August before heading east the entrepreneurs gathered in Denver and had themselves photographed. They called their meeting the "First Golden Rule Store Convention."[74] Among the sixteen participants were Tom and Alice Callahan, Hattie and Charles Ramsay, Jennie and Burr Fisher, Andy Murphy, Drury Keirsey, Dr. Mitchell and Ella Mitchell, C.C. Anderson and Mrs. Anderson, his mother, Miss Turner, Miss Lucy Green and two of her sisters who were milliners and sales ladies in several Golden Rule Stores.[75]

The owners and associates had good reason to be proud of their venture. Both R.G. Dun & Company's *Mercantile Agency Reference Book* and *Bradstreet's Commercial Reports* had given the Golden Rule Stores successively higher ratings throughout the early 1890s. The Longmont store was initially rated $0 to $500 in 1890. By 1893 it had risen to the $5,000 to $10,000 category. Fort Collins and Greeley Golden Rule Stores had the same rating as Longmont in 1893 while Canon City and Boulder Golden Rule Stores were in the $3,000 to $5,000 category.[76]

For the group picture the young women dressed in fashionable puffed-sleeve taffeta and lace dresses. Accustomed to wearing stylish clothing, they were examples for customers to follow. The confident businesswomen appear to play a more significant role during these early years than later on, as subsequent group photographs demonstrate. Gold watches and chains gave evidence of the men's status. Tom Callahan was practically hidden by his relatives, neighbors and employees; his demeanor gave no indication he had pioneered the risky venture or what his future plans might be.

Callahan's astute business sense had perceived the obvious—combine the buying power of the stores and obtain greater influence with suppliers. They could bargain for lower prices, larger discounts and receive more advantageous dating on invoices. Family ties and hometown connections made such cooperation a possibility. However, his idea could have died in selfish individualism and proud rivalry except for their mutual respect and the complete involvement of the Barnett sisters. They were very close to each other and thus drew their husbands closer together.

Doubtless, Callahan had been buying with Murphy and Ramsay ever since their stores were opened so it was logical to expand the procedure.[77] The husbands each contributed certain skills. For example, Murphy's previous experience in the boot and shoe business was quite helpful. Ramsay and Callahan had already worked as partners, and Keirsey had selling and bookkeeping experience from partnership in a Humansville agricultural implements store. The Fisher sons had worked with their father on various store and bank projects and were quick to learn the store business.

The buying arrangement became the means of achieving greater success. They quickly realized more stores meant more buying power. In the hard times their unusual success was a magnet drawing relatives and neighbors to join them. Often newcomers worked in one of the original Golden Rule Stores for a year or two before opening a new store. All new stores were patterned on the original ones.

In 1896, the same year several new stores were opened, the merchants subscribed to "Articles of Agreement."[78] In addition, buying committees were created to make the eastern trips more efficient.[79] These important organizational steps reduced the risk caused by more participants. The potential rewards were great. Their cooperative buying venture succeeded and in 1898 there were twenty stores.[80] Trade journals and newspapers referred to the sixteen merchants as the "Golden Rule Syndicate of Buyers," and proclaimed them to be the "heaviest buyers and most desirable kind of customers."[81]

The same year they placed a spring shoe order for $25,000 and a fall order for $35,000 with a fortunate St. Louis shoe manufacturer. The fall order was described as the "biggest order for shoes ever placed with a local dealer by the retail trade." Jobbers or wholesalers, the middlemen for retailers, were the usual buyers of such large amounts from manufacturers. The "Syndicate" eliminated these middlemen. Their fall order was actually $50,000 for it included several other shoe manufacturers' lines. Before Christmas 1897 Tom announced a "Clearance Sale of Shoes," and said, "No house in the country is in a position to make you as low prices as the Longmont Golden Rule Store." To back this claim he included prices: ladies' $3.50 vici kid shoes cost $2.48, little gents' $1.75 kangaroo calf shoes were $1.19, boys' $1.00 heavy shoes were only 59¢, and infants' shoes started at 13¢.[82]

The ad contained a picture of seven Golden Rule Store owners—Tom Callahan; Andy Murphy, now of Bozeman, Montana; Guy Johnson of Evanston, Wyoming; Edwin Middlebrook of Princeville, Illinois; W.C. Slagle of Grandin, Missouri; Oliver David Fisher; and Burr Fisher—inspecting shoes at the company in St. Louis. Middlebrook had married Julia Callahan and moved from Humansville to Princeville, a town twelve miles west of Chillicothe. Oliver David Fisher managed two Golden Rule Stores at Birch Tree, Missouri, site of the Cordz-Fisher lumber company camp.[83]

William Guy Johnson was a protégé of Callahan. He was born in West Virginia in 1858 but had lived in the Longmont vicinity since the early 1880s.[84] Before coming to work for Callahan in 1894 he had been in several small ventures, the latest being a confectionery shop. A big, confident-looking man, he displayed great talent as a dry goods merchant after joining the Golden Rule Store owners. In 1896 he became a partner with Charles E. Dimmitt and opened a Golden Rule Store in Great Falls, Montana. The next year, however, he and Callahan opened the Evanston store. Dimmitt became partners with Andy Murphy and several in-laws.[85]

Dimmitt entered the store venture directly from Humansville. The former partner of Murphy was experienced as a boot and shoe store merchant. Articulate and well-respected, Dimmitt was the author of the 1896 Articles of Agreement. His organizational skills and long experience eventually became a source of strength to J.C. Penney.[86]

All Golden Rule Store merchants followed similar practices. Next to their low cash-only prices, fashion was most important. Shoe ads and illustrations of clothing and hats were offered as proof they sold the latest styles at the lowest prices. They bought shoes, rubber goods, piece goods, trunks, men's hats, some ready-to-wear clothing, underclothes, corsets and overalls in the mid-west. Most ready-to-wear clothing for men, women and children—shirts, waists, suits, coats—as well as handkerchiefs, collars, gloves, laces, silks, millinery goods, umbrellas, lingerie, other fancy goods, notions and toys came primarily from New York City.[87]

The twice yearly buying trips lasted four to six weeks.[88] For most spring merchandise and some fall samples, they headed east in late January. Fall and winter buying was done in July and August. Goods were ordered to arrive over a period of several months, depending on size and purpose. Spring and fall millinery sales were always a special event at Golden Rule Stores.

By 1898 the total amount of merchandise purchased annually was reported as $900,000.[89] In January of that year the *Dry Goods Chronicle* gave notice to suppliers that the western buying syndicate had arrived in New York City.[90] A description of the Golden Rule Store owners' semi-annual meeting at the Broadway Central Hotel was included.

This hotel had become their New York headquarters. Located at Bond and Broadway, the spacious hostelry was near many garment makers and representatives for out-of-town manufacturers.

The merchants were also well known in other cities including Boston, Rochester and Chicago where salesmen "are anxious to show them samples and book their orders."[91]

Intense competition existed for their orders. "One of the largest, most bitterly fought for and most talked about shoe orders that is placed in any of the shoe markets of the country is the order of the Golden Rule Syndicate," was the opinion of the Boston *Boot and Shoe Recorder* in 1898.[92] This competition helped them obtain merchandise at bargain prices, and by selling for less than home town competition they continued to expand and prosper. The Golden Rule Store venture had literally turned into gold for them.

More prosperous every year, the merchants began traveling east together in a private train car. The July 1898 buying trip was one to remember. Upon returning the entire group stopped to see Yellowstone Park, enjoying their friendship and the striking scenery. It was also widower Guy Johnson's honeymoon trip with Lucy Green Johnson, a hat trimmer and cashier at Fort Collins and Longmont.[93]

America had just won the war with Spain and entered a new era. The Golden Rule Store owners' business methods suited the times, and they looked forward to many successful years together. To a St. Louis reporter Tom Callahan gave this justification of their buying system:

> Yes, we find we can secure better bargains by forming a syndicate, and all members buying any line of goods from the house that makes a better price by being brought into keen competition with all other houses, . . . We have not organized a trust. Of course, one of our members remarked in a friendly way 'if we don't do somebody, somebody will do us.' But, after all, the golden rule, even if it did originate with an ancient Grecian philosopher long before the time of Christ, is as fine a business motto as a merchant can follow.[94]

Certainly they had been successful beyond Tom's wildest dreams. From an idea born in Celia Callahan's Chillicothe store, combined with the Barnett family's involvement, and rapid western settlement based on the railroad, there were now related Golden Rule Stores in five states: Colorado, Wyoming, Montana, Illinois and Missouri. Owners were already opening additional stores. Their efficient modern practices, some common in big cities, had insured success in practically every small town they entered. With their buying power, they could out-buy and under-price almost every small town competitor and even challenge many urban department stores. Golden Rule Stores were destined to flourish for over three decades.

Besides relatives, Callahan encouraged salesclerks like Guy Johnson and Henry C. Stevens, just to name two, to become merchants. His early experiences had not been forgotten. Most likely influenced by Judge Barnett's example, he was willing to extend opportunities to others and trust them to make good. It was a form of enlightened self-interest for a partnership in a profitable store provided valuable income over the years. His perception and trust were rare, though, both then and now.

In early 1899 Penney was beginning to learn of the Golden Rule Stores' scope. His appreciation increased after hearing that Guy Johnson had been one of Callahan's sales clerks only a few years ago. He could hardly believe his good fortune when Callahan said he and Johnson planned to open more stores, and hinted that Penney, if he continued to work hard, might be one of their partners.[95] The developing, but by no means centralized or systematized, organization Penney joined made his dream much closer to reality. After meeting Johnson, who stopped in Longmont for a few days after an eastern trip, Penney was officially hired and prepared to move to Evanston.

Callahan was already a hero and model for the young clerk, and Johnson became another. He would strive to emulate them. One fact is clear: without Callahan's success story, Penney would never have begun building his successful chain of stores. When he died in 1940 Thomas M. Callahan was eulogized as the pioneer chain store merchant of Colorado. Even then, the story of the merchants from Chillicothe and Humansville was remembered by only a few.[96] Nevertheless, residents of these small towns had spread their stores and merchandising ideas throughout the west and midwest and made a remarkable contribution to twentieth-century retailing.

NOTES

1. Nevada State Department of Health, Division of Vital Statistics. Standard Certificate of Death #40-1285, Thomas M. Callahan; Interview with Hood family members in June 1979; *They Came to Stay*, p. 48.

2. Sharon Scott, *Chillicothe: The Way We Grew* (Chillicothe, Ill.: Chillicothe Historical Society, c. 1978), p. 2.

3. "Tom Callahan Dies in Reno, Nev.," *Chillicothe Bulletin*, 27 December 1940, p. 1; *Bradstreet's Commercial Reports* 42-45 (April 1878-April 1879), Chillicothe, Ill.

4. Interview with Mr. Thomas Hayden of Chillicothe, Ill., relative of Thomas M. Callahan, August 1979.

5. *Bradstreet's Commercial Reports* 66 (July 1884), Humansville, Mo.

6. *Chillicothe Bulletin*, 15 July 1884, p. 12, col. 1.

7. *Bradstreet's Commercial Reports* 71 (October 1885), Humansville, Mo.; Photograph Collection of Mrs. Ina Ramsay Fox—business card.

8. Mrs. Mary A. Owens, *My Town* (Lincoln, Mo.: Williams Press, 1976), pp. 1-2; *Humansville, Missouri 1872-1972, Centennial* (Humansville-Lincoln-Cole-Camp, Mo.: Williams Press, c. 1973), p. 4.

9. *History of Hickory, Polk, Cedar, Dade and Barton Counties*, Missouri (Chicago: Goodspeed Publishing, 1889), p. 624; National Archives, Pension Record for Union Service for John Briggs Barnett. Nos. 933674 and 831864. Includes clipping from *Humansville Star-Leader*, 26 March 1915, "Mr. and Mrs. J.B. Barnett Celebrate Golden Wedding Anniversary."

10. Ibid.; R.G. Dun & Co. (September 1873-January 1880); Herman Steen, *The O.W. Fisher Heritage* (Seattle: Frank McCaffrey, 1961), pp. 34-38.

11. R.G. Dun & Co. 49 (July 1880), Humansville, Mo.

12. *Humansville Centennial*, pp. 53, 66, 73; R.G. Dun & Co. 71 (January 1886), Humansville, Mo. reports population as 1,500; *Bradstreet's Commercial Reports* 75 (October 1886), Humansville, Mo., gives a population of 1,000. Railroad is the Kansas City, Clinton & Springfield Division, Kansas City, Fort Scott & Gulf Railroad.

13. Visit to Humansville by author in June 1978. Tour of town given by Mrs. Mary A. Owens, long-time resident and town historian.

14. Ibid.; Fox Photograph Collection and Fox Interview.

15. Fox Photograph Collection.

16. *They Came to Stay* (1971), p. 48; Interview with Mrs. Ina Ramsay Fox.

17. *1900 Census*, Humansville, Missouri, Andy Murphy and family, Vol. 75, E.C. 127, Sheet 2, Line 60.

18. *History of Hickory, Polk*, p. 624; Information and original advertisement for boot and shoe shop from Mrs. Blanche Miller, daughter of Charles E. Dimmitt; *Bradstreet's Commercial Reports* 78 (July 1887), Humansville, Mo.

19. *1900 Census*, Fort Collins, Colorado, for D.G. Keirsey and family, E.D. 213, Sheet 3; Steen, *O.W. Fisher Heritage*, p. 51.

20. Fox Photograph Collection.

21. Fox Interview.

22. R.G. Dun & Co., 1873+, Humansville, Mo.

23. *Bradstreet's Commercial Reports* 69 (April 1885), Humansville, Mo.
24. Steen, *O.W. Fisher Heritage*, pp. 40-42.
25. Fox Interview.
26. Ibid.
27. *Chillicothe Bulletin*, 28 September 1888, p. 5, col. 4.
28. *The Standard Atlas & Gazetteer of the World* (Chicago: Standard Publishing Co., 1888), p. 508, Chillicothe: 936 residents.
29. *Chillicothe Bulletin*, 27 March 1885, p. 1, col. 2.
30. Ibid., 13 April 1888, p. 6, col. 3, and 10 February 1888, p. 4, col. 3.
31. Ibid., 3 April 1885, p. 1, col. 3.
32. Ibid., 10 June 1887, p. 1; 3 June 1887, p. 5, col. 1.
33. Ibid., 5 February 1886, p. 2, col. 2.
34. Ibid., 8 April 1887, p. 8, col. 2.
35. Ibid., 18 February 1887, p. 8, col. 3, and 11 March 1887, p. 7, col. 1.
36. Ibid., 9 December 1887, p. 8, col. 1.
37. Ibid., 12 October 1888, p. 6, col. 2.
38. Fox Interview.
39. Ibid.
40. R.G. Dun & Co. 89 (July 1890), Longmont, Colo.
41. *Souvenir Industrial Edition*, p. 44.
42. *Longmont Ledger*, 18 October 1889, p. 3, col. 2.
43. Information from Mrs. Frank McDonough, Secretary of The Callahan House Board, Longmont, Colo.
44. *Longmont Ledger*, 17 January 1890, p. 3, col. 3.
45. Ibid.
46. Ibid.; 14 August 1891, p. 3, cols. 5-6.
47. Ibid., 14 August 1891, said "To The Cash Trade Only." Note: As early as 4 April 1890 they were saying in advertisements "No Goods Permitted to Leave the Store Until Paid For."
48. *Souvenir Industrial Edition*, p. 45.
49. *Longmont Ledger*, 1 May 1891, p. 3, col. 2.
50. *Boulder Daily Camera* (Boulder, Colo.), 6 October 1891.
51. *Dry Goods Chronicle and Fancy Goods Review* (New York) 13, No. 11 (March 12, 1892): 28.
52. *Fort Collins Express* (Fort Collins, Colo.), 23 April 1892, p. 1, col. 2.
53. Ibid., 30 April 1892, p. 1, col. 6.
54. *Longmont Ledger*, 18 November 1892, p. 3, cols. 2-3; 3 February 1893, p. 3, col. 2.
55. *Greeley Tribune* (Greeley, Colo.), 22 December 1892, p. 8, cols. 5-6; Fox Interview.
56. Ibid.
57. Colorado State Historical Library, Denver. *Dawson Scrapbook*, Vol. 59 "Businessmen Book I," pp. 326-27, "Colorado Millionaires. . . ." Article of December 31, 1904 includes a list of over 500 wealthiest citizens of the state.
58. *Boulder Daily Camera*, 18 July 1891, p. 4, col. 1; *Chillicothe Bulletin*, 29 July 1892, p. 4, col. 3.
59. *Chillicothe Bulletin*, 25 November 1892, p. 4, col. 1, and 16 December 1892, p. 8, col. 1.

60.   Ansel Watrous, *History of Larimer County, Colorado* (Fort Collins, Colo.: Courier Printing & Publishing Co., 1911), p. 306, Drury G. Keirsey; *Canon City Clipper* (Canon City, Colo.), 10 September 1897, p. 4, ad for Golden Rule Store; *Bradstreet's Commercial Reports* 102 (July 1893), Canon City, Fremont County, Colorado.

61.   Steen, *O.W. Fisher Heritage*, p. 49.

62.   *Encyclopedia of American History* (1965), p. 525; Kidwell and Christman, *Suiting Everyone*, pp. 111, 115, 119, 137.

63.   Fox Interview.

64.   Ibid.

65.   *Greeley Tribune*, 6 July 1893, p. 4, col. 1.

66.   *Boulder Daily Camera*, 17 July 1893, p. 1, col. 1; *Longmont Ledger*, 18 August 1893, p. 3, col. 4.

67.   Western Historical Collections, University of Colorado at Boulder. *L.H. Guldman Papers*. Bound V. Letter Books-1893 (April 18, 1893), p. 341 "Notice June 25, 1893; p. 359 LHG to Scheuerman & Bros., Des Moines, Iowa, June 30, 1893; p. 395 LHG to K. Mandell & Co., N.Y.C., July 11, 1893.

68.   Ibid., LHG to K. Mandell, 7/21/93, p. 437.

69.   Ibid.

70.   Ibid., LHG to Peerless Knitting Mills, Toledo, Ohio, 7/19/93, p. 426, LHG to Alpha Knitting Co., Schenectady, N.Y., 7/20/93, p. 434, LHG to N. Hatch & Co. of N.Y., 7/30/93, p. 430.

71.   *Longmont Ledger*, 15 September 1893, p. 3, col. 2.

72.   Ibid., 15 September 1893, p. 3, cols. 7-8.

73.   *Boulder Daily Camera*, 11 August 1893, p. 4, col. 1.

74.   Fox Photograph.

75.   Fox Interview.

76.   R.G. Dun & Co. and *Bradstreet's Commercial Reports*, 1890-1893.

77.   *Fort Collins Courier*, 28 July 1898, Special Edition, p. 3, full page ad; Note: Steen, *O.W. Fisher Heritage* on pp. 63-64 credits Burr Fisher with initiating the buying organization, but 1898 sources specify Callahan, i.e. *Shoe and Leather Gazette*, 11 August 1898, p. 22, and reprints in the *Fort Collins Courier*, July 28, 1898.

78.   C.E. Dimmitt, "Twenty Years Ago," *The Dynamo* 16 (April 1932): 6.

79.   *Fort Collins Courier*, 28 July 1898, Special Edition, p. 3.

80.   *Shoe and Leather Gazette*, 11 August 1898, p. 22.

81.   Ibid.; *Longmont Ledger*, 3 December 1897, p. 3, reprint of *St. Louis Republican* July 27, 1897 article about the syndicate.

82.   *Longmont Ledger*, 3 December 1897, p. 3.

83.   Ibid.; *Shoe and Leather Gazette*, 11 August 1898, p. 22.

84.   *1900 Census*, Evanston, Wyoming, for W. Guy Johnson and Lucy Johnson, E.D. 58, Sheet 11; *Shoe and Leather Gazette*, 11 August 1898, p. 22; *Fort Collins Express-Courier*, 23 November 1927, p. 1, obituary for William Guy Johnson.

85.   *Shoe and Leather Gazette*, 11 August 1898, p. 22.

86.   Dimmitt, "Twenty Years Ago," p. 6.

87.   *Longmont Ledger*, 14 October 1898, p. 3, cols. 6-8; 24 October 1898, p. 4; 18 March 1898, p. 3, col. 6.

88.   *Shoe and Leather Gazette*, 11 August 1898, p. 23.

89.   *Fort Collins Courier*, 28 July 1898, Special Edition, p. 3 ad.

90.   *Dry Goods Chronicle and Fancy Goods Review*, 19 February 1898, p. 11, col. 2.

91.   *Longmont Ledger*, 3 December 1897, p. 3.

92.   *Boot and Shoe Recorder* article reprinted in *Fort Collins Courier*, 28 July 1898.

93.   *Longmont Ledger*, 11 February 1898; *Shoe and Leather Gazette*, 11 August 1898, pp. 22-23.

94.   *Fort Collins Courier*, 28 July 1898, Special Edition, p. 3 ad. Article is reprint from *St. Louis Globe-Democrat*, 1 February 1898.

95.   Penney, *View from the Ninth Decade*, p. 47; Penney, *Man with a Thousand Partners*, pp. 25-26.

96.   D.S. McNeil, *The Story of Humansville* (Humansville, Mo.: Star-Leader Print, 1934), pp. 11-13 "The Golden Rule"; Jane Miller, "New York Woman Researches Local J.C. Penney History," *Chillicothe Bulletin*, 23 August 1979, p. 2, cols. 1-6.

YEARS OF PREPARATION
AND THE FIRST PARTNERSHIP

Johnson and Callahan opened the Evanston Golden Rule Store in spring 1897.[1] Evanston was the county seat of Uinta County and in addition to being on the Union Pacific Railroad main line, seventy-six miles east of Ogden, Utah, it was only six miles from Almy Mines, one of the largest coal beds in the west. Several lumber mills and railroad machine shops were located in the bleak-looking town by Bear River.[2]

Bear River winds through the 6,870-foot valley where Evanston was settled in 1868 and 1869. A train depot, business and residential streets were established south of the river. To the north across the railroad tracks and river was a substantial Chinese community.[3] In contrast with its somber landscape and plain architecture, Evanston's population was varied, colorful and far different from Longmont's more homogeneous composition.

In southwestern Wyoming there were large sheep ranches; timothy, wild hay, alfalfa, oats, potatoes and winter wheat were grown by Uinta farmers, but the majority of town residents worked for the mining company and railroad. Uinta County's population was the third largest in Wyoming. In 1900 it had 12,223 residents when the state's total population was 92,531.[4]

Frame buildings, from one to three stories in height, lined Front and Main Streets.[5] Brick buildings included the depot, Court House and several business firms such as Blyth, Fargo & Company, a successful general store, and the enlarged Golden Rule Store.[6] Clear skies with cold, dry air in mid-September gave warning of long, freezing winters. Wyoming temperatures ranged from 30° below zero in winter to 105° above in summer.[7] When Penney arrived at the end of March 1899, Evanston's 2,000 residents were eagerly awaiting spring.

The Golden Rule Store was first located in a small frame building; the stock was mainly notions. It was referred to as a "5¢ & 10¢" store, but, as in Longmont, this was only temporary.[8] Within a year a full line of shoes and clothes was offered. The move to larger quarters on Main Street in 1898 meant the Golden Rule Store was securely established and its cash-only policy accepted.

Due to Callahan's high standing with eastern credit rating agencies, the new store received the exact same rating in January 1898 as the Longmont store—$20,000 to $40,000.[9] By September 1899, it was rated at $40,000 to $75,000.[10] However, the new store had strong competition. Blyth, Fargo & Company which had a branch store in Pocatello, Idaho, was rated at $75,000 to $125,000. Beckwith Commercial Company, another general store that sold both wholesale and retail, had an even higher rating of $200,000 to $300,000. The owners were also bankers. I. Kastor sold clothing and furnishings, and his store was worth an estimated $5,000 to $10,000. James McKenzie and D.R. Cameron were tailors; both had ratings of less than $500. The town's two shoemakers, O. McVeigh and James Morganson, were in this same category.[11]

Under Johnson's managership and with the Golden Rule Syndicate's help the store was so successful its owners decided to open another one in 1899 at Rock Springs, Wyoming, a thriving railroad and coal mining town.[12] It was ninety miles east of Evanston and on the Union Pacific Railroad main line. The new store was expected to prosper in the town of 4,300 residents. Charles B. Smith, a former sales clerk from Longmont, was installed as manager.[13]

Johnson and Callahan planned to open another store as soon as they had the right man and found the right town. John Hood, Callahan's young cousin from Mason City, Illinois, had been working in the Longmont and Fort Collins stores for several years. In late 1900 or early 1901 he became manager of a Golden Rule Store opened in Pocatello, a prosperous Idaho town of 4,000 residents.[14] The firm name was originally "Johnson, Callahan & Co.," but within two years Hood was officially listed as their partner.[15]

Johnson's and Callahan's eagerness to open new stores was typical of other Golden Rule Store owners. After 1898 the country's financial mood was more confident, encouraging the entrepreneurs to expand faster than before. For example, in 1900 Charles Ramsay had stores in Delta and Salida, Colorado, besides Greeley. They were each rated above $20,000.[16] Ramsay was just opening a store at Rocky Ford, Colorado, and had several protégés who became partners in the new stores.

Columbus C. Anderson also had three stores: Central City, Colorado, and Boise City and Silver City, Idaho.[17] The Fisher family had its store at Boulder but they were about to close it and move to Montana. They purchased the Bozeman store of Andy Murphy, and were located in Missoula and Stevensville, Montana, by 1900.[18] J.N. McCracken & Son, former Humansville residents who followed their neighbors' footsteps west, owned successful Golden Rule Stores in Livingston and Billings, Montana.[19] Frank S. Jones, W.J. Lindsay, and members of the Akins, Willock and Worthington families, all from Humansville, were starting Golden Rule Stores, too.[20]

Golden Rule Stores were opened in central Illinois in Havana, Canton, Princeton and later in Kewanee by the Hood family. They sold similar merchandise and benefited from group buying with the western stores.[21]

The buying syndicate was in force, but now committees headed east to make large purchases instead of the entire group. As individuals opened more branch stores, however, they began buying more and more for themselves. Their long-time cooperation came more from home town and family ties than from a realization of the need for a centralized, modern organization. At heart, they were highly individual entrepreneurs as are most successful business people. There was plenty of room in the west and midwest for them to expand for many years. Other retailers began forming buying associations as well.[22]

Penney's few years in Evanston were crucial. He arrived determined to win Johnson's respect and to become as good a merchant as his employers. The close study and observation he undertook were characteristic. After arriving March 29th he began work as a junior salesman and earned fifty dollars a month, a fair salary. Sales of remnants and left-over merchandise became his specialty.[23] He enjoyed keeping stock neatly folded and would dust and sweep floors between serving customers. Given an hour for lunch, he rarely took more than thirty minutes.[24] He was quickly promoted to "first man" or chief sales clerk.[25]

Town residents were also impressed with his manner. In August
the Evanston *News-Register* described Penney as the "genial head
clerk at the Golden Rule Store," and reported he had made "a host
of friends during his short residence here."[26] The article
announced a major event in Penney's life—his marriage to Berta
Alva Hess, the young woman he met in Longmont. They were
married in Cheyenne on August 24th by Reverend S.C. Davis,
pastor of the First Baptist Church, during the city's Frontier Days
celebration.[27] This recreation of the "old west" of a few decades
earlier drew thousands of visitors from several states. At least ten
couples were married during the festivities. A special frontier style
wedding was one of the attractions, but the Penneys' marriage was
a simple, private ceremony.[28]

Frontier Days were colorful and exciting. "Polly Pry," an
enthusiastic reporter for the *Denver Post*, described one event:

> Around the corner swept half a hundred cowboys and girls.
> Down the wide street they came, floating hair, flapping
> sombreros, gaudy saddle cloths, jingling spurs, fluttering shirts,
> bright eyes and laughing faces, a tunder of noise, a swirl of color
> and just as they pass the hotel one big 'Ki-yi' and a yell that
> made the air tingle, while every rider brought her or his horse
> to a sudden standstill, and the crowd awoke to the fact that this
> was it—and testified its appreciation in proper form.[29]

Their brief honeymoon in Cheyenne was an auspicious
beginning to a happy marriage. Jim's marriage to Berta, however,
reveals more about his character than any action he had taken in his
twenty-four years.

Berta, a pretty five-foot-three-inch brunette, was a few years
older than Jim. The Hesses, of German descent, were hard working
but not wealthy. Her parents, William Osborne Hess and Ella Jane
Chatterson, had moved from Berkeley County, West Virginia, to
Canada to live with Chatterson relatives and later moved to
Detroit.[30] Berta's tragic and childless first marriage, made at age
nineteen, ended in divorce.[31] Jim had witnessed its final months
in Longmont. When he fell in love with Berta and asked her to
marry him, she responded with the love and loyalty of someone
given a new life.

Despite suffering severe attacks of asthma, Berta was a thrifty,
industrious person who admired Penney's ambition and principles.

His love for Berta, in an era when divorces were few and participants often regarded with suspicion and hostility, demonstrated independence and self-confidence. By following his feelings, he made one of the best decisions of his life. No secret to contemporaries in Longmont or to family members, over the years her previous marriage was known by only a few because Penney wanted to protect her.

Berta Penney, who once declared she would follow her husband anywhere, was an ideal helpmate for someone determined to succeed. She brought lunch and sometimes dinner to the store during busy sales times, advised him on selling from the woman's point of view and was as ambitious and determined as he was.[32]

In Evanston the newlyweds rented a small frame cottage on Main Street, about one-half mile southeast of the store. Their next-door neighbors were a Union Pacific linesman and a saloon keeper.[33] Berta joined the Methodist Church, and their first son, Roswell Kemper Penney, was born January 24, 1901.[34] The small circle of friends they enjoyed grew from Lucy and Guy Johnson to include customers and Evanston businessmen. At work, Penney served many ranchers and sheep herders as well as coal miners from other towns. His personality became more outgoing, befitting a top salesman.

As head clerk he was in charge of the store when Johnson went east on buying trips. He was responsible for cash deposits, daily sales records, and could draw up orders for merchandise.[35] Placing greater responsibility on him made him work harder, but he continued to ask questions and learn.

Penney said, "The days were not long enough, I was happy in my work and as deeply interested in the store as if it were my own."[36] He recalled, "Often I went home at night and was unable to sleep until I had got up, dressed, and gone back to the store to make certain that everything was in its place."[37]

Callahan was a frequent visitor to Evanston, and he and Johnson made efforts to encourage Penney.[38] He received salary increases, tangible proof of their confidence and interest. They were sincerely interested in seeing him improve, and he, in turn, did not leave them when the mayor made him a more lucrative offer.[39]

Once, when thinking about opening his own store, Penney computed how much the Evanston store's stock of shoes cost. The over $10,000 inventory was discouraging to say the least. It was all he and Berta could do to save several hundred dollars.[40]

In fall 1901 Johnson informed Penney that he and Callahan were opening another store. Penney was their choice for manager and one-third partner. They would be happy to loan him the amount needed.[41] This was the opportunity Penney had been hoping for, yet when it came, he was still overwhelmed by their confidence in him. The partnership offer had a striking impact on him, transforming him and awakening all the energy he possessed. He saw this as the opportunity of his life; it "fired my very soul with a desire and an ambition to be somebody."[42]

Truly the Golden Rule Stores were, as he described them, "an organization of great prestige and buying power." He had been trained by the store's pioneer and his protégé, and was now to become their partner. It was a time to rejoice, but he also knew he must not fail.[43] Certainly the relatives, neighbors and clerks who benefited from the first Golden Rule Store merchant's experience and interest were very grateful for their opportunities.[44] Many became highly successful, but only Penney made his name a household word, only Penney created the first nationwide department store chain in America.[45]

His appreciation of this first opportunity was one reason for his later success. Here was everything—partnership with successful merchants, yet a large degree of independence as manager, while the buying power, due to cooperation among at least two dozen merchants, almost assured success. In addition, low prices for quality merchandise, their cash-only and one-price policies appealed to him. Profits that came from rapid turnover of reasonably priced merchandise were more congenial to Penney than those from high mark-ups.

The Golden Rule Store name was much more than a clever advertising slogan. These merchants had high ethical standards. They were, like John M. Hale, merchants his father would have approved of. Before, Penney had desired success; he was now determined to obtain it. Assured of the endeavor's ethical practices, money became his primary concern as he strove to emulate his mentors. Every penny became important.

The new store's location had to be settled before partnership papers could be drawn up. Johnson tried to convince Penney that Ogden, a growing metropolis of about 20,000, was the place for a large Golden Rule Store. They toured the town, but Penney was far from sharing his boss's enthusiasm. In the first place, a large store would mean more capital invested, meaning more debt for Penney who had only $500 in hard-earned savings. Second, he was more familiar with small towns, even preferred them, and had recently become quite friendly with the miners, ranchers and railroad workers who frequented the Evanston store. From them he learned about several new towns on the Oregon Short Line Railroad, only fifty miles to the north.[46]

One named Kemmerer had been founded in late 1897 and was predicted to be a new county seat and boom town.[47] In fact, the Penneys had purchased property there in December 1900 apparently in anticipation of the coming boom as more coal mines were opened.[48]

Protesting that Ogden was too big, Penney attempted to convince Johnson and Callahan of his desire for a smaller town, a town like Diamondville or the adjoining town of Kemmerer to its north. Callahan arrived and after investigating these towns declared, "The woods are full of people," and recommended Kemmerer over Diamondville.[49] Many of these people travelled some distance to shop in the Evanston store, so a Golden Rule Store in that territory should do well. Since it was a growing area, it would not take many customers away from the Evanston store. But last-minute problems developed.

Callahan heard that other young businessmen, as hard working or almost as hard working as Penney, had failed in Kemmerer. He became concerned and asked Berta to convince Jim to change his mind. He told her about the town's saloons and frontier-type character. Berta, however, believed in doing what Jim wanted and would hear nothing of Callahan's suggestion.[50]

There were several financial problems to consider before opening a new Golden Rule Store. Confronting their cash-only policy was the railroad and mining companies' rule of paying once a month. Mining companies also used a "trading coupon" system whereby miners' families could purchase supplies and have the amount deducted from their pay check.[51] A cash store would be an anomaly in these small towns. It would also be short-lived according to Frank Pfeiffer, cashier of the First National Bank of Kemmerer.[52]

Both employers had large payrolls, though, and sheep ranchers and farmers were prosperous.[53] Wages were much higher in Wyoming than in the east, yet prices for goods and overall cost of living were only slightly higher than in eastern states due to excellent railroad connections and low freight charges. For example, railroad trackmen and day laborers earned $1.50 to $2.00 a day; conductors and engineers earned as high as $125 to $135 a month; coal miners averaged $35 to $75 a month; sheep herders earned $30 to $50 a month, which also included board.[54] Strengthening Penney's side were the buying power of the syndicate, his partnership with experienced merchants, a determination to succeed, and the region's bright economic outlook.

The Kemmerer Coal Company, whose mines were at nearby Frontier, was the brainchild of P.J. Quealy who had purchased the land in 1894. With the backing of Mahlon S. Kemmerer of Mauch Chunk, Pennsylvania, the independent firm was created and the town of Kemmerer was founded in 1897.[55] This company, however, was not the vicinity's only coal company.

At Diamondville, immediately south of Kemmerer, were mines owned and operated by the Diamond Coal and Coke Company.[56] The Union Pacific Coal Company had recently opened the Cumberland mines sixteen miles south of Kemmerer. In late March 1902 these mines were operating four days a week. In one day 3,000 tons of coal were recovered.[57] Miles of underground tunnels at Frontier and other sites teemed with activity beneath the brilliant blue sky and crisp air of the near 7,000-foot elevation.

As soon as spring arrived, oil drilling was expected at Fossil, ten miles west of Kemmerer.[58] Area boosters such as Quealy and the *Kemmerer Camera* editor said the long-awaited boom was around the corner.[59]

Kemmerer, population 900, had stark-looking stone and wooden buildings, numerous saloons and fancifully named dirt streets. Agate, Pearl, Emerald, Sapphire, Topaz and Garnet Streets crossed Pine, Cedar and Sage Avenues. To the east behind Hams Fork Creek rose scrub brush covered hills. Between the creek and town ran the Oregon Short Line Railroad tracks. A triangular-shaped park, just west of the depot, was in the middle of Kemmerer's business district.[60] About half a block north of the park, along Pine Avenue, was the frame building selected by Guy Johnson for the new Golden Rule Store.[61]

He had visited the town in mid-January prior to signing partnership papers on January 25, 1902.[62] Capitalization was $6,000, or $2,000 each. The senior partners offered Penney a $1,500 loan at 8 percent interest, but he obtained the money from a Hamilton bank at 6 percent, thus saving $30 a year.[63] Terms of the agreement were fairly typical and included:

> Books of account shall be kept and a full statement of business made to any partner; each of the partners shall share and share alike in the profits and losses of the business, and they may each, at their options and without penalty, engage in other business of like character or otherwise in any other locality.
>
> Neither of the said partners shall, without the consent of the others in writing, sign any note or accept or endorse any bill of exchange or other instrument for the payment of money for or on behalf of said partnership, nor shall either of them release or compound any debt or demand, due or coming to them, except for so much as shall actually be received and brought into the stock or cash account of said business. Neither of the partners shall, without the consent of the others in writing, sell or assign his interest or any part thereof in the business.
>
> The manager shall be required to make a statement to each of the said partners, on the first day of each and every month, showing the monthly sales, all expenses, amounts of cash on hand, bills receivable, bills payable and itemized statement of all moneys paid out, and such suggestions and information as may be proper for the good of the business. The manager shall not at any time draw more from the business than his fixed salary. He shall also use a uniform cost mark, known to all the partners, in marking all goods.[64]

The manager's salary was made part of the expenses, but as a partner Penney would also share in whatever profits he could produce. The agreement was titled "Articles of Co-Partnership" because the compact was between the firm "Johnson & Callahan" and J.C. Penney.[65]

In Kemmerer, the small store, only twenty-five by forty-five feet, was remodeled for $250 while Johnson ordered merchandise to stock it on his semi-annual buying trip.[66] He reached Kansas City January 31st and immediately began placing orders to arrive at Kemmerer "March 1st promptly." At Burnham-Hanna & Munger

Dry Goods Company, Swofford Brothers and J.J. Poindexter Mercantile Company and elsewhere his orders said "Terms—as Johnson & Callahan." Thus the discounts and good reputation established by them benefited the new store.[67]

Next, Johnson went to St. Louis, ordering goods from Rice, Stix Company, Hargadine McKittrick Dry Goods Company, Ely & Walker Dry Goods Company, Booger, Force & Goodbar, and American Manufacturing Jewelry Company, Herkert & Meisel Trunk Company, and Frolicht, Dunker & Renard Carpet Company. By far the largest amount of goods was ordered in New York City. After March 1st he was placing orders for ready-to-wear clothing and accessories with Rosenthal Bros. & Co., Max Solomon, Bendet Isaacs, J.L. Greenbaum & Co., Holzman Bros., Simon Epstein, Louis Marx & Bro., Excelsior Shirt Co., Knickerbocker Suspender Co. of Walker Street, and Lowenstein Bros. (for babies' caps) to name a few.[68]

The new store had to be introduced to some suppliers. For example Johnson added this note to his March 21st order at the Broadway Bargain House, 508 Broadway:

Mr. Austin,

> Kemmerer, Wyo., is a Branch store of Evanston. We guarantee all bills,

> Johnson & Callahan
> Guy Johnson[69]

The Golden Rule name was placed on many items he ordered so their identity was reinforced among suppliers and customers. For hats purchased from John B. Stetson Company of Philadelphia, he requested, "Please brand all hats Golden Rule Merc. Co., Evanston & Kemmerer, Wyo., and rush out as quick as possible." On hats ordered from Booger, Force & Goodbar of St. Louis the Golden Rule name was put in hats and on boxes, too.[70]

This year many shoes, a major item of the Golden Rule Stores, were purchased in Massachusetts. Companies were located in Lowell, Mechanics Falls, Haverhill and Lynn. Joseph P. Dunn & Co. of Denver also supplied shoes. Shoes were often put in special Golden Rule cartons. "Please ship out immediately" or "rush out immediately" was added to all order forms.[71] The new store was due to open in several weeks. The above orders, only a sample, were used to open the store. Fill-in orders and purchases of seasonal goods like furs and toys were made later.

The newspaper that announced the Golden Rule Store's opening also carried weekly ads for the Mountain Trading Company, a general store located in Diamondville, Oakley and Glencoe, two nearby smaller communities, and ads for The Frontier Supply Company, whose large general store was in Frontier. Kemmerer did not have a mining company general store, but Diamondville, Kemmerer and Frontier were within three miles of each other. The Golden Rule Store's chief in-town competitor was to be Blyth, Fargo and Hoskins, a branch of the successful Evanston and Pocatello firm. It would open shortly under the managership of Mr. Hoskins.[72]

Prior to April 14th, opening day, Penney distributed handbills listing prices and policies of the new store. He had the names of 500 miners from a friendly miner he had served in Evanston.[73] With some trepidation and anticipation, Penney, Berta and two sales clerks opened the store early Monday morning. Customers arrived all day long; by evening a total of $466.59, including $81.09 in shoes, had been sold.[74] Jim and Berta were excited and pleased. It appeared the partners had created another successful store.

Johnson was eager to help Penney. The two experienced merchants had great faith in the twenty-six and a half year old's ability. If the new store failed, their suppliers would hold them responsible for any unpaid bills, besides the $2,000 investment they could each lose. An example of the partners' close cooperation is seen in an April 21, 1902 letter:

> Mr. Penney,
>
> We send you by express this morning 2 pair of Spring Heel shoes size 3½ and 4 instead of 3 and 3½, but they are French Nos. and may answer your purpose just as well. They cost $1.60 each. Discount paid the freight so we charge you no freight. We will ship your freight goods today.
>
> Respectfully yours,
> Johnson & Callahan
> Per D[75]

Evidently, Penney sent a request to Evanston to satisfy a customer.

The new store was well stocked with work clothes and shoes as well as Sunday best suits, and materials, notions, and staple goods needed for everyday life. But in summer, when the mines were not worked as often, sales dropped. Penney had to discharge his clerks and spent time showing each customer the store's stock, explaining the good values to be had.[76]

To save money the Penneys lived above the store in make-shift quarters, using shoe boxes for chairs and other packing cases for tables. Water was drawn from a nearby well and hauled up by bucket and rope to their rooms. Roswell, only a year and a half old, slept under the counter while Berta waited on customers.[77]

One customer recalled the store's appearance:

> Your store was small but it was so full of merchandise—rough corduroys and sheepskin lined coats piled high on the center tables, and men's furnishings on your side of the store and ladies' and babies' dainty things on the wife's side.[78]

Penney, who was constantly straightening and rearranging stock, was "the nearest to perpetual motion of anyone I knew."[79]

Many customers came from a distance. One traveled from Green River, Wyoming, seventy miles to the east. Ranch owners became good customers, even if they only came to town twice a year. E.J. Brandly, a prominent sheep rancher near Granger, was one. Penney sold him and his outfit "scads of merchandise."[80]

The three towns were home to many immigrants from northern and southern Europe. Italians, English, Welsh, Scotch, Finns and some Chinese and Japanese lived and worked side by side.[81] The Golden Rule Store became the place where they brought relatives and friends to shop. The new arrivals purchased their first overalls, gloves, shoes and other western necessities from Penney.[82]

The store was open from 7:00 in the morning to almost midnight; they were always looking for customers. On Sunday they opened at 8:00. Whenever they had some free time, Jim and Berta borrowed a horse and buggy and visited nearby customers.[83] Now manager of his own store, Penney developed into a leader. A "busy, active atmosphere" pervaded the new store, reflecting his personality and attracting customers.[84]

He explained how he won customers' confidence:

To establish a reputation both for the store and myself in this new community was what I most desired. I made it my business to learn the names and places of residence of my customers, so that whenever they came into my store I could call them by name. Many of my customers came to town only once or twice a year. I made it a point to remember when they were last in the store and what they bought. This was not easy for me at first and I accomplished it only by persistent effort. This knowledge I found to be a tremendous asset. . . . I soon found that in case of regular customers, who made frequent visits to the store, I remembered much more than face and name.

I gradually built up a knowledge of the needs of the customer and of the family; for example, many times a wife would come in and say: I want shoes, a shirt or hat for my husband. Frequently, she would not know his size, but I made it my business to remember what size my steady customers were, and so was able to serve her. Though it is eleven years since I served these customers I can recall not only the names of many of them, but the sizes of hats, shirts, and shoes they wore.[85]

By January 1903, $28,898.11 of merchandise had been sold. Profits, to be divided three ways, were an impressive $8,514.36.[86] Penney had succeeded in turning over his original inventory of about $5,500 almost four times, a testimony to the merchandise selection, long hours and his personal style of salesmanship. When Guy Johnson arrived to examine the account books the newspaper quoted him as being "very enthusiastic over the amount of business done in Kemmerer."[87] Callahan and eastern credit rating agencies, which had given the new store the same rating as others owned by Johnson and Callahan, were not disappointed in their judgment.[88]

Because of his success, Penney was offered a one-third partnership in the Rock Springs Golden Rule Store if he would take over its management. Johnson and Callahan believed he could improve its so far mediocre profits. Twice each month Penney traveled fifty miles east to the larger town. Although he may have assumed some responsibility for the store in 1903, daily sales reports for Rock Springs did not appear in his record books until 1904.[89]

In mid-February 1903 he left Kemmerer just ahead of a paralyzing blizzard and journeyed to Kansas City to join the Golden Rule buying syndicate on their spring trip.[90] His first buying trip was a major step on the way to being a merchant. He had the benefit of Callahan's and others' valuable judgment and advice and was introduced to suppliers' representatives like Benton Heaton.[91]

Heaton was in charge of the western division of the large Hargadine-McKittrick Dry Goods Company in St. Louis. He was quite familiar with Golden Rule Store operations because the majority of owners had been his neighbors in Humansville. Nat Rounds of Ely & Walker, another well-known dry goods firm, became a respected friend, too.[92]

A group photograph commemorated their 1903 trip. Penney's copy became a treasured possession, recalling the associates who made his first dream possible.[93] Guy Johnson, Tom Callahan, Drury Keirsey and John Hood were pictured with Penney. Its caption was "The Golden Rule Mercantile Company," a name used by Callahan since 1897 to describe some stores he owned.

Two stores, first Pocatello, then Evanston, were incorporated using the name Golden Rule Mercantile Company. In September 1902, Johnson, Callahan and Hood created the first corporation. In June 1904, Johnson, his wife, Lucy, and a protégé, Roland W. Stevens, incorporated another company bearing the same name except for "The."[94]

Johnson and Callahan were experimenting with incorporating their holdings. Although their relationship with Penney did not evolve into a corporation, the name Golden Rule Mercantile Company, which appeared on letterheads, receipts and business cards, began replacing partners' names on these items at some store locations.[95]

The Fisher family had incorporated its stores in 1901.[96] The Fisher Mercantile Company remained in Montana, and the Fisher brothers were active in the buying syndicate. They became acquainted with Penney on trips like the 1903 buying trip.[97]

Penney returned to Kemmerer eager for spring sales. He wanted to improve his showing of the previous year. Although busy, family ties were as strong as ever. Pearl had been working in the store since October or November, and he urged Herbert, eighteen years old, to come west and work with him.[98] Roswell was a toddler and another baby was due in December, but Berta continued to work part time. These busy years were the happiest ones they had together.

Besides word-of-mouth advertising, handbills were the best way to reach customers. Once or twice a year he placed a full-page ad in the Kemmerer newspaper. The Golden Rule Stores' immense buying power, their cash-only and one-price policies were featured. Low prices, however, were what attracted customers' attention, and he proudly listed prices with descriptions of their good quality merchandise.[99]

Business increased rapidly at the small store when Kemmerer's population increased. The boom finally arrived: in 1904 its population had doubled to become 2,000.[100] Penney reached his goal of improving profits in 1903. They were $9,850.83, and in 1904 profits were $11,258.24. Jim continued his long hours and thrifty ways. He saved string and wrapping paper as well as money.[101] In August 1904, he moved the store into larger quarters and a better location.[102] He rented the left side of the first floor in a two-story stone building on the triangle. Counters lined its 25-foot by 140-foot length, while other merchandise hung from the ceiling as was the fashion.[103] An old photograph shows Berta on one side of the store and Penney on the other ready to greet customers.[104]

By this time they were living in a frame cottage on Pine Avenue across from the original store. It was the same property Penney purchased in late 1900.[105] Apparently they had rented it to others prior to moving in. The one-and-a-half-story house, covered with clapboard, was set back off the street. A front porch with scroll work made a pleasing façade. Berta, whose father was a millwright, built an enclosed back porch and finished the tiny loft area in her spare time.[106]

The Penneys' second son was born December 27, 1903.[107] He was named in honor of the partnership. Although Johnson Callahan Penney was known as J.C., Jr., the idea was a sincere tribute to his father's mentors.[108]

With the Rock Springs' Golden Rule Store under his supervision, Penney looked closer to home and discovered a new mining company town named Cumberland where rivals were establishing stores. He suggested to Johnson and Callahan that they open a store there, too.[109] Only sixteen miles south of Kemmerer, the town was owned by the Union Pacific Coal Company. It did not welcome competitors like the Golden Rule Stores. But in late 1904 or early 1905, Johnson, Callahan & Penney's Golden Rule Store opened outside the three-street town and drew a steady stream of customers.[110]

The Cumberland store was a significant step for it was Penney's first branch store, one he suggested and made successful. Johnson and Callahan began to realize Penney had a great amount of initiative. He was what they called a "hustler." Callahan had already recognized Penney's potential. In 1903 he mentioned his plan to open fifty stores in the Rocky Mountain states and offered his protégé managership of them. Although he was not ready for such a responsibility, the idea of a vast number of stores stayed in Penney's mind.[111]

In early 1905 Penney became a one-third partner in a store in Montpelier, Idaho. The Bear Lake County town of more than 2,000 residents was at the end of a division of the Oregon Short Line Railroad and had a large payroll. Area farmers found a ready market for their products in the Wyoming coal fields. Many of the industrious residents were Mormons.[112]

"Ersland, Penney & Callahan, Montpelier, Idaho" appeared on a letterhead in May 1905. For unknown reasons this brief venture was over by late June, and John L. Barney and Callahan became the owners.[113] Penney's readiness to expand, though, was a prologue to future ventures.

By 1905 Callahan had several new partners such as Barney and Katie and Tom Ryan who had worked for him in Longmont or Fort Collins. Other Golden Rule merchants were expanding. John Hood of Pocatello encouraged his sisters to close their Illinois stores and open ones in Idaho. C.E. Dimmett opened a store in Walla Walla, Washington.[114] There was little to stop their expansion during the years before 1907.

On the summer 1905 buying trip, Callahan, who had recently sold his Longmont store, acted in an advisory capacity for his protégés who had become competent buyers in their own right. Penney bought for the Kemmerer, Rock Springs and Cumberland stores. Callahan, however, was still their spokesman, as an interview in the *Dry Goods Economist* of July 1905 makes clear. After announcing the arrival of the "Far Western Buyers" and listing their names and stores, it quoted him on the western economy:

> Mr. Callahan reports business conditions in this section as excellent. In northeastern Colorado remarkable progress has been made due to the extension of irrigation facilities. There are six large beet sugar factories in that portion of the state and

large crops of other products are being raised. The high price of
wool has increased the prosperity of Wyoming, wool being the
largest product of that state. Mining conditions in Idaho are also
good.[115]

At Kemmerer, Penney's 1905 profits were up to $13,844.42, and
in 1906 they were $15,128.33.[116] They were divided three ways as
usual. R.G. Dun & Company rated the store at $125,000, the same
valuation given the partners' other stores. Profits from Rock Springs
and Cumberland were satisfactory, and the mining communities
continued to flourish. For example, eleven of the twenty-nine firms
rated in Kemmerer that year were saloons![117]

With cash in hand, Penney began to think more seriously about
expansion. He purchased Johnson's and Callahan's interests in the
Rock Springs store in January 1906.[118] Will Partin, a cousin from
Hamilton, became store manager and Penney sold him a partnership
interest by June 1906.[119] Partin's sisters, Belle and Anna, worked
in the store; an old picture shows them with Penney, all three busy.
Golden Rule Syndicate pictures were displayed in the plain but
neat-looking store.[120]

Many family members manned the stores, but sometimes
Golden Rule Stores' long hours were resented by Clerks' Unions
and other merchants. This had been a problem for the Hoods in
Pocatello in summer 1902, and the Rock Springs store had to
outlast a boycott because of its long hours. Reducing the number of
hours for clerks was a general movement across the west, in both
large and small cities. But the Golden Rule Stores' low margin of
profit meant they had to rely on volume of sales to survive.
Customers were their lifeblood, and to miss farmers and miners by
closing at 7:00 P.M. would have cut sales drastically. As the stores
became better established, workdays were shortened.[121]

By 1906 the Kemmerer store was firmly established, and much
progress had been made. But basic policies of cash only, one price
and low cost had not changed. Advertisements stressed low prices.
In 1904 Penney said his men's suits that sold at $2.49 and up were
50 percent cheaper than any other comparable ones; boys' suits
started at 49¢ as did ladies' wrappers and ladies' shoes; men's dress
shirts in any style were one third cheaper than elsewhere; hats
started at 49¢ while the best Stetson cost $3.45; suspenders cost 7¢,
12¢, 18¢ and 23¢, and Strauss overalls were 58¢.[122]

By comparison, summer weight men's Balbriggan underwear sold at the Kemmerer store for 15¢, 24¢ and 49¢, but at The Denver Dry Goods Company, the cheapest was 50¢. The latter store sold ladies' waists for 50¢ and higher. Mountain Trading Company in Diamondville did not have odd-cent prices either. Receipts for Rock Springs merchandise reminded customers of the Golden Rule Store policies. One slogan claimed they were "The Originators of Low Prices," and they declared: "We undersell every day of the year," and "We have the best shoe values on earth."[123]

Markup for all these Golden Rule Stores was low, an average of 33-1/3 percent on cost or 25 percent on sales price.[124] Work clothes might be sold near cost while better suits and some fancy goods had a higher than average mark-up. Buying and selling for cash, using their discounts with suppliers and maintaining long hours allowed them to keep this low mark-up.

They were careful not to overstock, one of the primary reasons for business failures, and purchased about 50 percent of their requirements in the market and filled in as goods were sold.[125] Penney was quick to question suppliers about merchandise he ordered. In November 1905 he wanted to know if the Kangaroo glazed skin shoes he ordered for the stores were genuine. The indignant supplier wrote back saying they were indeed Kangaroo and not Vici. He also learned by testing samples of materials.[126]

Only thirty-one years old, he had the example of his mentors to guide him. A new dream, one of a larger organization, began to form. He had several young men working for him who with more experience and responsibility might become his partners in new stores. Severt Tendall, A.F. Lieurance and Dayton H. Mudd were sales clerks at Kemmerer during 1906. Jim McDonald, a boyhood friend from Hamilton, was interested in becoming a merchant and had worked for him during 1905. Herbert worked in the Rawlins, Wyoming, and the Montpelier stores before coming to Kemmerer, and several others were learning the business.[127]

Penney was looking for people like himself who worked hard, had high standards and who would be motivated by the offer of partnership. The prospects were exciting, but his goal would take time to accomplish. Truly, he could say years later:

> I felt a deep sense of gratitude to Mr. Callahan and to Mr. Johnson. . . . In addition to the excellent training in

merchandising which I had received at their hands they had set me an example which was to bear fruit, yea an hundredfold.[128]

In reality, it was over a thousand-fold as his second dream took shape.

NOTES

1.   *Longmont Ledger*, 19 March 1897, p. 3, col. 2, "Home News."
2.   *Lippincott's* (1895), p. 1148 "Evanston."
3.   Author's visit to Evanston, Wyo., in Spetember 1978; *Wyoming. A Guide to Its History, Highways and People. American Guide Series* (New York: Oxford University Press, 1941), pp. 265-66; *Evanston Chinatown 1880-1922, Official Souvenir Program*, Chinese New Year 1976 Uinta County Wyoming Bi-Centennial Celebration (privately printed 1976).
4.   *Wyoming. Its Resources and Attractions* (Omaha: Passenger Department Union Pacific Railroad Company, 1903), pp. 101, 104; *1900 Census*, Evanston, Wyoming, Vol. 4, E.D. 58; *Wyoming, A Guide*, p. 445.
5.   *Evanston Chinatown 1880-1922*, photographs.
6.   Author's visit to Evanston; Elizabeth Arnold Stone, *Uinta County, Its Place in History* (Laramie, Wyo.: The Laramie Printing Co., 1924), p. 157.
7.   *Wyoming. Its Resources and Attractions*, pp. 11-12.
8.   Stone, *Uinta County*, pp. 156-57.
9.   R.G. Dun & Co. 119 (January 1898), Evanston, Wyoming.
10.   Ibid., 126 (September 1899), Evanston.
11.   Ibid., 119 (January 1898), Evanston.
12.   Ibid., 126 (September 1899), Rock Springs, Wyoming.
13.   Ibid.; *Lippincott's New Gazetteer of the World* (Philadelphia: J.B. Lippincott, 1906), p. 1561 Rock Springs; *1900 Census*, Rock Springs, Wyo., Vol. 4, E.D. 55, Sheet No. 10, Line 48; JCP to D.B. Woodyard, 15 March 1945, PHF I, F-3.
14.   Ibid., 134 (September 1901), Pocatello, Idaho; *1900 Census*, Fort Collins, Colorado, Vol. 12, E.D. 213, Sheet 14, line 100 (June 9, 1900).
15.   R.G. Dun & Co., 134 (September 1901), Pocatello, Idaho; Letterhead for Golden Rule Mercantile Company, 21 April 1902, lists "Johnson, Callahan & Hood, Pocatello, Idaho," PHF I, D-3.
16.   *Dry Goods Trade Directory of the United States 1900* (Newark, N.J.: Standard Book Co., 1900), p. 71.
17.   R.G. Dun & Co., 119 (January 1898), Boise City and Silver City, Idaho, Central City, Colo.
18.   Steen, *O.W. Fisher Heritage*, pp. 62, 70; *Dry Goods Trade Directory* (1900), pp. 147, 149, 150.
19.   *Dry Goods Trade Directory* (1900), pp. 149-50.
20.   McNeil, *Story of Humansville* (1931), "The Golden Rule," p. 12; *The Dry Goodsman and General Merchant*, 11, No. 16 (March 5, 1904): 49, refers to Mr. Atkins, of Atkins & Jones, Lewistown and Deer Lodge, Mont. and Astoria, Ore.
21.   R.G. Dun & Co., 127 (January 1900), Canton, Havana, Kewanee, Princeton, Princeville and Chillicothe, Ill. Note: Katherine, Julia and Frances Hood and Martin Hood were John Hood's sisters and brother, Interview with Hood family members, and newspaper articles in the Hood family collection.
22.   "A New Purchasing System," *Chicago Dry Goods Reporter* 33, No. 8 (February 21, 1903): 59.
23.   Penney, *Man with a Thousand Partners*, pp. 25-26.

24. Penney, *Fifty Years*, p. 46; Penney, *Man with a Thousand Partners*, p. 27.

25. Penney, *Man with a Thousand Partners*, p. 27.

26. *The Farmers' Advocate* (Hamilton, Missouri), 13 September 1899, p. 1, col. 4 (reprint of Evanston *News-Register* article.

27. Penney, *Fifty Years*, p. 46; Marriage License and Certificate of Marriage, James C. Penney to Berta A. Hess, *Book 5 of Marriages, Laramie County, Wyoming*, p. 352.

28. *The Cheyenne, Wyoming Daily Sun-Leader*, 24 August 1899, p. 4.

29. Ibid., 29 August 1899, p. 3, cols. 2-3.

30. *Penney and Allied Families*, p. 85; Author's files—correspondence with Mrs. A.B. Peak of Salt Lake City, Utah, a niece of Berta Hess Penney; correspondence with Mr. R.E. Penney, a nephew of J.C. Penney.

31. Author's files.

32. Penney, *Fifty Years*, p. 47.

33. Picture of Evanston home taken in 1930s; PHF I, C-4; *1900 Census*, Evanston, Wyo., Vol. 4, E.D. 58, Sheet 11.

34. *Penney and Allied Families*, p. 85.

35. *Dynamo* 10 (April 1926): 3.

36. *Dynamo* 5 (April 1921): 10.

37. Penney, *Man with a Thousand Partners*, p. 26.

38. Penney, "Man Training," *Dynamo* 15 (March 1932): 4.

39. Ibid.; Penney, *Fifty Years*, p. 47.

40. Penney, "Fruitful Years," *Dynamo* 15 (April 1931): 4; Penney, *Man with a Thousand Partners*, p. 27.

41. Penney, *Fifty Years*, p. 47.

42. Penney, "Looking Forward," *Dynamo* 11 (April 1927): 3.

43. Penney, "Fruitful Years," p. 4.

44. Interview with Hood family; Fox Interview.

45. William Dermot Darby, *Story of the Chain Store* (New York: Dry Goods Economist, 1928), pp. 15, 32-33.

46. Penney, "How Kemmerer Came to Be the Mother Store," *Dynamo* 5 (September 1921): 3; *Lippincott's* (1906), p. 1351.

47. Glen Barrett, *Kemmerer, Wyoming, The Founding of an Independent Coal Town, 1897-1902* (Kemmerer, Wyo.: Quealy Services, Incorporated, 1972), pp. 11-12; *Wyoming Press* (Evanston, Wyo.), 11 March 1899, p. 1, col. 1.

48. Warranty Deed #19447, Uinta County Records, Book O, 354. Note: Kemmerer became the county seat of Lincoln County in 1912.

49. Penney, *Man with a Thousand Partners*, p. 31.

50. Ibid., pp. 32-33.

51. Penney, *Fifty Years*, pp. 49-50.

52. Ibid.; Penney, *Man with a Thousand Partners*, p. 37; *Dynamo* 14 (April 1930): 9.

53. *Dynamo* 14 (April 1930): 9; Penney, *Man with a Thousand Partners*, p. 36.

54. *Wyoming. Its Resources and Attractions*, pp. 97-98.

55. "Twelve Miles Underground," "The Kemmerer Coal Company," *The Kemmerer Camera*, 27 May 1909, p. 5.

56.   Barrett, *Kemmerer, Wyoming*, p. 3.

57.   *Kemmerer Camera*, 29 March 1902, p. 1, col. 3.

58.   *The Weekly Pocatello Tribune* (Pocatello, Idaho), 2 November 1901, p. 1, col. 1 "Oil at Fossil"; *Kemmerer Camera*, 22 March 1902, p. 1, col. 3 "The Boom at Fossil."

59.   Ibid.; *Kemmerer Camera*, 1 February 1902, p. 1, col. 4 "Watch Us Grow."

60.   Author's visit to Kemmerer, Wyo., in September 1978; *Bradstreet's Commercial Reports* 139 (September 1902), Kemmerer, Wyo.

61.   Penney, *Man with a Thousand Partners*, p. 36.

62.   *Kemmerer Camera*, 18 January 1902, p. 1, col. 3.

63.   Penney, *Fifty Years*, p. 50.

64.   "Articles of Co-Partnership," PHF II, A-2.

65.   Ibid.

66.   Penney, *Man with a Thousand Partners*, p. 36; *Kemmerer Camera*, 25 January 1902, p. 1, col. 6.

67.   "Order Sheets for Merchandise for Opening Day, Books #1 and #2," PHF X, B-2.

68.   Ibid.

69.   Ibid.

70.   Ibid.

71.   Ibid.

72.   JCP to J. Peterson, 8 December 1970, PHF I, D-3.

73.   Penney, *Man with a Thousand Partners*, p. 35.

74.   Penney, "How Kemmerer Came to Be the Mother Store," p. 4.

75.   Johnson & Callahan to JCP, PHF I, D-3. Note: This is one of a dozen or more similar letters.

76.   Penney, "How Kemmerer Came to Be the Mother Store," p. 4.

77.   Bushnell, "J.C. Penney," p. 5. Note: Bushnell says J.C., Jr., but they had most likely moved into their cottage by the time he was born in late December 1903.

78.   I.T. Taylor to JCP, 4 November 1929, PHF I, D-3.

79.   Ibid.

80.   Mrs. A.C. Felton to JCP (1968), PHF I, D-3; clipping from *Kemmerer Camera*, 20 July 1951, "Penney Meets an Old Kemmerer Customer," PHF I, D-3.

81.   I.T. Taylor to JCP, 4 November 1929; Penney, *View from the Ninth Decade*," pp. 52-53; *Kemmerer Camera*, ads for the Mountain Trading Company, December 1905, includes text in Italian and Finnish.

82.   Penney, *Fifty Years*, p. 54.

83.   Penney, *Man with a Thousand Partners*, p. 38; Penney, *View from the Ninth Decade*, p. 57; Penney, *Fifty Years*, p. 53; JCP to E.V. Cline, 26 December 1968, PHF, EVM files; JCP to inquiry, 1 April 1941, PHF I, D-3.

84.   *Dynamo* 16 (April 1932): 11.

85.   *Dynamo* 5 (April 1921): 10.

86.   Balance Sheet for 1902, taken January 1903, PHF II, A-1.

87.   *Kemmerer Camera*, 17 January 1903, p. 1, col. 3.

88.   *Bradstreet's Commercial Reports* 139 (September 1902).

89.   JCP to R.B. Callahan, 10 April 1969, PHF, EVM files; Penney, *Man with a Thousand Partners*, pp. 46-47; Rock Springs correspondence, PHF I, F-3, and

Red Sales Book on loan to library, J.C. Penney Hall, National 4-H Headquarters, Chevy Chase, Md.

90.   *Kemmerer Camera*, 14 February 1903, p. 1, col. 2.

91.   JCP to Mr. Heck, 18 August 1937, PHF I, F-6; Dimmitt, "Twenty Years Ago," 6.

92.   Ibid.

93.   This photograph hangs in J.C. Penney's office at the Company's headquarters in New York City.

94.   Incorporation Records, Wyoming State Archives, #5367 "The Golden Rule Mercantile Company," September 1902, and #6174 "Golden Rule Mercantile Company," June 1904.

95.   Business Cards of the Golden Rule Mercantile Company, PHF I, D-2.

96.   Steen, *O.W. Fisher Heritage*, p. 64.

97.   Ibid., p. 212.

98.   1902 Daybook, Kemmerer, PHF, EVM files, October 6, 1902; *Penney and Allied Families*, p. 58.

99.   *Kemmerer Camera*, 30 July 1904, PHF Advertisements File.

100.   R.G. Dun & Co. (January 1905), Kemmerer, Wyo.

101.   Balance Sheets, Kemmerer, PHF II, A-1; Penney, *Fifty Years*, p. 57.

102.   *Kemmerer Camera*, 30 July 1904, ad and "Removal Notice."

103.   National Register of Historic Places Inventory— Nomination Form, Item Number 7, page one. Author's copy.

104.   PHF, Photograph Files.

105.   Warranty Deed #19447, and plat of Kemmerer.

106.   Bushnell, "J.C. Penney," p. 5.

107.   *Penney and Allied Families*, p. 85.

108.   Author's files, and alumni records from Peekskill Military Academy, Peekskill Library, New York.

109.   Penney, *Fifty Years*, p. 58.

110.   Ibid.; Plat of Cumberland, Evanston Court House, Land Records.

111.   Penney, *View from the Ninth Decade*, pp. 51-52.

112.   Rees H. Davis, *Bear Lake County, Its Past History, Present Prosperity and Grand Future* (Paris, Idaho: Post Press, 1903-04), pp. 4, 10, 12.

113.   Receipt dated 5/21/05, PHF X, B-6.

114.   *Longmont Ledger*, 17 March 1905, p. 5, col. 3; Author's files: Hood family collection and correspondence with Mrs. George Miller, daughter of C.E. Dimmitt.

115.   *The Montpelier Examiner*, 22 September 1905, reprint of *Dry Goods Economist* article of July 29, 1905, p. 49, col. 4.

116.   Balance Sheets, Kemmerer, PHF II, A-1.

117.   R.G. Dun & Co. (January 1905), Kemmerer, Wyo.

118.   Bill of Sale, Guy Johnson and T.M. Callahan to JCP, PHF I, F-4.

119.   Ibid., Rock Springs letters, and business cards.

120.   Rock Springs Store interior 1905 or 1906, PHF Photograph file.

121.   *The Weekly Pocatello Tribune*, 30 August 1902, p. 5, col. 6; Rock Springs Records, notes dated June 9, 1904 and July 24, 1904, PHF I, F-6.

122.   *Kemmerer Camera*, 30 July 1904, ad in PHF.

123.   *Denver Dry Goods Company*, Spring and Summer 1903 Catalogue—assuming prices were fairly constant for staple goods; December 1905 ad in *Kemmerer Camera* for Mountain Trading Company; Rock Springs receipts, PHF I, F-6.

124.   C.B. Ramsay, "Store Arithmetic," *Dynamo* 15 (July 1931): 18. The reference is to his father's store in Greeley. This is assuming markups were similar in other Golden Rule Stores since they all followed the same odd-cent prices and low cash-only policies.

125.   JCP to Mr. Heck, 18 August 1937, PHF I, F-6.

126.   A.W. Tedcastle to JCP, 27 November 1905, PHF X, Invoice Records.

127.   *Dynamo* 1-3 (c 1917-1919), listing of early workers.

128.   *Longmont Daily Call*, 12 February 1931, and Penney, "Fruitful Years," pp. 3-5.

SUCCESS ATTAINED AND QUESTIONED

On December 31, 1907, Penney became sole proprietor of the Golden Rule Stores at Kemmerer and Cumberland. Johnson and Callahan agreed to sell him their shares in the two profitable stores for approximately $30,000 plus eight percent interest. Their protégé gave them his personal note and paid the amount in full by February 1, 1909.[1]

Unlike the Rock Springs store purchase in 1906, Penney's acquisition of these stores was not planned. Guy Johnson and Tom Callahan decided, with little warning, to sever their ten-year partnership and even longer friendship.[2] Personal and business disagreements had developed between them, but they had no quarrel with Penney. In fact, Johnson and Penney continued to do some buying and advertising together, but Penney was never again a partner with either of his mentors.

Far from being disillusioned by their problems, he saw the partnership idea as having great potential. It had changed his life, turning a sales clerk into an expert merchant, and was making him financially secure. Its possibilities as a tool for expansion outweighed the risks involved. Although sorry to lose his senior partners, he had already become a mentor to new sales clerks at Kemmerer and Cumberland and was busy preparing them to be junior partners.

Selling was a highly personal business to Penney. He knew instinctively "the first thing a businessman has to sell is himself."[3] Understanding people was behind much of his success, and he practiced expert psychology when dealing with customers and clerks. By learning names and family needs he made customers feel important. It was a sincere interest, for, next to his family, loyal customers were the most important people in the world.

By observation, reading and native intelligence he had developed a shrewd but positive personality. Penney thrived on constant activity, and his firm handshake and genuine interest

109

impressed people of all ages. Speaking skills honed in Hamilton debates were put to good use. Known as a young businessman who was "bound to rise" much higher, Penney also set an excellent example for protégés.

Throughout 1908 he had full responsibility for both stores and was under pressure to pay the large debt. He explained: "I was cramped financially for a while, but that experience really 'made me,' for I worked day and night to get myself in shape, which I did in face of the 1907 panic and its later effects."[4]

Due to the twelve-month economic panic which started in March 1907, profits were down for the first time at Kemmerer. At the end of 1908, $17,393.73 had been earned while 1907 profits had been $21,217.41.[5] It was an opportunity to build good will for the stores, however, because low prices attracted more customers during hard times. As in 1893 the cash-only policy proved its weight in gold. Golden Rule Stores could withstand the often fatal blows of depressions and panics.

Their strength in the face of financial adversity confirmed Penney's faith in "progress." The work ethic, another heritage of his childhood and high school years, became a deeply-held conviction. Honesty, sobriety and hard work had brought him success. His experiences appeared to fit a logical pattern and his life had purpose and direction. During 1908 and 1909 Penney was more confident and optimistic than at any time in his life.

With the $30,000 note being paid off his dream had come true. At age thirty-three he was his own boss in a successful and satisfying business. Not content with this, the fifty stores Callahan had mentioned in 1903 now became an attractive goal, but considering the money and men needed, it was a seemingly impossible one. Nonetheless, he told an approving Berta he was ready to create a chain of stores in the mountain states.[6]

According to Barnett family tradition, about this time Callahan and Penney shared their dreams in a brief but fascinating conversation. Callahan told Penney he would, if still young, cover the nation with a chain of stores. Penney replied, "That's just what I'm going to do!"[7]

The dream was not impossible for several reasons. Penney had his mentors' example and that of other Golden Rule Store owners to guide him. Moreover, his family background was an important factor. His father had guided large civic organizations and persuaded others to follow his ideals. Like his father, Penney the merchant had the vital ingredient required to lead others—he had the courage of his convictions. Success-proven policies and partnerships with promising sales clerks gave his plan a solid foundation. Hard-earned savings were committed to the project.

Spring 1908 saw the establishment of two Golden Rule Stores by Penney. Bingham Canyon, Utah, a mining community near Salt Lake City, and Preston, Idaho, on the Oregon Short Line Railroad seventy miles northeast of Kemmerer, were their locations. Penney was two-thirds owner in both stores in 1908, while Mudd was his one-third partner at Bingham Canyon and Edward J. Neighbors was the one-third owner at Preston.[8] Mudd and Neighbors were carefully selected before coming to Kemmerer. Penney let his partners and contacts in St. Louis, such as Benton Heaton and Nat Rounds, know he was looking for hard-working, experienced salesmen who met certain other requirements.

Heaton's 1906 letter of recommendation for Mudd shows Heaton's regard for both men and one of Penney's important qualifications. Mudd, twenty-four, was described as a "good, conscientious, tireless worker," and Heaton added, "He possesses one of the most important requisites, according to your views, that are necessary for harmony with you, that is, he will not drink at all. He is a total abstainer."[9]

Neighbors, a tall lanky man who was as energetic as the more quiet-mannered Mudd, arrived in September 1907 on Callahan's recommendation.[10] Earl Corder Sams, a native of Simpson in north central Kansas, was hired in October of the same year through the "Business-Men's Clearing House," a Denver employment agency. Sams contacted them because his present position offered "no chance for advancement."[11]

In June the employment agent forwarded Sams' application to Penney at Kemmerer and reported back to Sams: "the opportunities for advancement with them are particularly good in as much as they frequently open up new stores and put some of their salesmen in the position of manager." At this time the Johnson, Callahan, Penney partnership was in effect, so the agent was actually referring to Golden Rule Stores operated by the three partners rather than Penney's. The agent added this interesting note to his letter:

We have also recommended you to the Ramsay Dry Goods Co. of Rocky Ford, Colo. This store also operates a chain of stores all of which are in Colorado. We think you would find the opportunities equally good if you made a connection with them.[12]

In one important respect the employment agent was wrong. Instead of placing clerks as managers in new stores, clerks became manager-partners. It was a rare opportunity indeed. In an era of family-owned businesses there was an over-supply of able but impecunious clerks seeking opportunities. Fear of anonymous jobs in large companies or factories haunted upwardly mobile workers who held to the ideal of independence and ownership.[13]

Sams had a detailed correspondence with Penney about the new position. Although often quoted, one of Penney's letters to Sams explains perfectly what he expected from clerks and why he was expanding. Almost every sentence provides insight to his goals and personality.

Kemmerer, Wyoming
7/4/07

Mr. Earl Sams.
Dear Sir:

Yours rec'd. Am very anxious to get a man as quickly as possible—I would rather wait a while and get a man that suits me than to get one who does not. I received a very nice letter from the Bush Hat Co., also the Beloit people concerning you, and I only reiterate what I have said previously that if you are the man we are looking for—one who can produce results, this would be the place for you. We want no man who is not competent and ambitious. In other words, we want "a live wire."

With your experience, and if you have the ability these people say you have—you certainly could climb just as fast as you like—the faster you climb— the better it suits us. One very pleasant thing concerning our methods, there are no restrictions against an ambitious man. In some places where I have worked there was 'jealousy' towards me for I was bound to succeed. But as soon as I studied these people's method, and knew that I would be unhampered regarding my advancement, I made a special effort to connect myself with them. Even though I was offered more in other places, I chose this, for I knew partly, what I was going into. I am proud to say even my fondest hopes have been more than realized and I wish I was in a position to tell you just what I and others have done. But it is unnecessary and to you, might have the appearance of boast.

I am very glad you are willing to come and see us, for I
consider a personal interview far more satisfactory.

I want a competent man for a permanent place and we
wouldn't want you to come out, not knowing what you were
coming into, any more than you would want to. You will then
see just what is what. I would like for you to make your
arrangement to be here not before Aug. 10th, as I may not get
home before then.

I am corresponding with another very seemingly capable
man. I have given you preference. This other party does not like
Sunday work—we are looking for a man who is anxious to work
any time of day—nights, Sundays, Holidays, or any other day.
One who knew no hours, and not particular about how much
work he does. Only this kind of men I consider make very rapid
advancements. My theory is to make "Hay while the Sun shines."
I am young and am anxious to fix myself so in my advanced
years, I will have enough to keep me comfortable and also to
provide amply for my wife and children in case of accident to
myself. I would be pleased to hear from you again, so I will
know what to expect from you.

> Very respy.,
> J.C. Penney[14]

Sams came for an interview and was hired. The twenty-three-
year-old Kansan was a farmer's son, but had worked in retailing
ever since high school.[15] He had ventured to Colorado City,
Colorado, where a former Beloit neighbor, Ira A. Foote, owned a
store. Foote wrote one of Sams' letters of recommendation. Later
on, Sams brought Foote into the growing chain of Penney stores.[16]

Sams, a short, confident-looking man with thick black hair, had
ability to match his demeanor. He and his wife, Lula Ammerman,
were in Kemmerer only a short time before Penney knew Sams was
determined to succeed.[17] Soon, Sams was sent to Cumberland to
manage the smaller store. During 1908 he and Lula, who worked as
a sales lady and kept house, saved almost $1,000 from their
combined salaries of $1,500. Their savings, which impressed Penney,
were invested in a Golden Rule Store opened in Eureka, Utah,
eighty-five miles south of Salt Lake City, in spring 1909.[18]

At Cumberland the first and many future manager-partners
tried out before opening a store. Initially an informal process, the
"try-out store" became a formal training stage after a few years.[19]
A few early partners, those with long experience in storekeeping,
moved directly from learning Golden Rule Store policies and

Penney's rules into store management, but the majority had to prove they could earn profits as a manager before any investment was made in a new store.[20]

Throughout 1908 letters of inquiry came to Penney at Kemmerer. Many were friends of new sales clerks or partners; others knew suppliers' representatives like Heaton. All were looking for an opportunity to get an "interest" in a store, and they were impressed with what they heard about Penney both from a personal and business point of view.[21]

For example, Bertrum Coffey of Olean, Missouri, and Christian Woidemann, a Scandinavian working in Beloit, wrote and were hired during 1908. Coffey learned of Penney through his friend Lieurance, while Woidemann was a friend of Henry E. Kendall, a neighbor Sams was urging to come west.[22] Woidemann assured Penney, "I am not afraid of work and I neither smoke nor drink."[23] Only twenty-seven, he had served a long apprenticeship in Denmark and had extensive knowledge of dry goods.[24]

Most applicants were in their early to mid-twenties but several were over thirty. George G. Hoag was thirty-seven and had been manager of the O.K. Clothing Company of Coffeyville, Kansas, for two years when he wrote to Penney, at Sams' suggestion, in spring 1909. Hoag had worked for the same firm since 1894. He explained why he wanted to leave: "Am desirous of connecting myself where there is a probability of something good for the future," and added, "am satisfied I can make good," but said he had no money to invest.[25]

After years of hard work, he like countless other men had not earned enough to have substantial savings and had little hope of becoming an owner or partner instead of an employee. However, the possibility of partnership Penney offered required no predetermined amount of money, although thrift and hard work were necessary.

William E. Collins and William B. Strawn were two salesmen at Kemmerer and Cumberland during these years. Penney's clerks earned on the average $75 a month, but most men mentioned here became partners and many were future incorporators of the company.[26] In almost every case they accumulated impressive wealth. On the other hand, clerks were fired for such obvious reasons as stealing from the cash drawer, leaving doors unlocked overnight, and also for not paying attention to the business. Only men who loved their work became Penney's partners.[27]

Speaking of love, sometimes romance developed behind the counter. In late August 1908 Pearl Penney and W.B. Strawn were married in Kemmerer. They moved into the Methodist Church parsonage and continued working in the store.[28]

Clerks and partners encouraged friends to apply because Penney needed men to continue expanding. New men were trained in Golden Rule Store methods and urged to save money to open stores. Many went to Kemmerer first, but Mudd, Neighbors and Sams, now partners, began training clerks as well.[29]

Penney was the focal point of everyone's hopes for he had the dream, the capital and the contacts. Protégés followed his style of personal salesmanship, and were required to operate neat, clean stores and be thrifty. Penney shared his experience with them by taking partners on buying trips and introducing them to suppliers' representatives in the midwest and east.[30]

Selection of towns was almost as important as having good men. Prosperous growing towns on or near railroad routes were chosen regardless of the competition. Cities over 10,000 population, though, were avoided for the time being.

Bingham Canyon where Mudd and his wife opened a store March 26, 1908, was a mining camp of 1,800 residents twenty-eight miles southwest of Salt Lake City.[31] It was a dramatic site; homes and business firms were perched precariously on a narrow road along the steep canyon wall. Mines yielded gold, silver and lead besides the copper it became famous for.[32] Although on a branch line of the Rio Grande Western Railroad, stage coaches and dray wagons were needed to reach town from the canyon's mouth.[33]

The Mudds lived above their twelve-foot by thirty-foot frame store.[34] Two general and dry goods stores were already doing business in Bingham Canyon. Miners' Mercantile Company and Bingham Mercantile Company each had an estimated value of $20,000 to $35,000. The Golden Rule Store, tiny and unimpressive looking, was valued at $75,000 to $100,000—a rating reflecting the value and credit of Penney's several stores.[35]

Similar to Johnson and Callahan, Penney was now an established merchant in the eyes of suppliers and eastern credit rating agencies. Both knew Golden Rule Store merchants bought in large quantities and paid bills on time. Often, payments were made early to obtain special discounts. Suppliers were happy to extend to new stores the same advantageous terms that were granted to ones in Kemmerer, Rock Springs and Cumberland. Thus, despite outward appearances, branch stores had great resources backing them.

One week after Mudd opened the Bingham Canyon store, Neighbors opened one in Preston, Idaho, a town of 1,500. Northwest of Kemmerer, it was on the terminus of the Cache Valley Branch of the Oregon Short Line Railroad as it wound through southeastern Idaho. The fertile, newly settled irrigation district was home for farmers and miners.[36] The twenty-five-foot by thirty-five-foot frame store, with a yellow and black Golden Rule Store sign painted on its side, opened on a capital of $3,900. Penney had a two-thirds interest or investment of $2,600, and Neighbors had invested $1,300.[37]

He met with hostility from local merchants who feared Golden Rule Stores' reputation for low prices and long hours. To discourage evening trade the town council, composed mainly of Neighbors' competitors, passed a 7:00 P.M. closing ordinance for Preston stores.[38] Despite these difficulties, Neighbors persisted in establishing the Preston store. His profits for 1908 were an impressive $7,861.80 and climbed to $9,205.91 for 1909 when his sales were $65,000.[39] Bingham Canyon profits were $5,423.90 in 1908 when sales were $28,043.41, but increased steadily to be $10,385.24 in 1910.[40]

Eureka in Juab County, Utah, was the site of Sams' first store. It opened in March 1909 with a capitalization of $6,000.[41] Again two-thirds of the investment was provided by Penney. The mining and smelting town of 3,300 residents was on the San Pedro, Los Angeles & Salt Lake and Tintic Range Branch of the Rio Grande Western Railroad.[42]

Articles of co-partnership for the "Sams & Penney" Golden Rule Store in Eureka included some more specific terms than the 1902 Johnson, Callahan and Penney Articles. Monthly reports and careful records of all expenses were expected along with business confidentiality and sharing of profits. But the manager had to maintain certain standards of conduct; he "shall at all times properly and becomingly demean and conduct himself, and for gross misconduct, intoxication, gambling or other incompetence shall be forthwith removed, and his accounts and interests settled at once."[43] Managers were not to engage in any similar business within a distance of one hundred miles of any of the partners' Golden Rule Stores. The latter restriction apparently was not in force, or was intended to provide room for each partner's "branch" stores. It was also specified that merchandise "shall be sold for cash only, and upon no other terms whatsoever."[44] Sams was happy to abide by the terms and the Eureka store flourished. On December 31, 1909, he recorded profits of $9,745.11 on sales of $56,129.04.[45]

Sams, Mudd and Neighbors realized they could be as successful as Penney and were eager to imitate him. As soon as new men were trained they were offered one-third partnerships, like the one Johnson and Callahan offered Penney in 1901. Penney was senior partner and major capitalist in almost every store as the chain literally mushroomed. By the end of 1911 he had outdistanced his mentors.

Ideally, stores were financed out of profits, but Penney often loaned the money needed for his protégés' one-sixth or one-third interest. Junior partners could pay off their notes as stores became profitable. Many, though, opted to start another store with their profits and delayed paying him.[46]

By operating in small but growing towns, keeping overhead low by renting small frame buildings, using packing case furnishings and maintaining long hours, they naturally increased earnings. But it was low prices for good quality merchandise that attracted attention. Kemmerer ads were typical of goods and prices being offered in all of Penney's stores. In colorful debating style an August 1908 advertisement declared:

> How in the name of common sense can you afford to pay competition such prices for your Dry Goods when you can buy them here and save 20 per cent on your purchase? Look around you. Money does not grow on trees. We Guarantee to Save You Money on Standard Goods.[47]

Several well-known name brands sold by Golden Rule Stores included Amoskeag, Fruit of the Loom and Lonsdale bleached muslins. Latest style Red Cross ladies' oxfords were $2.98 while other Red Cross shoes cost $3.50.[48] "Star Brand" and John Strootman lines sold from $2.98, but some ladies' shoes were as low as 69¢ and 98¢. $1.49 bought "a good, solid, honest shoe."[49] By comparison, Sears, Roebuck & Company's "The Great Price Maker" catalog for 1908 offered twelve styles of ladies' oxford shoes ranging in price from 92¢ to $1.68, manufactured in their Littleton, New Hampshire, factory.[50] Their prices were definitely competitive.

Golden Rule Store corsets included the "celebrated Warners" and "Just Right" standard high grade styles. Models selling for $1.25 and $1.50 elsewhere, according to Penney, were only 98¢ in his stores.[51] Sears' corsets ranged in price from 44¢ to $2.25 while the lowest priced ones at Kemmerer were 49¢ and 69¢. Golden Rule Stores had "Armourside" corsets for 98¢; Sears had two styles of this brand: one was 85¢, the other $1.25.[52]

The huge Chicago-based catalog company, whose sales for 1908 exceeded $40 million, also placed advertisements in local western newspapers as did the Denver Dry Goods Company. Mail-orders, of course, required customers to pay postage or freight charges and wait for merchandise, whereas Golden Rule Stores were much more convenient. Managers would send merchandise to distant customers, but they were known for a "cash & carry" policy.[53]

Exactly how much competition catalog sales were is difficult to determine. The profits and rapid growth of Penney's chain and other Golden Rule Store chains, however, proved they were filling a definite need as well as breaking the hold of company stores in mining towns.[54]

Golden Rule Stores were not the only chains selling dry goods in the region. For example, J.W. Hugus & Company was founded in 1882 and by 1908 had eight stores in western Colorado and Wyoming.[55] The already mentioned Blyth, Fargo & Company had stores in Wyoming, Utah and Idaho. These companies were expanding but not as aggressively as Golden Rule Stores. ZCMI (Zion Cooperative Mercantile Institution), a cooperative system of merchandising, had individual stores in numerous Mormon communities in the inter-mountain region.[56] But despite this organization's manufacturing facilities and buying power, Golden Rule Stores had no difficulty attracting customers in Mormon Utah and other predominantly Mormon towns in Idaho and Wyoming.[57]

Golden Rule Stores already had a reputation for low prices and good merchandise, and Penney was proud of the name. Occasionally a store opened with this name that was unrelated to the original organization, but merchandise and prices quickly distinguished them from the successful chains.

Why did customers continue to crowd their stores? In an October 1908 ad Penney admitted:

> Our only "Strong Hold" is the STRONG HOLD we have on those who have dealt with us once, on account of the superiority of our buying, advantages of our system of selling on low cash margins of profit, and strictly one price. . . .[58]

He claimed, "There are reasons for everything. Our growth has not been chance. It is the result of an adopted policy of giving more for the money than can be had elsewhere." Realizing some might think their merchandise was inexpensive because it was poor quality, he explained:

> At no time is Quality lost sight of. "Cheap Goods" are dear at any price. Our aim is to sell you Reliable, Staple, Dependable Merchandise at a less price than any other house in the country.[59]

As in the 1890s prices were figured on a "percentage basis of profit" and not "on appearance." Ads declared: "We offer no baits, every article is a LEADER." Other store items included notions, dress goods, men's shirts, gloves, hosiery, hats, men's shoes, ladies' skirts and waists, curtains, rugs and blankets besides staples like underwear. Best Stetson hats were still $3.45.[60] Their Strauss jeans were marked too low to suit the manufacturer, who, after 1910, refused to supply them to Golden Rule stores.[61]

The organization, quite personal and informal, was approaching a crossroads. Between 1909 and 1912 Penney made decisions that changed the internal structure of the growing company while its outward form of frame stores scattered apparently at random remained unchanged.

Another store opened in 1909. Neighbors and Penney, with the identical one-third, two-thirds partnership agreement, created a Golden Rule Store in Malad, twenty-two miles northwest of Preston.[62] It was the seat of Oneida County, a mountainous Idaho region drained by the Malad River and Deep Creek.[63] Eight new stores were planned for 1910.

During 1909 Penney hired George G. Hoag, A.D. Frost, W.O. Brown and C.J. Malmsten. Within three years they were one-third partners in new stores. During 1910 Roy L. Malmsten, the second of four Malmsten brothers who joined the company, Wilk Hyer and J. Whit Rickman were employed.[64] Penney was as inspired by the partnership idea as he had been in 1901. He later said:

> I felt that the plan had worked with me—it would work with others . . . I felt assured that the principle of allowing a man to share in what his labors produce is right and just, and that if we held strictly to having associated with us only moral, dependable men who had been properly trained and experienced along our lines, that success would crown our efforts.[65]

Certainly men already "on board" admired him. For example, in October 1909 Sams told a prospective employee, J.F. Deal:

> In reply to yours of the 28th ulto. beg to say that I have worked for Mr. J.C. Penney for 18 mo. as a clerk and always found him square in every circumstance. He is one of the best business men in the west without exception. I am now a partner of his and think more of him than any man on earth.[66]

He added, "I know nothing about your qualifications, etc., but if you are competent, as I judge you are, and are looking for something with a future, tie up with J.C. Penney if you can." But Sams cautioned, "If you are looking for a snap position without too much work attached don't do it."[67]

With preparations going ahead for 1910, Penney decided to move to Salt Lake City to be closer to large banks. Salt Lake City was also a practical distribution center with railroad connections to other states. His move to the large city was the first step on the steep path to a nationwide chain. It was the second crossroads in his life—the first had been joining Callahan in Longmont. Ironically, the turning points in his career were related to major events in his personal life.

Business was booming at the Kemmerer store, and a loom end sale was described by the local paper: "The Golden Rule Store is crowded every day to its utmost capacity and its corp of eight clerks find it difficult to wait on customers."[68]

"Penney to Leave" was a feature article in the same paper on May 6, 1909.[69] He was moving to the Utah metropolis to be full-time buyer for his growing chain. If the past was prologue, he would not be content with that role for long. In fact, friends who recognized his talent predicted a grand future for him and his family.

Berta Penney needed a "church letter" to introduce her to a Salt Lake City church and J.C. Bickel, Wyoming Mission Superintendent of the Methodist Episcopal Church, wrote Penney:

> Herewith I enclose church letter for Mrs. Penney. Please tell her I am very loath to see her leave Wyoming. However, I am sure Salt Lake City will give you a field for the great ability you possess as a leader in commercial lines. Indeed, as I have often told you you will be a millionaire. Among your fleet of stores you will need one in Salt Lake City. God Bless you both.[70]

Pleased by such votes of confidence the Penneys made a happy transition to Salt Lake City in early June. The capital of Utah presented a striking contrast to the railroad and mining towns they had lived in since 1899. Compared to those towns' muddy streets and barren hills, Salt Lake City in 1909 had boulevards, office buildings, and trolleys. Its dramatic Temple and domed Capitol high on State Street made the city unique. ZCMI's main department store was here too. Surrounded on three sides by mountains and hills, the city was in a wide flat valley, and the Great Salt Lake lay directly northwest. The city of 92,000 had a fresh, spacious aspect. The valley's wealth consisted of farms, mines, commerce of all kinds and industrious residents, the majority of whom were Mormon.

Penney selected a home on Seventh Avenue on a steep hillside with a view of the Wasatch Mountains and spreading city. Directly east of the Capitol, in 1909 it was one of Salt Lake's best residential areas.[71] Houses on Seventh Avenue were closely spaced, but wide porches and the hillside setting gave the impression of upper-middle class prosperity and security. The two-story brick house, lot, garage and connecting alleyway cost approximately $7,000.[72] Narrow porch pillars, carved wooden doors and expensive staircase panelling gave the house a touch of elegance. Photographs of children sitting on the porch and riding bicycles reveal some carefree hours spent there. Berta and Jim looked back with pride on a decade of accomplishment. Their tenth wedding anniversary was that August.

After arriving, the Penneys attended Sunday services at First Methodist Episcopal Church in downtown Salt Lake. Berta joined the church and the family became acquainted with its pastor, a tall vigorous-looking man, Reverend Francis Burgette Short. Penney, in fact, had been quite impressed by the first sermon he heard Short deliver, and deposited a generous check in the service collection. Reverent Short made a point to find out more about the new family.[73] When trouble came he proved to be a sensitive, concerned friend. Overall, he had a strong influence on Penney.[74]

Penney had always preferred small towns, but evidently frequent buying trips made him more amenable to large cities. The rolling green hills by Hamilton, however, were his favorite spot and he visited his hometown almost every year. More and more, his time was spent on buying trips or checking store locations. From June 1909 throughout 1910, he worked alone out of his home at 371 Seventh Avenue. Practically tireless, even he began to require assistance.

Some arrangements he now needed included accurate accounting of new investments besides increased buying and transportation of goods. Financing purchases became increasingly complicated and required larger lines of credit from banks plus perfect timing to repay short term loans and notes used to meet suppliers' discount deadlines. For now, his personal credit at Salt Lake banks sufficed.[75]

Penney worked at improving the buying end of the business by searching for bargains and staying in close touch with the New York market. As he stated in a 1908 ad describing the stores' rapid growth, "GOODS BOUGHT RIGHT ARE HALF SOLD." But his philosophy concerning sales was "Nor are we satisfied, we want to break all previous records."[76] Total sales for 1909 had climbed to $310,062.16 from $218,432.35 in 1908, so substantial progress was being made.[77]

Penney continued his mentors' shrewd buying procedure. In 1907 their suppliers were located in eleven states, from California to Massachusetts. In 1909 Penney purchased goods in nineteen states, but Kansas City, St. Louis and New York City remained his principal sources.[78] The five wholesalers traditionally shopped by Golden Rule Store merchants were Burnham, Hanna and Munger of Kansas City, Ely Walker, Hargadine-McKittrick and Company, Ferguson-McKinney Dry Goods Company and Rice-Stix Dry Good Company, all of St. Louis. These firms gave the successful owners sixty-day accounts, and Penney and his partners always paid their bills on time or early.[79]

In New York City in 1909 Penney selected merchandise from fifty-nine vendors.[80] Shoe factories in New England and the midwest provided these important items. But Peters Shoe Company and its successor, Roberts, Johnson & Rand Shoe Company of St. Louis, became their largest shoe supplier.[81]

Freight charges were part of the stores' overhead and were included in determining mark-up. Long haul freight rates which were reduced in 1911 by order of the Interstate Commerce Commission (over railroad protests) were already relatively low. Of course, any reduction was a boon to western businessmen like Penney and most likely encouraged them to expand. Before 1911, though, freight charges averaged ten percent of merchandise cost. By combining purchases and using the most efficient shipping routes this expense was kept down.[82]

Invoices and bills of lading for 1909 illustrate various western routes for eastern goods. Evanston and Rock Springs were on the Union Pacific Railroad main line, while crates bound for Kemmerer, Cumberland and Idaho stores were transferred to the Oregon Short Line branch at Granger, Wyoming, a junction point west of Rock Springs. Utah locations on railroad routes, plus use of dray and even automobile guaranteed arrival of needed merchandise. As earlier, if one store was short of a needed shoe or coat size, they could usually obtain it from a sister store.[83]

New York Packing Company at 14 Lispenard Street handled some 1909 shipments. They sent monthly bills for their service as middlemen between suppliers and railroad agents or steamship lines. Ocean Steamship Company of Savannah, Georgia, with offices in New York City, offered a combined steamer and freight express service to St. Louis, Kansas City and Denver which Penney used occasionally. Penney received and forwarded goods for other Golden Rule Store merchants such as Guy Johnson and C.C. Anderson in northwestern Idaho.[84] This arrangement did not last for more than a few years, though.

During 1910 Mudd and Penney opened two stores—at Midvale and Bountiful, Utah. Sams, Penney and Hoag opened a store at Provo, Utah, while Sams and Penney were partners in the Price store, also in Utah. Provo, with almost 9,000 residents, was the largest town they had entered. Penney opened a store by himself in Murray, six miles south of Salt Lake City. But these five stores were not the only ones started during 1910. J.S. Truex and Penney opened a store in St. Anthony, Idaho, and Woidemann, Neighbors and Penney had a Golden Rule Store in Rexburg, Idaho. W.E. Collins and Penney opened the chain's first store in Nevada, at Ely in White Pine County.[85]

The opening at Bountiful, eight miles south of Salt Lake City, was described by a participant, Roy L. Malmsten, then working in the Midvale store, ten miles south of Salt Lake:

> One afternoon [at Midvale] about 5 p.m. o'clock, Mr. Mudd came to me and said, "Roy, you go catch the street car and go up to Bountiful. You will help Mr. Wright (W.H. "Bill") open that store tomorrow." I took off and made connections with the Bamberger in Salt Lake City and rode to Woods Cross, three miles or more from Bountiful. It was well into the night and very dark as I got off the street car. I didn't know where I was going or how to get there, but then I saw most of the passengers going in one direction and I decided to follow the crowd. There was no sidewalk, just a path.
>
> After walking a short distance I noticed somebody ahead of me carrying quite a load, so I reasoned that if I gave him a lift with his burden he would tell me where I wanted to go. I stepped up to him and asked, "May I give you a lift?" And immediately came the reply, "You're _____ right you can give me a lift." It was W.H. ("Bill") Wright. He was carrying 10 bolts of Amoskeg Aprons Check and 10 bolts of calico. Rest assured I carried my part of the load. After two or three miles up that path we arrived at the store location. That store location was something for the book. It was at least three blocks up the street—away from the business section in what had been a saloon for years—attractive for the new adventure because of low rent. After a good night's rest in what was my bedroom, about 60 x 100 feet in size, we were up and at it bright and early in the morning to finish preparations for the Grand Opening of that store.
>
> About opening time, you [Penney] and Mrs. Penney and the two little boys arrived in your car which was loaded to capacity with merchandise from the Z.C.M.I. and Decker-Patricks. . . .
>
> During Opening Day you used Roswell and J.C., Jr., to go to the cash drawer and bring back the change to you. Mr. Wright was very disturbed because Zulick Co. had not shipped the children's shoes and we missed all that business. I was kept there about two weeks and then returned to Midvale.[86]

The addition of eight stores, although Penney sold his Rock Springs' interest to Partin, brought total sales for 1910 to

$662,331.16, more than double 1909's sales.[87] Undivided profits were $189,235.79.[88] Eight more stores were expected to open in 1911. Questions resulting from such rapid expansion grew throughout 1910, but difficulties on the horizon were small compared to the satisfaction Penney felt. He decided it was time to take a combined vacation and belated wedding trip.[89] As Christmas 1910 drew near the family prepared for a voyage to Europe and the Holy Land. Berta, Roswell and J.C., Jr., had been to Hamilton and New York on buying trips, but this would be their first overseas trip and a genuine vacation.

Berta had her tonsils removed after being informed this would ease her asthmatic condition and make the journey to low-lying, humid countries much more enjoyable. On her way home, immediately after the operation, she was caught in a sudden December rain storm. Within a week she had lobar pneumonia, a dreaded but not always fatal sickness.[90] After December 15, Dr. A.N. Hansen was in attendance, but the pneumonia spread and its accompanying high fever weakened her. Penney, taking care of last-minute business and checking new store sites in the Pacific Northwest, received a telegram describing Berta's serious condition. He rushed home, arriving a few days before Christmas, and was at her side when she died on December 26 at 11:25 A.M.[91]

Berta, energetic and capable—someone who had "no time for aches and pains"—left her loved ones in grief and shock.[92] Old friends in Kemmerer and new ones in Salt Lake were saddened by their unexpected loss and joined in praising her. Mittie, Penney's older sister, wrote to comfort him, and the Hesses, who had recently moved to Salt Lake from Detroit, were there to help.

Everyone offered sincere sympathy, but no one could answer the question screaming silently in Penney's mind, "Why?" Deeply attached to family and close friends, he was extremely sensitive to her untimely, senseless death. The sense of loss was so overwhelming at first he felt he was falling in slow motion into a vast empty space. Since 1899 Berta had been a helpmate and source of encouragement. Her unwavering confidence in him and enthusiasm had made the years of sacrifice and thrift years of adventure. Now she would not enjoy the results of their hard work. Successful in the eyes of the world, Penney, only thirty-five, felt "mocked by life," and was bitter.[93] His faith in God and belief in "progress," basic tenets since childhood, were badly shaken.

Eventually he emerged a stronger person, but the experience changed his personality, making him a quieter person.[94]

Eight years later his first biographer said, "This sudden bereavement was a great blow to Mr. Penney and for a time seemed to threaten his very life. Not even his best friends were aware of the intensity of his suffering."[95] One family friend, however, made it his job to provide comfort and wisdom. Years later Penney was still grateful to Reverend Short for helping him through this ordeal. In 1927 he wrote:

> I thought then that success meant the piling up of dollars, and then, you know what happened. The string that was so taut snapped, or nearly so. It is unnecessary to recount those experiences that for a time seemed to threaten my very existence. It is unnecessary to say anything concerning the comfort and help I got from you, Doctor Short, for you *know*; I have spoken to you many times from a full heart— words that might appear meaningless on paper.[96]

While Penney was questioning his life and goals, Short tried to instill some perspective on his talents and career. Two weeks after Berta's death he promised:

> I want to assure you that my relation to your family, from the first, has not been that of mere pastor, but rather with the feeling of a friend and brother in Christ. . . .
> Yours shall yet be a life of Christian victory and great usefulness to the honor of God and in lasting memory of my friend and your wife.[97]

Short started Penney thinking about philanthropy. He was very pleased when, in December 1911, Penney promised to pay a $10,000 mortgage on the First Methodist Episcopal Church in Berta's memory.[98]

His mother and Letha moved to Salt Lake and took care of Roswell and J.C., Jr. when he was away. Due to the tragedy Penney spent even more time in New York City. After completing the day's buying, he walked along dark streets near the Bowery. Wandering into the Bowery Mission he found inspiration from words spoken by a "rescued" businessman to a group of derelicts. Sometimes the weakness he abhorred haunted him. He was tempted to use alcohol to ease his pain and loneliness.[99]

Instead, he turned to work. Store openings, suppliers' and bankers' demands forced him into activity. The organization started to have a life and momentum all its own as partners hired new men and other qualified men contacted him. Everyone wanted an interest in one or more stores, and they looked to him for direction and leadership.

In 1911 the twenty-two stores had impressive sales of $1,183,279.96, but Penney envisioned at least fifty stores.[100] The stability and permanence of what they were creating now worried him and an intuitive ability for organization and foresight emerged. He decided to improve every phase of the growing business.[101] Financing purchases and expansion assumed primary importance. With a personal net worth of almost $100,000, but a less optimistic view of the world, Penney retained his ambition and energy.[102] Between 1911 and 1919, guiding the expanding chain and preparing it for the future absorbed his time.

In these same years fate brought him in contact with two of the great historic events of the twentieth century.

NOTES

1.   Receipts for payment in full for Kemmerer and Cumberland, dated January 13, 1908, February 1, 1908, and February 1, 1909, PHF I, D-5. Note: $30,000 amount is in question because the Rock Springs store is usually included in the 1907-1909 sale, as seen on p. 47 of Norman Beasley, *Main Street Merchant. The Story of The J.C. Penney Company* (New York: Whittlesy House, McGraw-Hill, 1948), when it actually occurred in January 1906. Records are incomplete in PHF.

2.   JCP to B. Corkern, 25 April 1967, PHF I, F-4; *Dynamo* 16 (April 1932): 20.

3.   Dorothy Sarnoff, *Speech Can Change Your Life* (New York: Dell, 1970, 1972), p. 6.

4.   JCP to Mr. Heck, 18 August 1937, PHF I, F-6.

5.   *Encyclopedia of American History*, p. 269; Financial Records, Kemmerer, PHF II, A-1; *Kemmerer Camera*, 3 October 1908, p. 4, full page ad, says: "We were in a position to take advantage of the extremely low prices that recently prevailed on account of the panic. . . ."

6.   Penney, *Fifty Years*, pp. 55-56.

7.   Fox Interview. The conversation took place at the Callahan home in Longmont where Mrs. Ina Ramsay Fox was a visitor.

8.   *Dynamo* 1 (June 1917): 5 (Bingham Canyon opening); ibid. (May 1917): 5 (Preston opening).

9.   Benton Heaton to JCP, 10 March 1906, PHF I, F-7.

10.   *Dynamo* 1-2 (1917-18) Records of early workers. Note: Neighbors was from the Longmont vicinity—assumption that Callahan recommended him.

11.   E.C. Sams' application form, Business-Men's Clearing House Company of Denver, May 1, 1907, PHF, EVM files.

12.   Business-Men's Clearing House to E.C. Sams, 4 June 1907, PHF, EVM files.

13.   Rodgers, *The Work Ethic*, pp. 28, 30, 35, 36, 39.

14.   JCP to ECS, 7/4/07, PHF I, F-7; reprinted in Penney, *Man with a Thousand Partners*, pp. 55-56.

15.   Penney, *Man with a Thousand Partners*, pp. 59-60. Sams had worked both as a clerk and manager, and, for a short time, was a bookkeeper; Clearing House application form, PHF, EVM files.

16.   Interview and Correspondence with Donald F. Foote, retired J.C. Penney Company manager in Loveland, Colo., and son of Ira A. Foote, Author's files.

17.   Penney, *Man with a Thousand Partners*, pp. 59-60; Penney, *Fifty Years*, p. 67.

18.   *Dynamo* 1 (July 1917): 5.

19.   Beasley, *Main Street Merchant*, p. 49.

20.   Ibid.; Penney, *Man with a Thousand Partners*, p. 68.

21.   PHF I, F-7, Application letters; Dr. Thomas Tapper, "Dayton H. Mudd," *Dynamo* 3 (September 1919): 4.

22.   Bertrum Coffey to JCP, 5/28/08, PHF I, F-7; Christian Woidemann to JCP, 7 June 1908, PHF I, F-7.

23. Ibid., Woidemann letter.

24. Christian Woidemann, *My Own Experience* (privately printed, c. 1924), pp. 7-10.

25. G.G. Hoag to JCP, 25 March 1909, PHF I, F-7.

26. PHF XX, Personnel Records, Early Penney Company workers; PHF I, F-7, Application letters; Penney, *View from the Ninth Decade*, p. 57.

27. C. Woidemann to E.J. Neighbors, c. 1910, PHF I, F-7; Penney, *Man with a Thousand Partners*, p. 40.

28. *Kemmerer Camera*, 5 September 1908, p. 4, col. 2.

29. Beasley, *Main Street Merchant*, pp. 73-74.

30. Ibid., p. 62.

31. *Bradstreet's Commercial Reports* 167 (September 1909), Bingham Canyon, Utah; *Dynamo* 1 (June 1917): 5.

32. *Lippincott's* (1906), p. 219.

33. Roy L. Malmsten to JCP, February 1965, PHF I, F-12, description of early Golden Rule Stores in which he worked.

34. *Dynamo* 1 (June 1917): 5.

35. *Bradstreet's Commercial Reports* (September 1909), Bingham Canyon, Utah.

36. *Dynamo* 1 (May 1917): 5; R.G. Dun & Co., January, 1910, Preston, Idaho; *Oneida County, Idaho (American Falls [Idaho] Advertiser*, n.d., c. 1905), n.p. foldout—Eastern Oneida.

37. *Dynamo* 1 (May 1917): 5.

38. Ibid.

39. Preston Financial Statements, PHF XXXIII, A-5.

40. Bingham Canyon Financial Statements, PHF XXXIII, A-5.

41. *Dynamo* 1 (July 1917): 5. Eureka Financial Statement, December 31, 1909, PHF XXXIII, A-5.

42. *Bradstreet's Commercial Reports* (September 1909), Eureka, Utah.

43. "Articles of Co-Partnership," Sams & Penney, PHF II, A-2.

44. Ibid. Note: Many Utah stores were opened within ten to forty miles of each other, but see also G.G. Hoag to JCP, 7/14/10, PHF I, F-8—contains a reference to the "new contract" and his concern that "there would still be some good territory for us."

45. Eureka Financial Statement, December 31, 1909, PHF XXXIII, A-5.

46. Ledger Book of JCP with loans and renewals, PHF X, C-3, c. 1911-1917.

47. *Kemmerer Camera*, 29 August 1908, Golden Rule Store ad.

48. Ibid., 3 October 1908, ad.

49. Ibid., 29 August 1908.

50. *Sears, Roebuck & Co. 1908 Catalogue No. 117, The Great Price Maker*, reprint, ed. J.J. Schroeder, Jr. (Northfield, Ill.: DBI Books, c. 1969), pp. 812-13.

51. *Kemmerer Camera*, 29 August 1908.

52. *Sears, Roebuck* (1908), pp. 996-97; *Kemmerer Camera*, 29 August 1908.

53. *Sears, Roebuck* (1908), p. 13; Boris Emmet and John E. Jeuck, *Catalogues and Counters. A History of Sears, Roebuck and Company* (Chicago: University of Chicago Press, 1950), pp. 150, 169; Ad "Information That Will Suit You" from St. Anthony, Idaho store c. 1912-14, PHF, EVM files.

54. Penney, *Fifty Years*, p. 102.

55.   J.W. Hugus & Company, *Souvenir History 1908* (Denver: Press of the Smith-Brooks Company, c. 1908), p. 6, says sales for 1907 will "crowd the million mark." Stores were in southern Wyoming and northwestern Colorado.

56.   Zion Cooperative Mercantile Institution, *Z.C.M.I., America's First Department Store: The One Hundredth Year 1868-1968* (Salt Lake City, ZCMI, 1968).

57.   Beasley, *Main Street Merchant*, p. 70.

58.   *Kemmerer Camera*, 3 October 1908, p. 4, "You Are Invited to become a member of our large Golden Rule Family" ad.

59.   Ibid.

60.   Ibid.

61.   Levi Strauss and Company to JCP, 21 September 1910; ibid., 22 September 1910, PHF I, D-3. The manufacturer had received numerous complaints from their customers in the same towns about Golden Rule Stores' cutting prices. These stores threatened to stop buying from them.

62.   Beasley, *Main Street Merchant*, pp. 74-75.

63.   *Oneida County, Idaho* (n.d., c. 1905), n.p. foldout.

64.   PHF XX, Personnel Records, Early Penney Co. workers.

65.   *Dynamo* 11 (April 1927): 3; 5 (April 1921): 10.

66.   ECS to J.F. Deal, 1 October 1909, PHF, EVM files.

67.   Ibid.

68.   *Kemmerer Camera*, 20 May 1909, p. 6, col. 3.

69.   Ibid., 6 May 1909, p. 6, col. 6.

70.   J.C. Bickel to JCP, 1 April 1909, PHF VII, C-1.

71.   Visit to Salt Lake City by author in September 1978; Interview with Mrs. A.B. Peak, niece of Berta Penney, Author's files.

72.   Ibid.; Salt Lake County Recorder's Office, Book 2-H Grantees Index, Warranty Deed, p. 135; Entry #246504, March 6, 1909.

73.   JCP to E.B. Short, 7 January 1927, PHF IV, C-7; Penney, *Fifty Years*, p. 88.

74.   Ibid.; also Penney, *Fifty Years*, pp. 86, 117.

75.   Beasley, *Main Street Merchant*, p. 77.

76.   *Kemmerer Camera*, 29 August 1908, ad.

77.   *Annual Report* 1951, J.C. Penney Company, pp. 8-9, PHF IV, H-File 2, number of stores and gross business from 1902 to 1951.

78.   PHF X, B-4, Invoices for merchandise.

79.   JCP to Mr. Heck, 18 August 1937, PHF I, F-6.

80.   PHF X, B-4, Invoices, 1909-1910, New York City.

81.   *Dynamo* 1 (November 1917): 22.

82.   Albro Martin, *Enterprise Denied. Origins of the Decline of American Railroads, 1897-1917* (New York: Columbia University Press, 1971), pp. 183-93; *New York Times*, 19 November 1911, Sec. 2, p. 9, cols. 1-2, "Freight Rates Cut on Western Lines." Rates had been 51¢, then 60¢, then 55¢ between 1910 and 1911 for through freight traffic from Atlantic coast to Missouri River Points.

83.   JCP to J. Westlund, 3 July 1912, and others, PHF I, F-6.

84.   PHF X, B-4, File 4, Invoices.

85.   Penney, *Man with a Thousand Partners*, p. 66; *Bradstreet's Commercial Reports* 178 (July 1912), Provo, Utah.

86.   Roy L. Malmsten to JCP, 14 October 1964, PHF I, F-12.

87.   *1951 Annual Report*, pp. 8-9, PHF IV, H-2.

88.   Balance Sheet, All Stores as of January 1, 1911, PHF II, A-1.

89.   Penney, *Fifty Years*, p. 75.

90.   W.A. Dorland, *The American Illustrated Medical Dictionary*, 9th ed. (Philadelphia: W.B. Saunders Company, 1918), p. 782.

91.   *Register of Deaths, Salt Lake County*, 1910, p. 412; *Deseret Evening News* (Salt Lake City), 27 December 1910, p. 2, col. 3; *Kemmerer Camera*, 28 December 1910, p. 3, col. 2.

92.   Ibid.; *Dynamo* 12 (July 1928), p. 7, quote from Nora Sammon Jones, early sales clerk in Kemmerer store and friend of Berta Penney.

93.   Penney, *Fifty Years*, pp. 76-77.

94.   Ibid.; *Dynamo* 2 (April 1918): 5.

95.   *Dynamo* 2 (April 1918): 5.

96.   JCP to E.B. Short, 7 January 1927, PHF IV, C-7.

97.   Short to JCP, 10 January 1911, PHF IV, C-7.

98.   Short to JCP, 14 December 1911, PHF IV, C-7; Penney, *Fifty Years*, pp. 77-78.

99.   Penney, *Fifty Years*, pp. 79-80.

100.   *Annual Report* 1951, pp. 8-9, PHF IV, H-2.

101.   Penney, *Fifty Years*, pp. 82-83; Penney, *Man with a Thousand Partners*, p. 89.

102.   January 1, 1912 Financial Statement, PHF II, A-1, reports "Individual Worth J.C. Penney Outside of the Company" as $98,942.87.

FROM PARTNERSHIP TO INCORPORATION:
1911-1913

The small chain was obviously thriving in the growing West. Population increases in the mountain and Pacific states between 1900 and 1910 were impressive and help explain the Golden Rule Stores' success. Utah's population increased by almost 100,000 to become 373,351 in 1910. Wyoming grew from 92,531 to 145,965, while Idaho more than doubled its population from 161,772 in 1900 to 325,594 residents ten years later. Nevada increased to 81,875 in 1910 from only 42,335 in 1900. Washington, Oregon and California as well as Colorado, New Mexico and Arizona matched their neighbors' growth.[1]

The expanding home population and arrival of casterners and immigrants meant greater demand for life's basic necessities—the clothing, shoes and household staples that were Golden Rule Store specialties. However, the population growth attracted the attention of many merchants. Instead of taking success for granted, Penney knew he and his partners had to be more efficient and work even harder to continue underselling other firms with quality merchandise.

Golden Rule Stores, in particular, benefited from western expansion due to size and flexibility. Stores, once opened, were rarely closed or moved. However, if necessary they could transfer stock from one store to another. Several years later, when the Union Pacific Coal Company closed the Cumberland mines, Golden Rule Store merchandise from the small store was moved to the Cokeville, Wyoming store on the Idaho border.[2]

Of eight stores opened during 1911, three were in Utah, two in Idaho and one each in Washington, Oregon and Nevada. Penney had a two-thirds partnership in three, as the one-third partnership plan was taking form.[3] In five of the new stores, Penney, an earlier partner and a new man each had a one-third interest. Potential partners not only worked as store managers, but also started training the newest arrivals to manage and open stores. A human chain was formed; loyalty to Penney and each other was its strength.

With no written rules or training booklets to study, policies were taught by example and discussion. Penney visited stores and talked to associates, encouraging them and seeing if they met his standards. When on buying trips, they corresponded by telegram and letter.[4]

Partners enjoyed the freedom of partnership, and they selected the merchandise mix best suited for their towns. Specific markups, although low, were also left to their judgment.[5] A believer in low markup and quick turnovers, Penney disapproved of eager manager-partners' higher markups.[6] Although his policy contradicted the old business adage of charging what the market will bear, Penney was being both idealistic and shrewd. He was serving the public and reaping profits from quick turnover.

Sharing in store profits and opening stores were powerful incentives to work hard. This group of men, who almost without exception possessed similar characters and backgrounds, developed an *esprit de corps* that outweighed dissension.[7] It was to everyone's benefit when new stores opened and succeeded. The result was greater buying power and more community recognition leading to larger sales and more profits.

By now Mudd, Neighbors and the ambitious Sams were partners in several stores. Penney, however, was committed financially in every store, and continued to lend capital to new partners.[8] Bankers regarded the organization warily for they questioned the stability of the one-third and two-thirds partnership arrangement and its rapid expansion. Penney then hired an accountant to organize and standardize his finances. With concise, accurate statements, he could approach new banks and also gauge store needs better.

John I.H. Herbert, a native of Union Star, Missouri, who was recommended to Penney, reported for work May 8, 1911.[9] He worked in a one-room office rented by Penney in the Kearns Office Building, an imposing new addition to Salt Lake's growing business district on South State Street.[10] Herbert, whose accounting experience was with the Burlington Railroad and a Missouri bank, saw financial statements scrawled on notebook paper and wrapping paper.[11] The partners were understandably busy, and he faced delays obtaining some records. Eventually centralized bookkeeping was established, but not until an attempt at centralized buying began.

One month after Herbert arrived, Penney incorporated his interests for the first time. The "J.C. Penney Company" of Utah was created June 9, 1911.[12] Total capitalization was $200,000; out of a total of 4,000 shares of capital stock, Penney subscribed to 3,996 shares. Herbert R. Penney, John I.H. Herbert, Arthur Lee Hess (Berta's younger brother who worked in the Bountiful store), and a lawyer, Eddy O. Lee, each subscribed to one share. Par value of shares was $50. Capitalization represented the "estimated aggregated valuation, exclusive of all indebtedness" of the incorporators' (Penney's) interests in nineteen stores. Three more stores were opened after June, bringing the total to twenty-two by December 31, 1911. The stores at Kemmerer, Cumberland and Murray were owned by Penney, while he had a two-thirds interest in stores at Preston, Malad, St. Anthony (Idaho), Ely, Pendelton (Oregon), Walla Walla (Washington), Eureka, Price and Mt. Pleasant (Utah), as well as at Bingham Canyon, Midvale and Bountiful. He also had a one-third interest in the Rexburg, Lewiston and Moscow (Idaho), and Provo and Richfield (Utah) stores.[13]

One purpose of incorporation, of course, was to protect the private property of stockholders from the businesses' debts, obligations or liabilities. Limited liability was the opposite of partnerships' unlimited liability, and the partners' power to act as their own business agents meant that Penney never had complete control over stores opened with his money. What existed now was a corporation doing business in partnership with twelve individuals—Neighbors, Woidemann, W.O. Brown, Coffey, J.S. Truex, Collins, A.D. Frost, Wilk Hyer, Sams, Hoag, Mudd and R.L. Malmsten. By definition a corporation has continuous existence, so Penney ensured the permanence of his dream, although what existed was complex and even contradictory.[14] He was president of the Company, Herbert Penney was vice-president, and J.I.H. Herbert became secretary and treasurer.

Two banks where Penney had accounts were Continental National Bank of Salt Lake City and Citizens Central National Bank of New York City.[15] The Salt Lake bank was his main source of funds at this time. Corporation assets were used as collateral for short-term loans needed for store operations. The partnerships naturally complicated Penney's efforts to obtain larger lines of credit. To resolve bankers' doubts, his partners, with a lawyer's help, signed over their store interests to Penney's care.

Penney explained it best:

> They joined in what is known in law as a Subrogation Agreement, underwhich they entrusted to me, as surety for whatever credits I might obtain from the banks, all that they owned in the stores, which for most of them was all that they owned in the world.

He added, "They gave me a vote of confidence which I prize next to the dying words of my father."[16]

This satisfied Salt Lake City bankers, who granted fairly large lines of credit, but it was not enough for the twelve store openings planned for 1912. New York City, the nation's financial center, was the obvious place to turn for more credit, especially since it was the location of many of their vendors and Penney spent most of his time in the metropolis. But eastern bankers' doubts about the western merchandiser continued for some time. Pleased to accept deposits for checking and savings accounts, they balked at granting large lines of credit.[17]

Fortunately, Penney's friendship with a supplier led to a temporary but effective remedy. Moe A. Isaacs, president of Isaacs Brothers Manufacturing Clothiers at No. 4 Great Jones Street and 686 Broadway, opposite the Broadway Central Hotel, offered his services as New York financial agent for the new corporation.[18] A "commercial paper" brokerage firm, Markwell & Springer of 35 Nassau Street, was also employed.[19]

J.C. Penney Company notes were not only new on the New York market, but their financial statement also included one overdraft which dampened buyers' enthusiasm and added ½ percent to the discount rate.[20] This was important because Penney wanted money at the lowest rate possible. Isaacs, whose firm was worth an estimated $500,000 to $750,000, advanced funds from his bank account, minus a discount. Markwell & Springer followed the usual route of advancing money, minus discount, and selling notes to banks, as well as collecting a commission fee.[21] Several months later, as notes came due, the Utah corporation either had money from new notes or had funds from the stores.[22]

From February 1912 throughout 1913 Isaacs and Markwell & Springer accepted notes and raised several hundred thousand dollars in New York for the rapidly expanding company.[23] Most of the money advanced was used to stock a warehouse in Salt Lake City, open new stores and pay invoices when due to obtain suppliers' discounts that ranged from 2 percent to 7 percent.[24] Salt Lake City was a major clearing house for western banks, and the majority of their suppliers accepted Salt Lake City bank checks without charging a collection fee. New York exchange (checks or drafts on New York City banks) was considered a superior form of payment, though.[25]

On sales of $2,050,642 in 1912, net profits were $286,317, and the company would have experienced little trouble selling their commercial paper or obtaining larger lines of credit except for the unusual incorporation and subrogation agreement.[26] The overdraft on a partner's book, separate from the corporation statement, led to complications that made Isaacs a valuable ally.

Isaacs admired Penney and was confident of the company's financial strength, but even he was taken back by demands made in March 1912. In one week, John I.H. Herbert, secretary and treasurer of the new corporation, drew on him for $60,000, making a total of $150,000 since January. Isaacs told him, "At the rate you have been drawing, why, it would take a National Bank to handle it." He advanced the money himself, but added, "Friend Herbert, don't you think that you are overdoing it? Don't you think that you are 'riding this horse too fast?'" Herbert quickly expressed his gratitude and wrote, "I want to ask your forgiveness for not writing you before as it was due to so many things to attend to."[27] Isaacs, in fact, could see a future time when the company's commercial paper would be in demand. On March 23, 1912, he wrote:

> In about two weeks time I am satisfied we can start over again getting you some more money at this end, but we must have an opportunity to sell what is unsold. I want to congratulate you on the success you have had in getting Mr. Neighbors and Mr. Sams to have all their business consummated at Salt Lake. Now, if you can only meet with the success of having the office moved to New York, getting a new statement of stock made out so that it will not show an overdraft in your bank account, why, I will consider the concern of J.C. Penney Co. as good as any firm or mercantile concern in the United States. With the high moral

standing of Mr. J.C. Penney and the reorganization of his
corporation on lines indicated by me when here, with a New
York Office, and a new statement, your paper will be sought for
by the finest institutions in America and you will be able to get
all the money you require and you will never have occasion to
have a sleepless night.[28]

Despite the company's high ratings from Bradstreet's and from
R.G. Dun & Company, the eastern financial establishment still
regarded the new firm as a dark horse from the "wild and woolly
west." It did not conform to their idea of a corporation.[29]

Suppliers like Isaacs, who dealt with Penney regularly, had few
doubts. Penney had the reputation of being "a very hard, close
buyer."[30] He admitted later, "It was a part of the game to match
one's wits against the 'other fellows' and try to buy at one's own
estimate of what the price ought to be based on the figure one had
fixed as the retail price."[31] Certainly, with such careful attention
being paid to suppliers' discounts, to every $\frac{1}{2}\cent$ on merchandise costs
and to $\frac{1}{2}$ percent discount rates on commercial paper, the
possibility of failure was remote.

In 1910 Penney's stores had been valued by the credit rating
agencies as worth $75,000 to $100,000, but by mid-1912 the rating
was $300,000 to $400,000. By comparison, ZCMI was worth an
estimated $1,000,000 and above. A new company in Salt Lake City
with ties to Penney, the E.H. Robinson Company, jobbers for dry
goods and notions, was rated at $35,000 to $50,000.[32]

The 1912 estimate of the net worth of Penney's stores reflected
an increase in number and inventory; a high credit rating showed
their bill-paying record was excellent. Financial arrangements in Salt
Lake and New York continued to be successful.

In summer 1911 Penney decided time and money could be saved
by operating a wholesale warehouse in Salt Lake City. By stocking
staple items most needed in stores, he could eliminate time-
consuming, expensive trips east by senior partners who bought for
several stores. Seeking to demonstrate the efficiency of centralized
buying to somewhat skeptical associates, Penney made the financial
commitment, but remained behind the scenes as the new business
was created.[33]

E.H. Robinson, a leading wholesaler for twenty years in St.
Paul, Minnesota, incorporated the business November 9, 1911 with
A.L. Hess and J.I.H. Herbert. Robinson was president, Hess, vice-

president and Herbert, secretary-treasurer.[34] Capitalization of $50,000 was increased to $100,000 in May 1912.[35] The new firm attracted attention as seen in a newspaper account:

> Plans New Business on A Big Scale—Leading Wholesaler of St. Paul Incorporates Company to open jobbing field here for dry goods and notions. Has Million Capital at Hand if Needed. E.H. Robinson Comes Here Unheralded and is Attracted by Possibilities of Building Up an Important Enterprise.[36]

Robinson's specialty was men's furnishings, notions and staple dry goods. The million dollars behind him was an exaggeration, but he did have Penney's complete confidence. In the newspaper account, Robinson cited lower freight rate schedules and Salt Lake City's position as a distributing center for many prosperous towns as influencing his decision.[37] At first they operated from the J.C. Penney Company office at 702 Kearns Office Building, and Penney introduced the wholesaler to his associates, suggesting they cooperate with him. He did not reveal his financial support of the project.[38] Opening for business in early March 1912 in a three-story building, the warehouse was one reason Herbert drew so heavily on New York funds. Financial backing existed, but from the beginning merchandise selection caused problems.

Robinson did not buy merchandise that the store partners wanted. He substituted brands and, while they might have been satisfactory, the merchants preferred tried and tested brands from their long-time suppliers.[39] For example, in June 1912 Mudd, on a buying trip in St. Louis, complained to Penney:

> Mr. Robinson writes that he is unable to make deliveries on Cherry Valley Shirts. If we are not careful we will not have any shirts to start the Fall trade with. I bought quite heavy [*sic*] for all the stores, but by using the stocking flannel will not use so many of the Cherry Valley.[40]

Brands and prices were of primary importance to store owners who believed they knew best what local customers wanted. Penney and his partners were proud of their record, too, as a group advertisement in the December 16, 1911 *Deseret Evening News* (Salt Lake City) reveals:

The Golden Rule Stores:

It May Be that there are Hundreds of People who are Unaware of the Fact that there is a Gigantic System of Stores Whose Total Sales Aggregate One and Three Quarter Million Dollars Annually operating in this and surrounding states. It is not a Trust however as competition is prone to describe us, organized for our own personal aggrandizement, but with the object of combining the purchases of our Twenty-Eight Busy Stores, for the sole purpose of buying in tremendous quantities in car-load lots, direct from the mill and factory, eliminating entirely the profits of the middle man.

The supporting of the middleman, or in other words the Jobber or Commission Man, is the one thing wrong with our economic system—The Buying of Goods on Credit by Merchants and the selling of them on a Long Time—Long Profit basis is another evil of our system. Our chain of stores fits right in and has been the means of saving the people of this inter-mountain country a great many thousand of dollars annually. In fact these stores have become the largest distributors of merchandise in the West. We can truthfully say without boasting or fear of contradiction that We have been instrumental in keeping at home thousands of dollars that formerly went to the mail order houses of the east.

Rated in the Mercantile Agencies as those who pay their bills on receipt of goods, rated as high as the highest. Controlled by men of the highest moral character—backed by merchandising of 20 or more years' actual experience—is in a position to not only BUY RIGHT BUT TO SELL RIGHT. Thus it is on this basis we solicit your future patronage and take this means at this time to thank our many loyal customers whose confidence and patronage has made this organization possible and effective.[41]

In addition, each customer was regarded as a walking advertisement for or against them, and "one price to all, cash only" and a "never swerving honesty of purpose" were their policies. Admitting, "We have the reputation of being 'price cutters,'" the ad explained, "It isn't that, it's merely the result of our knowledge HOW, WHEN and WHERE to buy. Then our system of distribution makes our prices possible." The lengthy advertisement, undoubtedly written by Penney, described the partnership plan as one reason for their success. He called the system a "profitsharing co-operative one." "In nearly every case the manager in charge is directly interested in the store of which he has charge. In conducting our business along these broad lines, it not only increases the efficiency of each manager, but he is alone responsible for the success of the business." Penney added one of his insights: "The first fundamental principle that he [the manager] is taught is the value of confidence. No great enterprise was ever built very high without that for a foundation."[42] These policies were the bedrock of the new company, and had been behind the success of every Golden Rule Store since the early 1890s.

The 1911 advertisement gave locations of twenty-eight stores, but six of them belonged to either Johnson or Callahan, who also had stores not included in the notice.[43] Penney's chain had by now outgrown other Golden Rule Stores chains although they too were expanding. In fact, Guy Johnson had fulfilled an ambition he nurtured since 1901. About 1908 he opened a store in nearby Ogden. Between 1900 and 1910 Ogden's population grew from 16,313 to 25,580.[44] Johnson and his partners opened a wholesale warehouse there as well.[45]

According to an agreement dating from the 1890s, possibly the 1896 "Articles of Agreement" written by C.E. Dimmitt, a Golden Rule Store did not enter a town where a "cousin" Golden Rule Store was in business. Penney and his associates adhered to this courtesy after their company had far superior buying power and financial backing. It would have been easy to disregard it for the other chains had little bargaining power.[46] A series of mergers eventually ended this remarkable chapter in retailing history. However, expansion and mutual respect reigned for many years.

In 1911 advertisements for individual stores echoed themes presented in the Salt Lake ad. In spring 1911 a Kemmerer ad entitled "A GOLDEN OPPORTUNITY" used rhyme to convey their philosophy: "'The Store for you,' where Lasting Satisfaction follows every Transaction." It was also "The Store That is always Looking Out for the Merchandise Welfare of its Customers."[47]

At Pendleton, Oregon, a store opened by Penney and A. Dennis Frost in spring 1911 used an attention-grabbing headline on a handbill: "How Much Can I Save!—is a very important question these days."[48] It continued:

> We can certainly help you to solve this perplexing problem.
> There is positively no sentiment in business. We expect people
> to spend their dollars with us because they get bigger and better
> values. We will not Indulge in Any Misrepresentation to Get

Your Business. We will Not sacrifice Quality for Price.
Everything Marked in plain figures. One Price To
Everybody.[49]

A fascinating "nutshell" history of the Golden Rule Store system
introduced readers to the new store:

Years Ago
In a little town in Colorado
the first little acorn was
planted, that has since
developed into a mighty oak.
Good goods, right treatment,
concerted action has placed us
in the foremost rank of
distributors of merchandise
in the West.[50]

A 1912 Preston, Idaho, ad referred to the Golden Rule Stores'
"scientific buying" and advised customers to do the same:

Now, why not employ the same principle of scientific buying to
your own individual needs. Investigate, compare qualities, prices
and values before you spend your money and it will not take you
long to find out that the Golden Rule always Has it For
Less.[51]

At Ely, Nevada, a first anniversary advertisement in April 1911
claimed, "Last Year We Proved to the Public that they had been
paying too much for merchandise." Other merchants had excused
their prices by blaming freight rates, but the Golden Rule Store,
which also had to pay freight costs, uncovered competitors'
"exorbitant profits." At the Golden Rule Store Crossett shoes, in the
latest styles, cost $2.98 to $3.98. Men's work shoes started at 98¢ a
pair. "All the new styles" in shirts, suits and ladies' ready-to-wear
were available. The store's motto was, "To please you, is to please
us."[52]

From beginning to end 1912 was a momentous year for the new
company. Twelve stores, four more than previously attempted, were
opened, and financial as well as buying arrangements were being
centralized. There were thirty-four stores in operation by the end of
the year, and Penney was one-third or two-thirds owner in all of
them. By December 31, 1913, however, several of his store interests

were sold to new associates, such as Arthur Lee Hess and John Firmage.[53]

John L. Firmage, the first of five members of the Firmage family to join the chain, was hired in spring 1911 to work at Murray, Utah. He was then transferred to Provo and trained under George G. Hoag.[54] The American Fork store in north central Utah, which Firmage managed in 1912 and became one-third owner of in 1913, was one of several stores in which Penney relinquished his interest either in part or in whole.[55] Hoag and Sams each owned a one-third interest in this store.[56] In future years other stores were opened without Penney's initial participation. By then the vision of a vast organization had caught everyone's imagination. A new form of incorporation, however, preserved many partnership features.[57]

During 1912 Penney's partners were on their own for several months. From late January or early February to June 1st, Penney was overseas on a vacation friends convinced him to take. Working relentlessly throughout 1911, he was truly exhausted by December and his poor physical condition was obvious. The mental stress caused by Berta's death was less obvious but real.

Before leaving business affairs behind, he hired George H. Bushnell, an accountant, to assist Herbert with store finances and warehouse supply records, and conducted a buying trip for partners and managers. Bushnell reported to work December 1, 1911, at a salary of $90 a month. He had been earning $175 plus expenses per month from an agricultural implements firm in Ogden, where he and his wife owned a house. Penney and Bushnell, thirty-four, had met in Idaho. A willingness to work long hours and mutual respect brought about the job offer.[58]

Bushnell hesitated at losing his comfortable salary, but he consulted a state senator who was acquainted with Guy Johnson and Tom Callahan. The senator had heard of Penney and recommended Bushnell seize the opportunity.[59] Penney believed in saving overhead costs whenever possible, and only wanted men who had insight into the new company's potential. While Bushnell was not a store partner, he, like the younger Herbert, would share in store profits from interests that Penney and others sold them.[60]

During 1911 Penney persuaded another experienced person to join his team. Charles E. Dimmitt of Walla Walla, Washington, had been out of the Golden Rule Store business since 1909.[61] Fifty years old, but sturdy and energetic, he was eager to re-enter merchandising and approved of Penney's conservative fiscal policies or at least most of them.

On the January 1912 group buying trip Dimmitt discovered just how frugal Penney was. In New York City seven men slept in each hotel room, they walked instead of using street cars, and ate the most inexpensive meals available. When Dimmitt decided to partake of a luxurious 25¢ breakfast and 35¢ dinner, Penney told him he was setting a bad example. Dimmitt returned to plain staple food![62]

The new organization Dimmitt and his son George joined actually had close ties to their home town, Humansville, Missouri. Many young managers were inspired by Dimmitt. He planned company ceremonies and conventions during the next decade and was a member of the Board of Directors. After retirement, he returned to the Board, serving in the Great Depression when strict economy was required once more.[63]

After the buying trip, Penney departed on an ocean voyage to visit Mediterranean countries and Europe. His guests were Dr. Short and Newell Beeman, a retired businessman from Evanston. Roswell, eleven, and J.C., Jr., nine, were taken out of school to accompany their father. Dr. Short arranged trip details and their itinerary included Cairo, Egypt, the Holy Land, Constantinople, Switzerland, Paris, and England.[64]

With Herbert, Bushnell, Isaacs and Robinson attending to business, Penney prepared to relax and regain his strength. He still questioned his goals, asking himself, "What was the purpose of life?" and "What had money meant for Berta?"[65] He hoped the trip and Dr. Short's companionship would provide some insight into life's meaning.

Among the "bon voyage" group at a New York dock were Mr. and Mrs. J.I.H. Herbert, E.H. Robinson, several supplier friends such as J.L. Greenbaum, Otto Golluber and possibly Moe A. Isaacs, and wives, children and other friends. Penney, in a dark overcoat with a wry smile on his face, had his head cocked characteristically to the right as Roswell snapped a group picture.[66] The trip that others had urged on him was to do more good than he anticipated.

In Constantinople by mid-March, they made a leisurely trip back to Paris. On April 15 they, with the rest of the world, were shocked by the sinking of the *Titanic*, and the tragic drowning in the North

Atlantic of 1,500 of its 2,206 passengers.[67] The previous evening, just before midnight, the largest, most luxurious ocean liner afloat scraped against an iceberg, and the fate of many rich and famous as well as ordinary passengers was sealed.[68] The Penney party was booked to sail on the *Titanic*'s second crossing.[69] Not being on the maiden voyage probably saved their lives, for only 315 men out of 1,662 male passengers were rescued.[70]

While Penney's group was still in Europe, a letter from Mrs. Short arrived. Her relief was obvious:

> I felt I must write you all just to tell you how glad I am that you will soon be starting this way. . . . We have not yet recovered from the terrible shock of the Titanic disaster, when I think of what our travellers have escaped and how they have been protected my heart is full of gratitude to our kind Father for his guidance and care over all of you. . . . I shall be very happy and greatly relieved when you shall all be landed safely in New York.[71]

The trip relaxed Penney and gave him a better perspective on life. As soon as he returned, he wrote to Mittie in Hamilton:

> Dear Brothers, Sisters and Families:
>
> Your dear letter of the 26th was awaiting my arrival from abroad. I will say that the thrill that I experienced when I caught sight of our own dear land is indescribable. The Statue of Liberty never looked so sweet to me before as she did on the morning of June 1st.
>
> While I was glad to get back I realized the trip that I made was the one thing for me to do and realized further that it has added years to my life, and I must say that I have come to the conclusion that I must take better care of myself if I expect to remain here.
>
> As you know, my duties are very onerous and it is only by the very greatest determination and effort that I have been able to hold myself together the past 18 months. I am fortunate in having in possession scores of friends from one ocean to another who are apparently very much interested in my welfare. It makes me realize that I have yet a great deal in life to live for.
>
> I have had a great deal of pleasure in having my boys along with me and had they not been able to make the trip there is no doubt in my mind but it would have worked a hardship instead of doing me an immense amount of good.

> I can now be classed in the heavy weight class, heavier than
> I have ever been, weighing 153 pounds, which, for a little fellow
> like me, is considered mighty good weight. . . .[72]

Trip details were given later, and he was pleased to learn his mother and sister Letha were on their way to New York City.[73] Broadway Central Hotel, popular with many out-of-town buyers, was Penney's usual New York headquarters, but letters were now addressed to him care of Isaacs Brothers at 4 Great Jones Street. He may have rented a house in New Jersey, travelling by ferry to and from the city each day.

Once more Penney felt genuine interest in the question, "Where are we going from here?" He learned to focus on his personal strengths and those of the company. In particular, he saw the evolving partnership plan as a basis for further expansion, even beyond the hoped for fifty stores.[74]

In early June managers, partners and new men reported business details to him. On June 2, L.M. Loll, manager of the Mackay, Idaho, store that Woidemann, Neighbors and Penney opened that spring, thanked Penney for the card from Paris and said:

> We have been doing a nice little business here since we started,
> our sales last month were 4027.46, shoe sales 881.47. I believe
> Mackay is going to make a good paying store.[75]

Regarding the competition, he noted:

> People are still in debt to the Lost River Commercial Co., but
> are trying to pay up, and buy from us, they are tired of paying
> double prices for their goods.[76]

Loll looked forward to a good fall trade. By December 1913 he owned a one-sixth interest in this store as Penney reduced his interest by half. Employed at Rexburg, Idaho, in 1910, he had trained under Neighbors and Woidemann before becoming manager in the central Idaho farming and mining community.[77]

Letters from Robinson and Herbert arrived as well. Herbert had successfully handled complicated financial transactions and met invoice and note deadlines. But financial and buying problems persisted.

A summer buying trip was in progress that June. Partners, accompanied by wives and children, left small western towns for Kansas City, St. Louis and New York City to select fall and winter merchandise and enjoy a reunion with Penney.[78] This trip included some luxuries. An old photograph shows twelve partners and their families perched happily on an open touring car ready for sightseeing in the metropolis of two and a half million residents.[79]

Before arriving in Salt Lake City in early July, Sams reported the latest sales at nearby Price, a store Sams and Penney had opened two years earlier. Total June sales were $9,921.70.[80] Of this, $2,388.20 were shoe sales.[81] Total sales for the first six months were almost $40,000, and Sams, now part-owner of eight stores and living in Salt Lake City, was obviously pleased with his progress.[82] He finished his report by saying:

> I am very anxious to get back. A man with so many stores has
> a hard time keeping in close touch with all of them especially
> when he is away for a time.[83]

Buying now occupied much more of Sams' time. Although he cooperated with E.H. Robinson, it was clear neither he nor the other partners coordinated purchases with the Salt Lake warehouse. They wrote to Penney asking him to obtain certain goods and prices. Robinson, too, wrote to Penney suggesting he take care of some items.[84] Robinson also needed money for goods sent to stores. However, J.I.H. Herbert either did not have the funds on hand or was delaying payments until Penney's return to Salt Lake.[85]

Back only two months, Penney realized the warehouse was not succeeding, but he was financially committed to support Robinson. He told Herbert to take care of the wholesaler's requirements, but returned to Utah sooner than planned to try to solve the problem.[86]

Happier news arrived from Great Falls, Montana, where his young brother Herbert was manager and part-owner of a store opened March 1, 1912. This Golden Rule Store had a capitalization of $12,000, one of the largest in Penney's chain. Penney had a two-thirds interest while Herbert had one third. The new merchant, only twenty-six, left Kemmerer in 1907 for Hamilton and Kansas City, but had returned in 1909 to work at Kemmerer, Eureka and

Spanish Fork, a new store in southern Utah.[87] Great Falls was his
first partnership interest and Herbert was eager to follow his older
brother's footsteps.

Travelling west by train, Penney planned to stop in Hamilton
and visit Mittie and Elie. Two of Mittie's sons, Frank and Russell
Whitman, were working for their uncle, and she was recommending
other young Hamilton men to her brother. Penney promised to
interview them while in town, but in response to Mittie's
admiration, said:

> Am very glad to know the high esteem with which you hold me,
> but you know a Sister is more liable to over rate a brother than
> the outside World; however it is not the opinion of people that
> govern my actions, I try to do the best each and every day and
> it is my aim in life to be of what assistance I can to those who
> are worthy, and are ambitious and energetic.[88]

In fact, the partnership plan, based on Penney's principle of
placing confidence in people, was proof of this statement. However,
Penney's idealism was extremely practical as a letter A.D. Frost
wrote him makes clear. Frost was concerned about store locations
and said, "But I will leave it to you for you know I am very anxious
to make a good showing for the more business I do is money for
both of us."[89] At first very informal, the partnership plan had
evolved into a system. As Mudd, Neighbors and Sams trained new
men and opened stores with them, these new managers, either
partners or becoming partners, trained more new men to open
stores. Training a store manager (future partner) now became a
prerequisite for obtaining a store interest. The organization was
thus constantly renewing itself from within.[90] Working up from
sales clerk to "First Man" or assistant manager, then to manager at
a try-out store and manager-partner in a new store took two to five
years.[91] Needed capital came from store earnings, but loans from
Penney and his senior partners often made stores possible. Loans
were paid back, however, from new partners' earnings.[92]

Kemmerer was the "Mother Store" to stores opened from its
surplus and to men who trained there or at Cumberland. Preston,
Bingham Canyon and Eureka were also "Mother Stores" for branch
chains developed by Neighbors, Mudd and Sams.[93] By January
1913 Sams had a one-third interest in ten stores, Mudd a one-third
interest in seven stores, Neighbors a one-third interest in six stores

and Hoag a one-third interest in five stores. Other partners each held one-third interests in one or two stores.[94] Penney had one-third or two-thirds interests in thirty-five of the thirty-six stores then existing.[95]

In the fall of 1912 it became clear that better financial arrangements were needed. Accounts had been opened at National Copper Bank of Salt Lake City, Chemical National Bank, and Importers & Traders National Bank, both in New York City, but large credit lines were still lacking. In November 1912 Penney had $100,280.06 in National Copper Bank; however, bank balances fluctuated as notes came due and invoices were paid.[96]

On November 22, 1912 Moe A. Isaacs, as interested as before in the company's future, wrote J.I.H. Herbert a letter summing up its problems and potential. Apparently referring to total assets of $750,000 to $875,000 and debts not exceeding $225,000, Isaacs said:

> I believe Mr. Penney is going to incorporate all the business under one head. I don't know this, but, he is thinking seriously of getting in that shape and have all those subrogation agreements done away with. Now if that can be done and will be done they will have a gross amount of merchandise on hand in all the stores with a cash on hand of say $750,000. and they will have an outstanding amount of say $8500.00, cash on hand $100,000. or $125,000. including the actual cash that is in the different banks in the different country towns besides the cash in the bank at Salt Lake and New York and if we don't owe over $225,000. with that kind of an asset we then will safely make a bankable statement which will make the paper marketable, quick salable, and at a very low interest rate. This is the position JCP wants to get into. This is what he is working towards and if you will help from your end to bring that result about, you can rest assured that my duties at this end will be well taken care of.[97]

On January 17, 1913, incorporation papers for a new J.C. Penney Company were filed in the Clerk's Office, Salt Lake County.[98] According to Utah corporation law, no corporation could take the name of an existing corporation, so on January 16th the June 1911 J.C. Penney Company Articles of Incorporation were amended, changing its name to Penney Stores Company.[99] The 1913 corporation consolidated Penney's holdings with the individual partnerships, ending the former complex organization. J.I.H. Herbert as well as bankers had not approved of the earlier business form, yet the new corporation did not meet with New York bankers' approval either. Capital stock was $1,100,000, divided into 10,000 shares of preferred stock with a par value of $100 each, and 10,000 shares of common stock with a par value of $10 each.[100] Any similarity to usual incorporation forms ended there.

Common stock was non-assessable and received no dividends. All 10,000 shares were issued to Penney as trustee. The preferred stock, or "classified stock" as it became known, was the important stock since it bore all expenses and received all dividends. It was divided into as many classes as there were stores. In January 1913 there were thirty-six classes of preferred stock representing the thirty-six stores, and each class was divided according to store ownership. For example, 150 shares of Kemmerer Class No. 1 represented the property value of the Kemmerer store, and 149 shares were issued to Penney and one share to J.I.H. Herbert. Sams received 50 shares of Eureka Class No. 11 while Penney received 100 shares in exchange for their respective one-third, two-thirds ownership of the store and merchandise.[101] Of the 10,000 shares of preferred stock, 3,690 were issued.[102] The new company had twenty incorporators.

However, the new company did not own or control any stock; dividends were declared for each class of stock, based on each store's earnings, not on overall company earnings. For dividends to be issued, however, a general surplus over and above the issued capital stock was required.[103]

Holders of a particular class of preferred stock had to bear all losses or deficits that individual store incurred, similar to the old partnership agreements. Preferred stockholders were also assessable for corporation expenses such as rent and salaries for buying and accounting offices. These were paid for by a general assessment of $20 a month, later amended to 3/4 of 1 percent of each store's sales.[104] It was a closed, privately held company and no stock was available to the public. If stockholders wished to sell their stock, they had to offer it to the corporation first.[105]

Preservation of as much of the partnership incentive as possible underlay the unusual form of incorporation. Sharing in what they helped create, training new men and opening new stores were an integral part of the corporation.[106] The Salt Lake City law firm of Powers, Marioneaux, Stott & McKinney received $1,500 for their services in drawing up the incorporation papers.[107] Apparently it was a unique form of incorporation, and Penney later admitted:

> The New York bankers still had their doubts. They and their attorneys had never seen anything like this instrument in which they detected a certain wildness of western freedom.[108]

About this time another famous twentieth-century company, the F.W. Woolworth Company, was incorporated. Although older and much larger, its corporate form was typical and helps illustrate by comparison the western corporation's structure. By 1911, 596 5¢ & 10¢ stores had grown from the original store founded by Frank Winfield Woolworth in Utica, New York, in 1879. Six separate but related companies were doing business in thirty-seven states. They merged into one corporation on December 15, 1911 with a capital stock of $65,000,000. The 650,000 shares of $100 par value each were divided into 150,000 shares of 7 percent cumulative preferred stock and 500,000 shares of common stock. Preferred stock represented the value of stores and merchandise while common stock represented good will and earning power. The capital stock of the six companies was exchanged for capital stock of the new corporation. A large amount of preferred and smaller amount of common stock was offered for sale to the public. Other stock was sold to company executives and store managers.[109]

The J.C. Penney Company with its $1,100,000 capital stock was small in comparison, yet rapid growth since 1909 was proof of its strength. The path was clear for tremendous growth. By issuing new preferred stock as new stores opened and making one-third interests available to new men, the stockholders became, in effect, partners who participated in the profits or losses of their individual stores with other owners of that class of stock. Although complex and unusual, the incorporation form was effective and insured cooperation. Merchandise appeal and low prices were the basis of customer loyalty, while sharing in profits guaranteed employees' or associates', as they were called, hard work and loyalty. A Board of Directors, elected by stockholders, wrote the by-laws and approved dividends, salaries, new managers, stock issues and stock sales. In January 1913, Penney who owned 2,054 of the 3,690 shares of preferred stock (55-2/3 percent) was elected President and General Manager; Sams, with 330 shares, was First Vice-President; Edward

J. Neighbors with 210 shares was Second Vice-President; Dayton H. Mudd with 235 shares was Third Vice-President; and J.I.H. Herbert with one share was Secretary and Treasurer.[110]

Of the thirty-six stores, two were in Wyoming, fourteen in Utah, seven in Idaho, five in Colorado, two in Nevada, two in Oregon, three in Washington and one in Montana. By the end of 1913, however, there were forty-eight stores in operation and fourteen more stockholders, making a total of thirty-four stockholders.[111]

A photograph commemorating the new company's first convention carries a caption of forty-seven stores, so the meeting was most likely held in fall 1913. Thirty-six proud men posed for the picture. Company conventions—after 1913 timed to coincide with the stockholders' Annual Meetings in January—were held in Salt Lake City until size necessitated regional conventions.[112] The convention was a perfect opportunity to instill company policies, discuss business and exchange ideas. New managers were initiated at the end of the week-long meetings. Company policies were put into writing now that the organization finally had a formal, centralized structure.

During 1913 Penney, C.E. Dimmitt and several others met in Salt Lake to draw up "The Original Body of Doctrine."[113] Dimmitt, the articulate and respected Golden Rule merchant who had written the "syndicate's" Articles of Agreement in 1896, was asked to sum up the principles guiding Penney's chain. The result was five, then seven, sentences:

1. To serve the public, as nearly as we can, to its complete satisfaction.
2. To expect from the service we render a fair remuneration and not all the profits the traffic will bear.
3. To do all in our power to pack the customer's dollar full of value, quality and satisfaction.
4. To continue to train ourselves and our Associates so that the service we give will be more and more intelligently performed.
5. To improve constantly the human factor in our business.
6. To reward the men and women of our Organization through participation in what the business produces.
7. To test our every policy, method and act in this wise: Does it square with what is right and just?[114]

It conveyed the founders' ideals and sense of purpose. At this same time Dimmitt created another document. "The Obligation" was an oath new managers took when initiated. This solemn pledge was regarded seriously by company officers, and because of it no manager was put under surety bond. Most business firms required those responsible for large sums of money to obtain bonding insurance to protect employers against theft or accidental loss. But in the new company a man's word was his bond.[115] The Board of Directors, of course, was empowered to dismiss a manager and could require a stockholder to surrender his stock for sale, allowing for a fair appraisal.[116] Men were carefully screened and still personally hired by Penney and senior partners. By now Penney was an expert in selecting his kind of people.

In New York City Penney returned to his typical work habits. In late January 1913, just after the incorporation, Dr. Short, writing from Salt Lake City, reminded him:

> I sincerely hope you are not plunging yourself into business affairs over your head so you can neither see nor sleep nor breathe. I would not for two worlds like this one discourage you but I want you to remember that your bundle of nerves cannot stand everything. There is a limit to your capacity of both endurance and business. Each of these depends upon the other, therefore, don't try to make all the money this year. There will be plenty to do and to make next year. DON'T KILL YOURSELF. You will serve your mission better by living longer even though you make a few less dollars per year. What will the product of fifty stores amount to for either you or your cherished plans, if you are dead? Say, I would rather have you around as a living clerk than a dead millionaire.[117]

Many exciting years lay ahead for the band of western entrepreneurs who had just incorporated and whose leader was dedicated to improving the business. Just how well Golden Rule Store methods and policies would fit into the twentieth-century world of "Big Business" remained to be seen.

NOTES

1.   *Historical Statistics of the United States*, p. 12.
2.   C. Watt Brandon, "Day by Day," *Kemmerer Gazette*, 9 May 1952.
3.   Beasley, *Main Street Merchant*, pp. 74-75.
4.   PHF I, F-8, Letters from store managers.
5.   JCP to O.A. Golluber, 12 March 1945, p. 2, PHF I, D-3; O.A. Golluber to JCP, 7 March 1945, PHF I, D-3; PHF Advertisement File.
6.   JCP to O.A. Golluber, p. 2, PHF I, D-3; Penney, explaining the Golden Rule Store principle, said certain embroideries could have been sold in much larger quantities at 49¢ than at 59¢, even though the 59¢ price was less than their competitors' price.
7.   Penney, *Man with a Thousand Partners*, p. 71.
8.   Ledger Book, 1911-1917, PHF X, C-3; Beasley, *Main Street Merchant*, pp. 74-75; Articles of Incorporation, 1913, PHF II, A-4.
9.   Dr. Thomas Tapper, "John I.H. Herbert," *Dynamo* 3 (December 1919): 5.
10.   Visit to Salt Lake City by author in September 1978.
11.   PHF II, A-1.
12.   "Articles of Incorporation of the J.C. Penney Company" filed with Secretary of State of Utah, 9 June 1911, #12859. Copy provided by the Wyoming State Archives, Records Management and Centralized Microfilm Division. (Certified copies were required by states where the corporation was doing business.)
13.   Ibid., pp. 2-4.
14.   Richard N. Owens, *Owens on Business Organization and Combination, Revised Edition* (New York: Prentice-Hall, 1940), p. 120-21, 123. Note: On p. 123 Owens says, "The nature of the partnership is entirely foreign to the theory of the corporation."
15.   January 1, 1912 Financial Statement, PHF II, A-1.
16.   Penney, *Man with a Thousand Partners*, pp. 73-74.
17.   Ibid., pp. 74, 77.
18.   Moe A. Isaacs to J.I.H. Herbert, 27 February 1912 through 15 November 1913, and J.I.H. Herbert to Moe E. Isaacs, 18 March 1912 to August 1913, PHF X, C-1.
19.   MAI to JIHH, 23 March 1912, PHF X, C-1; PHF X, C-2.
20.   MAI to JIHH, 23 March 1912, PHF X, C-1.
21.   R.G. Dun & Co., 183 (January 1914), New York City; MAI to JIHH, 12 March 1912, PHF X, C-1; Markwell & Springer to MAI, 26 December 1912, PHF X, C-1.
22.   JIHH to MAI, 30 March 1912 and 6 April 1912, PHF X, C-1.
23.   MAI to JIHH, 12 March 1912, PHF X, C-1; PHF II, A-1, July 29, 1912 record of J.C. Penney Company deposits and withdrawals.
24.   JIHH to MAI, 18 March 1912, 30 March 1912 and 6 April 1912, PHF X, C-1; Invoices 1902-1911, PHF X, B-4.
25.   T.M. Callahan to JCP, 25 January 1907, PHF II, C-3; JIHH to MAI, 5/7/13, PHF X, C-1. Note: Herbert said, "I am of the opinion that if we send one New

York check, together with these Salt Lake checks, it will cause the firms receiving same to want New York Exchange on all of their invoices."

26. *1951 Annual Report*, pp. 8-9, PHF IV, H-2; Summarized Financial Statement 1911-1925, PHF IV, H-1; Penney, *Man with a Thousand Partners*, p. 74; MAI to JIHH, 23 March 1912, PHF X, C-1; JCP to JIHH, 17 July 1912, PHF I, F-6.

27. MAI to JIHH, 12 March 1912, PHF X, C-1.

28. MAI to JIHH, 23 March 1912, PHF X, C-1.

29. *Bradstreet's Commercial Reports* 178 (July 1912), Salt Lake City; Penney, *Man with a Thousand Partners*, p. 74.

30. JCP to O.A. Golluber, 12 March 1945, PHF I, D-3.

31. Ibid.

32. *Bradstreet's Commercial Reports* (July 1912).

33. Penney, *Man with a Thousand Partners*, pp. 87-90.

34. November 1911 newspaper clipping on E.H. Robinson, Salt Lake City, PHF I, F-9.

35. Minutes of the Board of Directors of the E.H. Robinson Company, 1 May 1912, PHF I, F-9.

36. Newspaper clipping, November 1911, PHF I, F-9.

37. Ibid.

38. Ibid.; Penney, *Man with a Thousand Partners*, p. 90.

39. Penney, *Man with a Thousand Partners*, p. 90.

40. Mudd to JCP, 3 June 1912, PHF I, F-8.

41. *Deseret Evening News*, 16 December 1911, PHF, Advertisement File.

42. Ibid.

43. Ibid.

44. *The Library Atlas of the World, Volume I, United States* (Chicago: Rand McNally, 1912), p. xiv. Note: Ogden is 37 miles north of Salt Lake City: R.L. Polk & Co.'s *Ogden City Directory*, Vol. 1908-1909, XII (Ogden, Utah: R.L. Polk & Co., 1908), p. 244—Golden Rule Mercantile Co., 2275 Washington Avenue.

45. *Bradstreet's Commercial Reports* (July 1912), Ogden—The Johnson Stevens Co. W.D. Gds., Notions, valued at $200,000 to $250,000.

46. J.B. Byars to E.C. Sams, 24 January 1921, PHF II, F-1, and other letters in PHF II, F-1 and F-4.

47. Kemmerer "A Golden Opportunity" advertisement, PHF, Advertisement File.

48. Pendleton, Oregon, 1911 ad, "How Much Can I Save!" PHF, Advertisement File.

49. Ibid.

50. Ibid.

51. Preston, Idaho, 1912 ad, "The High Cost of Living," PHF, Advertisement File.

52. Ely, Nevada, April 1911 ad, PHF, Advertisement File.

53. Stock Certificate Book, PHF XXII, A-3; Beasley, *Main Street Merchant*, pp. 74-75.

54. PHF XX, Early Personnel Records.

55. PHF XXII, A-3.

56. PHF II, A-3.

57. Beasley, *Main Street Merchant*, p. 74; PHF XXII, A-3; PHF II, A-3.

58.   Penney, *Man with a Thousand Partners*, pp. 93-94; Beasley, *Main Street Merchant*, pp. 63-65.

59.   Ibid.

60.   Beasley, *Main Street Merchant*, p. 68; PHF XXII, A-3.

61.   Mrs. G.B. Miller to author, 23 March 1978.

62.   Dimmitt, "Twenty Years Ago," pp. 6-7.

63.   Ibid.; PHF XX, Early Personnel Records; Mrs. G.B. Miller to author, 23 March 1978; "Presentation of Gavel to Mr. Dimmitt," *Dynamo* 1 (March 1918): 7; Author's files.

64.   F.B. Short to JCP, 14 December 1911; Penney, *Fifty Years*, pp. 90-92.

65.   Penney, *Man with a Thousand Partners*, pp. 106-7; Penney, *Fifty Years*, pp. 76, 86.

66.   PHF, EVM files, 1912 photograph.

67.   *New York Times*, 15 April 1912, p. 1; 18 April 1912, pp. 4, 7.

68.   "The New Giantess Titanic," *New York Times*, 14 April 1912, p. 6; Walter Lord, *A Night to Remember* (London: Allan Lane, Penguin Books, 1976 ed.), pp. 17, 23.

69.   Penney, *Fifty Years*, pp. 91-92.

70.   Lord, *Night to Remember*, p. 33.

71.   Mabel H. Short to JCP, 1912, PHF IV, C-7.

72.   JCP to M.F. Whitman, 4 June 1912, PHF VII, E-2.

73.   Ibid.

74.   Penney, *View from the Ninth Decade*, pp. 78-79.

75.   L. Loll to JCP, 6/2/1912, PHF I, F-8.

76.   Ibid.

77.   *Dynamo* 1 (July 1917): 11; PHF XXII, A-3.

78.   E.H. Robinson to E.C. Sams, 27 June 1912, and EHR to JCP, 6 July 1912, PHF I, F-9.

79.   *Library Atlas of the World* (1912), p. xiv. *Pay Day*, April 1952, PHF XV, C.

80.   ECS to JCP, 7 July 1912, PHF I, F-8.

81.   Ibid.

82.   PHF II, A-3.

83.   ECS to JCP, 7 July 1912, PHF I, F-8.

84.   ECS to JCP, 18 July 1912, PHF I, F-3; EHR to JCP, 6, 8, 17 July 1912, PHF I, F-9; JCP to ECS, 22 July 1912, PHF I, F-8.

85.   EHR to JCP, 8, 17 July 1912, PHF I, F-9.

86.   JCP to JIHH, 25 July 1912, PHF I, F-6.

87.   PHF II, A-3; PHF XX, Early Personnel Records.

88.   JCP to Mrs. R.F. Whitman, 25 July 1912, PHF II, E-2.

89.   A.D. Frost to JCP (c. 1910), PHF I, D-3.

90.   Beasley, *Main Street Merchant*, p. 72.

91.   PHF XX, Early Personnel Records.

92.   PHF X, C-3, Ledger books; Beasley, *Main Street Merchant*, p. 75.

93.   PHF, File Box, cards with store openings listed.

94.   PHF II, A-3.

95.   Ibid.

96.   PHF X, C-3.

97.   MAI to JIHH, 22 November 1912, p. 2, PHF X, C-1.

98.   Articles of Incorporation, PHF II, A-3.

99.   Amendment included with #12859, Articles of Incorporation of the J.C. Penney Company (June 1911).

100.   PHF II, A-3.

101.   Ibid.; Penney, *Man with a Thousand Partners*, pp. 75-76.

102.   PHF II, A-3.

103.   Minutes of Meetings of the Board of Directors of the J.C. Penney Company, I, 110, 25 March 1913, By-Laws, Article XXI. Note: Source hereafter referred to as MBD.

104.   Ibid., 7 April 1914, p. 177; ibid., 12 September 1916, p. 297.

105.   PHF II, A-3. Restrictions were included on stock certificates.

106.   Penney, *Man with a Thousand Partners*, pp. 114-15.

107.   MBD I, 117, 25 March 1913.

108.   Penney, *Man with a Thousand Partners*, pp. 76-77.

109.   John P. Nichols, *Skyline Queen and the Merchant Prince. The Woolworth Story* (New York: Trident Press, 1973), pp. 76-79.

110.   PHF II, A-3.

111.   Ibid.; PHF XXII, A-3.

112.   Penney, *Man with a Thousand Partners*, pp. 127-28; PHF, Photograph Files, Conventions.

113.   Penney, *Man with a Thousand Partners*, pp. 127-28; Author's correspondence with Mrs. G.B. Miller; PHF II, B.

114.   Ibid.

115.   PHF II, C; Beasley, *Main Street Merchant*, p. 72; Penney, *Man with a Thousand Partners*, pp. 127-28. PHF II, C.

116.   MBD I, 25 March 1913, By-Laws.

117.   F.B. Short to JCP, 30 January 1913, PHF IV, C-7.

The Penney family in Hamilton, Mo., c.1888. From left to right: Mary Frances Paxton Penney, Herbert, Mittie, James (J.C. Penney), Elie, James Cash Penney, Sr. and Pearl. Courtesy of JCPenney Archives.

Penney family residence in Hamilton, Mo. Author's Photograph, 1978.

Berta Alva Hess Penney, who married J.C. Penney in 1899 and worked with him in the Kemmerer Golden Rule Store, c.1900. Courtesy of JCPenney Archives.

The Golden Rule Mercantile Company, c.1903. From left to right: J.C. Penney, Thomas M. Callahan, John Hood, Drury G. Keirsey, William Guy Johnson. Courtesy of JCPenney Archives.

The Golden Rule Store in Kemmerer, Wyo., c.1905. This was the second site of the "Mother Store." Courtesy of JCPenney Archives.

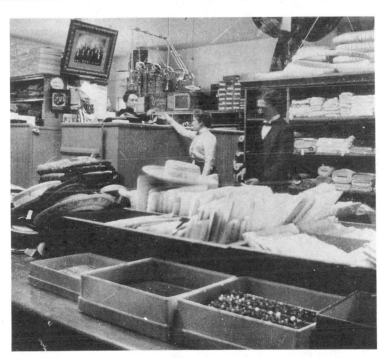

J.C. Penney working with his cousins Belle and Anna Partin at the Golden Rule Store in Rock Springs, Wyo., c.1906. A Golden Rule Syndicate group portrait from 1898 was prominently displayed. Courtesy of JCPenney Archives.

Mary Kimball Penney, who married J.C. Penney in 1919, with
Kimball Penney, c.1922. Mary Penney died in 1923. Courtesy of
JCPenney Archives.

#8 Belle Isle, J.C. Penney's winter home in Miami Beach, Florida,
during the 1920s. Courtesy of JCPenney Archives.

Caroline Autenrieth Penney, who married J.C. Penney in 1926, and J.C. Penney, c.1928. Courtesy of JCPenney Archives.

J.C. Penney at the Tucson Rodeo Parade in February 1937. Courtesy of *The Arizona Daily Star* and JCPenney Archives.

Earl Corder Sams, president of the J.C. Penney Co. from 1917 to 1946 and chairman of the board from 1946 to 1950. Courtesy of JCPenney Archives.

Albert W. Hughes, J.C. Penney Co. president and chairman of the board, with William M. Batten, J.C. Penney Co. president, chief executive officer and chairman of the board, c.1960. Courtesy of JCPenney Archives.

J.C. Penney, 89 years old, checks the fit of a pair of Easter shoes he sold to three-year-old Carmela Cota, in the downtown Tucson J.C. Penney Co. store in March 1964. Jack Sheaffer photograph.

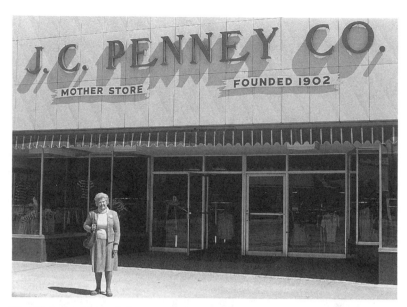

The "Mother Store" in Kemmerer, Wyo., and E. Virginia Mowry in June 1982. Author's photograph, 1982.

J.C. Penney Co. store #1180–9 at Wayne Town Centre, Wayne, N.J., November 1986. Courtesy of *The Star Ledger*, Newark, N.J.

BUILDING AN EFFICIENT SYSTEM
AND MODERN ORGANIZATION

> "We cater to the masses
> and we do it in a
> simple way."
>
> J.C. Penney
> 1 February 1914
> *New York Times*

What Penney and his associates accomplished in six short years is one of retailing's greatest success stories. The company expanded from forty-eight stores in seven states in late 1913 to one hundred and ninety-seven stores in twenty-five states by 1919. In these few years sales increased from $2.6 million to $28.7 million.[1]

Had the directors foreseen this phenomenal growth they might have been overwhelmed. Rapid expansion during the next few years demonstrated they were continuing to satisfy the needs of an expanding population.[2] The organizational problems they solved proved they were much more than fortunate entrepreneurs. The astute businessmen from small towns developed a most efficient system of distributing dry goods. The eager salesmen who became shrewd managers and buyers were now executives. Although neither students of finance nor part of the eastern business establishment, they learned fast.

Certain organizational problems were solved by ad hoc decisions. Other steps resulted from careful planning by directors and especially by Penney, the company's guiding force. Most important, they deliberately built a reputation and organization that made their 1920s nationwide system possible.

The incorporation preserved what already existed, but it made them eligible for increased credit and future expansion. However, New York bank credit still eluded them.[3] By now Penney was convinced their headquarters should be New York instead of Salt Lake City. He had to convince fellow stockholders of this insight.

Most of his time was spent in the metropolis, and he either returned to Salt Lake for directors meetings or sent telegrams approving meetings held without him.[4] Penney had a home in New Jersey near his mother and Letha. However, Mrs. Penney, seventy, was in very poor health. Despite doctor's care and a seaside residence at Ocean Grove, she died on November 2, 1913.[5]

Overall, her life had been quite satisfying. She had paid off farm and house mortgages and saw her middle son fulfill his first dream. After leaving Hamilton, Mrs. Penney lived in Kansas City and Salt Lake City, and she retained a lively interest in politics.[6] Dr. Short delivered the eulogy in Hamilton.[7] J.C. Penney Company Golden Rule Stores closed for the hour of her funeral and Penney received letters of condolence from many associates.[8] Respect and interest expressed by senior members gave newcomers the confidence to respond in kind.

The six Penney children's ages ranged from twenty-three (Letha) to fifty (Mittie).[9] At age thirty-eight, Penney was a handsome widower, father of two sons, and president of an organization that required most of his time.

Penney's determined work since Berta's death had brought results. He and his associates had opened new stores, increased profits, had a small accounting department and improved buying. Far more important was the merchants' sense of purpose and dedication. They saw themselves as performing a community service. The resulting sense of social usefulness was a powerful motivating factor.[10] The fine words of their advertisements were not an afterthought, but grew from Penney's experiences since 1902 and were a heritage from the 1890s' Golden Rule merchants. The focus on service, plus the natural attraction of low-priced, good quality merchandise would create legions of loyal customers.

Immediately after incorporation, a practical question arose: store dividends. Dividends were calculated on individual store profits, provided there was a general surplus. In February 1913, Kemmerer Class No. 1 had an impressive dividend of $27,572.[11] J.I.H. Herbert, with one share of Kemmerer stock received 1/150th or $184, while Penney received the remainder. The same day directors approved similar "special dividends" for thirteen stores. Preston, Utah, had a surplus of $24,000; Malad, Utah, $15,000; Wenatchee, Washington, $6,300; and Walla Walla, Washington, a new store, had $600.[12] As two-thirds owner of Preston classified stock Penney received $16,000, while $8,000 went to Neighbors, who also received one-third of the Malad dividend, or $5,000.[13] Grand Junction, Colorado, Class No. 33 and a new store, earned $4,500 in dividends in January 1913. Eugene C. Joclyn, who started in Kemmerer in spring 1909, was a one-third owner as were Mudd and Penney.[14] Sometimes dividends were declared twice a year.

When Penney sold classified stock to company members he relinquished future dividends. In January 1914 he sold George H. Bushnell nine shares in the profitable Price, Utah, store. That year it had a $21,000 surplus. At this time, Bushnell also became owner of ten shares of Midvale and Preston and seven shares of Eureka and Malad. In late 1913 Penney had sold Herbert and E.H. Robinson each a one-third interest in the Murray store, leaving Penney a one-third interest. They also became owners of 2/15ths and 2/9ths of the Kemmerer and Cumberland stock.[15]

All stock sales had to be approved by the Board of Directors.[16] By selling stock Penney set an example for others. As founder and principal capitalist he owned much more preferred stock than anyone else. His holdings, percentage-wise, however, were reduced when he could easily have increased them. For example, in January 1913 he owned 55-2/3 percent of the preferred stock or 2,054 of the 3,690 shares issued.[17] In 1916 he owned 3,253 of the 8,940 shares of preferred stock issued or 36-1/3 percent when there were 127 stores.[18] In the 1920s he maintained approximately a 20 percent to 15 percent ownership of the company's issued common stock.[19] New stock was sold at par value, $100 a share, but stock in previously established stores would have cost more. Records of loans to men who purchased "old" stock are not conclusive on this point. Sometimes men only borrowed part of the amount needed from Penney.[20]

Herbert's and Robinson's one-third interests in Murray were usually large for central office associates. For several reasons their interests were often smaller. Preserving a manager's incentive with a one-third interest was primary; other managers' and senior members' desire to open new stores with the original one-third partnership plan left little or no stock for non-management associates. Managers preferred men they had trained or men they trained under to be owners and make store decisions.[21] Penney, however, knew central office members' hard work was also essential to the company's success and believed in motivating them by providing opportunities for them to share store profits.[22] When the central office was small, this ad hoc arrangement was satisfactory. Large stockholders, mostly Penney but later Sams, Neighbors and Mudd, sold part of their classified stock in both old and new stores.[23] Small amounts of shares in a fairly large number of stores thus came to men like Herbert and Bushnell. A better system had to be devised as the headquarters office expanded.

The Board of Directors' first meeting in New York City was held in late November 1913 at 16 East 33rd Street. Provision had been made in the By-Laws for a New York office.[24] It had been conceived, however, as a place to record orders and view samples and eliminate operating from hotels. Penney suggested they move permanently to New York City to be full-time buyers. Among the many advantages of being near vendors and in the market daily were special bargains, discounts and more fashionable merchandise.[25] The company might become more credible in financial circles as well.

His associates, after spending several years in mining camps, enjoyed life in Salt Lake City and had a regional outlook.[26] Why not stay in the western city? It was near many stores and was a central distribution point. Close watch could be kept on store managers and new clerks, too. But Penney believed expert buying was necessary and improved transportation arrangements were possible if they attended to it in person instead of using agents. This major decision was Penney's idea alone. Supplier friends like Isaacs probably encouraged him and Penney persisted. However, he refused to force the move.[27]

The three other directors decided Penney and Sams should determine their headquarters location. While on a buying trip, Penney earnestly repeated the points favoring this step and Sams asked, "Are you sure of your judgment?" When he heard a confident "Yes," Sams said he would come east and the others would too. This often-mentioned and crucial scene in company history occurred while they were walking around the old Madison Square Garden in New York City.[28]

The directors sold Salt Lake City homes, rented apartments in New York City and leased a two-room office at 354 Fourth Avenue in early 1914. At first they continued buying for their "branch chains," but in a few months they joined forces. Each man then specialized in particular items. For example, Neighbors bought lingerie and ladies' ready-to-wear; Mudd bought notions and piece goods while Sams and Penney selected all other merchandise.[29]

In April Jim McDonald, who after working at Kemmerer in 1905 for six months had rejoined Penney's growing chain in 1911 and became manager and part-owner of the Centralia, Washington, store in spring 1913, came to New York to help Penney handle buying. McDonald was on Penney's personal payroll for some months. Eventually he would be put in charge of the company's buying department.[30]

The evolution to specialization in buying was a significant step towards efficient merchandising. Successful store managers were invited to join the buying staff in New York. A few outsiders were hired, but in May 1916 the Board of Directors resolved to employ as buyers only men who had started in the stores.[31]

The new buying staff, at first, did not replace managers' buying trips. Store managers always made the final selections from a variety of goods approved by the buyers.[32] Managers knew customers and community needs best, and this procedure preserved the concept of partnership. Indeed, managers were part owners of their stores due to the classified stock arrangement.

On April 1, 1914, twenty-two stores were added to the chain. Preferred stock was issued for each new store. All but five were capitalized at $6,000 or 60 shares.[33] Buying for the seventy stores was completed in late January. Although company stores were in far western towns, they were a thirteen-state operation and the arrival of thirty manager buyers in New York City was "news."

In early February a *New York Times* business reporter interviewed Penney. He was curious to discover how seventy stores could be operated smoothly in what easterners considered an underpopulated part of the country. In a lengthy interview Penney explained the store system in detail and gave many reasons for their success. He declared, "Co-operation in business means good team work, good team work means efficiency, and efficiency means success."[34] A "spirit of co-operation" dominated their operations, and was an inspiration to Penney. For example, he said:

> Every man is ready to help his brother manager at any time, and one man's idea or plan for the betterment of the business is the property of every other manager in the chain as soon as its practicability is proved.[35]

The ongoing buying trip was an example of this cooperation. Thirty men were as careful in selecting goods for others as for themselves.[36]

Only men of sterling character were hired, Penney said. In addition to a salary, they had up to a one-third interest in their store, their activities were "not curbed in any way," and they could open new stores with "bright assistants." "In short, it is a sort of endless chain proposition, and some of our men are interested in twelve to eighteen stores." Success was also due to low operating costs and low prices. They made no deliveries, had no fancy window trims or bargain sales. In the market they received jobbers' prices because of volume buying, and they turned over inventory four to six times a year. In early 1914 they were "decentralized" since finance was handled by the "western office" (but accounting and buying were soon consolidated in New York City). A week-long convention at the time of the January annual meeting revealed the men's "remarkable spirit and interest" in the chain's operation.[37]

The western region, with its dry farming, irrigation districts, fruit growing, grain harvests and rich mining areas meant the eastern recession was practically unknown. Penney concluded the interview by remarking:

> Our stores are now located in the West because they were started there and have made good. Some day we may extend our operations eastward, but it is too far distant to even hazard a guess as to when it will be.[38]

A national magazine for businessmen featured the chain in June 1914. *System* included a full-page picture of Penney hard at work and described how the company kept the cost of doing business extremely low. The average small town dry goods store had an overhead of 15 percent to 25 percent, according to the writer, while Golden Rule Store costs were 10 percent to 12 percent.[39] The chain's elimination of unnecessary frills, such as deliveries, might be tried by individual small stores who were now struggling with rising costs.[40] However, the interrelationship among low overhead, quantity buying, low prices and high turnover was such that individual store merchants would find it almost impossible to duplicate the chain's methods. They simply had fewer resources at their command, and it would necessitate changing their philosophy of retailing.

Despite financial strength, a major concern in 1914 was obtaining additional credit lines for expansion. Throughout 1913 and 1914 they opened bank accounts and strengthened their financial position. A second account was opened at Harriman National Bank in New York in spring. This bank extended them a $75,000 line of credit in late 1913.[41] In summer 1914, Herbert traveled to Chicago to arrange a line of credit with the Continental & Commercial National Bank.[42]

That same summer Penney, Letha, Roswell, J.C., Jr., and Vince A. Burns, the family chauffeur, were touring Europe by automobile.[43] While they were in Germany, World War I broke out. They became part of an often panic-stricken 150,000 American tourists scattered across Europe when the terrible onslaught began August 1st.[44] Borders were closed, citizenship papers demanded and car travel restricted. In Berlin on August 1st, they did not receive a transportation pass until August 11th.[45] After passing through war zones they headed home a few weeks later, having witnessed memorable events. Penney even received a partial refund from American Express in April 1915.[46]

In Manhattan, family life assumed a new routine. Penney rented an apartment at the Dorchester, at West 85th and Riverside Drive, one of several new apartment buildings on the breezy hillside overlooking the Hudson River. By 1915 all the directors had apartments on fashionable Riverside Drive, as did Dr. Thomas Tapper, a noted music educator, editor and author.[47] His book, *Youth and Opportunity*, attracted Penney's attention about this time and led to a mutually rewarding friendship.

Roswell and J.C., Jr., attended Peekskill Military Academy at Peekskill, New York, on the Hudson River. The boarding school, founded in 1833, was very highly regarded.[48] Included in his sons' tuition payments for fall 1915 were four scholarship payments for the school's use.[49] The boys, aged fourteen and twelve, had already traveled extensively in Europe. With Letha they visited Bermuda in 1913. In the next few years they became quite familiar with the western states as they accompanied Penney on cross-country summer automobile trips. Such long trips were something of a novelty. An old photograph shows family members, in goggles and dusters, seated in an open touring car at the Dorchester entrance.[50] A "New York to San Francisco" sign was on the running board!

For Penney these trips were a way to combine practical business and pleasure. Even though distances were vast, store visits served a most practical purpose. Just as other directors visited the stores that they had started, Penney wanted to impart his retailing philosophy in person. He also checked on business, stock-keeping and economic conditions. Although in constant touch by mail, sales reports and telegram, the trips continued for many years and inspired managers, assistant managers and sales clerks to keep working hard.[51]

As the company expanded, however, each store could not be visited every year. Additional steps were taken to impart ideals, knowledge and policy. Maintaining and improving communications in the far-flung store chain was a challenge the company met successfully. With eighty-three stores in thirteen states by spring 1915, the company had demonstrated its strength. That February the Board of Directors declared a surplus dividend for twenty-nine of 1914's seventy-one stores. Penney received $68,994 for his share of profits from twenty-six stores. His dividends ranged from $500 to $8,000, and the average amount was $3,000.[52]

They were the largest Golden Rule Store chain and had been for at least four years. Directors discussed the value of a name that could be confused with other less powerful but still expanding Golden Rule Stores, which also sold for cash, as well as the inevitable imitators. For the time being they continued using the original name, but J.C. Penney Company was printed either above or below the Golden Rule name in most cases.[53]

In 1915 a brochure reiterated the Golden Rule name to emphasize the service aspect of the company's operations. Their self-image of social usefulness was clear:

Some one from the New York office all of the time, and all of them some of the time, keep in personal contact with each of the eighty-three GOLDEN RULE STORES, studying the needs of each community, determining the kind of merchandise to buy for its people, getting acquainted with the people and really being a part of you. We take real interest in the welfare of our customers—something more than a mere commercial interest.[54]

They called themselves a business that was "doing unto others as you want to have them do unto you." A reproduction of a $65,895.75 check from the company's Chemical National Bank account to Roberts, Johnson & Rand (International Shoe Company) of St. Louis was used in the same advertisement together with a letter from the shoe manufacturer thanking them for the remittance and the fact that it came in "New York Exchange." The letter also stated, "There are few retail concerns in this country who can draw their check for this amount payable at one time and on one bank."[55]

Large buying power, buying and selling for cash, one price to all, testing merchandise—they cut open sample shoes, keeping managers up-to-date by conventions, and sharing profits was their interpretation of the Golden Rule precept. It was consistent with earlier ads like the one featured in the 1911 *Deseret Evening News*. Ever since 1902 or 1889, in fact, values and savings for customers had been stressed. Now, the service idea was made explicit. Penney realized service to customers and communities was equally important. This was the image he and fellow directors wanted to project; it was a reflection of their personalities. Store managers were encouraged to join local churches and become active in chapters of the Chamber of Commerce and Rotary International.[56]

How did this help the stores to be successful? Increasing population and prosperous towns helped all merchants to an extent. Their increasingly efficient system and improved central services made possible expansion, low prices, and good merchandise. By focusing on personal salesmanship and community involvement, however, the stores built outstanding local reputations.

The local manager's work never ended. The company was not built on forty-hour workweeks. Evening and Sunday work was common. Unpacking, marking and displaying merchandise, cleaning and "trimming" windows and record keeping were necessary.[57] The dream of being part-owner in a store had become reality for so many employees that new men did not question the difficult path to success.

One reason expansion continued was to provide the opportunities that attracted men in the first place. The understanding, not a written contract, was if they "made good," that is, worked hard, learned to run a profitable store and trained future managers, they could become a manager with a one-third stock interest in the store. Later, they could help open additional stores. Still, directors could have stopped expansion at any time. For example, a chain of one hundred stores in the mountain states and Pacific northwest would have been a significant accomplishment. Instead, a combination of ambition and obligation to hard-working clerks, assistant managers and managers brought them past the one hundred store mark in early 1916. Being conservative, they expanded out of earnings.[58]

Expansion posed challenges in all areas: finance, accounting, buying, transportation, testing and employment. In 1915 uniform daily cash reports for all stores were devised.[59] This made accounting and auditing much easier. The January 1915 convention was preoccupied with finances. There were general discussions on assessments and taxes, balancing cash, handling money left in local banks, and recording shortages and claims on invoices. Men were reminded to give close attention to letters and lists from the New York office, to keep a record of invoices sent to New York, and were told not to talk to various suppliers' "traveling men." They discussed "system and efficiency," and after the banquet at Salt Lake City's Commercial Club, George Bushnell explained trial balances and other accounting procedures by demonstrating them on a blackboard.[60]

At the first meeting of the Board of Directors after the 1915 combined annual meeting and convention, approval was given to open a store in Loveland, Colorado. West of Greeley and north of Longmont, Loveland was located below the Big Thompson River and residents had a beautiful view of Longs Peak in Estes Park. Ira A. Foote, Sams' former mentor, was appointed manager of store #74. It was capitalized at $6,000.[61]

When the world famous Cripple Creek gold mines near Colorado Springs closed during 1913, miners left town without paying their bills. Foote, whose own store sold on credit, was forced out of business. He was in his fifties when financial disaster struck and he had to start over again with nothing. Sams hired Foote and he worked at Provo and Eureka before becoming manager of the Loveland store where he soon obtained a one-third interest.[62]

The Foote family saga was typical. Within a few years three of Ira's sons, Mark, Donald, and Wyborn joined him. Mark opened the Longmont store in spring 1917. Donald, a graduate in electrical engineering from Kansas State, became a salesman and then was manager of the Loveland store after Ira moved to Denver in 1923 to open the company's first store in the state capital. Family members' hard work and merchandising skill brought them wealth as the company expanded. They, in turn, contributed generously to the communities that helped make their success possible.[63]

But success did not come easy. Ira Foote had to "fight for business," as son Donald recalls:

> The newspaper would not take his ads. Competition threatened to boycott the paper if they took our ads. We had to get our circulars out of town and distribute them ourselves in the country and town.[64]

What counted was that people liked their merchandise; despite initial difficulties the Loveland store grew and expanded.[65]

Many relatives and hometown neighbors continued to be hired. Firmages, Malmstens, many men from the Beloit, Kansas, area and others from Hamilton, like the large McDonald family, joined the company with alacrity. The number of men who owned classified preferred stock grew from thirty-four in fall 1913 to ninety by August 1916 when there were 127 stores.[66]

The new store network grew in the same fashion as in the partnership era. New stores opened from other stores' surpluses, and a profitable store became a "Mother Store" of many stores. Stockholders used either cash dividends or stock dividends to create new stores. The New York office, however, controlled the complex procedure.[67]

On paper an intriguing pattern developed. The Pittsburg, Kansas, store was opened from profits of the Laramie, Wyoming, store, and a store in Paris, Texas, opened from Provo, Utah, profits. Their western origins reversed an old American adage. An appropriate company motto would have been "Go East, Young

Man," as eastern stores opened from the profits of remote western stores. The first store in Illinois was at Moline in 1917. Wenatchee, Washington, was its mother store. In 1917 Shenandoah, Pennsylvania, was the farthest eastward. It had been opened by two Utah stores, American Fork and Springvale.[68]

Store managers witnessed history and survived rough and tumble western mining towns in this era. During a violent strike near Trinidad, Colorado, the Golden Rule Store, according to the manager's family history, was practically the only business firm that did not have to board its windows and barricade doors as angry miners stormed town streets.[69] Bisbee, Arizona, a bustling saloon-filled town, was famous for its copper mines during the World War I era. One day, two women entered the store; one pulled a gun from her handbag and tried to shoot the other! Fortunately, she missed and the manager took the deadly weapon away.[70]

Many stores were in small to middle sized trading centers surrounded by scattered farming communities. Saturday evening was shopping day for farmers and stores stayed open to 10:00 P.M., even 11:00 P.M., to accommodate them. With the advent of the Model T, farm families came to town with increasing frequency. They also traveled to larger towns, but returned to the Golden Rule Store after discovering much higher price tags for similar fashions in the big city.[71]

Loss-leaders, selling merchandise for less than cost to attract business, were not used, but at different times goods were sold at cost or net. For example, in spring 1915 all rubber goods were to be marked "net."[72]

In spring 1916, a year of transition, over forty stores opened, bringing the total to 127.[73] In May, as stores in twenty-two states promoted spring and summer merchandise, the Board of Directors held a special meeting in New York. Nine directors, the original five plus George Bushnell, C.E. Dimmitt, Jim McDonald and George Hoag who had been elected at the January stockholders' meeting, discussed amending the Articles of Incorporation.[74]

Except for 1,060 shares, the original 10,000 shares of preferred stock had been issued. At most, the directors could open twenty new stores and they faced the first of several turning points in company history. They needed larger lines of credit, but most bank officers remained skeptical of the 1913 incorporation form. They told Penney and Sams to issue common stock in the company's name, instead of having separate stock classifications. At a special stockholders meeting in August amendments proposed in May by the directors were unanimously approved. Instead of following the bankers' advice they resolved to maintain and continue "the present general plan and system of classifications of stock."[75]

Penney's 10,000 shares of common stock were retired, the preferred stock was eliminated and classified common stock replaced it. Each store would continue to issue dividends to its individual owners. Capitalization was increased to $3 million, making 30,000 shares of $100 par value of common stock of which 21,060 were available for new stores.[76]

Fifteen of the ninety stockholders in August 1916 held 6,804 of the outstanding 8,940 preferred shares (renamed classified common). The remaining stockholders held an average of 28 shares each. Penney owned 3,250; Sams, 745 (up from 330 in January 1913); Mudd, 485; Neighbors, 470; Hoag, 390; Herbert, 135; and Bushnell, 88.[77] It remained a tightly controlled corporation. No stock was available to the public, but several widows of managers owned stock. Astute conservative leadership, increasingly professional merchandising and motivation through stock ownership provided the inner resources to grow so rapidly. The only question was where would they stop?

Other important events occurred during 1916. Penney resigned as General Manager, and Dimmitt was promoted to the time-consuming post. Deciding the word "sale" implied prices were marked down from an artificially high earlier price, they resolved to stop using the word in ads and stores. Prices, which stayed the same all season, were offered at the lowest possible markup at the season's beginning. This policy would reassure customers and they would not delay purchases waiting for special sales.[78]

Their store name was questioned again. Lawyers were consulted to ascertain if using "J.C. Penney Company—Operating 125 Golden Rule Stores," gave them exclusive right to the Golden Rule name in a town. The name problem would be resolved at the 1917 Annual Meeting.[79]

Related Golden Rule Store chains continued to flourish. Idaho had numerous Golden Rule Stores scattered throughout its mountainous terrain and river valleys. Hood family members had stores in seven towns; C.C. Anderson had a prosperous Golden Rule Store in Boise.[80] In 1916 the J.C. Penney Company opened four Idaho stores in addition to ten already in operation. They were in Coeur d'Alene, Shelby, Jerome and Sandpoint.[81] In 1916 the company entered Iowa, Wisconsin, Minnesota, South Dakota and Kansas. These few stores were harbingers of a flood.[82]

In late January 1917 sixty-seven manager-buyers arrived in New York City; their spring purchases totalled $2 million. Immediately after the January Annual Meeting and convention in Salt Lake City, a special five-car train was used for the eastern buying trip. After being stalled by a Wyoming blizzard, they proceeded to Kansas City and from there went to Hamilton. Everybody walked up Davis Street to Hale's Department Store, and Penney introduced them to his former boss, John M. Hale. Old and new managers saw in person the origin of Penney's legendary rise from $2.27 a month apprentice to head of the growing chain.[83]

Fifty new stores were opened that spring. This required fifty managers and assistant managers. Several clerks, a bookkeeper and cashier were usually hired for larger stores; the latter were often women. The manager actually wore three hats, as supervisor, top salesman, and record keeper. Despite unending work, men were eager to be hired. However, few were selected. Those who were hired had most of the same qualities possessed by the founders. Recruiting from relatives and home towns had been helpful in the early years, but after 1916 occasional advertisements began appearing in newspapers and magazines.

The company had stayed in towns with populations of less than 20,000, but in 1917 a store was opened in Salt Lake City. Store #155 was capitalized at $21,000, or 210 shares of classified common stock and was under Frank R. Payne's management.[84] Payne, an experienced merchandiser, joined the company in spring 1915. From a trainee at Murray he became the Midvale manager until 1917. The Salt Lake store quickly became one of, if not the most, profitable stores in the chain. It proved company policies and merchandise were popular in large cities. From a surplus of $7,000 in February 1918, two years later its profits were $50,000.[85] Obviously, larger stores offered great potential.

If 1916 was a year of transition, then 1917 was one of expansion in all directions. It was a turning point for Penney as well. At the January Annual Meeting, he tendered his resignation as president and asked for a vote for a successor. Earl Sams was unanimously elected.[86] Sometimes this event is cited as the date of Penney's retirement from company activities, but records make clear he undertook even greater efforts to plan company policies and make its future secure. Leaving day-to-day operations to others freed him for recruiting, training and perpetuating his business philosophy. He became Chairman of the Board of Directors.[87]

It was also an act of trust and recognition. Sams, whom he had known for ten years, was a dedicated leader whose ambition and foresight almost matched Penney's. Actually Penney was ahead of his time and was practicing modern psychology in leadership development by providing his subordinates with opportunities for growth and advancement.[88]

To continue expansion they needed men—men who had to be trained for several years before becoming managers. Penney devised two solutions to this challenge. First, he engaged in extensive job interviewing. In early 1917 over 5,000 applications were examined and several hundred were selected for interviews. During 1918 and part of 1919, Penney interviewed at least 5,000 men in person. Second, a remarkable company publication, *The Dynamo*, was created with his initiative.[89]

Free to all associates, the monthly publication first appeared in April 1917. Penney called it an "ambassador" from the central office to their hundreds, soon to be thousands, of store employees. It was an outgrowth of directors' store visits and of Penney's bulletins to managers in which he included mimeographed articles from the *New York Times*.[90]

The new magazine contained biographies of men like Frank Vanderlip of National City Bank, Frank W. Woolworth, Carnegie, Wanamaker and Edison, but it emphasized company history and introduced the chain's executives, managers and buyers. Executives wrote inspirational articles about the company's potential; information on fashions and materials as well as business and personal anecdotes were included. Each issue stressed their increasingly professional approach to merchandising. Over seventy years later *The Dynamo* remains informative and inspirational reading.

In late 1916 or early 1917, Penney placed William M. Bushnell, a younger brother of George Bushnell, on his personal payroll.[91] William Bushnell was editor of *The Dynamo* for three years and helped Penney interview and hire men. Dr. Thomas Tapper was also closely involved in developing the magazine. He and Dr. Short eventually became editors of the publication.[92]

For the initial issue, Short wrote an article, "Where Are You Going?" Tapper wrote, "The Two Sides of a Job" and later in October contributed, "What is Efficiency?" Old adages, good habits, hard work, rendering service, efficiency and scientific planning were stressed. Arthur Frederick Sheldon, president of the well-known Sheldon School—Penney and Sams had taken its business correspondence course—wrote a special article, "Knowledge, When Applied, Is Power," for *The Dynamo*'s June 1917 issue. He had read earlier issues and thought the magazine would meet company needs most effectively.[93] Associates were encouraged through *The Dynamo* to form good reading habits, and Bushnell was happy to provide reading lists. Within three years an extensive company business training course developed from *The Dynamo*'s successes and failures.

St. Louis became the company's employment center. Advertisements had appeared in dry goods journals in late 1916, but in 1917 a sixteen-page brochure titled "Men Wanted" was distributed. Inside the front cover was a quote by Penney:

> I will have no man work for me who has not the capacity to become a Partner. Any man whom I employ must understand that as soon as he has proved his ability, he will become a Partner in one or another store.
>   I will give him an interest and he shall pay for it out of his earnings.[94]

Under the headline "Men of Sterling Qualities Wanted," the brochure proceeded to explain the requirements: "EXPERIENCED men are wanted who are EMPLOYED; who KNOW their BUSINESS; who feel that a CHANGE in necessary for BETTERMENT. They must have the MIND and MORALS of a Christian, be INDUSTRIOUS, AMBITIOUS, OF GOOD HABITS, OF HIGHEST REFERENCES."[95]

Penney's requirements were the same as in 1906 and 1907, but the brochure explained:

> The objection to gambling, smoking, drinking, indolence, and the like is not hysterical. It is scientific. It is known from many years of observation, test and experience that these habits are

> dangerous air bubbles in the steel rails of business, which is but
> another name for MEN.[96]

High salaries were not offered to newcomers, but opportunities for advancement were. They had just opened fifty stores and were now committed to expansion, depending on business conditions.

Although the pamphlet's tone was almost intimidating, readers were reassured the company was looking for ordinary people:

> A man of ordinary mind and body and of meagre attainments,
> inspired and led on by some high ultimate ideal, accomplishes
> far more in life, than the man of finest mental and physical
> equipment, splendidly trained, who drifts.[97]

And the company's service concept was mentioned, as Penney explained, "Money is always the by-product of a useful service."[98]

In St. Louis, Penney was assisted by F.J. Bolger, a former manager, and William Bushnell. It was difficult to find the right men. Out of 300 who were being seriously considered in spring 1917, sixty-three were employed.[99] If a man's wife was likely to object to his long hours, small pay check and life in a distant town, he was quickly eliminated.[100]

As Penney, now Chairman of the Board, entered personnel areas, his name began appearing on more and more stores. At the 1917 Annual Meeting a solution to the name problem, suggested by a committee of J.W. Rickman, Wilk Hyer and A.F. Lieurance was approved. Its terms were:

> We, the committee, suggest that all stores that are in
> operation and are to be established hereafter, must be known as
> the J.C. Penney Company, after January 1, 1919.
> We further suggest that until January 1, 1919 all stores
> have the privilege of opening up and operating under the name
> "Golden Rule" or "J.C. Penney Company" . . .[101]

At its manager's discretion, however, a store could make this change anytime between 1917 and January 1, 1919. Penney always liked the idealistic name, and he had some reservations about eliminating it. The new name did cause some problems. When the Towners opened the Pittsburg, Kansas, store in 1917, people confused the name with penny coins and thought the store was like a "5¢ & 10¢" store![102]

In many respects 1917 was an eventful year. The E.H. Robinson Company had been liquidated in 1915, but the need for a warehouse and distribution center remained. In early 1916 an arrangement was made with the Lindeke Warner Company, a St. Paul, Minnesota, wholesaler known to Jim McDonald. D.G. McDonald, a store manager and brother of Jim, opened the company's St. Paul office in March to oversee this operation.[103] Penney Company buyers and Lindeke Warner buyers worked together on some items, and many orders were filled from St. Paul.

The same month another buying office was opened. Wilk Hyer, an experienced, well-respected manager and buyer, started the company's St. Louis office and was placed in charge of all shoe purchases.[104] D.H. Mudd joined him and took charge of staple goods' purchases made in the Midwest.[105] St. Louis was also the site of their "employment office."[106]

The St. Paul and St. Louis buying offices were the beginning of decentralized buying and shipping, but administrative, accounting (the department now had thirty-four employees) and other purchasing remained in New York. Separate departments, designated by letters of the alphabet, developed within the purchasing department. For example, in 1918 "Department D" included silks and dress goods.[107] The vast buying operation continued to be broken down into smaller components.

Buying and finance departments were making good progress as Penney turned more time and attention to employee needs. The highly personal nature of the company continued. In fact, for several years Penney paid for group life insurance for all associates.[108]

During these years Penney's home life was not entirely neglected. In February 1917 a wedding breakfast was held at his Riverside apartment. His sister Letha married Roy H. Ott, a store manager who soon joined the New York office.[109]

Since late 1915 Penney had lived at Riverside Mansions, an attractive building at 410 Riverside and West 113th Street. But he left the spacious eight-room apartment and was at 210 Riverside Drive the same year.[110] Roswell and J.C., Jr. now attended The Hill School, a college preparatory school in Pottstown, Pennsylvania. Founded by Reverend Matthew Meigs in 1851, the school had risen to national eminence under the guidance of John Meigs, and sons of many prominent men attended it in the World War I era and later. Penney's nephews, Richard E. Penney and

Harold Penney, Elie's sons, came from Missouri to study at The Hill School. They spent vacations with Penney in New York or at his Pocono Mountain home.[111] At The Hill School, the boys became well acquainted with a Latin teacher named Albert W. Hughes. Hughes, while tutoring J.C., Jr., learned more about the J.C. Penney Company and asked Penney for a job which, many years later, brought him to the chain's presidency.[112]

After receiving a discouraging life insurance policy report, Penney made an effort to stay in good health. He took early morning horseback rides in Central Park and regained his health and childhood interest in livestock.[113] Recalling his high school ambition to attend college, he embarked on a private tutoring program starting in March 1918, which occupied his time for one-half a day for twelve to eighteen months. English grammar, literature and essay writing were practiced to prepare him better for the training programs he wanted to develop.[114] Dr. Thomas Tapper was his tutor and was closely involved in *The Dynamo* and business courses unveiled in 1921. During this time, Tapper accompanied Penney on store visits, and they, with several others, planned an educational program for all associates.[115]

Penney's contributions to *The Dynamo* reflected an increasing self-awareness, although this was a quality he had never really lacked. For example, in October 1918 he wrote about "Organization" and said that success is not by chance, rather "the man who succeeds is the man capable of analyzing himself and his requirements. He must as well analyze the possibilities of the future."[116] He tried to inspire others and give them credit as seen in some remarks made on *The Dynamo*'s first anniversary in April 1918:

> Bear in mind that I alone could not have built this great business. I have had some wonderful assistants and associates.[117]

Altogether, 1917 was a most successful year for the company as sales and profits increased. Throughout 1917 advertisements continued to stress "economy." Prices ranged from extremely low to moderately high. Some ladies' waists sold for 98¢ but other crepe de Chine models were $3.98. However, they guaranteed to save customers one third off similar quality merchandise in other stores.

At Kemmerer in 1917, ladies' shoes sold from $2.49 to $7.00. The expensive models were described as "8-inch lace, white washable Kid, high or low heel, white Ivory soles," and "8-inch lace, Grey or Ivory Kid, Leather Louis heels."[118]

Competition included firms like Philipsborn, a popular mail-order Chicago firm that specialized in women's and children's clothing and shoes. Their colorful Fall and Winter 1917-1918 catalog carried the "fashion endorsement" of Mrs. Vernon (Irene) Castle, a noted dancer, actress and arbiter of fashion.[119] It described her as "The Best Dressed Woman in America" and portrayed her in Philipsborn fashions and quoted her approval of them. The catalog featured high button or lace ladies' shoes costing from $3.00 to $5.98. An example of the latter was "'The Colonel' Boot in soft, grey kid, with black kid trimming, Leather Louis heel and close edged sole. Hi-cut, laced style. Medium vamp."[120] Most shoes sold for $3.98 to $4.98, and Philipsborn prices, quite reasonable, included all delivery charges.[121]

Philipsborn had an estimated two and one-half million customers, and forty-eight "state representatives" were employed in Chicago to answer customers' fashion questions.[122] The mail-order specialty house, which had been in business for twenty-seven years, gave an "absolute guarantee of unqualified satisfaction or your money instantly refunded."[123] Philipsborn dresses, waists, trimmed coats and shoes were certainly attractive and popular.

While women's ready-to-wear fashions were not the J.C. Penney Company's only line, with competition from Philipsborn and other similar firms, the chain's interest in fashion grew. The New York buying office kept store merchandise up-to-date and informed sales clerks of seasonal changes as well as what fashions New York retail firms had on display in store windows. *The Dynamo* was a perfect medium for sharing this information from the nation's fashion center.

Articles by E.J. Neighbors and A.E. Kretschmer, an experienced ladies' ready-to-wear buyer and one of the few outsiders hired, and Christian Woidemann, who became a buyer after starting several Idaho stores, began appearing in spring 1917 under the title "With The Buyers."[124]

In May, Kretschmer said he knew women in small towns wanted the newest styles too. His aim was to provide the latest styles in good assortments, but in small units to promote rapid turnover.[125] In June, Woidemann made a mid-season report and said that foulards, Georgettes and other light materials would remain strong throughout the summer and were being shown in "high class shops." He had noted, "Zephyr gingham and combination gingham dresses are very popular, and the stores show them up to as high as $35 to $40 a garment." Furs were going to be even more popular than last year and a few advance styles of winter coats were being shown, but he promised to write more on this subject later.[126]

In October 1918, Kretschmer noted World War I's impact on prices and material conservation. Longer skirts were in question, and of course the military influence was strong on jackets, hats, coats and pocketbooks.[127] World War I also served to make men more fashion conscious as farmers' sons came into contact with large cities and traveled overseas for the first time.[128] In 1917, the J.C. Penney Company's popular brand of "Marathon Hats" sold for 98¢ to $2.98.[129] They had secured the "Marathon" trademark in early 1914.[130] In the 1920s many distinctive company brands were proudly featured in stores. These items were manufactured according to buyers' specifications.[131]

Besides seasonal large orders, buyers handled daily orders from stores. *The Dynamo* articles about fashions and large company purchases gave sales clerks self-confidence when talking to customers. As years went by two-column articles developed into two- and three-page spreads with titles like "What's What in Fall Fashions."[132] By then, the Company had accomplished editor Bushnell's April 1917 aim:

> Let us, through the pages of this magazine, work together to make the J.C. Penney Company, not only the greatest concern of its kind in the United States, but the most unique in the world.[133]

This goal, incredible as it was, was actually achieved by 1926. On December 18, 1925, the New York *Daily News Record* said that the company "today is accepted as the world's largest chain department store organization."[134] The company was just moving into its newly completed New York headquarters, an eighteen-story office building at 330 West 34th Street.

Throughout the pages of *The Dynamo* in 1917 can be seen the rudiments of advertising and standardization, both necessary to building the nationwide organization. F.J. Bolger gave concise advice on writing store advertisements. He said, "Balance your displays, simplify your wording, make name and location prominent, omit negative copy and phrases and standardize the 'signature cut' or store name." The aim was to make an ad "attractive, interesting and convincing." Their yellow and black store fronts were another form of standardization.[135] A carry-over from the Golden Rule era, it was an important recognition factor in these years.

Associates contributed articles, although not as many as Bushnell wanted, about fixing window displays, gave sales tips and sent in copies of ads.[136] Starting in September 1917, at the suggestion of Ben M. Kendall, manager at the Witchita Falls, Texas, store, women employees were given a special department in *The Dynamo*.[137] The magazine was truly a window on store activities and promoted interest and cooperation as well as professionalism.

The goal, set by Penney and pursued by company officials and associates, was constant improvement.[138] As Sheldon explained in his June 1917 article:

> Business is a profession—a science today. The old rule of thumb methods will no longer work. The law of survival of the fittest is working all the time and overtime.[139]

The addition of fifty stores in spring 1917 had naturally greatly increased sales. At the company convention in January 1918, Sams gave an enthusiastic welcome address. He said, in part:

> We have just concluded the most phenomenally successful year in the history of our existence. We have accomplished a vast amount more than our fondest dreams of a year ago. Fortune has played fair with us, and our sincere and extraordinary efforts have been rewarded. We all come here feeling very, very happy, and I want to bid you a very hearty welcome that we may enjoy together that happiness which we all feel.[140]

The convention, held as usual at Salt Lake City, was both serious and lively. Quartets sang, and for the first time, evidently, company buttons with H.C.S.C. and the company name printed on them were distributed to store managers and executives. The letters stood for company ideals of Honor, Confidence, Service and

Cooperation.[141] After a week of discussions and talks, the Obligation ceremony, a banquet and an official convention photograph, men returned to small town stores to continue their hard work. There were now 123 stockholders of classified common stock, the only stock.[142]

Sales for 1917 were $14.9 million, up from 1916's $8.4 million. Profits were $900,466, after an income tax of $847,822.[143] This was the first year they had to pay an income tax which was a high rate because the Revenue Acts of 1916 and 1917 included an excess profits tax to help pay war expenses.[144] A tax abatement was applied for and received in 1920; it was used as a credit against 1922 taxes.[145] However, the company's retained earnings in 1918 totalled $1.8 million, up from $439,797 in 1913.[146] With no contingent liabilities, the company was in a sound financial position.[147]

The United States had entered World War I in April 1917; by June wartime efforts began affecting business firms across the country. Men enlisted or were drafted into the Armed Forces, and supplies grew scarce for retailers like the J.C. Penney Company as government orders for shoes, uniforms, blankets and other articles received priority from manufacturers.[148] Steps were taken by directors to cope with wartime shortages and other related problems.

Patriotic fervor sweeping the country was evident in the New York office. On June 12, 1917 the company purchased $100,000 worth of Liberty Bonds, and increased that amount by $50,000 that October. Directors and associates were encouraged to purchase bonds held by the company. In 1918 "Thrift" or "War Saving stamps" were purchased by stores.[149] Men leaving the company to serve in the armed forces or overseas with the Red Cross, Y.M.C.A., Knights of Columbus or Salvation Army were paid a monthly salary of fifteen dollars.[150] On their return, a position would be available.[151]

Despite Sams' happy words at the convention, business conditions were worsening. In January 1918 Jim McDonald, speaking at the convention, warned managers:

> The market conditions have changed entirely in the last two years. As a rule we have a buyers' market, but today it is

absolutely a sellers' market. It is impossible for a buyer to get
what he wants if he is after large quantities. . . .[152]

Manufacturers were taking orders subject to restrictions and made allocations; but market fluctuations could change prices overnight. Shipping problems occurred as well. Even though prices were high due to demand, suppliers could not furnish goods. The government was buying millions of socks, underwear and uniforms, and mills were expected to be tied up with these orders until October. Buyers told managers to give the New York office all latitude possible in filling orders and to be reasonable in their expectations.[153] The situation, however, affected all dry goods retailers.

Nonetheless the company opened twenty stores in 1918; sales were $21,336,796, but total gross profit was only $2 million more than in 1917. Net profits were down to $695,754, but this was after "compensation" amounting to $857,121 and an income tax (later adjusted) of $1,305,360. The company's surplus of retained earnings increased to $2,064,342.[154]

While dividends were declared from net profits and after taxes, "compensation," an amount based on 30 percent of each store's earnings and distributed proportionately among stockholders, was treated like a salary or operating expense.[155]

Wartime conditions prevailed, but company officials declared they could have sold $1 million more of merchandise except for the dangerous influenza which began to sweep across the nation in late 1918.[156] Very wisely, the January 1919 convention was cancelled to avoid possible contagion. No new stores were opened in 1919, but preparations went ahead to open one hundred stores in 1920.[157]

They were already operating in twenty-five states, and the future looked fairly bright. Directors now had salaries of $10,000, except Penney who had not taken a salary since 1909.[158] Buyers' and other top New York officials' ranged from $3,500 to $8,500— quite substantial for the time.[159] After analyzing their financial situation, however, directors decided to raise money by issuing stock to sell on the New York Stock Exchange. Taxes, increasing operating costs and requirements of 100 new stores necessitated this.

In July 1919 they proposed increasing the company's total authorized capital stock from $3 million to $15 million, or from 30,000 shares to 150,000 shares of $100 par value. One hundred thousand shares or $10 million worth of stock was designated seven percent Cumulative Preferred, and 50,000 or $5 million became classified common stock. Thirty thousand of the 100,000 seven percent preferred stocks were to be issued and sold for company purposes.[160] A sinking fund was established for its retirement.[161] It was listed on the New York Stock Exchange in late 1919 after a special meeting of stockholders approved these amendments to the Articles of Incorporation.[162]

In early February 1920 there were 15,810 shares of classified common stock (the important stock) outstanding, and 145 stockholders. Penney held 5,387½ shares; Sams, 1,215; Hoag, 686; Mudd, 610; and Herbert Penney, 360.[163] But, despite carefully laid plans, 1920 proved to be a most difficult year for the young chain.

In 1919 and 1920 Penney's name became better known to the public. *Good Housekeeping*'s October 1920 issue featured his picture and asked readers, "Would you go with your husband if Penney should choose him?" The author then explained "Penney's Plan" and the merchant's stiff requirements and the important role a wife played in her husband's career.[164]

The popular *American Magazine* carried Penney's article, "It is One Thing to Desire—and Another to Determine," in its August 1919 issue.[165] Penney described his experiences in interviewing men. He added these words of advice:

> Real success has never yet been obtained except through sacrifice. My job is to try to develop men into good merchants; and someone asked me the other day how these men could help themselves in this process of development. My reply was: "By study, more study, and then some more study."[166]

Out of 5,000 interviews, only one hundred men were selected, and "character" was the decisive quality he looked for.[167]

No doubt these articles stimulated more than a few job inquiries, which was fine with Penney. In 1920 William Bushnell began to work full time on employment in St. Louis, leaving *The Dynamo* in other hands.

Obviously, by 1920 a complex and sophisticated system was emerging to provide direct, "simple" service to millions of customers.

NOTES

1. *Summarized Statements, 1911-1925*, PHF IV, H-1. Note: Net profit in 1913 was $333,609.73; in 1919 it was $1,804,775.38 after an income tax of $1.06 million and $1.2 million in "compensation."

2. *Historical Statistics of the United States*, p. 12.

3. Penney, *Man with a Thousand Partners*, p. 77.

4. MBD I, 78.

5. *Penney and Allied Families*, p. 53; Obituary notice and related materials on Mrs. Mary Frances Paxton Penney, PHF I, A-2. She and Letha had also lived in Ridgewood, New Jersey.

6. JCP to Pearl Strawn, 3/13/20, PHF VII, C-3.

7. Obituary notices, etc., Mrs. Penney, PHF I, A-2.

8. PHF III, E-2, Correspondence with managers.

9. *Penney and Allied Families*, pp. 54-62.

10. Jennings, *Anatomy of Leadership*, pp. 172-73.

11. MBD I, 55.

12. Ibid., 57-74.

13. Ibid, 194-209.

14. Ibid., 57-74.

15. Ibid., 130; PHF XXII, A-3.

16. MBD I, 96; By-Laws, Article XV, Section 2.

17. PHF II, A-3; PHF XXII, A-3.

18. MBD I, 284-85.

19. Ibid., II, 469-70; in 1924 he owned 16,553½ classified common shares out of a total of 92,445 or approximately 18 percent, PHF IV, H-1 and C-1; JCP to W.T. Kemper, June 1932, PHF VI, G-1—immediately before certain banks disposed of his stock, which had been used as collateral on personal loans, he had a reported 385,200 shares of common stock and 9,000 shares of preferred stock out of 2,468,984 outstanding shares of common stock and 199,215 shares of preferred stock outstanding. This made his common stock holding approximately 15.6 percent.

20. Ledger Book 1911-1917, PHF X, C-3; Ledger A (J.C. Penney Company General Office Ledger, 1913-1915), J.C. Penney Personal Account, p. 55, PHF, EVM Files.

21. Beasley, *Main Street Merchant*, p. 68.

22. Ibid.

23. MBD I, 216, 422.

24. Ibid., 130, 49 (By-Laws).

25. Beasley, *Main Street Merchant*, p. 83.

26. Ibid., pp. 83-85.

27. Ibid., pp. 83-84; Penney, *Man with a Thousand Partners*, pp. 124-25.

28. Beasley, *Main Street Merchant*, p. 85.

29. Richard G. Price and Beth Bohling, *The J.M. McDonald Story* (reprinted from *Guernsey Breeders' Journal* for the J.M. McDonald Foundation, Inc., c. 1950), pp. 6-7, PHF IV, C-6; Penney, *Man with a Thousand Partners*, pp. 124-25.

30. Penney, *Man with a Thousand Partners*, p. 125.

31.   MBD I, 258.

32.   "How a Chain of Stores Is Run—Buy and Sell for Cash, Have No Deliveries, and Do a Business of Millions Yearly," *New York Times*, 1 February 1914, Sec. 8, p. 10, cols. 5-6.

33.   MBD I, 159-60.

34.   *New York Times*, 1 February 1914, Sec. 8, p. 10, cols. 5-6.

35.   Ibid.

36.   Ibid.

37.   Ibid.

38.   Ibid.

39.   "James C. Penney, Who Runs Seventy Stores," *System. The Magazine of Business* 25 (June 1914): 637-40. Note: The same issue featured an article about Andrew Carnegie.

40.   Ibid.

41.   Beasley, *Main Street Merchant*, p. 106.

42.   MBD I, 184.

43.   *Dynamo* 5 (July 1921): 3-4.

44.   Ibid.; Alden Hatch, *1850 to 1950, American Express, A Century of Service* (Garden City, N.Y.: Doubleday, 1950), pp. 109-19; *New York Times, Index* for July and August 1914 shows the tourists' plight.

45.   Citizenship Document issued August 1, 1914 by Embassy of the United States of America in Berlin, Germany to James C. Penney and sons, PHF, EVM Files. They were "approved for transportation" on August 11, 1914.

46.   Ledger A, 1913-1915, J.C. Penney Personal Account, April 23, 1915 entry, PHF, EVM Files.

47.   Ibid., p. 89; *Trow's General Directory of the Boroughs of Manhattan and Bronx City of New York* (1910-1920). Note: Two Thomas Tappers are in the directories, assumption the Tapper Penney met later was on Riverside Drive. He and Penney met at 354 Fourth Avenue, however; *Bakers' Biographical Dictionary of Musicians* (1958), p. 1617; PHF I, G-3, Tapper file.

48.   Correspondence and conversation with Reference Librarian, Sylvia Saltzman, The Field Library, Inc., Peekskill, New York, author's files; *1926 Alumni Directory, Peekskill Military Academy*, Peekskill, N.Y.

49.   Ledger B (1915-1918), J.C. Penney Personal Account, p. 287, October 18, 1915, PHF, EVM Files.

50.   PHF III, A-2, J.C. Penney photograph file.

51.   *Dynamo* 1-2 (1917, 1918) reports of trips; Note: Penney's store visits continued throughout the 1920s and 1930s, and into the 1960s; Interviews with retired J.C. Penney Company store managers in Colorado, Utah and Illinois made by the author in 1978 and 1979, author's files.

52.   MBD I, 192; Ledger A, J.C. Penney Personal Account, p. 14, PHF, EVM Files.

53.   PHF, Advertisement File; also store pictures.

54.   PHF, Advertisement File, 1915 four-page ad-brochure.

55.   Ibid.

56.   Interviews with retired store managers, author's files. Note: Many J.C. Penney Company managers became presidents of local chapters of these organizations, served on bank boards, etc.

57. Ibid.; *Dynamo* (1917-1932).

58. MBD I, 240-41 (establishing new classifications of stock #s 87 to 127); Penney, *Man with a Thousand Partners*, p. 82.

59. MBD I, 187.

60. Ibid., 188.

61. Ibid., 190.

62. Author's correspondence and interview with Donald A. Foote, son of Ira A. Foote; author's files.

63. Ibid.

64. Ibid.

65. Ibid.

66. MBD I, 284-85.

67. Ibid., 96; II, 491-92, 494 (distribution of both stock and cash dividends, 16 March 1920).

68. PHF, File Card Records of Store Openings.

69. Information Courtesy of Gerald H.S. Kendall of Sarasota, California. His father, Henry E. Kendall, was manager and one-third owner of the Trinidad, Colorado, store at the time of the Ludlow massacre.

70. *Dynamo* 2 (April 1918): 29.

71. Interviews with retired managers, author's files.

72. MBD I, 187.

73. Ibid., 240-41.

74. Ibid., 258.

75. Beasley, *Main Street Merchant*, p. 107; MBD I, 261.

76. MBD I, 260-61.

77. Ibid., 284-85.

78. Ibid., 245.

79. Ibid., 237.

80. Hood Family Collection, business cards c. 1915.

81. MBD I, 240-41.

82. MBD I, 246; PHF V, B, 1920's booklets with lists of stores by state.

83. PHF I, G-1; *Dynamo* 8 (January 1925): 22.

84. MBD I, 315-17.

85. MBD I, 395; II, 494, 513.

86. Ibid., I, 310.

87. Ibid., 310, 314; Beasley, *Main Street Merchant*, pp. 100, 101.

88. Notes from a talk by Dr. Harry Levinson, "A Psychologist Looks at Executive Development," given January 14, 1980, National Retail Merchants' Annual Convention, New York City. Levinson said the central task of leadership is to develop new leaders, and that is what Penney began doing. Perpetuation of an organization is an executive's main problem; this is more important than increasing profits, according to Levinson. Other points made by Levinson included the importance of leaders having high standards, subordinates having trust in themselves, and everyone having a transcendent purpose. Penney practiced all these principles. Author's files.

89. *Dynamo* 1 (April 1917): 13; J.C. Penney, "It is One Thing to Desire—And Another to Determine," *The American Magazine* 88, No. 2 (August 1919): 51; Penney, *Man with a Thousand Partners*, p. 180; Beasley, *Main Street Merchant*, p. 117.

90.   Penney, *Man with a Thousand Partners*, pp. 160-68; "Bulletin No. 180," 1916, PHF I, F-8.

91.   MBD I, 362. On September 1, 1917 the directors decided to place Bushnell on the company payroll. He received $4,000 per annum. Note: The magazine was twenty to thirty pages in length and was printed on expensive paper. Bushnell's aim for *The Dynamo* was to make it the "best publication of its kind in the United States, intensely interesting from cover to cover, at the same time inspiring to one and all." (September 1917 *Dynamo*.)

92.   Penney, *Man with a Thousand Partners*, pp. 168-80.

93.   *Dynamo* 1 (April, June, October 1917).

94.   "Men Wanted" (published by the J.C. Penney Company, 1917), 16 pages, PHF, EVM Files. Dr. Tapper was the author.

95.   Ibid., p. 5.

96.   Ibid., p. 16.

97.   Ibid., pp. 7-8.

98.   Ibid., p. 9.

99.   *Dynamo* 1 (April 1917): 13.

100.   Penney, "It is One Thing to Desire," p. 51.

101.   MBD I, 310.

102.   Clipping from Pittsburg, Kansas, newspaper, c. October 1969, quoting Mrs. John B. Towner, PHF I, F-5.

103.   *J.M. McDonald Story*, p. 7; MBD I, 304.

104.   MBD I, 324.

105.   Ibid.

106.   *Dynamo* 1 (October 1917): 15.

107.   Ibid., 2 (September 1918): 12.

108.   Ibid.

109.   Ibid., 1 (April 1917): 16.

110.   Ledger B (1915-1918), p. 290, J.C. Penney Personal Account, PHF, EVM Files; 1917 *Trow's New York City Directory*; Visit by author to typical apartment at 410 Riverside.

111.   Correspondence and conversations with Mr. R.E. Penney of Modesto, Calif., Author's files; Paul Chancellor, *The History of The Hill School 1851-1976* (Pottstown, Pa.: The Hill School, 1976), pp. xi, 30, 31, 49, 50; Information from The Hill School Alumni Office, courtesy Mrs. Nelson M. Vaughan, Alumni Secretary, Author's files.

112.   Beasley, *Main Street Merchant*, pp. 110-11; "Personality: The Quiet Caesar of J.C. Penney," *New York Times*, 24 June 1956, clipping, Hill School files.

113.   "How J.C. Penney Makes a Principle Work," *National Magazine: Mostly About People*, June 1927, p. 419.

114.   PHF I, G-3, Dr. Thomas Tapper file.

115.   Ibid.; Penney, *Man with a Thousand Partners*, p. 169.

116.   *Dynamo* 2 (October 1918): 5, 16.

117.   Ibid., 2 (April 1918): 14.

118.   Kemmerer 1917; Salem, Ore., 1917, PHF, Advertisement File.

119.   *Philipsborn, The Outer Garment House-Chicago, Fall and Winter 1917-1918* (Chicago: Philipsborn, 1917), pp. 10, 11, 15.

120.   Ibid., p. 168.

121. Ibid., pp. 158-71, order form after p. 230.
122. Ibid., pp. 10, 81.
123. Ibid., pp. 9, 27.
124. *Dynamo* 1 (April 1917): 14.
125. Ibid., 1 (May 1917): 16.
126. Ibid., 1 (June 1917): 17.
127. Ibid., 2 (October 1918): 19; ibid., 3 (May 1919): 17.
128. Ibid., 3 (May 1919): 17.
129. Salem, Ore., 1917, PHF, Advertisement File.
130. MBD I, 179.
131. Beasley, *Main Street Merchant*, pp. 155, 157.
132. *Dynamo* 13 (September 1929): 20-21.
133. Ibid., 1 (April 1917): 12.
134. "J.C. Penney Co. to Occupy New Home Early Next Month," *Daily News Record*, 18 December 1925, p. 8, Daily Dry Goods News Section, PHF I, G-1.
135. F.J. Bolger, "Advertising Ideas," *Dynamo* 1 (June 1917): 16. Note: Standardization of prices for men's clothing and overcoats occurred in January 1918, MBD I, 388.
136. *Dynamo* 1-2 (1917-1918).
137. Ibid., 1 (September 1917): 15.
138. Penney, *Man with a Thousand Partners*, p. 89; "Penney Idea."
139. *Dynamo* 1 (June 1917): 3.
140. Ibid., 1 (March 1918): 8.
141. MBD I, 384-89.
142. Ibid., 381.
143. *Summarized Statements, 1911-1925*.
144. "Petition," p. 1, PHF IV, after H-3; *Encyclopedia of American History*, p. 278.
145. "Petition," pp. 2-3.
146. *Summarized Statements, 1911-1925*.
147. *Annual Reports*, PHF IV, H-1.
148. *Encyclopedia of American History*, p. 309; *Dynamo* 1 (March 1918): 18; 1 (August 1917), the "Honor Roll," company employees who were in the armed forces, was listed for the first time on the inside back cover.
149. MBD I, 357, 418, 420.
150. Ibid., I, 420. Note: They had to be regularly employed by the company for at least three months to be eligible.
151. *Dynamo* 3 (January 1920): 30.
152. Ibid., 1 (March 1918): 18.
153. Ibid.
154. *Summarized Statements, 1911-1925*; MBD I, 392.
155. MBD I, 426.
156. *Dynamo* 2 (February 1919): 15.
157. MBD I, 435-36; II, 494, 514. Note: One hundred stores were opened in spring and fifteen more that fall.
158. MBD I, 408.
159. Ibid., 433.
160. Ibid., 442-43.

161.   Ibid., II, 453.
162.   Ibid., II, 459.
163.   Ibid., II, 469-70.
164.   R. Dickinson, "Penney's Plan," *Good Housekeeping*, October 1920, 55.
165.   Penney, "It is One Thing to Desire," 51.
166.   Ibid.
167.   Ibid.

FLORIDA, FARMING AND PHILANTHROPIES

Summer 1919 brought a happy change to Penney's life. On July 29th he married Mary Hortense Kimball of Salt Lake City, the daughter of Edwin Kimball and Geneva Hartwell Kimball.[1] A fifty-acre estate named Whitehaven in White Plains about twenty miles north of New York City became their home.[2]

Mary Kimball, thirty-nine years old and four years younger than Penney, was a member of a prosperous Utah family. Edwin Kimball left Massachusetts for California in the Gold Rush of 1849 but earned substantial wealth by transporting ore from Utah mines. Elliott Hartwell, Geneva Kimball's father, had also been a "'49er."[3] Penney became acquainted with Mary on his 1912 or 1914 European trip. His friend, Dr. Short, may have introduced them. The attractive dark-eyed brunette attended Mary F. Stevens School in Germantown, Pennsylvania, and Bryn Mawr College in 1899 before studying French and music at Paris and Dresden.[4] She was a student of the noted Marchesi. In Europe throughout World War I, she worked for the Y.M.C.A. with the American Expeditionary Force.[5] Soon after returning to America she and Penney were married. On September 28, 1920, a son, Kimball, was born to them. Two years later a photograph shows Mary, in a satin dress, fur boa and stylish bobbed haircut, proudly embracing her tiny, curly-haired son.[6]

Penney's marriage to Mary Kimball marked his entry into Florida commercial and philanthropic activities. For almost a dozen years he was deeply involved in agriculture, real estate and banking. Although Penney's interests were by no means confined to Florida, he, with many others, saw the "last frontier's" great potential.[7]

In November 1919, Dr. Short, preparing to leave his Portland, Oregon, ministry to become Educational Director of the J.C. Penney Company, wrote his friend:

> I want you to have the following quotation, in your clipping file, which is on the monument of George Peabody in London, from his own sayings: "What I spent I had; what I left I lost; what I gave away I have still." This I thought you might like to hide away as a worthy follower of one of the world's most conspicuous philanthropists; though you may not have yet equaled his gifts, you will in time.[8]

Concerning the new position, Short said he and Mrs. Short "can hardly believe our own feeling of regrets to leave here and anticipation of being there." He looked forward to rendering a "satisfactory and helpful service."[9]

Their friendship had remained quite close during these ten years as Penney's September 16, 1920, letter reveals. He referred to Short's welcome letters that reflected the minister's personality and high standards. It was Penney's forty-fifth birthday. He noted the fact with humor in an otherwise serious letter:

> These milestones in my career are coming, it appears to me, too frequently. But I suppose if I were not wrapped up in my work and happy in the execution of my duties, time would drag; so I find in that a consolation. Sometimes I feel my efforts fall far short, though I never become discouraged.
>
> If I could only live and do the things I'd like to do—render a service to humanity worth while—not for the sake of eulogies made about me after I am gone, I should be very happy. I appreciate the fact that you seem to think that I have rendered you some valuable financial assistance while in the pastorate. I regret now that I didn't do more, for no doubt these past years you could have rendered even a greater service to those in need, had you known you could have had my support.
>
> But then, I realize, too, I have not been free from financial worries of my own till now. I am depending on you largely to help me distribute wisely a portion of my wealth, so that I may see with my own eyes some of the results of a life of intensified effort.[10]

Penney concluded, "I am happy today, Doctor, thankful to the Giver of all things for I feel I have had gifts showered upon me most generously—not material things do I speak of—but those things that money can not buy, Doctor."[11] Contentment from friendships, a happy marriage and financial security were clearly his as the new decade began.

In 1912 Penney had made a winter visit to Palm Beach, Florida, hoping the sunshine and sea air would aid J.C., Jr.'s health.[12] Afterwards he visited there occasionally staying at "The Breakers" or in the rapidly growing town of Miami and adjacent Miami Beach. In May 1921 he purchased a two-story mansion from the Henkel family, owners of a large Detroit flour milling company.[13] The estate of several acres was on Belle Isle, immediately west of Miami Beach. Visits lasting from December to early April became part of his routine.

Although he kept in close touch with the New York office, these visits were also a chance to relax, go fishing and enjoy the social life he had missed. He and his talented wife earned a reputation for gracious entertaining.[14] Mary Penney had a three-manual "Aeolian" pipe organ and grand piano installed in the Florida mansion's two-story domed music room. In winter 1922 Artur Rubinstein gave a recital at their home and Clarence Eddy and his wife performed as well. Mary hoped to make their home a "musical mecca" and increase appreciation of music.[15] Many people enjoyed these entertainments at the elegant estate overlooking Biscayne Bay.

Belle Isle was originally a mud flat named Bull Island. Renamed by 1913 it had been bulkheaded and filled in. In the mid-1920s eight private estates were located on the 1600-foot diameter island.[16] When the Venetian Way causeway, a $2 million structure, replaced the 1913 Collins Bridge in early 1926, several new "islands" were created.[17] Belle Isle became the last of a series of small round islands on the two-mile causeway route from Miami across Biscayne Bay to Miami Beach. Belle Isle's mansions were modest compared to John Deering's imaginative Vizcaya south of Miami, but the mud flat had been transformed into a semi-tropical garden.

It was not hard to be impressed with southern Florida in the carefree days before the devastating September 1926 hurricane. In the early 1920s Miami's winter population reached 120,000 from a quiet 29,000 year-round residency.[18] There were speed boat races and parades; famous Americans—millionaires, politicians and preachers—added to the city's glamour.

Miami was nicknamed "The Wonder City." It was no surprise to city boosters that Dade County, which included Miami, was the fastest growing county in the United States. Dixie Highway brought automobile owners south from Detroit and Chicago.[19] The Illinois

Central ran special trains south and its "Floridan" contained as many as fourteen pullman cars.[20] Millionaires, like the Deering brothers of International Harvester, and ordinary tourists began arriving the first week in December to enjoy the scenery and sunny, warm weather. Coconut and royal palm trees, tropical flowers and forests of pine greeted visitors fleeing northern ice and snow. Grapefruit, orange and mango or avocado groves filled the countryside. R.L. Polk's City Directory for 1924 proudly stated that Miami's mean annual temperature was 75.1 degrees and that only five days in the year were without sunshine.[21]

The Penney home was #8 Belle Isle. The two-story house of reinforced concrete was built on the island's southern half in 1915, but in summer 1922 the Penneys added a third story with a colorful frieze to complement the mansion's stark white walls.[22] Of Italian Renaissance style, the house had a roof of apricot-colored tiles. Its white walls and tall arched windows, sparkling in the sunlight, contrasted with the bright green lawn, graceful palm trees, tropical flowers and shrubbery.[23] White stone paths led past rose gardens to a pavilion and boat house on the edge of Biscayne Bay.

Across the bay, in the midst of the sunlit silvery ripples, one could see Flagler Monument. The island memorial was built in the 1920s to honor Henry M. Flagler, "oil baron" and pioneer developer of Florida. Beyond the aqua green bay was downtown Miami.

Dark mahogany woodwork and antiques from Italian villas gave the interior a dignified simplicity to match its outside elegance.[24] Above the music room was a twenty-five-foot by fifty-foot ballroom with a painted carved ceiling.[25] The constant but gentle breeze, tropical plants, sun and sea air created a relaxing dream-like atmosphere for the Penneys and their guests.

Among the famous people who made Miami their winter home for one or more seasons were three-time presidential candidate William Jennings Bryan, who built a home in Brickell Avenue after 1913 and became one of Miami's most noted residents; James and Charles Deering; James Whitcomb Riley, the Hoosier poet and writer, Alexander Graham Bell; William K. Vanderbilt of railroad fame; the trust-busting lawyer, Samuel Untermeyer; Andrew Carnegie; and John Wanamaker. A Texan, Mrs. Percy V. Pennybacker, author and president of the General Federation of Women's Clubs in America, was also proudly included in a list of Miami's winter guests in 1916.[26]

When Penney made Belle Isle his winter home, he was just becoming a national figure. A January 1922 Miami newspaper summed up his life in these words: "Had Rough Time Getting to Be Most Modest Millionaire."[27]

The head of the 371-store chain doing $50 million worth of business a year in twenty-nine states was not yet well known to the general public, especially in the east. Expanding a life insurance policy to $3 million, however, focused attention on Penney. According to the Miami newspaper only three other persons in America carried larger insurance policies—Adolph Zukor, Rodman Wanamaker and Pierre DuPont.[28]

In 1980, all that remained of Penney's Belle Isle home was the #8 on a sturdy concrete wall beside the isle's tree-shaded sidewalk. Through missing gates, a weeded path led to a crumbling sea wall; dying palm trees and rubble have replaced the mansion and landscaped grounds. In the distance, though, Flagler Monument stands surrounded by silvery, aqua green water. High rise apartment buildings frame the empty lot, but Belle Isle, lying between two crowded cities, retains its pleasant, calm atmosphere.[29] In the 1920s it was the site of happiness and tragedy for the merchant.

Penney's journey through middle-age was filled with as many ups and downs as earlier years. Despite his single-minded drive and energy, he was constantly being reminded his life was not under his control. When Kimball was four months old, Pearl Penney Strawn died in childbirth at her home in Roseburg, Oregon.[30] Her death on February 14, 1921 was a shock to the Penney family and particularly to her older brother. Vivid memories of growing up in Hamilton and of years spent in Longmont and frontier-like Kemmerer returned.

Roswell, twenty, about to enter Princeton University, and J.C., Jr., completing his preparatory course at The Hill School, spent winter vacations at Belle Isle.[31] During the 1922-1923 winter season, business correspondence occupied most of Penney's hours. But he found time to reminisce in a January 2, 1923 letter to George Bushnell, now comptroller of the Company:

> While my mail has been quite heavy, I have not stuck to my desk quite as closely as I did last year, though I haven't got started yet to playing golf as I hoped that I would before this. I have been out fishing once to try out my Christmas present

which Mrs. Penney and the boys gave me. I am glad to know that you closed the year's business with nearly five million dollars cash on hand. That certainly will look mighty good on our statement. It looks very much to me as if the stores would make more money than we had figured.[32]

He continued by referring to Bushnell's "splendid letter of some few days ago," and said:

Words cannot express my feelings toward the men who have worked with me so closely in the building up of this great business. I cannot tell you how I appreciate this association and how I miss it. I have plenty of time down here to meditate and there is not a day that goes by but my thoughts are with you.[33]

Correspondence continued throughout the month. On January 25th Penney informed Sams he would probably miss a February Board of Directors' meeting. After discussing managers and store business, he closed with best wishes and settled back to enjoy a pleasant, sunny February.[34]

The idyll was abruptly interrupted. Shortly after noon on February 15th, Mary Kimball Penney died at their Belle Isle home.[35] Although confined to bed for a week with abdominal pains, her condition was not considered serious. After breakfast that morning she had violent stomach pains. Three doctors arrived but could do nothing as internal bleeding and pain made her unconscious. One half hour before she died, Penney learned how critical her condition was. The doctors discussed operating but were not sure it would save her. Her sudden death was attributed to "acute indigestion."[36]

Sams and his family had just arrived in Miami and were on hand to help Penney. Mary's long-time friends and Penney's sent condolences to the widower and his small son. Her sudden death was a "deep shock" and caused Penney much grief for their marriage had been extremely happy. However, he adopted a more philosophical attitude towards this tragedy than at Berta's death. Some months later he wrote to his cousin Will Partin saying he was "happy in the fact that I had the privilege of knowing her intimately and enjoying her love and friendship for the short three and one half years."[37]

Young Kimball, plus memories of their happiness and Mary's "noble character," remained to inspire him. Mary had an interest in orphans and before her death she had made a large contribution to a Salt Lake City orphanage in her mother's memory.[38]

Penney still found it difficult to understand why Mary had to die. Dr. Tapper and Dr. Short tried to help him by imparting their philosophy of life, and he appreciated their efforts. At Easter, Dr. Short sent this advice, "While you think of your loved ones who have left you, I want you to think of them as still living in God's own keeping."[39]

Letha and her two children, who with her husband, Roy H. Ott, moved into the White Plains home in spring 1923, returned with Penney to Belle Isle next winter. Although the house held many memories, Penney did not live in the past. Letha's two young children, near in age to Kimball, became his playmates, and they had "quite a little Kindergarten."[40] The children's cheerfulness was refreshing as Penney began to involve himself more in Florida and philanthropy.

Mary's death, in fact, increased his interest in helping others. Soon after she died, Penney wrote one of her close friends:

> Her departure has impressed me with the necessity of living each day as if it were the last, besides it has brought me into a closer realization of the power of God. It has also made me feel that I have not rendered the service to my fellow man that I should have done and from now on it shall be my endeavor to put forth a greater effort.[41]

In December 1924 Penney, Kimball, Letha and her children arrived in Miami on the first "Floridan" with James Deering and 280 other passengers. A *Miami Herald* reporter noted, "Aboard the train was J.C. Penney of Belle Isle, nationally known as the head of the Penney chain of stores more than 500 of which are in the United States." The report continued. The merchant was "another of Miami's most welcomed homecomers," and his career resembled "one of those tales of Horatio Alger that spurred on the youth of the former generation." It concluded by remarking, "In Miami Mr. Penney is known and esteemed for the pleasant approachability of his personality. The dignified elegance of his home on lovely Belle Isle is one of the city's prides."[42]

Penney had been in another section of Florida only a few weeks before. Mittie and her husband learned why:

> I made a rather hurried and unexpected trip to Florida two weeks ago Sunday night from which I returned the early part of the week. You will open your eyes when I tell you that I am in on a deal for 120,000 acres of land there. Now, you may have the idea that I once had about Florida land, that most of it is under water. True, there is a lot of such land, but this is high, dry, with 10,000 acres cleared, much of the ground cultivated ready for potatoe planting, etc. It is a big proposition and would take quite a while to tell you of all it consists. If the deal goes through, and I will know in about thirty days, I will send you some literature regarding the tract.[43]

He was on the verge of entering one of the largest, most creative projects of his life. He had in mind a model farming community. This new dream was related to his father's efforts to help farmers. Penney saw an opportunity to aid a distressed sector of the economy and put into practice the successful business methods used in building a chain of stores. It was almost as complex and personal as the retailing endeavor.

The millionaire merchant remained in many ways a Missouri farm boy. After 1919 he returned to farming on a small scale at Whitehaven. The estate was purchased to aid his ailing health, and he discovered raising sheep, pigs and poultry was relaxing and healthful.[44] That venture foreshadowed extensive involvement in agriculture and stock raising. In December 1921 he purchased the 720-acre Emmadine Farm at Hopewell Junction, Dutchess County, New York.[45] Its limestone based soil was excellent for dairy cattle raising; within six years Emmadine Farms and its Foremost Guernseys were nationally famous in agricultural circles. For example, his livestock won first and second prizes in the Guernsey Breeder's Young Herd at the 1928 National Dairy Show. These were just two of countless prizes awarded the pure-bred Guernseys developed at Emmadine under the management of Jimmy Dodge, a noted breeder, with Penney's personal interest and financial backing.[46]

Penney's childhood in rural Caldwell County and father's stock-raising led him to dairy farming. The location of many J.C. Penney Company stores in the midwest dairy farming region also influenced him. Penney discovered on his many cross-country trips the dairy industry could use improvement, and statistics proved him right. Poor grades of cattle, low average yields of buttermilk and milk could be improved by proper breeding. With the purchase and development of the Dutchess County farm, his avocation became Guernsey breeding. He hoped "to contribute something worth while to the dairy industry of the nation." Permanent improvement of this breed in America was Penney's ambition. It was an educational venture in part. Although the farm had to be self-supporting, he saw it as a distributing center and a demonstration of what could be accomplished. Costs for breeding were minimal, and 4-H Clubs were welcome visitors.[47]

To insure the permanence of the pure-bred herd at Emmadine Farm and its availability to dairy farmers for improving their stock, Penney endowed it. Although he had never heard of this being done before, "that made no difference," and his lawyers proceeded.[48] By the decade's end his goal was reached, but improvement of the herds naturally continued, and Penney extended livestock activities to his Missouri home and began to widen his agricultural interests even further. Farmers' problems, Penney decided, included the need for careful business methods, greater diversification of crops and more truck gardening to meet personal needs. Close attention to detail, required by all successful businesses, was one of the most needed business methods. Standardization and cooperation were equally vital.[49]

The acquisition of 120,000 acres in northern Florida in February 1925 was not with the intention of subdivision and sale. Instead, developing an ideal cooperative farm community seized Penney's imagination.[50] When enthusiastic, he moved fast. In this case he committed large sums of money and enlisted experts to carry out the project. It was in working order within a year.

Better farm products and a higher standard of living for farmers became twin goals for the idealistic merchant. Of course, there was a practical connection between farmers' and commerce's prosperity. He thought he had devised a practical way to aid farmers in America and around the world. The enthusiasm of journalists, academic and government officials matched Penney's. "Penney Farms" attracted attention across the nation, but the former farm boy had mixed success as he took on the land, weather and a depressed market for farm products in the 1920s.[51] The odds were against him, but that fact never stopped Penney. He was inspired by his father's dream of helping farmers. Wide-sweeping plans had the same appeal to the son as they had to the dedicated community leader who crusaded in vain for "Free Silver." The large land purchase was also proof of a change in Penney's attitude about Florida. Previously he had kept a distance between himself and the state's rampant land speculation. But the lure of Florida proved too strong. However, Penney's aim, except for outright philanthropies supported since 1911, was to help others help themselves.

The 120,000 acres he purchased for $400,000 in early 1925 included almost one-third of sparsely populated Clay County, on the west bank of the St. Johns River twenty-eight miles southwest of Jacksonville.[52] Property in the county seat, Green Cove Springs, included a well-known mineral spring, the "Qui-Si-Sana" Hotel plus waterfront property and cottages remaining from the Dowling-Shands Lumber Company operations.[53]

A noted resort town in the 1880s and on the Atlantic Coast Line Railway, Green Cove Springs was a pleasant but sleepy town of less than 3,000 residents alongside of St. Johns River.[54] Far from the excitement and crowds of Miami, Penney launched three projects: a model farming community, an agricultural institute to promote scientific farming, and a remarkable memorial to his parents.

Seven miles west of Green Cove Springs along a rutted sand and dirt road surrounded by scrub brush and cut over timber lands was a tiny community named Long Branch.[55] Originally part of a tract of land owned by the Southern Cattle Feeding Company whose venture failed during World War I, Florida Farms and Industries Company spent a reported $3 million clearing the land and advertised it as fertile farm land.[56] The town of Long Branch was platted in 1922.[57] Sixty to seventy families arrived but the company was indicted for false advertising and the enterprise went into the hands of a receiver.

By 1925 tall weeds grew everywhere, houses and buildings, like "Taterville" depot, had tumbled down and the railroad tracks were rusted.[58] The community and surrounding land plus property in Green Cove Springs came into Penney's possession in February 1925. He decided to build the model farming community around Long Branch. According to a report in the *Manufacturers Record* in spring 1926, the new project was founded on "well-tested lines."[59]

Men would pay for their farm out of its operating profits like Penney Company managers who paid for store interests from earnings. Selection of colonists was made by project directors; no land was for sale as in an ordinary real estate venture.[60] Approximately $500 to $1,500, however, was needed to defray the cost of a new farm house, poultry house, trees, seeds and equipment rental.[61] A try-out period of one year was part of the plan. If a dissatisfied colonist decided to leave, any money he had invested would be returned.[62] Otherwise, provided he was acceptable to project directors, the farmer agreed to a schedule of payments for the pre-determined farm cost. Tracts of twenty-acre farms were considered most efficient, but a few tradesmen had smaller lots.[63]

Transportation, soil analysis, crop advice and equipment were available, and a grammar and high school were built. The experiment, an attempt to remove "guesswork from agricultural processes," was off to a fine start by spring 1926.[64] The idealistic plan had a few critics. Some saw it as "paternalism" and even "socialism."[65] To Penney, however, cooperation and "helping others to help themselves" was good business. He declared the farm development contained the "soundest of purely American business principles."[66]

Farm relief plans, the McNary-Haugen Bills, were being debated in Congress. According to project supporters, though, the way to stabilize farming was to put it on a "firm business basis."[67] Overexpansion during World War I led to mortgages farmers could not pay off; overproduction caused falling farm product prices in the 1920s, and numerous farm families were in trouble.[68] It was a situation Penney understood only too well, and it was only natural he would try to solve it with methods he knew were successful.

Their aim was to create self-supporting, self-respecting farmers. To achieve this, proper selection of men, attention to details and a central organization providing scientific resources and educational information were necessary. The concept included standardizing operations and economical production, which were the same concepts involved in the development of the by now nationwide J.C. Penney Company chain.[69]

A 1927 farm booklet explained their plan:

> The J.C. Penney-Gwinn Corporation has adopted the plan of
> the J.C. Penney Company in making available to farmers the

services of its organization, in buying seed, plants, trees, shrubs,
fertilizer, mules, equipment, farm machinery, home furnishings
and the like, and in assisting the farmers in marketing their
products. In order to achieve this result, the Corporation
maintains a staff of expert agriculturists, who, without charge to
the farmer, cooperate with him in analyzing his soil, testing
seeds, planting crops, developing drainage and irrigation
systems, and in applying modern science and business principles
in connection with any and all problems which may arise.[70]

An Institute of Applied Agriculture was created in the midst of
the Long Branch community, renamed Penney Farms in 1927.
Twenty thousand acres of the large tract had been cleared, and part
of this was devoted to the Institute's experimental farming. Among
crops tested were peppermint, grapes, corn, blackberries, cowpeas,
persimmon trees, napier grass, pecans, blueberries, satasuma orange
trees and tung oil nut trees. Hundreds of acres of potatoes and
ordinary garden vegetables were planted by the colonists as staple
crops.[71]

A large modern dairy farm of 463½ acres had 40 Guernsey
cattle in residence by 1927, and the number would increase to 100.
A demonstration poultry plant with 4,000 birds, and modern nursery
with some of the demonstration crops mentioned above were in use.
The railroad connecting them to Green Cove Springs and the
Atlantic Coast Line Railroad was rebuilt. One hundred miles of
well-kept roads, twenty-five of which were paved, including the road
to Green Cove Springs, improved transportation greatly. A large
canning factory, a general store, post office, garage and machine
shop and gasoline station were also in operation. Of the
approximate 300 houses existing, 125 were suitable for the farm
families. As more colonists arrived, new farms and houses were
created.[72]

Many of the first settlers came from either Berea College in
Kentucky or were recommended by J.C. Penney Company store
managers. Of the original thirty-nine settlers, thirty-four remained
after the first year, and there were one hundred colonists at Penney
Farms in 1927. Up to 6,000 families were anticipated.[73]

The second annual banquet at Penney Farms was held on
February 18, 1927. The 400 guests heard Francis O. Clark, Director
of Farm Operations, describe "The Folks We Want":

> We are selecting a very high class of people. We are primarily interested in finding middle-aged to young married men with experience on farms who have been successful in saving a little money, but not much; men who are willing to take advice from others; men who do not think they know all that is to be known about farming; men who are high-spirited and not too easily discouraged. . . . We are all here to learn. We are going to bring to this community people who believe in education, who refrain from the use of liquor, who believe in religion and go to Sunday School, and we prefer those who can get along without the cigarette. We are selecting farmers on about the same basis as the Managers of the Penney Stores are selected.
>
> The Corporation (J.C. Penney-Gwinn Corporation) is doing the advance work in experimenting on all the things that are untried. We are all good listeners and good observers of the experience of our native friends who have been here before and who have succeeded, as well as those who have failed. All we have to do here is to see what others are doing to succeed and then find men who are open-minded and progressive enough to be willing to do things in a new and better way.[74]

The average education of the settlers was a respectable two years of high school.[75] However, the project leaders Penney recruited were among the nation's best educated and most talented administrators. For example, Clark was the former head of the Vocational Department of Berea College in Berea, Kentucky. Albert A. Johnson, head of the Applied Institute of Agriculture, was former head of the Farmingdale School of Agriculture of New York, and D. Walter Morton, resident business agent at Penney Farms, had been dean of the School of Commerce and Accounting at the University of Southern California.[76] Burdette G. Lewis, in charge of the J.C. Penney-Gwinn Corporation Florida office, had a distinguished career in running institutional facilities. Most recently, he was State Commissioner of Institutions and Agencies of New Jersey.[77]

Visitors to Penney Farms included the Secretary of Labor of the Coolidge cabinet, James J. Davis. Davis enthusiastically supported the plan's ideals.[78] Richard T. Ely, noted economist at Northwestern University, spoke at the 1927 banquet. His remarks proved the significance of the project:

> We are gathered together because we desire to recognize suitably the progress made in a vast enterprise of national and

world-wide significance. These words I have just uttered may
seem exaggerated, but to those who understand the situation of
agriculture in this and other countries, and who appreciate the
urgency of our farm problems, and who at the same time know
what it means to have an undertaking like the Penney Farms
conducted on a large scale and under competent leadership, in
order to point the way to improvement through experimentation
and demonstration, will not be inclined to dispute me when I say
that I have measured my words carefully.[79]

Ely hoped successful standards and methods for the nation
would be established from this experiment. He noted one of the
most ironic aspects of the farmers' problem. Farming was now a
profit-making business and surpluses drove product prices down. In
former times farmers were self-sufficient and produced both food
and clothing for their families. Once they became consumers like
other parts of society they needed money to buy merchandise. The
giant J.C. Penney Company store chain, in fact, was built on this
inevitable change in social life as farm families desired reasonably
priced ready-to-wear clothing and other necessities of twentieth-
century life.[80]

Despite increased production, Ely realized better methods and
standards could achieve harmony, lead to wiser selection of crops
and result in less economic distress for farmers. It was a complex
problem with no easy solution, and the economist concluded his
remarks by saying, "Success to Mr. Penney and his associates in a
new and most difficult field of service."[81]

As the J.C. Penney Company expanded in the 1920s Penney had
an impressive annual income from cash dividends and what was
called compensation, although he drew no salary.[82] Compensation,
in effect from 1918 to 1925, was distributed as part of company
expenses before dividends were declared. It was in addition to
regular salaries and dividends yet it was based on an individual's
amount of stock ownership.[83] In 1923, Penney received $444,698
in compensation; in 1924 he received $524,666. The latter year his
total earnings were $1,572,666, a combination of compensation and
dividends, before personal taxes.[84]

Thinking his financial future was secure, Penney channeled vast
sums into Florida projects, the New York dairy farm and created a
foundation. Although thrifty by nature, Penney did enjoy pleasant
surroundings like Belle Isle and deluxe late model cars, and he gave

expensive gifts. In 1922, Mary's Christmas present was a Tiffany silver service.[85] In contact with many famous people, Penney continued to pursue special interests with perception and enthusiasm. He preferred useful projects to involvement in "society."

Ralph W. Gwinn, a graduate of Columbia University's Law School and General Counsel for the J.C. Penney Company after 1920, was Penney's partner in many of his 1920s ventures. When the J.C. Penney-Gwinn Corporation was formed, Gwinn was listed as owner of one-eighth of the Clay County, Florida, tract.[86] Gwinn attended to certain business details, but the corporation had a treasurer, C.L. Rood, Penney's private secretary in New York, and secretary, Howard E. Moore. Gwinn and Burdette G. Lewis were vice-presidents while Penney was president.[87]

The J.C. Penney-Gwinn Corporation was incorporated in Florida in 1925.[88] It was one of two organizations that implemented Penney's personal business and philanthropic activities. The J.C. Penney Foundation, planned since 1922 and operating by 1925, was the other.[89]

Dr. Daniel A. Poling became secretary and director of the J.C. Penney Foundation in early 1926.[90] Of the many talented people helping Penney, Poling was the best known. A nationally recognized religious and temperance leader, he had been active in the United Society of Christian Endeavor since 1915 and became its president in 1925. Renamed International Society of Christian Endeavor, the organization would eventually have 400,000 members. Poling was also pastor of Marble Collegiate Church in New York City during the 1920s.[91]

Political as well as religious leaders respected Poling. He and Penney met in 1923 at a Washington, D.C., dinner creating the "Committee of One Thousand," a cross-section of national leaders who promoted adherence to the 18th Amendment and Volstead Act.[92] At this time, Penney became well acquainted with William Jennings Bryan and began attending Bryan's Sunday school classes when in Miami.[93] Poling and Penney had similar interests and a close friendship developed. It resulted in Poling's involvement in Penney's philanthropies and Penney's involvement with *Christian Herald* magazine, an important interdenominational magazine, and with the world-wide Christian Herald Association Charities.[94] Poling became editor-in-chief of *Christian Herald* in 1926.[95]

In 1924 and 1925 Penney emerged as a respected national figure. *The American Magazine* described his rise from farm boy to millionaire merchant, calling him "The Man with 1,000 Partners," and countless newspaper articles featuring some aspect of his life began appearing.[96] One of the proudest moments of these years occurred when the J.C. Penney Company opened its 500th store in 1924 in Hamilton, Missouri. Penney had always wanted a store in his hometown, but he waited until his former boss, John M. Hale, in poor health and bankrupt, finally closed his store in August 1923. The new store occupied Hale's old location. Penney's hometown ties had remained strong. A few years earlier he provided most of the funds for the small community's public library. It was dedicated to his parents.[97]

In 1925 Kansas Wesleyan University at Salina, Kansas, awarded Penney a Doctorate of Science in Business Administration. It was the first time they had granted that degree, and it was certainly an appropriate award.[98] Penney also began corresponding with merchants like Edward A. Filene, and politicians like Franklin Delano Roosevelt, who was a Dutchess County neighbor.[99]

Penney's fame naturally drew more attention to his northern Florida venture. During 1925 and 1926, the company's new eighteen-story modern office building and warehouse between 8th and 9th Avenues on West 34th Street in New York City also attracted national attention to him and the chain.

In May 1925 the *Kemmerer Camera*, which had followed Penney's career with pride, announced:

> Today, his picture, together with a sketch of his life is appearing in national magazines and sent out through news service bureaus for use in newspapers of the nation, pointing out his success. Next to Henry Ford his work is being held up to the people of the nation today as one of the greatest examples of success for one man, through organization.[100]

Penney maintained close ties to the small Wyoming town, as the article made clear:

> Recently Mr. Penney sent a check of $12,000 to the Kemmerer Post, American Legion, for use in the erection of a building to be known as the "Berta Penney Memorial," which will be the home for the American Legion in Kemmerer, provide a huge

auditorium, and in which the post hopes to be able to establish a library at a later date.[101]

Rendering service while being practical could have been Penney's motto. Unfortunately, the idealism of several Miami ventures was later questioned.

At Penney Farms in northern Florida in early 1927 another project was almost complete. It was a sixty-acre community with twenty-two new apartment buildings for retired ministers, lay church workers, missionaries, Y.M.C.A. and Y.W.C.A. secretaries, their wives and families.[102] On June 22, 1926, Memorial Home Community was incorporated; although located in the center of Penney Farms, it was independent of the farm project.[103]

Penney had been inspired by three dozen empty cottages near the sawmill site on his Green Cove Springs property. While at Qui-Si-Sana Hotel in summer 1925 he had a vision of providing rent-free housing for retired church workers who in many cases had little savings and even faced poverty after years of hard work.[104] He announced the cottages' availability and by November 1925 seventeen families had arrived. The neglected cottages needed some repairs but D. Walter Morton was overseeing the project. The small but growing group of retired ministers quickly developed an *esprit de corps*, helped fix the cottages, planted gardens and created an organization, Penmor Place Association, named in honor of Penney and Morton.[105]

In mid-March 1926, as the farm project was growing, Penney and Dr. Poling attended a prayer meeting at Penmor. At the meeting's conclusion, Poling made a dramatic announcement on Penney's behalf. A modern apartment building, housing up to one hundred families, was being constructed as a permanent home for them. The three-room apartments would have modern facilities and would be rent-free.[106]

The Green Cove Springs' apartment building idea was transformed into a campus-like community at Penney Farms. By November 1926, only nine months later, the first retired church workers were moving into brand new "cottages." Within a few months, there were twenty-two individual buildings each containing three to five apartments consisting of three rooms plus a bath.[107] Quite appropriately, a church at the end of Poling Boulevard was the heart of the new community. The church held up to 450 people, had a large community room and library.[108]

The "cottages" were actually sturdy, one-and-a-half and two-and-a-half story houses. Outside, buildings had yellow, red and purple tile roofs, dormers, large panelled casement windows, and enclosed porches. Hollow tile walls were covered by orange-tan colored plaster. Curved walks led past individual buildings, garden plots were available, and palm trees, azaleas, ivy, and other shrubbery were planted by houses and avenues. The grounds were maintained at no charge to residents.[109] Inside, apartments were completely furnished and included kitchen and laundry equipment, such as refrigerators and either electric or oil stoves. Electricity and "water works" connections were made in September 1927. There were "Murphy" beds and fireplaces. Heaters were installed later.[110] The families in residence by dedication time in April 1927 and those who arrived later were quite fortunate.

The new project was not an "old-age" home, but a carefully planned residential community—perhaps the first in a state that has since become famous for retirement communities. It was another example of Penney's foresight and perception.[111] Interdenominational in character, the community had a variety of Protestant religions, and an intellectual climate prevailed. Ministers took turns delivering Sunday sermons.

Young farm families, school children, the retirement community and faculty of the agricultural institute made Penney Farms a well-balanced, interesting community. Socials, receptions and lectures were well attended. New arrivals were noted by the county paper. By September the twenty-two buildings were almost filled.[112] Dedicated to Penney's parents, the retirement complex was named "Memorial Home Community." The church was "Memorial Home Chapel," but was also called "Church of the Seven Gables." The architectural style was Norman-French; the placement of buildings around the church was to recall village life in thirteenth-century Normandy. Alan B. Mills and Arthur E. Davis, Jr., were the architects and builders.[113]

On June 13, 1926, Penney laid the cornerstone of the church and less than one year later the entire community—twenty-two buildings and church—were dedicated. On April 22-24, 1927, Penney Farms was the scene of a large dedication ceremony. Distinguished visitors, such as the Governor of Florida, and U.S. Senator Duncan

U. Fletcher, were happy to join many university and religious leaders, Dr. Daniel Poling presiding. Dr. Short came for the three-day ceremonies and delivered one of the many addresses.[114]

In March Penney revealed his satisfaction with the project when he wrote, "I am looking forward to the event with happy anticipation. As I think you know, Doctor Short, this has given me more joy than any thing I have ever done before in my life."[115] In fact, Penney had best expressed his emotions at the cornerstone laying ceremony. He took that occasion to explain his feelings about his parents, and said:

> All I am I owe to my father and my mother—How thankful I am for my parents and for their example. I feel that I am but carrying on the work which my father started. This group of buildings is to be dedicated to God's own purpose. All that you see here is nothing more than my father would have done. This Memorial will express the religious faith and purpose of my parents, and perpetuate the ideals for which they lived.[116]

The April 1927 ceremonies, however, were among the most emotional moments of Penney's life and made his years of tireless work worthwhile. During the ceremonies, Roswell and J.C., Jr., dedicated a large, carved wooden screen to their mother's memory.[117]

Memorial Home Community cost Penney approximately $1,125,000 to create.[118] It was supported by the J.C. Penney Foundation, and Dr. Poling oversaw its financial needs, while Morton became resident superintendent.[119]

Penney's personal and business interests crossed paths often. In January 1925 a week-long company-wide convention was held in Atlantic City, New Jersey, at the Ambassador Hotel. Nine hundred people, including wives, attended. Highlights were speeches by William Jennings Bryan and Russell H. Conwell. Conwell gave his world-famous "Acres of Diamonds" inspirational sermon, which reflected many of the precepts of the company's directors.[120] Although constantly moving forward with modern, efficient methods, it was the precepts of the nineteenth century that motivated them. Penney, Sams and other senior executives wanted to perpetuate important aspects of their success, especially hard work, cooperation and making the most of every opportunity.

Because of his wife's illness, Bryan at first refused Penney's invitation. But Mrs. Bryan urged her husband to attend and the famous statesman, who had only several more months to live, made the winter trip north.[121] Bryan, in his opening remarks, however, said that he would not have come for anyone else but Penney. His address, an overview of political changes he had seen, also dealt with religion and material wealth, and was broadcast over an Atlantic City radio station to the public.[122]

Penney's brief introduction ended with:

> I have the honor of presenting to you a man who, in all the years of his public life, has never had the finger of scorn raised against his character—a man with whom, on some questions, we have not always agreed, but who, on all questions in which morals are concerned has always been known to be on the right side. It is a privilege to know and to have such a man for a friend.[123]

Groups of Penney managers, carrying banners with their state name and an H.C.S.C. emblem, posed for pictures while enjoying a stroll along the famous boardwalk in the chilly seaside air.[124] Wives were bundled in fur coats, and even a few children came. Planned to renew and instill in newcomers the company's sense of unity and purpose, the large convention required detail and planning to execute. Since 1921 they had held regional meetings. For this meeting, the company's Traffic Department arranged for six "J.C. Penney trains," three from the west coast, to bring participants east.[125]

The organization, quickly becoming immense, retained its personal character due to similar efforts. Store visits, *The Dynamo*, letters from executives to managers, the business training course, and yearly regional meetings created a team spirit. At the beginning of 1925 there were 571 stores and in December 1927 there were 892, and the company was still growing. In the mid-twenties the company was in excellent financial shape; the 1919 preferred stock issue was being retired, and it was still a closed corporation. Year after year annual reports stated no contingent liabilities, and their surplus or retained earnings kept increasing.[126]

Relaxing after the busy convention, Penney had time to reflect. Family life was changing somewhat. Roswell would graduate from Princeton in spring, J.C., Jr. was a student at the Ivy League school, and Kimball, four, was at home.[127] Old friends who meant so much to Penney stayed in touch. Hearing that Tom Callahan had some stores to sell, Penney wrote him and noted the older merchant's influence:

> I remember I thought so many times of your varied experiences and I recall very often your relating your early experiences and what a difficult time you had to get a start. Might I say in all earnestness, Mr. Callahan, that I feel your life has been an inspiration to me.[128]

Penney's large Florida project was in the planning stage, the foundation was in operation, but his involvement with Dr. Poling and Poling's numerous activities was just starting. Both Poling and Penney were interested in helping young people. The vocational guidance nature of many of the foundation's activities reflected this. Overall, everything seemed to be under control and proceeding smoothly. He was doing exactly what he hoped to do when the decade had opened.

In early 1926, newspapers described the foundation's purpose:

> The J.C. Penney Foundation is to be increasingly the social, educational and religious expression of both the spirit and fortune of its Founder. Its plan provides for a conservative beginning with a comprehensive program which aspires to strengthen in the direction of self-help the enterprises it may support. It will lay particular emphasis upon research and counsel in the field of vocational training.[129]

From its headquarters in the new J.C. Penney Company building at 330 West 34th Street, the foundation supported several of Poling's projects like the "Young People's Radio Conference." A vocational guidance and personal advice program, it was broadcast from the Waldorf Astoria Hotel every Sunday afternoon from October 1 to May 1. By underwriting part of the broadcast's expenses and handling many requests generated by the program, the foundation made a valuable contribution to this pioneering youth guidance project.[130]

There was a "J.C. Penney Foundation in Christian Vocations," established in association with the United Society of Christian Endeavor. A vocational guidance department at Grinnell College in Iowa was also supported with foundation funds. In Manhattan, in conjunction with the Judson Health Center, there was a "J.C. Penney Foundation for the Cure of Malnutrition and Incipient Rickets," and the central foundation also contributed in smaller amounts to 125 organizations during 1926. Another interest, less emphasized than vocational guidance but related, was the field of industrial administration and the "science and art of distribution."[131]

In the midst of business and outside activities, Penney married a young woman whose energetic personality matched his. Caroline Bertha Autenrieth and Penney were married in Paris, France, on August 10, 1926. She was his wife for forty-five years.[132] Mrs. Penney's parents were Charles E. Autenrieth and Marie Autenrieth, cousins who emigrated to America from southern Germany in the 1880s. They went into the hotel business in upstate New York, and then moved to Arizona to help improve a son's ailing health. Caroline grew up in Phoenix, then a fairly small town and health haven. Although their father died in 1904, the four Autenrieth children, ambitious and talented, thrived. Caroline came east to study music. She also did church work and was working for the American Methodist Episcopal Bishop in Paris in August 1926.[133]

Penney, who had been acquainted with her for a year or two in New York, traveled to Paris that summer to marry the petite, gray-blue eyed woman who was twenty years younger than he. On May 28, 1927, Mrs. Penney became the mother of a baby girl, Mary Frances, who was named for Penney's mother. After three sons, Penney was delighted with his little daughter. Caroline became Kimball's mother, too. In spring 1927, J.C., Jr. graduated from Princeton, and Penney, although busy, wrote that he was very proud of his family.[134]

A series of short articles written by Penney began appearing in *Christian Herald* magazine after April 1927. "Lines of a Layman" gave his business philosophy and precepts for living. The inspirational messages showed a growing desire to communicate deeply held convictions. Poling, in his introduction, described Penney, now 52, as "one of the youngest men of great achievement in the commercial world."[135]

Penney, idealistic and with a strong religious background, believed religious principles were necessary for success in business. His speech at the 1925 convention in Atlantic City was "The

Spiritual Meaning of Business"; in September 1928 the *Saturday Evening Post* carried his article entitled, "The Bible in Business." It was, in part, a defense of wealth, for he said:

> Another unmerited rebuke is to the effect that every man who reaches the crest does so at the expense of his brothers; that in the mad rush he tramples the weak and travels over their financially, dead bodies to supremacy, pocketing the spoils as he goes.
>
> No man, in my opinion, can pull himself up by his own bootstraps, favorite theory to the contrary; he is hoisted by his personal efforts and the cooperative efforts of his friends, and the latter are benefited and not battered. . . . In business, true, there is a survival of the fittest, but the fittest is synonymous with the one who practices most consistently and conscientiously the cardinal virtues of being patient, humble, diligent, charitable and honest. To my idea, the one rule to which an ambitious young man or woman can adhere and remain morally safe, is the Golden Rule. In it are encompassed all commandments and conventions; through it and it only, I think, success and happiness can be derived.[136]

Penney was known for bringing others along with him on his journey to success, and the cooperative nature of the company he founded with its profit-sharing opportunities gave his words a firm foundation. The chain store controversy, in which chains such as J.C. Penney Company were accused of driving smaller firms out of business, was gaining strength at this time, too, but years-old policies of service and community involvement stood the company in good stead.

In 1928 Penney became president of *Christian Herald* and the Penney Foundation assumed the magazine's past and future deficits.[137] Although Penney's acceptance remarks were cautious, he was fully committed, saying he believed in the magazine and its mission. He concluded:

> I accept this new responsibility only after careful deliberation and with some reluctance, but my decision finds me conscious of a great opportunity, in which I invite you all to join. Help us make the Fiftieth Anniversary of *Christian Herald* a golden year. . . .[138]

If only similar careful deliberation had kept him from accepting chairmanship of City National Bank in Miami in 1928, he would have been spared much grief. However, even his perception had blind spots. In the bright days of 1928, no one knew the country's financial institutions were headed for disaster.

Penney lived at #8 Belle Isle during winter months, but he traveled back and forth to New York frequently, making short stops at Penney Farms. After 1926, the J.C. Penney-Gwinn Corporation extended its activities into Miami. To Penney his involvement in the Miami Shores development and in City National Bank in Miami were practical and idealistic. The J.C. Penney-Gwinn Corporation wanted to make itself a strong factor in the development of Florida housing, commerce, and agriculture. Marketing of Florida fruits and vegetables was vital to give the state a sound economic base.[139]

In Miami, several large housing developments were underway before the building boom collapsed and suffered long-term damage from the September 1926 hurricane. In December 1924, real estate sales for "Miami Shores" property, from 87th Street north to about 105th Street and fronting on Biscayne Bay, broke a Florida sales record. Seventy-five salesmen sold more than $2.5 million worth of lots on opening day. Shoreland Company was the owner of this bonanza. It was one of the largest residential projects ever to be placed on the southern market, according to the *Miami Herald*. Approximately 2,500 acres were to be developed; 50 miles of sidewalks and 25 miles of streets, plus attractive landscaping were being completed.[140]

In December 1924, Penney apparently had a very small investment in the project. This grew in spring 1926 and by early 1929 the J.C. Penney-Gwinn Corporation was the second largest holder next to a reorganized Shoreland Company.[141] Although Miami boosters in early 1929 foresaw a prosperous future for Miami, it did not arrive as soon as they hoped. The September 1926 hurricane, in fact, had severely damaged not only property but also many outsiders' interest in southeastern Florida. The city had received a strong blow to its progress and prosperity.

Penney's increased participation in Miami affairs came after the hurricane. He believed in the area's future, as well as in northern Florida's potential.[142] As a result he and the J.C. Penney-Gwinn Corporation entered banking, marketing, and supported real estate loans between 1928 and 1930. These were risky ventures even for someone as wealthy as Penney.

In 1927, in connection with increased earnings and "The New Plan," which ended the original classified common stock in favor of company-wide stock, the company split the common stock ten for one.[143] The number of stores increased from 892 in late 1927 to 1400 by fall 1929, sales and profits were up, there was a $25 million surplus and no contingent liabilities.[144] Thus, Penney's stock holdings grew in value. To raise large sums of cash needed for his outside projects, he borrowed money from five banks using his company stock as collateral.[145]

City National Bank in Miami was originally organized in early 1926; that June two other banks merged with it, and the new bank, after the hurricane in September, was left holding worthless loans, mortgages and notes as real estate was either destroyed or dropped in value. When bank examiners checked the bank's assets in 1927, they recommended reducing its capital structure and eliminating some of this "bad paper." Real estate values continued to drop, and in late 1927 another adjustment was required. At this point Penney and the J.C. Penney-Gwinn Corporation entered the picture.[146]

On February 10, 1928, they purchased a majority interest in the bank. As real estate values kept declining, bank examiners said losses had to be offset. By contributing a million dollars that February and in March 1929, plus reducing the capital stock, the new owners tried to strengthen the bank. In April 1930, through the Tarrier Corporation, created by Penney and the J.C. Penney-Gwinn Corporation, another one million dollars was contributed to the bank. During April and May 1929, the bank was considered in sound financial condition, and deposits grew. On June 10, 1930, as the Depression tightened its grip, the Bank of Bay Biscayne closed and depositors in all Miami banks began withdrawing money. Penney sent a telegram saying City National Bank was strong and that he stood firmly behind it.[147] Depositors were reassured, but the other bank's closing foreshadowed future problems.

Later, harsh accusations were made against Penney and the bank's directors claiming the bank made loans to poor risks, such as the reorganized Coral Gables Corporation, and to certain individuals. Accusers said J.C. Penney-Gwinn Corporation deposited money and then withdrew it.[148]

In 1928 when Penney and the J.C. Penney-Gwinn Corporation assumed control of the bank, their intentions were, "to aid in the recovery of Florida and in the development of its agriculture and commerce." At this same time Penney and Lewis, who headed the corporation's Florida operations, decided to join forces with the Florida United Growers, Inc., a cooperative marketing organization which arranged for citrus fruit and vegetables to be sold outside of Florida. "Proper organization and development of Florida growing and marketing" was Penney's and Lewis's aim.[149]

They wanted Penney Farms, still prospering, to be an "essential part" of the marketing, and foresaw a federation of cooperatives throughout the south to aid marketing.[150] Another project was added to this list about 1929. Foremost Dairies Products, Inc., was organized to control production and marketing of dairy products in southern states and some northern ones. Described as a "huge merger" and a "$5,000,000 subsidiary" of the J.C. Penney-Gwinn Corporation, it was called the largest dairy company in the South." Equalizing distribution of dairy products in five southern states was its aim.[151] Thus in early 1929, Penney was fully committed to Florida and his interests were spreading to adjoining states. There was no indication of pending disaster. Like quicksand, over the next few years financial problems slowly drew Penney down to the point of ruin.

In late January 1929, Penney and his Belle Isle home received coverage in newspapers across the nation. President-Elect Herbert Hoover and his wife were making #8 Belle Isle their pre-inaugural home. Although he considered himself a Democrat, Penney supported Hoover during the recent campaign. Penney made his views clear in statements to magazines, newspapers and to political leaders like his Dutchess County neighbor, Franklin Delano Roosevelt. Prohibition was one of Penney's major concerns; he also believed an urban leader like Governor Alfred E. Smith did not understand rural America and the farmers' pressing needs.[152]

Arrangements for Mr. Hoover's visit had been concluded after the November election. The Penneys were thinking of selling the estate and Lewis decided the publicity resulting from Hoover's stay would help sell it.[153] Publicity certainly came. Full-page features of the house and grounds appeared in numerous papers. Miami benefited as well, for reporters came from everywhere to cover the Hoover story. While this occurred the Penneys were on a world cruise of several months' duration.

When Penney returned he resumed his series of "good-will" tours around the nation.[154] On one of these trips, he made a stopover in a small Ozark town, Humansville, Missouri. Charles E. Dimmitt, temporarily retired from the J.C. Penney Company, invited Penney to the dedication ceremony for the "George Dimmitt Memorial Hospital." This expensive structure was built in memory of the Dimmitts' son who died in 1928.[155]

As he walked the town's narrow streets, the same streets where the Barnett daughters, Tom Callahan and many other Golden Rule merchants once walked and dreamed dreams, memories of them and of his start as a merchant arose. The roots of the giant J.C. Penney Company chain and his legendary career were embedded here. Carrying happy memories, he left Humansville, with no idea that his personal fortune and everything he had tried to accomplish with it were in jeopardy.

NOTES

1.   *Penney and Allied Families*, p. 85.
2.   Penney, *Fifty Years*, p. 120.
3.   Clippings, letters and miscellaneous information on Mary Kimball Penney and the Kimball family, PHF VII, C-3.
4.   Obituary Notice (Miami[?] newspaper), PHF VII, C-3; Dorsey, "Missourians Abroad," p. 559; Alumnae Records, Bryn Mawr College, Author's files; *Penney and Allied Families*, p. 58.
5.   Ibid.; *Grove's Dictionary of Music* (1955), p. 570, Marchesi family.
6.   *Penney and Allied Families*, p. 85; Photograph and letter about its date, JCP to Mrs. A.J. Gorham, 20 April 1923, PHF VII, C-3.
7.   Penney, *Fifty Years*, p. 121.
8.   F.B. Short to JCP, 7 November 1919, PHF IV, C-7. Note: Short, born in 1868, had received the following degrees by 1920: A.B., University of Delaware, 1891, and D.D., Puget Sound College, 1913. He is listed in *Who Was Who in America 1897-1942*, p. 1121.
9.   Ibid. Note: He was becoming editor of *The Dynamo*.
10.   JCP to FBS, 16 September 1920, PHF IV, C-7. Note: JCP had been contributing a yearly $3,500 fund for Dr. Short's use during the 1913-1915 period according to Ledger book entries.
11.   Ibid.
12.   Penney, *Fifty Years*, p. 120.
13.   Robert Henkel to JCP, 16 May 1921, PHF VII, D-1; Penney, *Fifty Years*, p. 121.
14.   Obituary notice, PHF VII, C-3.
15.   Ibid.; Miscellaneous clipping on Eddy, no date—assume 1922/23, PHF VII, D-1; PHF VII, D-1a, Florida.
16.   Polly Redford, *Billion Dollar Sandbar* (New York: E.P. Dutton & Co., Inc., 1970), pp. 69, 83, 90; *Plat Book of Greater Miami, Florida and Suburbs* (Philadelphia: G.M. Hopkins Co., 1925), Belle Isle; JCP (office) to Col. H.A. Mann, 16 November 1928, PHF VII, D-1.
17.   *The Herald* (Miami), 17 January 1926, in Microfilm File, "Venetian Causeway," Florida Collection, Miami-Dade Public Library.
18.   R.L. Polk & Co., *Polk's Miami City Directory 1924*, Vol. 13 (Jacksonville, Fla.: R.L. Polk, 1924), p. 8.
19.   Ibid.
20.   *Miami (Florida) Herald*, 4 December 1924, p. 14-A, cols. 2-3.
21.   *R.L. Polk's Miami* (1924), pp. 8, 11.
22.   Pages from *Florida—The East Coast—Its Builders, Industries and Resources*, "The Residence of J.C. Penney, Miami, Florida, pp. 203-5, c. 1927, PHF VII, D-1a.
23.   Photographs and newspaper pictures from the 1920s, PHF VII, D-1a.
24.   *Florida—The East Coast* (c. 1927).
25.   Ibid.; JCP (office) to Col. H.A. Mann, 16 November 1928, PHF VII, D-1.

26.   *The Miami Metropolis*, 2 March 1916 in Clipping File—VIP's in Miami, at Historical Association of Southern Florida Library, Miami, Fla.
27.   Clipping from Miami newspaper, 27 January, PHF I, D-2.
28.   Ibid.
29.   Author's visit to Belle Isle, Miami Beach, March 1979.
30.   *Penney and Allied Families*, p. 58.
31.   Ibid., p. 85; JCP to C.L. Rood, 26 December 1922, PHF VII, C-3.
32.   JCP to G.H. Bushnell, 23 January 1923, PHF IV, C-1.
33.   Ibid.
34.   JCP to ECS, 25 January 1923, PHF IV, C-1.
35.   *Penney and Allied Families*, p. 85; Obituary notice, PHF VII, C-3; Dorsey, "Missourians Abroad," p. 559.
36.   JCP to Miss J. Sands, 2 April 1923, PHF VII, C-3; Dorsey, "Missourians Abroad," p. 559.
37.   JCP to W.M. Bushnell, 9 March 1923, JCP to Mrs. D. Woidemann, 23 March 1923, and JCP to Will Partin, 17 January 1924, PHF VII, C-3.
38.   Obituary notice, PHF VII, C-3.
39.   JCP to E.S. Atwood, 28 March 1923, PHF VII, C-3; F.B. Short to JCP, 31 March 1923, PHF IV, C-7.
40.   JCP to E.S. Atwood, 28 March 1923, and JCP to Will Partin, 17 January 1924, PHF VII, C-3.
41.   JCP to E.S. Atwood, 28 March 1923, PHF VII, C-3.
42.   *Miami Herald*, 4 December 1924, p. 14-a, p. 1-B.
43.   JCP to Mitt and Ross (Mr. and Mrs. R.F. Whitman), 28 November 1924, PHF VII, E-2.
44.   J.C. Penney, "The Purpose Behind Emmadine Farm," An Address at Wisconsin Guernsey Breeders' Association, June 21, 1928, in *Addresses and Manuals 1928* (New York: J.C. Penney Company, Inc., 1928), pp. 10-11.
45.   Date of deed given in "Agreement between J.C. Penney (1st part), Ralph W. Gwinn (2nd part) and J.C. Penney-Gwinn Corporation (3rd part)," 8 December 1925, p. 2, PHF IX, A-1; Penney, *Fifty Years*, p. 122.
46.   J.C. Penney, "The Purpose Behind Emmadine Farm," frontispiece and p. 12.
47.   Ibid., pp. 7-17.
48.   Ibid., pp. 17-19.
49.   Ibid., pp. 8-9.
50.   Dr. Thomas Tapper, "A Successful Store-Chain System Applied to a Farming Project," reprinted from the *Manufacturers Record*, 18 March 1926 in *J.C. Penney-Gwinn Corporation Farms, Independent Farm Ownership on a New Plan* (Green Cove Springs, Fla.: J.C. Penney-Gwinn Corporation, 1926), pp. 9-10. Note: Date of land sale was either February 20 or February 24, 1925; see *J.C. Penney-Gwinn Corporation Farms* (St. Augustine, Fla., 1927), pp. 2-3. Note: All model farm project booklets are in PHF.
51.   *J.C. Penney-Gwinn Corporation Farms, Independent Farm Ownership on a New Plan* includes reprints of short articles that appeared in the *Manufacturers Record, Miami Herald, Florida's Man Power, Zion's Herald* and Jacksonville newspapers. An article about Penney's purchases in Florida and farm community appeared in the *Wall Street Journal*, 1 May 1926, PHF IX, C-Miami Shores.

52.   Arch Frederic Blakey, *Parade of Memories. A History of Clay County, Florida* (Jacksonville: The Clay County Board of County Commissioners, 1976), p. 209. Utilizes material from Philip Alton Werndli, "J.C. Penney and the Development of Penney Farms, Florida (1924-1934)," master's thesis, University of Florida, 1974; F. Reisner, "A Unique Undertaking," reprinted from *Zion's Herald*, 28 April 1926, in *J.C. Penney-Gwinn Corporation Farms* (1926), p. 45.

53.   Blakey, *Parade*, pp. 212-13; *J.C. Penney-Gwinn Corporation Farms, Penney Farms Clay County Florida, A Unique Agricultural Demonstration* (St. Augustine, Fla.: Record Company, c. 1927), pp. 3-5.

54.   *Life More Abundant. The Story of a Retirement Community at Penney Farms, Florida* (Penney Farms, Fla.: Penney Retirement Community Association, 1973), p. 6.

55.   Percy Hamilton, "Memories Light Up Fading Sermons," *The Florida Times Union Jacksonville Journal*, 28 November 1976, p. B-1, in Penney Retirement Community Historical Society Files (PRC).

56.   Reisner, "A Unique Undertaking" (1926), p. 45.

57.   Percy Hamilton, "Penney Farms Retirees Close Jail, Cut Taxes," *Jacksonville Times Union*, 10 October 1976, PRC; Plat, "Long Branch City," PRC.

58.   Reisner, p. 45; John C. Snowhook, "How One Man Is Solving the Farm Problem for Hundreds," reprinted from the *Manufacturers Record*, 10 February 1927, in *The Unique Farm Project of James C. Penney 1927* (Green Cove Springs, Fla.: The J.C. Penney-Gwinn Corporation Farms, 1927), pp. 7-8.

59.   Dr. Tapper, "A Successful Store-Chain System."

60.   *J.C. Penney-Gwinn Corporation Farms* (1927), p. 13; Snowhook, "How One Man Is Solving," p. 8.

61.   *J.C. Penney-Gwinn Corporation Farms* (1927), p. 24.

62.   Ibid., p. 19.

63.   *The Unique Farm Project*, pp. 23-24, reprint from *Florida Farmer* (Jacksonville, Fla.), 15 March 1927, "Where Money Alone Will Not Buy a Farm."

64.   Dr. Tapper, "A Successful Store-Chain System," p. 13.

65.   Snowhook, "How One Man Is Solving," p. 10.

66.   Ibid.

67.   *J.C. Penney-Gwinn Corporation Farms* (1927), p. 48, E.C. Sams' speech at 1927 banquet.

68.   *Encyclopedia of American History*, p. 509.

69.   Dr. Tapper, "A Successful Store-Chain System," p. 12.

70.   *J.C. Penney-Gwinn Corporation Farms* (1927), p. 19.

71.   Ibid., pp. 18, 26, 42-43.

72.   Ibid., pp. 8-9, 15.

73.   Ibid., p. 26; Dudley V. Haddock, "Clay County Shows Rapid Advancement," reprint from *Florida Times Union*, 23 March 1927, in *The Unique Farm Project*, p. 44.

74.   *J.C. Penney-Gwinn Corporation Farms* (1927), p. 27.

75.   Ibid.

76.   Snowhook, "How One Man Is Solving," pp. 8-9.

77.   *J.C. Penney-Gwinn Lectures* (c. 1928), PHF IV, C-7; *Who Was Who in America* (1961-1968).

78.   *J.C. Penney-Gwinn Corporation Farms* (1927), p. 45; *The Unique Farm Project*, p. 18, copy of telegram sent by Davis in 1927.

79.   *J.C. Penney-Gwinn Corporation Farms* (1927), pp. 36-37.

80.   Ibid.

81.   Ibid.

82.   MBD I, 433.

83.   Ibid., 426.

84.   G.H. Bushnell to JCP, 15 February 1923 and G.H. Bushnell to ECS, 12 March 1925, PHF IV, C-1; Summarized Statements 1911-1925. Note: Total compensation in 1924 was $2,246,766.91, and net profits were $4,523,348.02 on sales of $74,261,343.00.

85.   JCP to C.L. Rood, 26 December 1922, PHF VII, C-3.

86.   December 8, 1925 "Agreement," pp. 2-3.

87.   *J.C. Penney-Gwinn Corporation Farms* (1927), inside front cover.

88.   December 8, 1925 "Agreement," pp. 2-3. Note: Evidently the corporation was created prior to the "Agreement," but not before February 1925.

89.   "Child Placing Agency of the State Charities Aid Association" to J.C. Penney Foundation, 21 May 1925, and W.H.D. Pell to JCP, 28 December 1922, PHF VI, C-1; Penney, *Fifty Years*, pp. 128-29.

90.   *Dynamo* 11 (April 1927): 28.

91.   *National Cyclopedia of American Biography* 54 (1973), 120.

92.   Penney, *Fifty Years*, pp. 128-29.

93.   JCP to Will Partin, 17 January 1924, PHF VII, C-3.

94.   Daniel A. Poling, "President J.C. Penney!" *Christian Herald*, 7 January 1928, p. 3; *Dynamo* 11 (April 1927): 28-29.

95.   *National Cyclopedia of American Biography* 54 (1973), 120.

96.   John Monk Saunders, "The Man with 1,000 Partners," *The American Magazine* 98 (October 1924): 19, 171-77; also "James C. Penney, A Portrait in Photogravure," 18.

97.   "Letters to the Editor," Joan Gosnell to A.L. Chadwick, *The Hamilton Advocate*, 1/9/91 (Hale had asked Penney in March 1923 to buy his remaining inventory as a "favor," but Penney, in mourning for Mary, either did not receive the letter or else delayed answering it. J.M. McDonald, who forwarded the letter to Penney, had already refused Hale's request, citing previous company commitments); *J.C. Penney Memorial Library and Museum* (1975), p. 8.

98.   Dorsey, "Missourians Abroad," p. 561.

99.   PHF VII, H-1, H-2, Correspondence with Presidents and Other Prominent Persons.

100.   *Kemmerer Camera*, 29 May 1925, PHF I, D-2.

101.   Ibid.

102.   *Life More Abundant*, p. 8; Charter of Memorial Home Community—a corporation, not for profit, pp. 1-3, typescript dated 7/21/26, PRC; Penney, *Fifty Years*, pp. 146, 147.

103.   Ibid.; Blakey, *Parade*, p. 215.

104.   *Life More Abundant*, p. 3.

105.   Ibid., pp. 3-5; Blakey, *Parade*, p. 214.

106.   *Life More Abundant*, pp. 5, 8.

107.   Ibid., pp. 11-12.

108.   Ibid.; Visit by author to Penney Retirement Community, Penney Farms, Florida, in April 1979.

109.   Dr. George A. Smith, "Apartments," reprint from *Clay County Times* in *The Unique Farm Project*, pp. 38-39; *Life More Abundant*, pp. 12, 13, 44-45. Note: Pp. 44-45 report that in September 1964 Hurricane Dora arrived, but the buildings suffered no damage although the grounds did; 1979 visit.

110.   Ibid.; *Clay County Crescent*, 9 June 1977, reprint of page from *Clay County Crescent*, 16 September 1927.

111.   Author's interview with Dr. Paul P. Hagen, Executive Director of Penney Retirement Community, in April 1979, Author's files. Note: "Moose Haven," a home for retired members of this organization, was started two years earlier at Orange Park, north of Green Cove Springs on St. Johns River. This, however, was an "old folks home," an institution, not a retirement community.

112.   *Clay County Crescent* reprint.

113.   *Life More Abundant*, p. 15; Dedication Plaque in Church.

114.   Blakey, *Parade*, p. 215; *Life More Abundant*, p. 12; PHF VI, C-3, Francis Burgette Short, D.D., LL.D., "Dedicatory Address of the Penney Memorial Homes Community" (4 pages).

115.   JCP to Dr. Short, March 1927, PHF VI, C-3.

116.   *Life More Abundant*, p. 17.

117.   Ibid., p. 14; Author's visit.

118.   Penney Retirement Community Historical Society Archives, "Charter," p. 3, reports "highest indebtedness $1 million," "amount of real estate $2 million"; Blakey, *Parade*, p. 216, reports Penney spent about $2 million on the retirement community.

119.   *Life More Abundant*, pp. 18-20; *Dynamo* 11 (April 1927): 28.

120.   *Dynamo* 8 (February 1925), convention issue.

121.   PHF, EVM files, JCP's Introductory remarks.

122.   *Dynamo* 8 (February 1925).

123.   PHF, EVM files.

124.   *Dynamo* 8 (February 1925).

125.   Ibid., back cover.

126.   PHF, H-1, Annual Reports.

127.   *Penney and Allied Families*, p. 85.

128.   JCP to T.M. Callahan, 11 February 1926, PHF III, C-3.

129.   Daniel A. Poling, "The J.C. Penney Foundation," *Dynamo* 11 (April 1927): 28.

130.   Ibid., p. 29.

131.   Ibid., pp. 28-29.

132.   *Penney and Allied Families*, p. 86.

133.   Information courtesy of E. Virginia Mowry, J.C. Penney Company. Note: Source also noted as EVM in chapters.

134.   *Penney and Allied Families*, pp. 85-86.

135.   Daniel A. Poling, "James Cash Penney—A Personality," *Christian Herald*, 23 August 1927, p. 3.

136.   J.C. Penney, "The Bible in Business," *The Saturday Evening Post*, 22 September 1928, p. 105.

137.   Poling, "President J.C. Penney!" p. 3.

138. Ibid.

139. *Dynamo* 11 (July 1928): 21.

140. *Miami Herald,* 5 December 1924, p. 1, cols. 2-3.

141. C.L. Rood to JCP, 9 December 1924, PHF IX, C-Miami Shores; *Wall Street Journal,* 1 May 1926 (clipping); *Miami Herald,* 7/28/29 in Biography Clipping File, Florida Room, Miami-Dade Public Library.

142. *Dynamo* 11 (July 1928): 21.

143. MBD (Delaware Corporation) I, 348 (22 March 1927).

144. *Annual Report* 1929, PHF IV, H-1.

145. JCP to C.L. Rood, 17 August 1932, PHF V, G-1.

146. "Memorandum—Re: City National Bank" by Ray M. Earnest (Stockholder in Tarrier Corporation), PHF V, G-1.

147. Ibid.

148. Clippings, i.e. *Miami Daily News,* 30 April 1935, "$2,000,000 Fund for Depositors Sought in Suit," PHF V, G-1.

149. *Dynamo* 12 (July 1928), 21-22.

150. Ibid.

151. *Miami Herald,* 7/28/29 (clipping).

152. "Democratic Head of Great Chain Store Organization Supports Hoover," *Manufacturers Record* (Baltimore), 27 September 1928, p. 51; PHF VII, H-1, Correspondence.

153. PHF VII, D-1b, Florida, Herbert Hoover's Occupancy.

154. *Dynamo* 14 (August 1930).

155. *Humansville, Missouri 1872-1972,* p. 105. Author's interview with Mrs. Mary Ann Owens, Humansville Town Historian.

A NATIONWIDE INSTITUTION

When the annual convention of managers and executives was held in February 1920, senior members looked forward to a decade of expansion. They knew how difficult the task would be. Lew V. Day, manager of the Everett, Washington, store and protégé of C.E. Dimmitt, gave a convention talk that set the stage for the new decade. He spoke on "The Manager: His Duties and Responsibilities," and demonstrated the perception that made the company a household word across America well before 1930.[1]

Individual store managers were the key people in the widely scattered chain. Central office work centered around managers' needs. Buying, accounting, shipping and administrative departments were improving and expanding their services, but the front-line people were the manager and his small group of associates. They had to establish and maintain profitable stores. Daily progress depended on their individual ability.

Although buyers provided information and made valuable suggestions, they had to be informed of what customers wanted, what was selling and what was not. Managers made the final merchandise selections for their stores based on community needs. Their low-priced merchandise required rapid turnover to make profits. The demanding job of manager received particular oversight from executives who were former store managers.

Day said, "The mere making of money in the individual store" was not the manager's only task. A company manager should develop four talents: merchandising skill, financial knowledge, personal character building and teaching skills. Salesmanship, advertising and display expertise came under merchandising. He warned, "Today competition is keen" and said the company's methods were being copied by the competition. On the plus side, though, the Penney chain prided itself on "personal, courteous service," an aspect often neglected by their competitors.[2]

He explained past successes and future possibilities:

> We must admit that our strongest factor in securing business up to now has been because we have attempted to keep our prices lower than competition. The problem for us to solve in the future will be, to hold our customers and increase our business and keep our expenses down still doing business outside of the high rent district, with but little difference between our price and the competitor's price. . . . The new basis of competition is service. It is for us to go one better and make a broad distinction between Service and J.C. Penney Company Service. . . . We must establish our reputation on distinctive personal service.[3]

During the war years, higher wages led to a desire for better, higher priced merchandise, which the company provided. The $7.00 shoes at Kemmerer were one example. A "race" for higher prices was occurring, but this was not their policy. Day cautioned:

> Possibly the day of men's all-wool suits at $9.90 is gone forever, but the principle still lives, and if we are to continue successfully in the conduct of our business we must adhere strictly to that principle. . . . Give your patrons the greatest possible values for the money. Hold your expense down and don't forget that money is made in rapid turnover, not in carrying big stocks.[4]

Old rule-of-thumb methods no longer sufficed. Day posed some tough questions and warned his listeners that economic conditions could change. He asked,

> Gentlemen, are we the real keen merchants that we should be? When business runs smoothly—when trade comes easily—when conditions are favorable, we are apt to give ourselves credit for a success that is not justly earned. The test comes, my friends, when conditions become adverse. When the unexpected happens—when prices fall and stocks are large. When competition meets us with price and quality.[5]

These were prophetic remarks.

Training new managers and those who would be eligible for central office jobs, however, was the managers' "extremely serious duty." If new men sent out were not well trained, then instead of progress they had created "stumbling blocks." He emphasized, "The responsibility of the financial status of this company for the year

1920 positively rests with every one of us." The training of those under a manager to be even better than he was was their last and most significant challenge.[6]

Men were carefully hired but were then assigned to a store to learn all aspects of the job. It was an on-the-job training program; there were no formal training sessions in New York or St. Louis. A complete business training correspondence course was being created by the Company that same year and the first lesson was sent out in March 1921. For the time being, however, there was the informative *Dynamo*. To this, Penney added a personal note of encouragement; it symbolized the direction he wanted managers to take. At the end of the 1920 convention, after the important Obligation Ceremony, he gave everyone a book titled "Salesmanship and Business Efficiency."[7] Obviously, study was a vital element in their success strategy.

Before the Company could advance very far in its journey, a severe recession occurred in the fall of 1920. The 1920 drop from wartime high prices or the "sellers' market" McDonald had described left retailers stocked with merchandise purchased or ordered at the earlier high rates. To clear inventories, merchants had to take markdowns causing a loss on already narrow profit margins. Nationally, four million were unemployed, over 20,000 business firms went bankrupt, and it was the first year the company did not show a gain in earnings.[8]

Opening 100 new stores plus high purchasing costs helped cause the drop in earnings. Even though total sales volume was $42.8 million, cost of merchandise was $37.1 million, leaving little room for expenses.[9] In 1920 no compensation or dividends were issued. Dividends were precluded by the agreement with preferred stockholders, but a payment called "advance compensation" was approved by the Board of Directors in early 1921.[10] Retained earnings, which were $3.6 million in 1919, dropped to $2.2 million in 1920, but they made up for this reduction.[11]

Advance compensation was the only mention of difficulties during 1920 in the official Minute Books, but a few letters survive which show some uncertainty but also the basic confidence of the directors. As Penney admitted in a mid-June 1921 reply, "In these times, we do not, any of us, know just where we stand." In the same letter to Mrs. Woidemann, who was caring for her ailing husband, he added, "We feel we have our business in first class shape."[12]

When 1921 drew to a close the company's business was thriving again. They had weathered their first major economic storm. It proved the large chain had the same flexibility that allowed the smaller Golden Rule Stores to survive in 1893 and 1907-1908. What the buying public did not see, though, were the smoothly run accounting, merchandising, shipping, real estate, sales and educational departments supporting every single store from large ones like Salt Lake City to those on side streets in mining towns and farming communities.

An important component of this smoothly running merchandise machine was *The Dynamo*. When Dr. Short became head of the Educational Department in early 1920, he became editor of *The Dynamo*.[13] He had contributed articles to it for several years and gave speeches and memorial services at conventions. As editor he worked with Dr. Tapper to present a well-rounded picture of the company. He followed the path blazed by William Bushnell and provided both information and inspiration.

Penney's aim for *The Dynamo* was to increase the power and efficiency of all associates, and readers of the monthly issues undoubtedly felt as if they belonged to one big family striving for improvement. Sometimes up to 50,000 issues were printed to be given to customers as good-will gestures and company advertising. Each year's Christmas issue, often printed with green ink or on green paper, was given free of charge to interested customers.[14]

Short and Tapper also worked on the training program wanted by Penney and the directors. To expand, the company needed managers and associates who understood and upheld company policies, who trained others and motivated them to work efficiently and cheerfully. Together *The Dynamo* and the business course, free to all associates, became major factors in their rise to nationwide strength. Company executives, primarily former store managers, followed Penney's leadership and, besides promoting the Golden Rule operating policies, they began to envision a much larger organization.

William Bushnell had proclaimed the Company's possibilities in 1917; his older brother, George H. Bushnell, was equally progressive. As First Vice-President and Comptroller, Bushnell had an annual salary of $10,000 and a growing number of classified common stock shares. However, he was not isolated in the New York office. Through annual conventions, which had been transformed into twice-yearly regional meetings at three to six cities, he became well known and even more respected.

Bushnell helped organize the company's financial affairs and had been in daily contact with Penney and Sams for the past ten years. He developed into an expert on the company's management needs. Daily sales reports, inventory records and operating expenses came through his office giving him an accurate, detailed picture of both individual managers and overall problems and progress.

His first record keeping system was pronounced flawless by a professional accounting firm in 1916. The New York firm of Marwick, Mitchell, Peat & Co., after making an extensive check of stores, inventories and all records, said the company's financial statement was of the highest standard.[15] Bushnell's auditing and accounting background made him an expert at detail work, which was precisely what the expanding organization needed.

He spoke at the spring regional conventions in 1922, 1923 and 1924. At St. Louis, St. Paul, Portland and Salt Lake City in April 1922, Bushnell called "man-training" the "great problem that confronts us."[16] He advised managers to:

> Train your men carefully and patiently. Remember they are your partners of the future. We are in business to build men as well as to build surplus of money. Both are essential to our mutual success but the man comes first, for all else depends upon his character, vision and industry.[17]

At meetings like this, Bushnell did not talk down to his audience of managers. Instead he talked to them as they were—actual or future partners and stockholders. As such they were entitled to know company data and the "inner workings" of the central organization.

At the fall 1921 conventions, Sams explained their Articles of Incorporation in detail. Bushnell, in spring 1922, added the newest information on stock expansion. In March they amended the Articles of Incorporation, he explained, from $15 million to $20 million, increasing the amount of classified common stock by 50,000 shares or $5 million "to take care of future expansion."[18] After saying they had retired $300,000 of the already issued $3 million preferred stock, he noted they could handle any emergency that might arise since they were authorized to issue an additional $7 million of preferred stock whenever necessary. They were in a strong financial position that spring.

Bushnell's talk on "Character" summed up the company's direction during the coming decade:

> The future of our Organization devolves upon you Managers more than upon anyone else. Development of our future Managers is up to you. It is your responsibility. The success or failure of these men largely depends upon you. You must diligently train your men so that our expansion may go on without being delayed by the lack of men who should be coming along or by the poor management of half-trained men. Do not recommend to the Board of Directors that we elect a man to managership unless you feel sure that the man will reflect your training in his management and in the development of the men in his store.
>
> I can see a thousand J.C. Penney Company stores within a very few years, all manned with thoroughly competent men. Ten years from now I can see our Organization the largest chain store system of any kind in the world, not only larger in number of units but larger in its service-giving capacity to the public, greater in its influence for the moral uplift of every community in which we operate and stronger financially than any mercantile institution in existence.[19]

After describing their commitment to the Golden Rule and the company policy of "rewarding every one in proportion to his contribution," he counseled patience in obtaining a store interest. "The ultimate success of our business," he declared, "depends upon our guaranteeing its security through wise and patient work." The fact that men who acquire an interest obtain it at par cost, that "no good will is charged" and they are "allowed to pay for this interest out of earnings" shows that "our Company is unusually liberal and unselfish."[20]

Bushnell was very proud of the company's financial strength. They could now obtain a $5 million credit line without collateral and only a few years earlier they were fortunate to obtain $50,000.[21] Their policy of expanding through earnings assured their security. Managers were to learn as much accounting as possible to analyze their store's position at any time. They were to follow their leaders' plans, but "every manager must support the whole Organization and never lean upon it."[22]

Among their leaders' plans was a new, extensive business training course which, despite its emphasis on "man-training," was for both men and women. It was expensive to initiate and carry through, and the people who created it were paid substantial salaries. Dr. Short was receiving $7,500 a year as Director of the department, and Dr. Tapper, at first a half-time department employee, became full time in September 1921 and received a $7,200 salary.[23] Dr. D. Walter Morton, who was later at Penney Farms, was on the staff, and Dr. Harold Whitehead, department head of Sales Relations at Boston University, served as a consultant.

The Educational Department, later called Education and Research Department, made its first report to the Board of Directors on February 21, 1921, and the first lesson of the "Business Training Course" was sent to associates March 4, 1921.[24] Titled "The Unfolding of Business," it contained a foreword giving the Course's purpose, and a brief section on how to study. In the Foreword, Dr. Short stated:

> One objective has inspired this work—that all our Associates may become efficiently trained Salesmen, Merchandising Experts and Business Partners; that they may fit themselves for the larger positions of trust and responsibility in our Organization.[25]

Both Penney and Dr. Sheldon had "read, constructively criticized and unqualifiedly approved" of the lessons.[26] Short urged planning a study schedule, and lessons were deliberately made pocket-sized to be easily carried.

Lesson I contained a twenty-one page history of commerce's development from primitive man to the chain store. Advantages and disadvantages of each phase, such as the department store and mail-order catalog, were listed. No disadvantages of chain stores were listed, and the J.C. Penney Company's special advantages were proudly described.[27]

Booklets were shipped to store managers who handed them to store associates who wanted to enroll. Of course, the manager was expected to take the course. Answers to questions listed after each lesson were returned to managers who sent them to New York to be corrected and returned.

How was the experiment greeted? In the 1920s correspondence schools of all kinds flourished. Besides the popular Sheldon School courses, the Alexander Hamilton Institute offered a series of excellent business courses. Competition was keen, and lessons from the better known schools were concise, clear and gave important insights and practical advice on subjects ranging from letter writing to advertising to difficult accounting courses.

Self-improvement was popular in the growing population and increasingly competitive business world. In an era when a college education was equated with money and the leisure class, a certificate from an established correspondence school was a path to success for ambitious but less wealthy young men and women. Working by day and studying by night proved their determination and interest. No doubt many successful people emerged from these courses.

The J.C. Penney Company correspondence course was designed to fit its particular needs, but its standard was equal to the Sheldon and Alexander Hamilton Institute courses. Penney's high standards plus the experienced judgment of Sheldon, Tapper and Short with Morton and Whitehead, all well-educated men, assured the lessons' quality. What was amazing was the response. By August 1921 over 90 percent of the company's entire 2,500 associates, or 2,361, had enrolled for the free course. The Educational Department was flooded with answer sheets. Several employees corrected papers all day long at the Company's new office at 370 Seventh Avenue, in the heart of Manhattan's "garment district."[28]

The correspondence course promoted the all-important aims of good will and good service. In spring 1921, Salt Lake City had the largest "class" enrolled in the new business course. Manager Payne had twenty-six students. Naturally not everyone who started the seventeen-lesson program completed it, and it was not mandatory for anyone. One and a half years to two years were required to complete it, and many associates took longer. A graduation certificate and name printed on a special page, with other graduates, in *The Dynamo* were part of the honor of finishing it.

Far more significant was the knowledge and insight obtained from the lessons. They emphasized practical over theoretical information, but used psychology, positive thinking and self-analysis as well. A blend of old and new, of inspirational and scientific language, held readers' attention.

Lesson II described in detail the "Company Principles and Policies." The two foundation principles were the Golden Rule and Potential Partnership.[29] Lessons III and VIII dealt with aspects of salesmanship.

Lesson IV was devoted to "Personal Analysis" as applied to salesmanship. Aspects of personality were described and the authors explained how spiritual, mental and physical qualities were interwoven. A personality that was forceful, yet pleasing—one that attracts others—was most desirable in a salesperson. Salesmanship was "creative" and a natural expression of one's developed personality or character traits. It was important not to copy anyone else's personality, and readers were admonished "not to memorize and repeat to customers any sales talks or phrases which they may read in these Lessons or in any book on Salesmanship."[30]

Personality could be cultivated, and traits that were desirable for company associates to develop included: "activity, ambition, carefulness, cheerfulness, common sense, co-operation, courage, courtesy, economy, health, healthfulness, honesty, industry, initiative, knowledge, loyalty, lucidity, and tact." Of these traits, co-operation was most important to the progress of the company. Associates and managers had to cooperate in the stores; stores cooperated with each other and with company officials. The lesson stated, "It is clear greater results are to be obtained when all pull together." Advice on keeping a healthy body and mind was also given, and initiative was stressed as necessary for "development of executive ability."[31]

Lesson VI in the salesmanship group was on "Knowledge of Goods" but stressed service to customers as well. *The Dynamo* was cited as a good source for "up-to-the-minute information on merchandise, manufacturing processes and market conditions."[32] Every possible need of the customer regarding merchandise use and care was emphasized. Extra store service, such as being able to supply train and trolley schedules, letter and parcel post rates, a free checking service for small items, and if a customer was moving to another town (where there was a company store), that store manager should be informed so he would be ready to greet them. An ability to comment intelligently on current topics was necessary, but no gossip should be indulged in. Be cheerful, smile, exchange merchandise or give refunds promptly, and treat all customers as though they were invited guests at your home were some obvious but important points.[33]

Students were told, "the most important service we can render our customers is to sell them the best merchandise at the lowest possible prices and to show them how they can get the best use out of what they buy," yet the extra small services "cost nothing but a little time and some study" and the overall effect on the public "is splendid."[34] The company's policy "is to give customers such efficient personal service and such exceptional value for the money that they will return."[35]

An amusing but necessary section was on unwanted mannerisms that one may not be aware of. These included repetitious speech patterns, such as "Do you see what I mean?" "You bet!" and "Sure thing!" "Don't you understand me?" and continually using meaningless adjectives like "bully, fine, great or dandy." These tend to drive customers away.[36]

Mannerisms of action that were objectionable were gum chewing, candy eating or carrying a toothpick in the mouth. The lesson gave two examples illustrating the point if only we could see ourselves as others see us:

> A certain salesman in a department store used to amuse and, no doubt, irritate customers, for whenever he became interested in anything he would keep flicking the end of his nose with his forefinger. . . .
> Some salesmen feel that they must emphasize everything they say by waving the hands. One salesman had to be dismissed because he offended many customers by pointing a threatening forefinger at them, whenever he wanted to emphasize anything.[37]

Not every action was a "mannerism," but it was a "safe rule to err on the side of quiet demeanor."[38] Any peculiarity of dress which distracted attention from the merchandise was to be avoided also.

Both the obvious and not so obvious were dealt with lucidly and gave readers much to consider. The Course was not easy and concluded with Lessons IX through XVII which explained the buying procedure and need to study a community. These lessons also covered stockkeeping, business English, letter writing, thrift, personal organization and the partnership process.

The eager participation of women store associates in the course most likely influenced the directors' decision to start a "Bonus Plan" for them that November. Sales clerks, cashiers, bookkeepers and alteration experts were included. Length of service and productivity, adjusted for non-sales help, were compiled in a complicated formula. Length of service was rewarded by a percentage point per year up to ten years. Salaries were usually $70 a month for full-time sales clerks. Most stores were not in large cities and salaries, although low, were competitive with other local firms. Directors hoped the bonus would encourage loyalty and efficiency.[39]

The Dynamo, the correspondence course, and the team spirit created by most managers resulted in many long-time, satisfied women associates. Marriages and births had a special column in *The Dynamo*, and letters from women clerks describing how they made a special sale or dealt tactfully with an irate customer appeared regularly. But women did not become department managers until the 1960s and store managers until after the 1960s.

Labor questions also arose in the 1920s. Unions were struggling to survive, and what was called the "American Plan" opposed them. Many J.C. Penney Company customers were members of unions, and often stores were located in a strong union town. Just as frequently, however, they were located in a conservative agricultural community or in a town where there was strong anti-union sentiment. On March 3, 1922, the Board of Directors resolved that "the corporation maintain strict neutrality with reference to all labor questions."[40]

In early 1924, Sams stressed the need to maintain neutrality "for the reason of our wide geographical distribution of stores." He added, in this letter to a store manager who had to deal personally with a union representative:

> We have never questioned the right of people in our employ belonging to the Unions, if it is their desire to make such affiliation. Nor are we unwilling to work with the Union in matters of labor hours, opening and closing of the store and such other reasonable considerations as tend to promote our mutual well-being. In fact we are anxious to cooperate with them in these matters.
> We value highly the work Unions are doing for the improvement of labor conditions and for many of the standardizations they are seeking to establish. And in all of this

constructive work they have our best wishes and such reasonable
cooperation as we can consistently give.[41]

Projecting and checking sales figures based on community
income studies and published statistics were also important tasks for
managers. For example, it was estimated that one sixth of an
average annual income was spent on clothing, and the per capita
expenditure for shoes was $10. If a community had 10,000 members,
then there should be $100,000 worth of shoe business in the town.
If there were three stores selling shoes, J.C. Penney Company store
should have shoe sales of at least $33,333. That would be the
average volume, and the company expected to do much better due
to its prices, good quality shoes and good styles.[42]

That was just one example of how old rule-of-thumb methods
were no longer satisfactory. Accurate, mathematical gauges of
business were required. Census of children and types of customers
had to be made. Farmers' needs were much different from those of
lumbermen or miners or immigrants. In mining towns, men did
most of the buying, whereas in other areas women did 75 percent
of it. Advertisements had to vary according to communities and
shoppers.[43]

Communities could change too. Associates were urged
repeatedly to observe, study, compare and investigate. Eagerness
and enthusiasm were important, but logical reasoning and
understanding how best to serve customers' needs were stressed.
Everywhere the manager's importance was underlined. The training
course lesson on buying stated, "The manager is the keystone in the
buying arch—he must know his community and order what he
determines is desired by the customers in his community."[44] While
the buyer is the scout for new styles and novelties, the manager is
the judge of quantities, colors and sizes. Buyers, who presented
samples of merchandise at regional conventions, only ordered what
the manager specified.

During these years the manager was responsible for computing
the markup on merchandise. They were expected to earn a 10
percent net profit, which required a 25 percent to 30 percent
markup on the selling price.[45] However, as in earlier years, this
was the average. Items such as overalls, sewing threads and cotton
gloves earned them practically no profit, as did some domestic
staples, outing shoes and certain socks. As "leaders" they were

marked up only high enough to cover operating expenses and freight charges, or about 15 percent. In turn, other more profitable lines were marked up to 50 percent and higher.[46]

The New York office sent out "pocket-size Profit Charts" but specific markups were made by managers.[47] Merchandise arrived marked with its cost price so managers could determine the selling price. Turnover was essential to creating a profitable store, and it was also the manager's responsibility. Markup helped determine turnover, but selection of merchandise was equally important. At the 1924 spring conventions, one manager explained:

> A Manager can hardly expect the Turnover in his first year that he should get later on. Coming into a new community, it is natural to expect some mistakes in buying, for communities differ in the types and qualities of merchandise they demand. . . . But after he has been in a community a while, studying its needs, his mistakes in purchases ought to decrease, with a corresponding increase in his Turnover.[48]

The same manager declared:

> I do not believe that it is possible to lay down any hard and fast rules, the application of which will assure us a satisfactory Mark-Up and Turnover. Were this possible, there would be little need of having Managers at all. Retail prices could be marked in the Wholesale Department and the stores run on the cafeteria plan. Every community has its own individual characteristics and each Manager has his own problems to solve. . . .[49]

The Dynamo, Business Training Course and conventions were each vital factors in the company's personal improvement program. Besides executives, managers participated in conventions by giving talks on such subjects as markup and turnover, loyalty, standardization of forms, etc. Neither effort nor money were spared in this learning process. Exactly why was stated succinctly in the summer 1924 *Dynamo*: "This is necessary to carry on the business policy that has given the company the praiseworthy place it occupies in the commercial life of the times."[50]

In May 1924 George Bushnell spoke on "The Building of a Merchant," and said the company could not afford "to mortgage its future with incompetent men."[51] The same "man-training" theme had been stressed in his spring 1923 convention talk on "The

Creative Process in Business." He said, "What we need is the thinking, planning, creating, devising type of man who is ever seeking new combinations out of familiar things and operations and who by so doing succeeds in making service on the one hand and money on the other."[52]

This intensive training resulted in 54 new stores in 1922, bringing the total to 371. In 1923, 104 stores were opened; in 1924, 96 stores opened; and in 1925, 105 new stores opened for business.[53] Sales went from $42.8 million in 1920 to $91 million by the end of 1925 when there were 674 stores. Retained earnings grew from $2.2 million in 1920 to $9.46 million in 1925.[54] More expansion was planned as they set their sights even higher.

In 1924 several changes to the Articles of Incorporation were approved, almost all of the central departments were established and a new office building was planned. William Bushnell, Director of Employment, maintained, "Closer attention must be given to the training of the coming managers, for we must be ever mindful that the right kind of training is the strongest possible foundation on which to build for a successful future."[55] Besides the book learning, it was still on-the-job training. Practical results were wanted.

As of December 23, 1924, they began doing business as a Delaware corporation.[56] Delaware incorporation laws and inheritance taxes were less stringent than Utah's; many companies made Delaware their legal residence because of the state's accommodating laws.

Instead of two there were now four types of stock: 1) 100,000 shares of First Preferred (the 1919 issue); 2) 150,000 shares of Class A Preferred, subordinated to both First Preferred and classified common stock rights, worth $15 million, par value $100 per share; 3) 100,000 shares of classified common stock (same class numbers and par value as earlier); and 4) 100,000 shares of unclassified common stock, without nominal or par value. A seven percent dividend payable quarterly was assigned the First Preferred as earlier, while a six percent dividend payable semi-annually was assigned to Class A Preferred stock.[57]

In a complicated maneuver, stockholders who were not store managers turned in their classified common stock (which was more than one year old and whose rate of net earnings equalled at least one-half the rate of net-earnings for the entire classified stock issued as of December 31, 1924). In return they received Class A Preferred stock and cash or unclassified common equal to the dividends they would have received in 1925 on their 1924 classified common stock. Other holders of classified common stock, that is the store managers, received the Delaware corporation's classified common stock under the same class numbers and in the same amounts as they held in the Utah corporation.[58]

Problems of providing stock interests for non-managers were increasing and many former managers were now no longer directly connected with operating stores they owned interests in. A transition was occurring to company-wide stock for all stockholders. In 1927 "The New Plan" resolved remaining problems. The underlying principle of sharing in what they helped create stayed intact for all associates, however, particularly for store managers.

In 1924 the classified common stock was used:

> To preserve the benefits of the original J.C. Penney plan for individual responsibility in the management and conduct of stores and the participation of the profits and in the assumption of losses of the store with which they are personally identified and in which they are financially interested.[59]

Losses had always been the other side of the classified stock plan, and these deficits or losses naturally increased as the number of stores grew so rapidly. Individual stockholders were assessed to make up these losses, in proportion to their holdings in that particular store. Sometimes it took three years for a store to start showing a profit.[60] Although all efforts were geared to earning profits, losses were not rare.

By March 1923 the Company was in twenty-nine states, and was just beginning to move into the northeast and south. "The Solid South" was described by the company's Real Estate Department as "economically sound" and a "land of opportunity for the J.C. Penney Company plan of merchandising." As they moved into new towns and territories, the Advertising Department, functioning since 1922 and under the direction of Glen G. White, provided materials for a "campaign." They had "an unusually strong series of institutional advertisements and introductory propaganda."[61] It would make the company name familiar. The stores would then prove in person that they did have better merchandise at lower prices as well as better service than competitors.

Since January 1922 "Ad-Man Bulletins" had been sent to every store providing them with ideas and institutional materials. The "Window Display Division," created in 1923, made original displays and sent photographs of them to stores. Being in New York City gave this division of the Advertising Department the advantage of observing large retailers' displays and utilizing some of their ideas for smaller sized J.C. Penney stores.[62] Pictures of attractive fashionable merchandise arranged in modern window displays began appearing in *The Dynamo*, with the store's name and the manager's name proudly listed.

All headquarters departments had expanded greatly by 1924. The Merchandising Department had been busy. J.C. Penney Company began featuring its own brands and many were special trademarks. By June 1924 these included: Honor Brand cotton piece goods; Nation Wide cotton piece goods, sheets, pillowcases, worksuits, workshirts, overalls and children's playclothes; Big Mac workshirts, Checkers children's garters; Gentry men's and boys' ready-to-wear clothing; Gladio cotton piece goods, especially percales; H.C.S. ginghams, Kyber men's shirts and Lady-Lyke women's corsets and underwear.[63] They also had Majestic men's garters; Marathon men's hats, Pay Day overalls and workclothes; Pay Time men's and boys' workclothes; Penco cotton piece goods, sheets and pillowcases; Pen-I-Net hair nets; Waverly men's caps; Union Leader men's and boys' workclothes; Ramona cotton piece goods.[64]

By November 1924 another brand of bleached muslin had been introduced. In a single month 150,000 yards of it were sold. The buyer for Department "A" described the difference between new "Belle Isle" muslin and an older brand:

> Our Honor Bleached Muslin has what is known as a pure finish (with no dressing), while Belle Isle Bleached Muslin is slightly sized or back filled, and this gives it a substantial feel and attractive appearance, although it has a little lower count and weight.[65]

The new selection had become quite popular because it gave good value for its "very moderate price," according to the buyer.[66]

Other items such as ready-to-wear women's clothing, shoes and special brands of women's hose had J.C. Penney Company labels. Only a very large store would have all the trademark items, but most had some. Good will, control of prices, and customer convenience were reasons for the trademarks. These goods, like others with the company name label, had been made to meet certain specifications and were carefully tested for quality and, in the case of workclothes, for durability. A "Merchandise Testing Center" was developed at company headquarters about this time.[67]

By January 1925, the date of the company-wide convention in Atlantic City, there were 571 stores in 41 states.[68] They had begun calling themselves a nationwide organization in late 1922 when they had 371 stores and were on both the Atlantic and Pacific coast. But it was only after entry into the South and New England that they had complete coverage and were nationally recognized. Becoming a household name and an American institution would be accomplished by their Silver Anniversary in 1927.

Regional conventions were efficient but many managers missed the one-big-family atmosphere of the pre-1920s. Penney and the directors decided to hold a 1925 convention of all executives and managers at the oceanside resort from January 20th to the 24th. The idea was not to discuss business but rather to "listen to men who give all a broader conception of life."[69]

Certainly with Bryan and Conwell (almost eighty years old) this desire was fulfilled. There were, of course, many other speakers. Penney's speech, "The Spiritual Meaning of Business," was a history of his personal development from making money to realizing the important aspects of life. He urged his audience to develop the spiritual side of their natures.[70]

At the end of Sams' introduction, all 900 people present stood up briefly as a gesture of honor and respect to Penney. He, in turn, gave an unusual speech. He told them it would be intimate, and to illustrate the need for more than material goods in this life, he related once more the history of Kemmerer.

This time he added small details, like Berta on her hands and knees scrubbing the store floor before opening day. He had been so eager to earn money that he neglected his family. He never stopped working on Sundays or evenings or even on so-called vacations. Every one of those early years stood out clearly in his mind! Penney then said, "I am not ashamed to say that on my recent visit to Kemmerer, I stood in front of where the little old store stood—looked across the street to the little house—and cried."[71]

Berta's death at Christmas had shocked him, but he described how he went ahead with the January buying trip. Late at night, while his partners slept, he struggled with his grief. The point of the talk was to urge everyone to develop a balanced outlook on life, to become more giving instead of being selfish. It was also helpful for him to speak like this and express some long felt feelings of remorse, even some guilt, before such a large, friendly group.

Penney's personal odyssey was entwined with the company's development. His business philosophy was more thoughtful because of his sensitive personality, and he had learned that his business and personal life were bound together. No one listening to him could "stand in his shoes" but his words gave them something to consider and remember. It was a talk meant for friends and partners. In late 1924 there were 472 stockholders and 571 stores. Penney had an approximate one-third interest in 276 or 48 percent of the stores, giving him a 17.9 percent ownership of the classified common stock before the incorporation change.[72] It was still much more than anyone else's holdings. The group was unusually close due to the stock ownership plan, the need for close cooperation and the apprenticeship training for all new managers. Careful selection (only 4 percent of all applicants were hired), team spirit and the potential of partnership gave them strong morale.[73] However, changes in the pattern of trust were slowly occurring.

Before 1925 the company had never used traveling auditors. Penney told his audience how disappointed he was by their reports of losses and problems. Still, no manager was required to post bond.[74]

The modern organization remained distinctive in many ways. Selection of store locations was one. In a new publication, *Chain Store Age*, started June 1925, Glen G. White, now head of the Real Estate Department, explained how the J.C. Penney Company system differed from that of other chains that were completely controlled by a central organization. He explained:

> We are sometimes confronted with the unique problem of finding a town and a store suitable for a particular store manager rather than the more usual chain store task of finding a suitable manager for a particular store.[75]

He added:

> The success of the Penney stores has been due in a large
> measure to the personal contact with the communities which the
> managers have been able to develop. It is the policy of the
> company not only to operate successful stores but to develop
> worthy men able to contribute to the welfare of the communities
> which the stores are established to serve. It has been found that
> that policy can best be achieved in small and medium-sized
> towns where a store manager of the right kind of personality can
> soon make his store part and parcel of the community. In the
> large cities that is not so easily accomplished.[76]

White thought their kind of merchandise sold best in medium
sized towns, and as a general rule, cities of more than 25,000 were
regarded as too large to meet their requirements. However, they did
operate quite successfully in Portland, Salt Lake City and Denver,
all well over 100,000 in population. Whereas other chains would not
consider towns of less than 8,000, that was not the Penney
Company's policy. A town's surrounding territory was vital, as was
a manager's personality.[77]

He related the inner workings of his department. Eight "scouts"
investigated and reported on potential sites. Good locations were
sought, but not the most expensive ones. Proximity to a 5¢ and 10¢
store or department store had proven to be helpful. A middle of the
block site on "Main Street" was fine, but corner locations on the
same street were too expensive. More than seventy of their stores
were located in Masonic Temple buildings.[78]

White stated, "Strangely enough, until five years ago the J.C.
Penney Co. had no real estate department at all."[79] Expansion now
compelled them to be more systematic and methodical, but he
admitted:

> It is a fact significant of the inherent skill and merchandising
> judgment of our store-managers and other executives who,
> without any special training, formerly selected the sites for our
> new stores, that remarkably few of the stores we have opened in
> the years that have passed since the first Penney store . . . have
> had to be abandoned. Perhaps in some cases they have
> succeeded despite poor locations, but in the light of the
> importance which merchants place today on the proper location
> of their stores, that is hardly likely.[80]

In April 1927, the company's Silver Anniversary, 773 stores were
doing business in 45 states. By the end of the year there were 892

stores and total sales were $152 million.[81] The sales total in 1926 had been $116 million, so 1927 was a spectacular year. It was a year for reflection and prediction. Penney declared that sales of $1 billion were quite feasible in another twenty-five years.[82]

It was also a year of change. Classified common stock was replaced with company wide or unclassified common stock and six percent preferred stock, both established in 1924. The seven percent preferred stock was retired. Managers, after converting their classified stock, would receive both common and preferred stocks to equal its value and a special contract guaranteeing them a share of their store's profits, equal to its old percentage share. They were eligible to buy "expansion stock" in the company at a discount, and a retirement plan was included to provide them with two-thirds of their active earning power.[83] As could be expected, it was a complex procedure. Booklets carefully explained why and how, and stockholders approved the "New Plan" at a February 21, 1927, special meeting.[84]

There were many reasons for the change. Basically the company had become too big and too old to continue its original plan. Many managers and executives were at the age when they could become inactive, yet would still own store stock. New men becoming managers in these stores would find it difficult to obtain an interest unless an older stockholder gave up part of his interest and earning power. Expansion to larger cities, of increasing interest, meant greater risk due to larger investments. It would be better if the company as a whole would establish these stores instead of individual stockholders. The "Mother Store" system might be holding back an able man from opening a store, if other stores in its branch chain had poor results. They were considering doing business in Canada, and again company-wide resources should back that endeavor.[85]

The "New Plan" did preserve the concept of partnership or "sharing in what one helped produce" by the generous contracts. Non-managers were eligible for expansion stock as often as the Board determined, and in the 1930s a profit-sharing plan for more employees was developed.

The Board of Directors had discussed changing the classified stock plan as early as November 1922. Manager Payne, a new Board member, had missed one of the meetings and Sams informed him of their actions:

> The discussion that carried with it, to my mind, the largest degree of importance, had to do with our Organization of the future. It seems to me, and I think I am voicing the sentiment of most of the Directors, that our present plan of co-ownership of stock is not going to suffice when we are handling five hundred or more stores. We all believe that for the present, and for the past, our plan is the most ideal that we can think of. But when it begins to develop that some men become inactive, other stockholders drop out for other purposes, and when deaths begin to occur, then our troubles are going to begin.[86]

The 1924 changes had been a compromise, but they were definitely looking ahead. Hiring and expansion of business training courses proceeded. In 1924 a special course just for managers was devised, but interest in all the self-improvement projects remained strong.

As the twenty-fifth anniversary year began the company was in excellent financial shape. In 1926, dividends on the unclassified common stock, still a relatively small block of stock, were an amazing $59.61 per share. Cash dividends were declared on over 500 stores. These ranged from $500 to $21,000. The latter was for the Salt Lake City store, still under Payne's management. The Lubbock, Texas, store had an $18,000 dividend; at Breckenridge, Texas, the dividend was $15,000. Approximately $2.7 million in dividends were declared to classified stock holders in 1926.[87]

In January 1927 there were 85,200 shares of classified common stock outstanding. No more classified common stock was to be issued; however, as of January 1, 1927, it could be converted for a combination of common and preferred stocks, according to the "New Plan." All classified common stock was to be converted by December 31, 1931.[88]

Starting in April 1927 Silver Anniversary advertisements featured the company's growth and its policy of SERVICE. An institutional ad in the summer proclaimed: "GOOD VALUES ARE NOT UNUSUAL HERE. The J.C. Penney Company's idea of Service is to serve all its customers in all its 885 Stores as well as it can Every Day—At All Times." Part of an early Kemmerer ad was used to emphasize their consistent policies.[89]

A twenty-six piece set of Rogers' silverplated tableware, packaged in a silver-colored cardboard box, was sold for $5.90. This memento of their anniversary, in a simple but elegant special pattern, was designed and priced for everyday use.[90] The same ad said, "The Proof of Good Service is Constant Growth," and explained:

> The J.C. Penney Company has become a household word throughout the United States for quality in General Dry Goods, Outer-Apparel, Millinery, Corsets, Dress Accessories, Clothing, Hats, Furnishings, Footwear for the entire family, and also well-known notions at 4 cents and 8 cents. . . . Our great buying advantages and cash purchases save millions of dollars every year. These important savings are passed on to our customers in better quality at lower prices.[91]

A small paragraph at the bottom of the ad read:

> Salesmen Wanted—experienced in our lines, to train for Co-partner Store Managers, providing for the continuous growth of our Company and especially the expansion planned for 1927. Write for particulars.[92]

Obviously they did not miss an opportunity to attract potential employees, and made good use of expensive advertising.

Nationwide success brought problems as well as benefits. Continued rapid expansion in the next three years attracted strong competition from large mail-order catalog firms who had decided to open retail stores. This expansion brought them into the midst of the "chain store question" and led to increased centralized authority. It was a tribute to the leadership that the personal interest and trust so evident in the chain's early years were maintained to so great an extent.

The late 1920s were in general a period of business consolidation, and the Penney Company's acquisitions reflected this.[93] The majority of the stores they purchased, however, shared a common origin for they were the "cousin" Golden Rule Store chains that were still flourishing in the midwest and west. Their owners wanted to retire, or decided it would be beneficial to join the larger company. The J.C. Penney Company wanted to open stores in most of these towns, and do it before other competitors became established.

Between 1927 and 1929, approximately 230 stores were purchased.[94] In 1927 eight Hood-Van Engelen Golden Rule Stores were purchased along with three Samsel's Golden Rule Stores and

Golden Rule Stores at Medford and Ashland, Oregon. Also J.H. Akin's Golden Rule Store at Lewistown, Montana, and fifty F.S. Jones' Golden Rule Stores joined the company.[95] Jones was another successful Humansville merchant.

While "clearing the decks" for expansion in 1927, however, the Company had another concern to deal with. The Board of Directors resolved:

> Whereas the state of Georgia has passed a statute discriminating in the matter of taxation against chain stores, and Whereas similar legislation has been proposed in a number of different states, Resolved, counsel for the company, Messrs. Gwinn & Pell, be given full authority to take such steps and being such action as may be necessary to contest the validity and legality of the Georgia statute. . . .[96]

Chain stores of all kinds were spreading across America and independent merchants were losing trade. Jobbers and other middlemen in the distribution process were being eliminated because large chains bought directly from many manufacturers. Volume buying by chains provided lower prices and many groups began arguing this price advantage was unfair and even against the law. Independent retailers said they were being discriminated against in the matter of price, and tried to get laws through state legislatures to destroy the vast system of chains that served millions of customers.[97]

If the chain system were destroyed customers would lose access to moderately priced, good quality merchandise, food and other items. In 1927 the controversy was just beginning to heat up; it would reach a boiling point in the 1930s. Earl Sams became a nationally known spokesman for the chain stores, and gave many addresses in these years explaining how the J.C. Penney Company developed and what it was trying to accomplish.[98]

A more elaborate organizational structure was established in 1928 and 1929. The company had been divided into two divisions for spring and fall conventions. Previously they had met in six cities, but by 1928 size required eleven meeting places, and they were separated into Eastern and Western Divisions.[99] By spring 1929, they were holding conventions in fourteen cities and had created a Central Division as well. The Divisions and convention regions were evidently forerunners of a system of Districts (and later Zones) that were created after March 1928 to aid communications between the "field" and New York.[100]

In spring 1928 a representative from each of five tentatively established districts attended spring conventions in the Eastern Division to discuss their new responsibilities and were an immediate success.[101] This led to a company-wide system of District Managers by spring 1929. George Bushnell gave his view of the new officials' job:

> The most important task for these District Managers is to approach our men in the spirit of helpfulness rather than that of authority—to plan with and assist every Manager in realizing the greater possibilities in his unit of our business and, finally, to assist him whenever necessary in the upbuilding and unifying of his personnel group.[102]

With rapid expansion, a better system of checks and controls were required, yet the individual manager's initiative remained essential.[103] The number of stores had greatly increased—at the end of 1928 there were 1,023 stores and by the end of 1929 there were 1,395 stores.[104] Sales reached $209,690,000 that year, but would not be that high again until the end of 1934. However, they were well prepared for any unforeseen difficulties.

As of April 1, 1929, the Personnel Department reported the company had a total of 21,999 employees. Of these 20,478 worked in the stores; 1,213 of the latter were store managers.[105] With the exception of 100 to 150 who received a brief course in company methods because of prior managerial work in the F.S. Jones' and J.B. Byars' stores, all had risen through the company's extensive apprenticeship-business correspondence course program.

In spring 1929 three acquisitions were made that were of historic interest. The smallest had the longest, most intriguing history. It was Miss Celia Callahan's Golden Rule store in Chillicothe, Illinois. Celia inherited the store when her mother died in 1908. Tom Callahan visited Chillicothe every year and when she decided to retire, he negotiated the sale and building lease with the company.[106]

In the same location since 1889, it was also the tiny store that gave Tom Callahan his idea for a western dry goods and notion store. The Barnetts and numerous Humansville residents provided the man- and woman-power and financial backing while Chillicothe supplied Tom's idea. It was very appropriate that this small store came into the larger chain. The original Golden Rule Merchants and their "offspring" had been reunited.

The other acquisitions were the large 116-unit J.B. Byars company and six stores belonging to William Barnett and his wife. Like the F.S. Jones company, Byars men became, in most cases, Penney managers after learning company procedures. Byars' total included the recently purchased twenty stores of Lindsay and Company, also Golden Rule Stores.[107] Byars was C.H. Ramsay's protégé and had become major owner when Ramsay retired about 1916. After a store purchase, it took about six months to make it a J.C. Penney Company Store. For example, the new Chillicothe store opened in November 1929.

Penney attended Board meetings regularly and made store visits that were also "good will" tours. On these trips, he not only spoke to managers and associates and before civic organizations, but he also sized up the competition. Some trips were a little out of the ordinary! For example, in 1927 or early 1928 he brought several prize-winning Guernsey cattle with him to Portland, Oregon. Large displays of their trophies were installed in store windows in several Oregon stores. Evidently, this did increase good will and interest among the area's farmers and stock breeders.[108]

On September 10, 1929, the Board of Directors resolved "that application to be made to the New York Stock Exchange for the listing of the Common (no par value) and Preferred Stock of this corporation."[109] However, they were already listed on the "New York Curb Exchange," a forerunner of the American Stock Exchange, with both common and preferred stock as early as September 4, 1929.[110]

October 22nd was the date of their last listing on the Curb Exchange, for on October 23rd they appeared on the higher rated New York Stock Exchange. A "Nationwide Stampede to Unload," as the *New York Times* described it, was occurring just as they entered the market and went public for the first time. Stock prices slumped a reported $14 billion between October 22nd and October 29th. J.C. Penney Company common stock, which had been as high as $124-1/2 per share on the Curb Exchange earlier in the year, had dropped to $97-3/4 by October 29th.[111]

At a Board meeting that same day, the crisis was discussed, and members resolved to put in a bid to purchase shares at $87-1/2 but not to exceed $90, for up to 10,000 shares of common stock. The amount was later increased to 40,000 shares. They took this action because the crisis "may have a serious effect upon the welfare and prosperity of the stockholders of this company, and as such may result seriously to the detriment of the company itself."[112] Surplus funds of the company were used to try to reestablish a fair market price for the company's common stock. No one had any idea the stock market would continue to drop slowly but steadily for the next 32 months. Both the company and Penney were in for a period of readjustment.

It would be fair to say that the high standards set by Lew V. Day in 1920 had been met by 1929. George H. Bushnell's vision of one thousand stores had more than come true. They had not created "stumbling-blocks" to progress but stepping stones to greater success. The small town western and midwestern merchants made their dream of a nationwide institution reality by using two powerful methods: 1) placing confidence in the manager's intelligence and personality, and 2) pursuing constant improvement by studying all aspects of merchandising.

With such a "steel reinforced" structure and a foundation of old Golden Rule Store policies—time tested and previously depression-proof—Board members were guardedly optimistic as the new decade opened. The "Roaring Twenties" were left far behind; an atmosphere of national and world-wide economic uncertainty prevailed.

NOTES

1.   Lew V. Day, *The Manager: His Duties and Responsibilities* (New York: J.C. Penney Co., 1920), pp. 3-36. Note: Delivered in Salt Lake City February 6, 1920.
2.   Ibid., pp. 8-9.
3.   Ibid., p. 11.
4.   Ibid., pp. 12 13.
5.   Ibid., pp. 13, 16-17.
6.   Ibid., pp. 19-24.
7.   MBD II, 480.
8.   *Summarized Statements*, 1911-1925.
9.   Ibid.
10.   MBD II, 532-33.
11.   *Summarized Statements*, 1911-1925.
12.   JCP to Mrs. C. Woidemann, 23 June 1921, PHF III, C-4.
13.   PHF XX, Early Personnel Records.
14.   *Dynamo* 5 (December 1921): 3-4.
15.   Beasley, *Main Street Merchant*, p. 68; MBD I, 308.
16.   George H. Bushnell, *Fundamentals in the Development of Our Organization* (New York: J.C. Penney Co., 1922), p. 26.
17.   Ibid., p. 27.
18.   Ibid., pp. 10-11.
19.   Ibid., p. 23.
20.   Ibid., pp. 12-13, 33.
21.   Ibid., p. 24.
22.   Ibid., pp. 24-25.
23.   MBD II, 501, 551.
24.   MBD II, 529; *Dynamo* 5 (March 1922): 15.
25.   *Business Training Course* (New York: J.C. Penney Co., March 1921), I, Lesson I, 3. (Hereafter referred to as BTC.)
26.   Ibid.
27.   Ibid., Lesson I, 22-27.
28.   *Dynamo* 5 (August 1921): 14; 5 (July 1921): 17; 5 (May 1921): 15; MBD II, 527. The former location was 354 Fourth Avenue.
29.   BTC I, Lesson II, 32.
30.   Ibid., Lesson IV, 22, 23.
31.   Ibid., 28, 33, 35-37.
32.   Ibid., Lesson VI, 25.
33.   Ibid., 38, 39.
34.   Ibid.
35.   Ibid., Lesson V, 6.
36.   Ibid., Lesson VII, 6.
37.   Ibid., 6-7.
38.   Ibid., 7.
39.   MBD II, 554-57.
40.   Ibid., 571.

41.   ECS to W.C. Carroll, Kelso, Washington, 16 February 1924, PHF III, E-2. Note: On 5 April 1921 the Board of Directors resolved that "Sunday labor be regarded as unnecessary, and that we look upon it with disfavor, except in those extreme cases where an absolute loss would obtain," MBD II, 538.

42.   BTC, Lesson X, 27.

43.   Ibid., 35-36.

44.   Ibid., Lesson XII, 52.

45.   *Store Meeting Manual* for 1927 (New York: J.C. Penney Company, 1927), p. 53, June Men's Meeting.

46.   *Mark-Up and Turnover* (New York: J.C. Penney Company, September 1924), p. 10.

47.   Ibid., p. 13.

48.   Ibid., p. 12.

49.   Ibid.

50.   *Dynamo* 8 (July-August 1924): 10.

51.   George H. Bushnell, *The Building of a Merchant* (New York: J.C. Penney Company, 1924), p. 16.

52.   George H. Bushnell, *The Creative Process in Business* (New York: J.C. Penney Company, 1923), pp. 18-19.

53.   Beasley, *Main Street Merchant*, p. 222.

54.   *Summarized Statements*, 1911-1925.

55.   *Dynamo* 8 (October 1924): 13.

56.   MBD II, 706.

57.   Ibid., 707.

58.   Ibid.

59.   MBD I (Delaware), Article IX, 13.

60.   For example, in May 1925 deficits existed in 21 stores, MBD I, 54.

61.   A.C. Bernard, "The Solid South," *Dynamo* 8 (June 1924): 7.

62.   Jack T. Chord, "The Window Display Division," *Dynamo* 8 (October 1924), 8-9.

63.   W.H. Dannat Pell, "The Value of Trademarks to the Company," *Dynamo* 8 (June 1924): 3-4; Note: Since early 1921 the Company had been manufacturing corsets. The Crescent Corset Co. in Cortland, New York, was their only venture into manufacturing. MBD II, 527 (Utah Corporation).

64.   Pell, "Trademarks," pp. 3-4.

65.   G.H. Childs, "Belle Isle Bleached Muslin," *Dynamo* 8 (Nov. 1924): 7.

66.   Ibid.

67.   *Store Meeting Manual* (1927), p. 77; Beasley, *Main Street Merchant*, p. 170. (In 1929 a fully equipped testing laboratory was established.)

68.   *Dynamo* 8 (January 1925): back cover.

69.   Ibid., 8 (February 1925): 3.

70.   J.C. Penney, "The Spiritual Meaning of Business," *Dynamo* 8 (February 1925): 12.

71.   Ibid.

72.   G.H. Bushnell to ECS, list of all stockholders, copy to JCP, as of December 31, 1924, PHF IV, C-1.

73.   For example, see Earl C. Sams, *Reciprocity in the Business Organization* (New York: Madison Square Press, 1922).

74. Penney, "Spiritual Meaning," p. 10.

75. Glen G. White, "Picking Sites for Penney Stores," *Chain Store Age* 1, No. 2 (July 1925): 5.

76. Ibid., 5.

77. Ibid., 5-6.

78. Ibid., 7, 24.

79. Ibid., 24.

80. Ibid.

81. *Summarized Statements*, 1911-1925.

82. *Dynamo* 11 (April 1927): 3.

83. "The New Plan and Proposed Amendments to Certificate of Incorporation of J.C. Penney Company 1927" (New York: J.C. Penney Company, January 20, 1927), Exhibit "B," pp. 5-8.

84. MBD II, 249-86.

85. "The New Plan" (1927), Exhibit "A," pp. 1-4.

86. ECS to F.R. Payne, 14 November 1922, PHF III, E-2.

87. MBD II, 326-27, 338.

88. "The New Plan" (1927), p. 5.

89. PHF, Advertisement File, 1927.

90. Ibid.

91. Ibid.

92. Ibid.

93. *Owens on Business Organization*, p. 285.

94. PHF II, F-1-4.

95. MBD II, 247, 323, 374-75, 385.

96. MBD II, 388.

97. *Owens on Business Organization*, pp. 659-71.

98. PHF III, F-1, Articles by E.C. Sams, including "The Relation Between Chain Stores and Local Chambers of Commerce," Address delivered before The Annual Convention, U.S. Chamber of Commerce, Washington, D.C., 8 May 1928.

99. *Dynamo* 12 (April 1928): 15.

100. *Dynamo* 13 (May 1929), "Convention Number"; W.A. Reynolds, "The District Representatives at Convention," *Dynamo* 12 (June 1928): 3.

101. Ibid.

102. George H. Bushnell, "How We Can Make the Best Use of Our District Managers," *Dynamo* 13 (July 1929): 3.

103. Ibid.

104. Beasley, *Main Street Merchant*, p. 222.

105. *Dynamo* 13 (June 1929): 35.

106. MBD III, 575; Author's visit to Chillicothe, Ill., August 1978, and *Chillicothe Bulletin*, February-April 1929.

107. MBD III, 586, 588.

108. *Dynamo* 11 (February 1928): 13.

109. MBD III, 616.

110. *New York Times*, 4 September 1929, p. 46, listed under "New York Curb Exchange."

111. Ibid., 29 October 1929, pp. 1 and 41.

112. MBD III, 622.

A FULL BUT GROWING CIRCLE

When Penney returned to Belle Isle in early spring 1930, the *Miami Herald* described him as a "philanthropist, merchant, banker, farm developer and all-around business man."[1] A half-page photographic survey of the attractive estate was combined with a detailed description of his state-wide activities. Penney had also recently become quite interested in the University of Miami. The article, positive and admiring, was typical of others written about his life and accomplishments.[2] However, the estate where Herbert Hoover and Lou Henry Hoover rested for four weeks would soon be listed with a real estate agency. The sale of #8 Belle Isle symbolized the end of an era for Penney.

In spring 1930 many business people like Penney were optimistic despite unsettled stock market conditions. In early 1929 the company had opened its thirteen-story warehouse in St. Louis.[3] The St. Paul office and Lindeke Warner connection were ended several years earlier, but the New York City headquarters with its fourteen-story warehouse could no longer handle all the merchandise now being purchased. A record breaking 375 stores had been opened during 1929.[4]

With 25,000 employees by January 1930, the company required more centralized control.[5] Business training courses, conventions, and "apprenticeships" were not enough. The Personnel Department had been keeping "rating reports" on each potential manager ever since the 1927 reorganization.[6] A new business training course that reflected the decade's progress was issued in December 1929.[7] Salesmanship was stressed and graduates of the first course were urged to take the new one. A total of 11,081 employees had enrolled in the 1921 course and 2,246 had graduated. The Education and Research Department said it had examined 78,944 lessons![8]

The rating reports, sent in by managers every six months, were designed to standardize training. Up to the mid-twenties, store

managers used training ideas and methods that had worked well for
them, and new managers usually stayed in the "Mother Store's"
branch chain they had trained in. Now, stores followed Personnel
Department guidelines and new men could be assigned anywhere in
the company.

Although the company's growth proved "a thorough job" had
been done in the past, growth also brought changes.[9] The manager,
though, was still responsible for training and recommending men.
Lew V. Day, now director of the Personnel Department, said the
managers' guideline should be "The Golden Rule." They should
follow the example of their founder by dividing responsibilities and
giving men a "fair chance to make good."[10]

Day explained that Penney was "not afraid to choose men who
were capable or more capable in some ways than he and then he
made them responsible for the development of the business."[11]
Day, who had to consider all possibilities, warned managers:

> Before recommending a man for store management be sure he
> would be an acceptable partner to you and to our Company. Be
> sure he knows all that he should know about store management,
> merchandising, and successful store operation. Don't
> recommend him just to get rid of him. His future performance
> will reflect either favorably or unfavorably upon you.[12]

In May 1930, Day explained how the company had been built
"chiefly with MEN and IDEAS." From the beginning he said Penney
has placed "greater emphasis on the human factor in business," and
that the "secret of Mr. Penney's success is in his ability to pick the
right type of men; to pile upon their shoulders all the responsibility
they can carry; and to turn over to them absolutely and completely
the jobs they are to fill."[13]

The four factors that made a successful store manager in 1930
were almost identical to the 1920 requirements. In spring 1930, Day
said he must have 1) mercantile ability, 2) executive ability,
3) training ability, and 4) character. Diligent, regular study plus the
hard work and long hours of earlier days were necessary. Starting
salaries were low but these few years should be regarded as an
expense paid "college" course in expert retailing methods.[14]

Roy H. Ott, director of the Public Relations Department,
explained to *Dynamo* readers that increased size made creating
"good will" even more important. He emphasized the manager's vital

role in establishing friendly relations with their communities. Ott also remarked that many of Penney's dairy and farming activities had become a source of free publicity by putting the company's name in the national news. He estimated that more than 2 million lines of publicity had resulted from his projects in the last two years. Another source for earning favorable public sentiment was participation in State Fairs. Several nearby stores would pool resources to create large displays and hold "style shows."[15]

To maintain close contact with such a large number of associates, more conventions were planned. Sixteen were held from March 31 to May 5, 1930. Penney attended all of the Eastern Division meetings in Atlanta, St. Louis, Chicago, Cleveland and Philadelphia. Sams spoke at all the Central Division conventions while George Bushnell attended Western Division conventions.[16]

While in these cities, both Penney and Sams were asked to speak before many civic groups. The company enjoyed an unusual amount of "good will." Due to lack of time many of these outside requests had to be refused, but Penney did speak in Atlanta, St. Louis, Indianapolis, Springfield, La Salle, Elgin, Chicago and Philadelphia.[17] Anti-chain store sentiment and legislation did not affect Penney's and Sams' popularity.

Although laws were being passed in several states that would tax chains to death, the company's response was low key.[18] It continued to emphasize service and values for customers. As Day stated in May 1930, "It isn't the purpose and it isn't the desire for our organization to embarass or to destroy the independent merchant. Our job is to serve well a community through our plan of economic distribution."[19] Sams became a recognized national spokesman for the chains, and Penney gave radio talks, such as one in July 1930 that was broadcast on thirty-six stations.[20] The chain stores' economic contributions were stressed. At the same time the nation's economy was in increasing trouble.

In early April 1930 the editorial page of *The Dynamo* quoted a source on the economy. It stated: ". . . the downward trend of commodity prices since January 1 proved to be a greater factor than anticipated."[21] The continued downward price trend resulted in a company-wide "readjustment" or clearance of merchandise that July. It was necessary to reduce inventories of merchandise purchased at earlier higher prices. Managers, "first men" and sales clerks were cautioned to "avoid all appearance of a cheap bargain sale." "Big Values" was to be their theme.[22]

After the readjustment, actually similar to one undertaken during the 1920-1921 recession, the company quickly adapted to depression conditions. They could purchase goods at lower prices and attract customers with even better values. Their long established cash and carry policy was a strong factor in their quick recovery. They also cooperated with National Recovery Administration (NRA) guidelines for retailers. Although sales totals declined for several years, profits began to increase and by the end of 1934 were higher than in 1929.[23]

Annual Reports with Sams' careful explanations of business factors and trends reveal how well positioned the company was. For example, sales in 1930 were nearly $17 million less than in 1929 and profits were just over $4 million less. However, they had taken full depreciation on inventory, adjusted selling prices as replacement costs were reduced, paid the common stock dividend for 1929 and distributed 1930 dividends in quarterly payments during 1930. Sams reassured stockholders with the following statistics:

> Cash on hand and in banks at the close of business in 1930 totaled $12,270,083.07, which is substantially higher than any other year in the history of the Company. The ratio of our current assets to current liabilities at the end of 1930 was in the proportion of 12 to 1. During 1930 we have focused attention to a large degree on reduction of general operating costs. The full advantage of operating cost revisions could not be applied against the entire twelve months of 1930, but we find ourselves at the start of 1931 in a position to apply these savings against operations for this year. Your Company is in a strong financial position, ready to take full advantage of the present low commodity prices, and with the added advantage of having adjusted merchandise stocks to a position where any necessary future inventory write offs will be reduced to a minimum. The business of your Company, being nation-wide in scope, with 1452 separate retail units, is geographically diversified, and not dependent to a vital degree on the opportunities offered by any particular section of the country.[24]

In 1931 sales dropped by $19 million, reflecting the recession in prices, but net profits after Preferred dividends and common stock dividends had risen to $7.7 million from 1930's net profits of $7.1 million. Cash on hand and invested in U.S. Treasury bonds was

$13.7 million. Inventory on hand was kept higher than in 1930 "to maintain through to the end of the present period the good will of our trade which has been steadily built during the last 30 years."[25] No "extensive program" of expansion was planned, but the Board was accepting leases for new locations that would be advantageous in the future.

While sales decreased in 1932, costs were declining and sales per unit had increased. Profits after preferred stock dividends were down to $3.9 million, or $25.51 per share on preferred stock outstanding and $1.57 on common stock issued. Reductions in cost of merchandise sold were continuing; they decided to adjust the book values of fixed property carried by the company which would lower operating costs in future years. However, with cash on hand in the banks equalling $22.8 million, the Board of Directors decided:

> That such an amount of cash was in excess of that conservatively needed for contemplated operations. It was therefore decided after consideration of the various opportunities afforded to purchase for retirement a portion of the Company's 6% Preferred Stock.[26]

By purchasing 96,000 shares at $103 a share, annual dividend charges were reduced by about $576,000. After this purchase, the company's ratio of current assets to current liabilities was approximately ten to one.[27]

Despite this financial strength, the price of the company's common stock on the New York Stock Exchange continued to decline. As its sale value declined so did the worth of the collateral Penney had given five banks. In June 1930 when the Bank of Bay Biscayne closed, J.C. Penney Company common stock was selling for $63.50; in December 1930, when City National Bank closed, the stock was selling for $30.50. As recently as October 1929 it had been selling for $110.00 per share.[28]

The value of Penney's collateral, 385,200 shares of common stock, began to equal the $7 to $8 million he had borrowed from New York banks for J.C. Penney-Gwinn Corporation projects and his other projects. Once it reached these amounts and became less valuable than the loans, bank nominees took control of his collateral and could sell it to recover the loan amounts.[29]

When City National Bank had heavy withdrawals December 19th and 20th, the Board of Directors of the bank voted not to open its doors Monday morning December 22, 1930. "Malicious rumors," it was felt, had caused these withdrawals. Depositors' funds were considered safe and the closing was to assure an "orderly liquidation in the interests of all the depositors and stockholders." Reorganization was a possibility as well.[30] By December 25th the bank was in the hands of federal official H.J. Spurway, receiver of insolvent national banks. The preceding day an explanation had been given for the bank's closing:

> Failure of the City National Bank in Miami to open Monday was placed directly on the refusal of J.C. Penney and his associates in New York to further support the institution, in a statement issued yesterday by N. Vernon Hawthorne, state's attorney, after a conference of more than four hours with Hugh H. Gordon, Jr., president of the bank.[31]

Penney's statements in April and June 1930 were cited as evidence that he was fully committed to supplying needed funds to the bank. On December 24th, the bank president said:

> . . . on last Friday when he noticed heavy withdrawals from the bank he caused to be communicated to Mr. Gwinn in New York the situation and requested that sufficient money be placed in the Federal Reserve Bank in Atlanta Saturday morning to meet this emergency, and was told that the matter would be looked after. He said that Saturday morning when he learned that the money had not been so placed in Atlanta he again tried to get in touch with Mr. Gwinn by telephone and failing immediately called Mr. Penney who advised him that the matter had not been called to his attention and that there was no reason why the money should not have been placed there. Mr. Penney informed Mr. Gordon that he would immediately talk to Mr. Gwinn and call the Miami banking officials later in the day. Mr. Gordon says that much to the great surprise of himself and other officers of the bank, later in the same day he was advised by both Mr. Penney and Mr. Gwinn that they would not comply with the request to meet the financial emergency by furnishing further funds.[32]

When Penney's stock collateral fell in value and almost equalled his outstanding loans, bank officers in New York refused further loans. Penney had no way to raise the money needed by the Florida bank. The situation became worse as stock market prices declined throughout 1931 and 1932. In a futile attempt to refinance his loans in June 1932, he described the situation as "an unnecessary catastrophe." It was, too, for the stock market price of $13 to $16 a share in no way reflected the intrinsic value of company stock.

Penney had no control over "this most perplexing problem" after August 1932. Two banks sold him out completely, another wanted to sell part of his collateral. Chemical Bank and National City Bank of New York were willing to wait, and he was most appreciative of their confidence. Between December 1930 and July 1932, Penney had to watch his personal fortune and personal reputation, due to the Florida bank closing, suffer almost irreparable damage. By December 1931, he was on the verge of a nervous breakdown.[33]

He attended Board meetings regularly and continued the convention and "good will" trips, but by the time he reached Battle Creek, Michigan, in early December 1931, a severe mental depression had set in and he had a bad case of the skin disease shingles. While on yearly store visits, a brief stopover at the Kellogg Sanitarium at Battle Creek had become routine. A former Hamilton schoolmate, Dr. Elmer Eggleston, would check his physical condition and send him on his way. On this visit the doctor insisted he check in and rest for some time.[34]

Nervous and unable to sleep very well, Penney was walking the sanitarium halls very early one morning when he heard a small group of patients praying and singing in a chapel. They were singing hymns he had not heard since he was a child in Hamilton. The words, "God will take care of you," drew him into the little sanctuary. Here, he asked God to help him, and what occurred next was so personally dramatic he liked to call it a miracle. He felt as though a heavy burden, all his fears and worries, had been immediately lifted from his shoulders.[35]

Although the worst, financially speaking, was yet to come, Penney's self-confidence and optimism returned. His health also returned and the doctor agreed he could leave to be with his family for Christmas. The Penney family now included a second daughter, Carol Marie, who was born in April 1930. Penney was back working in the New York office by December 31st.[36]

As 1932 opened, difficult decisions had to be made. Money was no longer available to continue to support Memorial Home Community, the Agricultural Institute and other ventures related to the model farm community. Nor could he continue to underwrite, through the Foundation, all the expenses of *Christian Herald*. His assets, chiefly his common and preferred stock, were tied up in the banks. An expensive life insurance policy was cashed in to raise some money, and he drew a salary from the Company for the first time since 1909.[37]

Loans received from three good friends helped him buy back some of the company's common stock that began flooding the market after June 1932. Wilk Hyer, Mary Hess, the widow of Arthur Lee Hess, Berta's younger brother who had died in 1929, and Herbert Penney each loaned him $52,000 without requiring any collateral. After three years he stopped taking the salary, and although he never owned as much stock as before 1932, by 1940 Penney had 51,193 shares of common stock.[38]

Store visits, plus careful observation of retail store competition from Sears, Roebuck and Co. and Montgomery Ward & Co., articles and talks on business, religion and ethics occupied his time during the 1930s.[39]

A suit brought by depositors in City National Bank was finally resolved in 1941. At that time a Federal judge reversed a "special master's" 1940 report, which had concluded Penney "did not violate either the National Banking Act or the Federal Reserve Act," and held Penney liable for the depositors' losses.[40] The *Miami Herald* summed up the Judge's decision as follows:

> Penney, he held, was "grossly negligent" as chairman of a board "most of the directors" of which were "mere dummies." The court made it clear that, no matter how well-intentioned were the acts of directors not qualified to serve, Penney was responsible for losses because he permitted them to serve.[41]

The directors were not bona fide because their $1,000 worth of qualifying bank stock was actually owned by Penney, and thus they had not complied with national banking law requirements.[42]

The reversal shocked Penney. His lawyers were willing to appeal the case, and after a series of negotiations a settlement of $1.5 million was reached. Penney, through the J.C. Penney-Gwinn Corporation and the Tarrier Corporation, had contributed $3 million to the bank between 1928 and 1930. This money was gone, and Penney now had to pay more for his confidence in Florida. It was many years before he wanted to return to the city he had once been so enthusiastic about.[43]

The Penney Farms farm cooperative disappeared, but Memorial Home Community was able to support itself. It received a quit-claim deed in 1932, and with strict economy survived some difficult years. Foremost Dairies Products, Inc. was reorganized by Paul Reinhold, who also purchased most of the Clay County land of the J.C. Penney-Gwinn Corporation. The J.C. Penney Foundation curtailed its activities, but did not close.[44] Penney's great interest in livestock continued. In the late 1930s he began buying the "Home Place" farm outside Hamilton, and Emmadine Farm was thriving. After 1932, Penney was much more cautious about money, and devoted more of himself personally to "Christian" movements such as Laymen's Movement for a Christian World.

The success of the company in 1934 and 1935 was impressive. Reports showed a net profit in 1934, after preferred dividends, of $16.1 million, up from $14.2 million in 1933, and up from $3.9 million for 1932.[45] The growth in profits was due to increased efficiency, increased sales and retirement of the preferred stock.

Changes continued to occur. A six-story company store, their seventh department store sized outlet, was opened in Seattle, Washington, in August 1931.[46] After February 1931, managers no longer computed their store's markup. From now on "proper mark-up and mark-down figures" were the responsibility of the New York office.[47] Managers were still the men on the "firing-line," however, and "Man-Training" was a vital part of their responsibilities.

In March 1932 Penney wrote a two-part article for *The Dynamo* on this important subject. "Man-training," he declared,

> is, more than any other one factor the basis of the success of the J.C. Penney Company. In the past our Company has come ahead almost solely through its ability to train men. That was the one condition under which new stores were opened. . . . In the future it will be the basis on which further new stores are opened and increasing development founded.[48]

In late 1933 Penney went on another of his combination store visits, good will and convention trips. He visited Kemmerer for the first time in several years. Wyoming newspapers proclaimed: "A MERCHANT PRINCE WITH WORLD WIDE FAME WILL

VISIT HIS OLD HOME TOWN," and said that "Memories Recall Humble Beginning."[49]

Here he first practiced, as a merchant, the "Golden Rule" policies of his mentors and made them his own. Here he dreamed of a chain of stores to cover the mountain states, and when he and Berta, Roswell and J.C., Jr., left Kemmerer in June 1909, people were already saying he would be a millionaire. The giant chain of over 1,400 stores was definitely the product of his Kemmerer dream.

One mentor, Guy Johnson, had died in 1927—soon after selling his chain of twenty stores to the company—but Tom Callahan and Penney remained close. In 1931 Callahan wrote an article for *The Dynamo* about Penney. He stated, "Mr. Penney's habit of using every good business idea which is better than his own, immediately and instantly, is one of the principal reasons for his success." Callahan noted that most people will not accept others' ideas.[50]

Study, observation, investigation and analysis were the foundation of Penney's success, and he made them company policies. He was neither a "Merchant Prince" nor "benevolent tyrant." Penney was what those who worked with him during these years would later say, the smartest man they ever met.[51]

Penney's greatest strength was astute management. He was a merchandising genius and a determined leader who saw his goal clearly and the means needed to reach it. He readily discarded old ideas for better ones and was eager to "choose men as capable or more capable in some ways than he" for the growing company.

The rise of the company from its Kemmerer origins proves that Penney was a risk-taker. Each new store he opened was in a sense a gamble on the new manager and his business acumen. Failures in the early days would have ruined their credit ratings. It would have been easier to proceed more slowly than they did. As late as 1931 Penney was telling conventions and *Dynamo* readers that "We have not begun to tap our vast resources of unlimited possibilities."[52]

Both the company's evolution and Penney's life reflect many of the changes America experienced between 1875 and 1935. The transformation from a self-supporting rural, agricultural economy to a consumer-oriented, urban, industrial economy was the most obvious and significant change, and it had occurred within the lifetime of many people. Yet these changes did not guarantee business success, for thousands of companies disappeared in recessions and depressions.

Penney's character was a blend of heredity, childhood experiences and observation. He was conservative in that he maintained traditional values of hard work and believed in "progress" and religious precepts. These were products of the late-nineteenth-century culture and values stressed by his parents and high school teachers.

He followed his father's teaching on Prohibition, but he was also influenced by his father's example as a liberal thinker and political leader. Reverend Penney was a risk-taker—he sacrificed his health to support Populist principles and he sacrificed his Log Creek Church affiliation when he developed more modern views. The son valued money very highly and yet believed money should be used for creative purposes.

Penney's experiences between 1930 and 1932 changed his character to an extent and made him much more aware of the strength obtained through faith. Despite his previous close ties to ministers and church-related philanthropies, after 1931 Penney realized he had to have more faith and give more of himself personally, rather than rely on money to show his beliefs.

He had always been sensitive to the needs of others. From its founding the company had relied on close, personal relationships. Penney's faith in people, with few exceptions, was amply rewarded. Under his leadership, the company's emphasis on partnerships and profit sharing, on employee training, and on cooperation and communication gave the chain amazing inner resources. Their low-priced quality merchandise was always popular and, although the term "service" was no doubt overused by many businesses in the late 1920s, the J.C. Penney Company's system of efficient mass distribution did contribute to raising the nation's standard of living.

When the Great Depression arrived with its paradoxical mixture of over-capacity and unfilled demand, Penney saw the problem as one that proper distribution could solve. In a 1931 business autobiography he declared:

> Distribution is today an international problem. It cannot be solved by revolution or by force of arms. It can be solved only by the persistent application of scientific intelligence sustained by the spirit and practice of the partnership idea.[53]

It was typical of Penney to think in such wide-sweeping terms. If he had not done this as a young man in Kemmerer and persisted in it, the giant chain would have remained just a dream. Of course, all his dreams did not succeed as well as the nationwide chain of department stores, but he tried to improve inequitable conditions he saw and was willing to commit vast amounts of money to implement his projects.

After December 1931, he returned to the faith of his ancestors. They had never questioned God's will and were constantly preaching God's words to their neighbors. When Penney assumed personal involvement in movements like Laymen's Movement for a Christian World he had actually traveled full circle back to his heritage as the son, grandson and great-grandson of preachers. Ethics in business and high standards had always been his principles, and he continued to promote his special views on business and religion, on sharing profits and public service until his death on February 12, 1971.[54]

He became famous not only nationally but also world-wide. Awards and honors came, but he always liked to return to Hamilton and visit his Caldwell County farms. Here he was at home. In New York, he proceeded to work, write and lecture in his independent, self-confident manner, although he was now tempered by experience. Store visits continued unabated.

The nationwide institution he founded thrived; its success was a tribute to his genius and leadership development skills, and to the many associates he insisted on giving credit to. In 1935 he had thirty-five more years filled with joys and sorrows ahead of him, but he now had an additional source of strength from faith in God—the same faith held by his proud ancestors.

NOTES

1. *Miami Herald*, "Chain Store Founder Spends Winters," p. 7B, 30 March 1930, PHF VII, D-1.
2. Ibid., clippings, magazine articles.
3. *Dynamo* 13 (August 1929): 10.
4. Ibid. (January 1930): 9.
5. Ibid.
6. Ibid. (October 1929): 27.
7. Ibid. (December 1929): 18.
8. Ibid. (November 1929): 15.
9. Ibid. (October 1929): 27.
10. Ibid. (May 1929): 9.
11. Ibid.
12. Ibid.
13. Ibid. 14 (May 1930): 5.
14. Ibid., 6-7.
15. Ibid., 13 (April 1929): 6.
16. Ibid., 14 (April 1930): 15.
17. Ibid. (May 1930): 19.
18. Ibid.
19. Ibid., 6.
20. *Chain Store Age* 6, No. 7 (July 1930): 73.
21. *Dynamo* 14 (April 1930): 8.
22. Ibid., 3.
23. *Annual Reports* 1929-1935, PHF IV, H-1. *Kemmerer, Wyoming Gazette*, 17 November 1933, PHF I, D-2.
24. *Annual Report* 1930, PHF IV, H-1.
25. *Annual Report* 1931.
26. *Annual Report* 1932.
27. Ibid.
28. *Miami Herald*, 11 June 1930, p. 12; *New York Times*, 22 December 1930, p. 29; *New York Times*, 4 September 1929, p. 46.
29. JCP to W. Kemper, June 1932, PHF V, G-1.
30. *Miami Herald*, 22 December 1930, p. 1, col. 8; ibid., 25 December 1930, p. 1, col. 1.
31. Ibid., 24 December 1930, p. 1, col. 8; p. 5, col. 1.
32. Ibid.
33. JCP to W. Kemper, June 1932, and JCP to C.L. Rood, 17 August 1932, PHF V, G-1; Penney, *View from the Ninth Decade*, p. 118.
34. 1931 Diary, 4 December 1931, PHF IX, E-Diaries; Penney, *View from the Ninth Decade*, p. 121-23.
35. Penney, *View from the Ninth Decade*, pp. 121-23.
36. 1931 Diary, 22 December 1931, 31 December 1931.
37. *Life More Abundant*, pp. 21-22; Penney, *Fifty Years*, p. 170.

38.   JCP to A.E. Otis, 23 January 1956, PHF X, G-1; Proxy Statement, Annual Meeting of Stockholders, 21 March 1940, PHF II, E-3.

39.   JCP to ECS, 9 November 1933, ECS to JCP, 10 November 1933, PHF II, F-3. Penney sent some of their competitors' ads to headquarters. Note: In 1928, mergers with Montgomery Ward & Co. and with Sears, Roebuck & Co. were under consideration, but were not approved. Beasley, *Main Street Merchant*, pp. 126-37.

40.   Clipping, *Women's Wear*, 4/16/40, and clipping, *Miami Herald*, c. February 1941, PHF V, G-1; see also "City National Bank in Miami vs. J.C. Penney," Harold Harper, Special Master decision and evidence, U.S. District Court, Southern District of New York, copy in PHF VI, A-1.

41.   Clipping, *Miami Herald*, c. February 1941, PHF V, G-1. Note: Total amount claimed by depositors, including interest, was $2.9 million. Special dividends totalling 40 percent of deposits had been issued in 1931 and 1934, reducing the original claim from $3.5 million to approximately $2.2 million. Interest brought their claims up to $2.9 million by 1940.

42.   Ibid.

43.   Penney, *Fifty Years*, p. 143.

44.   Penney, *View from the Ninth Decade*, pp. 116-19; Blakey, *Parade*, pp. 212, 216.

45.   *Annual Report* 1934, PHF IV, H-1.

46.   *Dynamo* 15 (September 1931): 3-4.

47.   MBD III, 801-3.

48.   *Dynamo* 15 (March 1932), 3-5.

49.   Clipping, *Kemmerer, Wyoming Gazette*, 17 November 1933, PHF I, D-2.

50.   T.M. Callahan, "Mr. Penney's Commencement Exercises," *Dynamo* 15 (April 1931): 8.

51.   Interviews with retired J.C. Penney Company managers, Author's files.

52.   *Dynamo* 15 (June 1931): 13,

53.   Penney, *Man with a Thousand Partners*, p. 215.

54.   Isadore Barmash, "J.C. Penney, Founder of Chain Stores, Dies at 95," *The New York Times Biographical Edition*, 18 February 1971, pp. 389-91.

"KING OF THE SOFT GOODS"

Between 1935 and 1957, Penney company sales increased from $225.9 million to $1.3 billion; their net income increased from $15.4 million to $49.4 million, and the number of stores increased from 1,481 to 1,694.[1] Stores continued to sell "soft" or dry goods; textiles, clothing, footwear, notions and accessories for the family and household were sold to millions of customers. The only new merchandise offerings were in housewares departments in stores opened in metropolitan areas.[2]

By 1950 the company had become the largest retail outlet in the world for blankets, sheets, textiles, work clothes, men's shirts, women's hosiery and housedresses. A typical housedress sold for $2.79 in 1949, but they sold six million of them. Its own private label brands accounted for most customer purchases. Many of the approximate 30 private brands had been introduced in the 1920s; the most popular items were Towncraft men's shirts, Town-Clad men's suits and coats, Brentwood dresses, Marathon men's hats, Nation-Wide sheets; Gaymode hosiery, Pay Day, Foremost and Super Pay Day work clothes. Private label goods were manufactured to strict specifications set by the company. Staple goods were regularly tested in the company's testing laboratory for wear, fading, shrinkage, flammability and other effects.[3]

Ever since 1935, however, Penney stores had faced increasing competition for customers from Sears, Roebuck and Company, and Montgomery Ward & Co., Inc. America's two largest mail order catalogue firms had opened retail stores after 1925 and were now located in many of the larger communities served by Penney. Their mass distribution systems meant low prices on soft goods, occasionally lower than Penney's prices. Sales figures indicate how popular their items were. Sears net sales in 1935 were $385 million, of which $243 million came from retail store sales; their net income from all sales was $21.5 million. In 1935, Montgomery Ward's net sales from its catalog and retail stores were $293 million, the largest in its history; net income was $13.5 million.[4]

Of the nationwide department store chains in 1935, only Penney did not sell "hard goods" such as furniture, refrigerators, tools, automotive supplies, paint and similar items. Penney also did not have mail order catalogs at a time when catalog sales were almost one-third of Sears and Montgomery Ward's total sales.

Besides competitive clothing prices, Sears and Montgomery Ward had credit payment plans that attracted millions of customers, who might otherwise have shopped at Penney stores. Penney had a popular "Lay Away" plan, but items could not leave the store until payments were completed. By comparison, credit plans allowed qualified customers to have items immediately. In the early 1930s, Montgomery Ward began selling clothing, which was previously a "cash merchandise" item, on their "Time Payment Plan," a credit plan. Sears began selling clothing on its credit plan to selected credit customers in the mid-1930s and to all its credit customers in 1939. By 1941, credit sales were 28.4 percent of Sears total sales, up from 16 per cent in 1935.[5]

Despite this competition, Penney's remained with its cash only policy and soft goods merchandise. Company officers concentrated on improving success proven methods to sell "quality products at the lowest possible prices." In the 1941 *Annual Report*, president Earl Sams described the company's objective as "still to offer the best possible values to the clerical worker and the skilled mechanic—the farmer and the wage earner—the home builder, and, in fact, the working man and woman of every class. These constitute the largest group of American consumers."[6]

Policies that were successful in 1902 in Kemmerer continued to provide good values in the 1940s: there were no charge accounts and no deliveries; expensive buildings and fixtures were avoided. When a new store was opened or an older store remodeled, advertisements described them as serving "people who live simply, but well." In 1941, the company slogan was: "The Penney Idea is: To serve the average American family with the merchandise it wants. . . . Every dollar buying the fullest measure of real value!"[7] An equally important company objective, Sams said in 1941, was to continue to "attract and maintain an outstanding personnel." Sharing in store profits motivated management, while competitive salaries and bonuses for non-management associates resulted in relatively low personnel turnover. There were about 40,000 full time associates in the early 1940s.[8]

Loyalty and good morale existed among managers and associates due to these personnel policies and to store managers' leadership skills. In about five percent of the stores, however, sales people became members of unions. There were approximately 88 "unionized" stores at any one time during these years and in later decades. As in the 1920s, some of these stores were in strong union towns; more frequently, though, unions were successful because store managers were either not close to their co-workers or else had not treated them in an entirely acceptable manner.[9]

In the 1930s, the company took several steps to provide for increased profit sharing and retirement security for management and non-management personnel. Company stock, called expansion stock, was sold below market value to store managers, buyers and executives after 1936. A profit sharing retirement plan for non-management associates was established in 1939 and approved by stockholders in 1940. The plan also included a compulsory retirement age of 60 for active, salaried associates, including store managers and Central Office officers and executives. However, the plan was not implemented until 1945.[10]

The chain had remained highly decentralized. Despite increasing guidelines on merchandise selection and initial price markup from the Central Office, the company's success relied on individual store manager's final judgment in these matters. But company officers, directors, and personnel department members did not rely on paperwork results to judge individual store progress. Personal visits were made to every store.

Throughout these years, J.C. Penney, Chairman of the Board, visited stores and attended company conventions and store openings. Sams, who was President, and Albert W. Hughes, who became Executive Vice President in 1943, handled day-to-day operations, but Penney was much more than a figurehead. He was a working executive, spokesman, salesman, and a newsworthy attraction. By the mid-1930s, Penney, in his sixties, had resumed a full work schedule and had a busy family life with his wife, Caroline, and two young daughters, Mary Frances and Carol Marie. Kimball was at The Hill School and entered Harvard University in 1937.

His daughters' reminiscences about their childhoods revolve around ordinary family activities and add another dimension to Penney's story. The family lived in White Plains, a community north of Manhattan, at "Whitehaven," the small estate that Penney purchased for a summer residence about 1919. Home was a large two-story white clapboard house with dormer windows. Penney retreated here after his fortune vanished in the early 1930s; he reduced expenses by closing most of the house, did without household servants, and had a garden to save money. As he reestablished some financial security, Whitehaven was restored to full use. On its 50 acres Penney kept a small herd of sheep, had riding horses, and planted crops like watermelon. The daughters had ponies and a pet doe.

Mary Frances, born in 1927, and Carol Marie, born in 1930, recalled their father's physical vitality at Whitehaven. Penney was always active; on weekends his idea of relaxing was to pick rocks out of a field and cut down weeds. With his daughters he planted watermelon, went fishing and horseback riding. The daughters would happily gather worms from manure piles for fishing expeditions.[11]

The family visited Arizona each winter, usually staying in Phoenix where Mrs. Penney's mother and other relatives lived. Penney and Berta's youngest son, J.C., Jr., had relocated to Phoenix about 1934 and became a citrus fruit grower. In winter 1936 the family stayed in Tucson, Arizona for several months, where the daughters also attended school.

They no longer stayed in Miami Beach for several reasons. Penney's Belle Isle mansion was sold in the early 1930s when his finances were at low ebb, and Penney had also lost his enthusiasm for visiting the popular city. Legal problems caused by the closing of City National Bank of Miami in 1930 continued through the 1930s and were not resolved until 1943. That year a U.S. Circuit Court of Appeals reduced the amount Penney owed bank depositors from $1.4 million plus interest and costs to $596,000 plus interest and costs. Finally, Penney could put the matter to rest.[12] During the 1930s, Penney's financial situation had slowly improved. For several years, about 1932 to 1935, he received a salary from the company for his work. Eventually purchases of company stock and holdings in other companies, such as Foremost Dairies, Inc., provided enough dividend income to maintain an increasingly comfortable lifestyle. But Penney never regained the fortune he had in the 1920s.

Penney, "The Man with a Thousand Partners," was already a legendary figure when his daughters were growing up. Strongly held principles were the basis of his "dominant yet undemanding" personality. However, the daughters did not take their father's "sermons" as seriously as they might have. Mary Frances and Carol, whose personalities and outdoor interests made them very similar to their father, even suspected Penney might have embellished some of his early history, including the famous butcher shop story. More than anything else, it was Penney's work ethic that made the strongest impression on them. His philosophy was "you worked and you achieved." Both daughters worked hard and pleased their father with their achievements, including academic honors, university degrees and careers. But Penney's competitive personality and example discouraged sons Roswell, J.C., Jr. and Kimball from following in the footsteps of their larger-than-life father.[13]

Penney was a strong believer in the virtue of thrift, said his daughters. At home, he was the same as at work; he would unknot ribbons and cords, fold up wrapping paper, and never leave a room with a light on. He was an original advocate of recycling, and reused paper bags and strings. Penney believed deeply that thrift builds character, and that no matter how much money you have, it was wrong to be wasteful.[14]

In the midst of their pleasant childhoods, however, family tragedy struck again. On June 7, 1938, J.C., Jr. died from pneumonia at age 35, after a three-day illness. He was best known as the aviation enthusiast who had introduced gliding and soaring as a sport to America in 1928. After the Great Depression, the young man whose name had been selected to honor Guy Johnson and Tom Callahan became a citrus farmer and was selling insurance when he suddenly became ill. J.C., Jr. was buried beside his mother in Mt. Olivet Cemetery, Salt Lake City.[15]

Penney's memories of Berta had remained strong all these years. During Christmas time in the 1930s, his daughters recalled Penney not joining in the festivities wholeheartedly and being a "grump." Later, they learned Christmas held sad memories for him because Berta had died on December 26th. During weekdays and on many weekends, though, Penney had no time for family activities or memories of what might have been. He was travelling across the country on company business, relying on his "boundless physical energy" to maintain a tight schedule. The constant train travel would have tired a much younger person, but Penney thrived on visiting stores, meeting associates and greeting customers. He never lost an opportunity to stand behind the counter and sell merchandise; his skill at recalling people's faces and names, even after intervals of 30 and 40 years, was astonishing.

What appeared to be straightforward store visits, however, had a more serious purpose, according to William M. ("Mil") Batten, a 1932 graduate of Ohio State University who joined the company in 1935 and was its Personnel Training Director in the early 1940s. Batten, who later became Chairman of the Board and architect of the modern J.C. Penney Company, travelled frequently with Penney before and after the war. He confirmed that visiting stores was a vital means of communication and contributed strongly to the company's success. Since the company now had stores in all 48 states, constant travelling was required of many executives. Batten's schedule consisted of trips lasting three to five weeks at a time.

Store managers, the company's "front line" in communities, were under constant scrutiny by the Central Office. The outwardly simple task of introducing associates to Penney and Batten revealed a tremendous amount of information about the store manager and the store itself. How much the manager knew about his associates indicated how interested he was in them, and what the store's level of morale was. Based on his observations from a single store visit, Penney could accurately predict if a new manager would succeed or fail. Batten said:

> Mr. Penney was a keen judge of human beings. It was like a sixth sense. I have heard and I believe it is true that he hired and released 50 men before he found Mr. Sams. I would say Mr. Penney's talent for picking people was one of his greatest talents.[16]

In late April 1940, Penney returned to Kemmerer, Wyoming, after an absence of seven years. He wanted to "refresh his memories, renew old acquaintances and mark the 38th anniversary of the company's founding." Penney spent most of the day waiting on customers in the "Mother Store" and meeting old friends. That evening, he spoke before the Kemmerer Lions Club and was made an honorary member. This trip was the first of almost 20 years of annual visits to Kemmerer and Evanston. The visits usually coincided with his attendance at annual reunions in Salt Lake City of the Utah Consistory, a statewide meeting of the Scottish Rite Freemasons, a branch of the Masonic Fraternity. Old friends who met him on these trips commented, "He is much the same individual as he was in those early days. Affluence and success have not tinged his character."[17]

Another event in 1940 turned Penney's thoughts to his early years in Colorado and Wyoming. In December 1940, Tom Callahan died in Reno, Nevada, where he had moved several years earlier from Longmont. Callahan, 82, was eulogized as the "pioneer chain store merchant of Colorado and other states," and as the person who taught many clerks, including J.C. Penney, the retailing business and then became partners with them in new stores.[18]

As the company's 40th anniversary approached it seemed to be a good time to look forward, though, instead of backwards. Steady growth in sales and profits made the new decade look full of opportunity. However, world events intervened, and America entered World War II after the bombing of Pearl Harbor on December 7, 1941. Expansion and modernization efforts were halted as the nation began its total war effort. The company's history, however, made it better prepared than some firms for the new environment. It was not difficult to select the company's anniversary theme. Appropriately, it was Penney who gave the keynote address at a company convention in April 1942. He said:

> We have chosen thrift as the theme of our 40th anniversary because it seems to us particularly timely to stress the need for our return to pioneer simplicity. . . . Now in wartime, because of the tremendous job ahead of us, we must learn again to work hard and to live simply—to put into the preserving of America what we once put into the building of it—to return to the old ways of thrift and savings that were the general rule at the beginning of this century.
>
> We feel that the Penney company is well equipped to make a substantial contribution toward the thrift and savings of the nation—because the Penney company knows from long experience what thrift is all about. Thrift is nothing new to the Penney company—it is our stock in trade. . . . Our first little store in Kemmerer, Wyoming, was dedicated to thrift, and all through the years, as our business has grown, thrift has continued to be our guiding principle.[19]

As World War II opened, company officers and directors had good reason to be proud of their progress during the 1930s. At the end of 1941, there were 1,605 stores, an increase of 124 since 1935 including 19 in 1940; 171 stores had been modernized during 1940 as well. Sales had grown to $377.5 million, and net income was a solid $17.1 million. The company paid dividends of $5.00 per share on the 2.7 million common shares outstanding in 1940 and 1941, and maintained this dividend level throughout the war. Common stock was the company's only outstanding security.[20] However, the company, since it was classified as a nonessential industry, began losing thousands of personnel to the defense effort in 1942. Only workers in war industries, agriculture, the clergy, and hardship cases could be deferred from the military draft, which included men from ages 18 to 38. Like other retailers, the company was also affected by merchandise scarcities and new government regulations. Merchandise scarcity was reflected in the company's inventory levels. By the end of 1942, its year end inventory level had declined $23 million from 1941; it increased by $21 million in 1943, only to decline by $10 million in 1944. Staple goods, including work clothes, sheets and blankets for military personnel, were purchased by the government from manufacturers, leaving smaller quantities available to retailers. In 1943, shoes joined the list of items that were rationed and only limited amounts could be purchased. Maintaining records of the company's compliance with the Office of Price Administration controls, War Production Board regulations and wage stabilization rules added even more work to Central Office and individual store operations.[21]

At the end of 1942, there were over 3,200 associates serving in the Armed Forces; of these 41 were store managers. As in World War I, the company supplemented military salaries with quarterly checks and also forwarded the new company magazine, *Pay Day*, to them. By the end of 1944, there were 5,529 associates serving in the military, including 97 store managers and 390 Central Office associates. Women assumed increased responsibilities in the stores as they replaced men who had been department managers. Women associates were praised by Penney and Sams for their skill and dedication. During the war, Sams said, "Penney women have kept the company in business," explaining that "hundreds of our stores do not have a single trained Penney man besides the manager. Women are writing orders, trimming windows, making show cards, keeping stores clean, selling most of the merchandise, doing every job in the stores." In a speech after the war, Penney said, "it was the women who really kept our stores going throughout the war years. We had over 5,000 men in service—and women did men's jobs and did them well!"[22] After the war, though, men who served in the military were entitled by law to return to their prewar positions, and women returned to their traditional non-management jobs in companies like Penney and elsewhere.

Officers and directors saw the company's role in wartime as helping maintain citizens' morale and being "quartermasters to the civilian population." Fashion was still important and restrictions on materials resulted in new styles for women. Skirts and coats were made shorter; sleeveless dresses and smaller hats became popular; cotton and rayon stockings replaced silk stockings. Besides selling apparel and staple goods, stores were active in the war effort in their communities. The U.S. Treasury Department gave special recognition to the Penney Company for selling over $8 million in War Bonds in July 1942; this was the best record for the year 1942 among the retail industry. In 1943, sales of War Stamps and Bonds to customers and associates in their 1,610 stores and Central Office totaled almost $75 million. That same year, several hundred store managers joined local rationing, draft and price panel boards, and about 600 managers assisted in salvage drives and other defense work. As in the 1920s, managers were encouraged by the Central Office to assume leadership roles in their communities. As a result almost 20 percent of all managers were either current or past presidents of their local Chambers of Commerce or Merchants Associations in the 1940s.[23]

Staffing their stores was difficult due to the labor shortage, and many women went to work in defense related industries. However, competitive salaries and benefits, which were available to the majority of associates, helped retain and attract workers. Benefits for sales associates included paid vacations, sick leave, free death benefits, bonus payments and the opportunity to participate in the company's Thrift and Profit Sharing Retirement Plan. Profit sharing proved its value as store managers achieved solid results with the help of women associates.[24]

Financial results told the story best. In 1942, when there were 1,611 stores, sales were a record $490 million and there was an $18 million net income. Sales fell slightly in 1943 due to a combination of shortages and store closings. 1944 became the first year in the company's history that sales exceeded one half billion. By 1945, although there were nine fewer stores than in 1942, sales had increased to a record $549 million. Net income in 1945 of $17.4 million was less than three years earlier, but taxes were almost $8 million more than in 1942. Income figures soon rebounded. At the end of 1945, stockholders, who numbered about 20,000, evidently approved of the company's progress and voted in favor of a stock split of two for one. The outstanding common shares were increased from 2.7 million to 8.2 million.[25]

During the war the company's ratio of current assets to current liabilities was approximately two to one. In 1943 cash on hand and in banks was $60 million and an additional $10 million was held in short term government securities. The company's "strong liquid financial position" was seen as essential to their future. Cash reassured stockholders and gave company officers a degree of flexibility and confidence during uncertain business conditions. There were no outstanding bank loans, notes or preferred stock; there was not even a category for long term debt on its balance sheet from at least 1940 to the 1960s.[26]

Penney and Central Office personnel continued visiting stores during the war to monitor business and boost morale. During the month of May 1942, District Manager Maurice J. Wright travelled with Penney visiting stores in Utah, Wyoming and Idaho. Wright, who said Penney "loved stock work," had previously managed the company's Evanston, Wyoming store, where he met many customers who recalled Penney working as a salesman for Guy Johnson and Tom Callahan. One news report of Penney's May 1945 visit to the Kemmerer store also summarized his family's activities. The family circle was scattered due to the war and school: Mrs. Penney, who was doing volunteer work for the Navy League in New York City, said she was looking forward to visiting Kemmerer after the war; Kimball, 25, was a Navy lieutenant serving in the Pacific where he was in charge of an LMS landing boat; Roswell, 44, was managing a 220,000 acre farm for his father in Florida; Mary Frances, 18, was majoring in chemical engineering at Massachusetts Institute of Technology in Boston, and Carol Marie, 15, attended Foxcroft, a boarding school near Middleburg, Virginia.[27]

After the war, Penney, 70 years old in 1945, maintained his busy schedule of visiting stores, attending company conventions, and store openings. His daughter Mary Frances described a store meeting in the Washington, D.C. area that she attended with her father. Early in the morning before the new store opened to the public, Penney stood in the center of a group of associates and gave them a "pep" talk. He was like a coach, telling each associate "you can do it." Talks to associates were given without notes, and he liked to make his point by using analogies like "the profit is in the last shirt in the box."[28] Penney's speaking style was effective; his voice was distinctive and, by including personal anecdotes, he held the attention of audiences ranging from store meetings to company conventions. Now a wider arena was opening for him through the medium of lectures to the public, articles and books. Penney became a popular speaker at civic and religious organizations.

By the mid-1940s, Penney's life had returned to the pattern established in the 1920s. Materially, it was on a smaller scale, while spiritually, he saw it as being on a larger scale. Interests such as dairy farming, education and youth were now supplemented by a desire to reach a wider audience with his views on religion and business. At this time Emmadine Farm in Dutchess County, which he had purchased in 1921, was home to Penney's Foremost Guernsey dairy herd; by 1945, he also owned eight smaller farms in Caldwell County, Missouri; five of these were operated as partnerships with local farmers. He also held an interest in Foremost Dairies, Inc. which owned properties near Penney Farms in Florida. A new interest, the Laymen's Movement for a Christian World, an international nonsectarian association of businessmen, and an older one, the Christian Herald Association, were the main beneficiaries of his philanthropy. In 1946, Penney was on the board of directors of both the Laymen's Movement for a Christian World and Allied Youth, Inc., and he was on the board of managers of the Y.M.C.A. schools.[29]

Penney's title became Honorary Chairman of the Board in April 1946 when Sams became Chairman of the Board, and Albert Hughes was promoted to President. But the new titles did not signal a change of direction, nor did it mean Sams and Penney cared less about the company's progress. Sams, 62 years old, said he was looking forward to continuing his service as a director. The

company's 1946 *Annual Report* reassured stockholders that no
drastic changes in the company were under consideration. The
problem was no one could predict how the economy would react to
pent-up consumer demand and the return of millions of military
personnel to civilian life. After World War I, there had been a
serious business recession, and Penney Company officers
remembered it as the only year, prior to the Great Depression, that
the company did not show an increase in earnings. Inflation was a
major concern once price controls were removed, but the company's
cash only policy was described as a deterrent to inflation and a
means of reducing expenses.[30]

While the Penney company took a middle road, its competitors,
Sears and Montgomery Ward, reacted in opposite ways.
Montgomery Ward, whose management was expecting a serious
postwar recession to lower real estate prices, did not open a single
new store between 1941 and 1956. Sears, however, saw great
opportunities for expansion and immediately began opening new
and larger stores across the country.[31]

In March 1947, over 24,000 stockholders were informed of the
Penney company's postwar direction:

> The present plans of the Company call for no radical
> developments in the type of merchandise carried. Broadly
> speaking, the selection of merchandise is controlled by the
> fundamental policies on which this business has been built: of
> selling on a cash-and-carry basis and of avoiding the expense of
> service departments necessary to the satisfactory sale and
> installation of some items.[32]

Compared to 1945 sales, 1946 sales were a record $676.6
million, an increase of $127 million over 1945, with net income of
$35.5 million, compared to $17.4 million in 1945. Stockholders
received dividends of $2.70 per share on the newly split stock, and
$13.2 million was added to the company's surplus increasing
retained earnings to $82 million. Sams proudly noted that 85
percent of the associates who were released from military duty at
the end of 1945 had returned to employment with the company by
Spring 1946. Merchandise that had been scarce was also returning
to store shelves; inventories began returning to normal levels, and
new fashions reflected peacetime conditions. More materials were
available; longer and fuller dresses and skirts appeared in stores. In

1947 the "New Look" in women's fashions by Christian Dior became popular in America, and Penney stores quickly had a low priced version of the tiny waist, full skirted dresses available for shoppers.[33]

Although one of the world's largest retail department store chains, it still had the outward appearance of a small town organization to its customers. In 1947 its 1,603 stores were solidly established on Main Streets in towns whose populations ranged from less than 1,000 to over 100,000. However, there were only 11 stores in the former and 78 in the latter; the greatest number of stores, 575, were located in towns of 2,500 to 7,500 population. By 1947 there were 50,000 full-time and more than 75,000 part-time associates serving an estimated 35 million customers.[34]

The manager's role was still all important, and it was not any easier to become a manager in the 1940s than it was in the 1920s. Batten, who had worked as a trainee from 1935 to 1940 in the Lansing, Michigan store, recalled those years, saying, "There was no leisure time. All we did was work and sleep. We worked evenings and Sundays when the store was closed. It is like joining the Marines."[35]

Between 1946 and 1950, because of these managers' hard work and an expanding economy, sales grew from $676.6 million to $949.7 million. Net income for 1950 was the highest in the company's history, $44.9 million, up from $35.5 million in 1946. A population increase starting in 1946, families moving to "suburbia," customer demand for goods after wartime rationing, and larger stores all contributed to these yearly sales increases. In summer 1950 the start of the Korean War also caused increased buying by customers fearing wartime shortages. Reflecting the growth of suburban areas across the country, a new type of Penney store was established at Hampton Village Shopping Center outside of St. Louis, Missouri. Each store at the "new drive in shopping district" was designed in a Colonial Williamsburg style. Opened in 1949, it has been generally known as the first Penney store situated off "Main Street" and the forerunner of present-day shopping mall stores. But Penney stores in suburban locations or shopping centers on the Pacific Coast had been operating successfully "for many years" according to the 1953 *Annual Report*, indicating it was a pioneer in the movement to suburban locations.[36]

The late 1940s and early 1950s were a time of increasing recognition for the company as its 50th anniversary approached, and for Penney personally. The publication of *Main Street Merchant, The Story of the J.C. Penney Company* by Norman Beasley in 1948 provided publicity for the company and Penney, especially on the East Coast where the company was not as well known. Besides describing the company's history, it was a defense of chain stores. Sams and other chain store executives remained wary of legislative efforts designed to halt the expansion of chain stores and to heavily tax nationwide chains.

The Federal Anti-Price Discrimination Act, also called the Robinson Patman Act, had become law on June 20, 1936. The new law made illegal unreasonably low prices that tended to destroy competition. It was intended to limit the price advantage chain stores received on large volume orders from manufacturers and wholesalers. Chain store executives argued that lower costs meant lower prices for customers, and chain stores attracted customers for independent merchants on "Main Street" as well. Federal legislation that would have taxed chains based on their size had been submitted by Congressman Wright Patman in 1938, but it was defeated in 1940.[37] In theory, restrictive legislation could be reintroduced, and continued good will towards chain stores was an important aim of company officers and directors.

For his part, Penney was embarked on a one-man good will campaign, outside of business hours, that contributed to the company's visibility among political as well as business and religious leaders. An honor that attracted worldwide and national attention was given to Penney when he was invited to participate in the 1949 series of Green Lectures at Westminster College in Fulton, Missouri. In 1946, Winston Churchill delivered his famous "Iron Curtain" speech at this same forum. Penney spoke on the "Significance of the Spiritual Factor in American Destiny and Development," which was consistent with his interests as well as reflecting the contemporary fight against the atheistic values of communism.[38] Not surprisingly, the topic had some elements in common with his 1893 high school graduation oration on American Progress, but it was even more similar in theme to James Cash Penney, Sr.'s graduation oration at Pleasant Ridge College in 1859.

Penney also began writing an autobiography, *Fifty Years with The Golden Rule*, and continued to produce weekly articles for *Christian Herald* magazine. The articles were later published as a book in 1956 titled *Lines of A Layman*. He was giving more talks to civic organizations and church groups. Penney's religious talks included details of his parents' lives, and his experience in the chapel at Battle Creek Sanitarium in December 1931. In 1949, Penney gave 28 talks in just 23 days in locations from Canada to Florida; his subject was "Christian Principles in Business." In 1951, he gave over 200 speeches on the topic "to love God and to love your neighbor as yourself."[39]

In retrospect, his talks were affirmations of traditional values of family and church; however, the pioneer virtue of self-reliance was not helpful unless religious faith came first. Penney's business talks always emphasized that his success came from letting people share in what they helped build. The original one-third partnership plan and its profit sharing successors were examples of The Golden Rule operating in business.

Despite his increasing fame, Penney never lost interest in Hamilton, the family's hometown, and he donated money to help build a modern high school. At the cornerstone laying ceremony at the Penney High School in October 1949, he spoke about the importance of wanting an education and said that the "will to do" is the most important factor in obtaining an education.[40] Through a new foundation he established in 1954 with his wife and children, Penney continued to provide substantial financial support to Caldwell County schools. Returning to New York from store visits in the Rocky Mountain states, Penney made stopovers in Hamilton to visit store #500. He looked at sales figures, sold merchandise and showed sales clerks how to wrap packages.

Nineteen fifty, only two years before their Golden Jubilee celebration, was an important year for the company in many respects. Ironically, one month before a *Fortune* magazine article titled "Penney's: King of the Soft Goods" appeared, one of the people most responsible for the company's preeminence died. Earl Corder Sams, who was not well known to the general public, died in New Rochelle on July 23, 1950, at age 66. Sams had been associated with the company ever since Penney hired him in 1907; he was the company's President and operating officer from 1917 to

1946. Penney once told Batten that he selected Sams to take over day-to-day operations of the company because Sams was a more prudent person than Penney. Penney believed that Sams would not jeopardize the company's future by taking the kind of big risks Penney might.[41] Considering the major risks Penney took to build the early chain and the projects he developed in the 1920s until the Great Depression halted him, this explanation appears to be accurate.

Batten, who worked on the 17th floor with Sams at the Central Office on West 34th Street in New York City, said Sams deserves more recognition for his role in managing the company. Sams was very important in the rapid growth of the company, but outside the company, most of the attention was given to Penney, said Batten. Batten remembered Sams as being "warm and friendly, and easier to relate to than Mr. Penney. Mr. Sams reached out to people more and was an easy person to be around." Although Penney made himself be an extrovert, he was a more quiet person than Sams and much more formal. Sams was highly respected by his peers in the chain store industry, and he testified on the industry's behalf before a Congressional committee. As Sams became wealthy, he became a philanthropist. He was president of the Earl C. Sams Foundation, a member of the national council of the Y.M.C.A., and a member of the Board of National Missions of the Presbyterian Church in the United States. His philanthropies included substantial gifts to New Rochelle Hospital, Boy Scouts of America, and he gave the Sams Auditorium at Wesleyan University in Salina, Kansas, in honor of his parents.[42]

Fortune magazine in September 1950, however, described the nationwide store chain as "a company that nobody runs," and said a "kind of intentional planlessness" pervaded the company's leadership.[43] But the magazine's observation was as misleading as the chain's small town image on "Main Street." The apparent openness and flexibility among top executives came from knowing that everyone in the field followed certain tenets. Individuals who became managers had been carefully trained to work and sell in the Penney way. Managers and stores were constantly monitored through visits from Central Office personnel. Maintaining communication within the far-flung chain was a Central Office priority, and training programs for all personnel were continuously updated.

One section of the 1950 article that probably interested readers more than Central Office planning or lack of it was the amount of money earned by store managers. Managers received from one-sixth to one-third of their store's net income, but actual dollar amounts were not generally known outside the company. *Fortune* reported more than one-third of all store managers earned over $15,000 annually, and it was "not uncommon" for store managers to earn between $30,000 and $50,000 annually. In 1950 the average family income in the United States was approximately $3,000, so these figures seem remarkably high. Nonetheless, they were in line with the profit sharing policy of the company. Central Office executives earned a maximum of $10,000 in salary and received a percentage of overall company profits for the rest of their earnings.[44]

In 1950, company officers and directors were pleased that their goal of being the largest store of its type in the world had been met; the title "King of the Soft Goods" was a tribute to their policies and to the hard work of tens of thousands of associates. Of the major nationwide nonfood retailers in 1950, Penney was number three; only Sears and Montgomery Ward were larger.[45] As in 1935, these firms sold hard goods, had mail order catalogs and sold on credit. Despite the Penney company's great success, however, it was inevitable that changes in fundamental policies would occur. The seeds of the new company were already planted in the postwar population growth, in the general increase in prosperity that started in the late 1940s, and within the company itself. Executives like Batten, who became an assistant to President Hughes in 1951 and Vice President in 1953, analyzed these changes and considered how the company should respond.

The same *Fortune* article described the company's founder as "vigorously active in the company's behalf," adding "his greatest triumph is the fact that the company still follows his principles, though he has not been its top executive officer for over thirty years."[46] Two good examples of Penney's efforts receiving widespread media attention were a *Life* magazine article in May 1951, and a store opening in Indiana a few months earlier. *Life*, with a circulation of over five million, recorded one of Penney's annual visits to the Kemmerer store. Although readers may not have known it, the photo story titled "Salesman Penney Sells Again" was definitely not a staged event. Penney actually failed to sell shoes to some customers, although he was successful selling other items. In February 1951, when Penney and his wife Caroline attended the opening of a new Penney store on Monument Circle in Indianapolis, it was described by shoppers as "the next thing to the Oklahoma land rush." As Penney cut the ceremonial ribbon, the governor of Indiana stood by his side; Mrs. Penney, other officials and executives surrounded Penney.[47]

Penney's 1927 goal of $1 billion in sales was reached in 1951, just on time for the start of the company's Golden Jubilee year.[48] Special sales events were held in stores across the country and the sculptor Julio Kilenyi designed a medallion to use in conjunction with the 50th anniversary celebrations. Its logo was "Growing with the Nation," and certainly with 40 million customers, one-fourth of America's entire population, shopping at Penney stores, it was an appropriate theme.[49]

April 1952 found Penney, now 77, in Kemmerer for the historic occasion. The *Kemmerer Gazette* described him as a "merchant prince, gentleman farmer and breeder of blooded stock." Penney stood behind the counter, sold goods and visited with customers for several hours during the day. Then he had lunch with local businessmen at the Kemmerer Cafe. In his informal talk to the group, he praised Berta for her hard work in the first store.[50] Penney celebrated the 50th anniversary in another way, too. In April 1952, he donated his Foremost Guernsey dairy herd, considered one of the finest purebred herds in America, and his farm properties at Emmadine Farm, Hopewell Junction, New York, to the University of Missouri. Penney's Foremost Guernsey Association, Inc. had been incorporated in 1936 to ensure its continuance. Property at Hopewell Junction was to be sold to endow the herd, which was moved to a University farm. The gift was valued at $750,000.[51]

Company sales in the Golden Jubilee year were a record $1.08 billion. But net income was $37.1 million, about $8 million less than in 1950. The primary reason for this decline was an increase in taxes. On July 1, 1950, new federal taxes on corporations and an Excess Profits Tax had gone into effect. The company's federal, state and local taxes had climbed from $49.4 million in 1950 to $64.3 million in 1952.[52]

Sales were $1.109 billion in 1953 and net income was $38.5 million. However, in 1954, when sales dropped slightly to $1.107 billion, net income rose to $43.6 million, reflecting the expiration of the Excess Profits Tax on January 1, 1954.[53] Officers and directors appeared satisfied with the results; certainly, as President Hughes commented in the *Annual Report*, "Sales of over one billion, one hundred million in cash do not just happen these days."[54] Under Hughes' direction, the company was moving forward at a steady pace by opening more stores and modernizing others. Hughes, though, realized that even more expansion was needed to keep pace with current conditions. In March 1955, he gave an optimistic forecast to stockholders about the state of the country and company, saying:

> Our country is surging with growth. Our standard of living is rising; national income is rising. Families are growing in number and size. In this atomic age, American science and industry are surpassing all past achievements. Social and technological changes are producing ever-changing patterns of taste and living. The Penney Company's plans for growth are geared to these changes and to the country's ever-quickening pace.[55]

Eighteen stores were opened in new locations and eight smaller stores had been closed during 1954. But with $133.2 million cash in banks, another $33 million in short term government securities and retained earnings of $196.3 million, company leaders decided to increase the pace of store openings. In 1955, thirty new stores were planned to open in areas not already served by the Penney company. Ohio received the most, six, and then California received five new stores. California, which already had 146 stores, and Texas with 125 stores, however, continued their longstanding record as the states with the largest number of stores.[56]

One direct effect of the increasing national prosperity noted by Hughes was more shoppers wanted to wear the latest fashions. A side effect of the new prosperity was an improvement in how goods were distributed to stores. Store managers responded to customers' interest in fashionable apparel by placing smaller, more frequent orders based on photographs of new items selected by the Central Office buyers. Company suppliers now shipped merchandise by truck or air freight to six consolidation points where items destined for stores in one area were combined; boxcars and trailers were used to provide rapid and direct deliveries. In 1953 the company closed its Manhattan warehouse, and in 1954 it closed the St. Louis warehouse.[57] These closings symbolized the end of an era dominated by trains and telegraphs, and the start of an era of increasingly rapid communications of all kinds. While officers and directors discussed what additional steps were needed to respond to the rising level of wealth, Penney was also taking steps to adjust to the new era.

With his financial status steadily improving, Penney decided to establish a new foundation to better organize his philanthropies. On September 17, 1954, the James C. Penney Foundation, Inc. was incorporated in New York State, and its directors were Penney, Caroline A. Penney, Roswell K. Penney, Mary Frances Penney Wagley and Carol Penney Guyer. At the directors' first meeting on December 9, 1954, Penney was elected president, each family member was elected a vice president, and Floyd F. Eldred was elected secretary and treasurer.[58] The new organization, which was not affiliated with the Penney Company, was not intended to duplicate the extent of the 1920s' J.C. Penney Foundation. However, organizations like Christian Herald Association, with which Penney had close ties since the mid-1920s, received annual donations for many years. As a family foundation it supported the broader interests of family members. Caroline Penney was a strong supporter of the Y.W.C.A., and gifts to this organization were among the earliest large donations made by the foundation.

Two thousand shares of common stock of Foremost Dairies, Inc. that Penney donated to the foundation were its only assets; the shares were subsequently sold to raise operating funds. The first year of gift giving was 1955, when $27,000 was donated to fifteen organizations. Of this amount, $25,000 was a gift to the Hamilton, Missouri public school district, reflecting Penney's continuing support of education in his hometown. Smaller gifts were made to religious or church affiliated groups and to health, children, civic and local charitable organizations.[59]

In 1953 and 1954, Penney received several prestigious awards in honor of his unstinting work on the company's behalf. In early January 1954, Penney received the highest honor given by the National Retail Dry Goods Association. The Tobe Award for Distinguished Contributions to American Retailing was given to Penney at the Association's annual meeting and dinner. He received the Horatio Alger Award from the American Schools and Colleges Association in 1953, and the Boston Conference on Distribution named him to its Hall of Fame in Distribution that same year. Penney was truly a living legend. But this status did not change his dedication to work and religion; instead it opened more doors for him, even in other countries.[60]

Penney's 80th birthday on September 16, 1955 was a feature picture story in *Life* magazine. "A Party for Penney" described the outdoors celebration and dinner at Whitehaven; five hundred friends, family members and business associates attended and watched Penney open presents like a golden ruler from the company and a gold wristwatch from the president of Foremost Dairies. Penney, described as a "triumphant tycoon," waltzed with Caroline, and posed for photographs with Caroline and his four children. Kimball, who was in the U.S. Naval Reserves, had come from San Francisco; Roswell had arrived from his home in Daytona, Florida; Mary Frances came from her home in Baltimore, Maryland; and Carol returned from India for the special occasion.[61]

Herbert Hoover and Bernard Baruch sent telegrams congratulating Penney on his birthday, and Thomas J. Watson, chairman of International Business Machines, was a guest along with other company executives. Flowers arrived from as far away as Hawaii and Seattle; many stores in the chain sent representatives to deliver associates' well wishes in person.[62] The lovely sunny day, filled with admiring family and friends, ended with a sit-down dinner under a huge striped canopy. It was truly a milestone for Penney. The difficult journey back to prosperity and renown from the Great Depression years of the early 1930s was completed. He had fought to make a new life for himself at age 56 and had succeeded. Now, at age 80, Penney was filled with plans not only for next year, but also for two more decades. He enjoyed excellent health and had no intention of retiring from company work.

During the next two years, the company and its stockholders were also looking forward to many healthy and happy years as national prosperity helped increase sales. In August 1956, business magazines reported national incomes were up 6.4 percent from the year before, and this figure was reflected in company sales and profits.[63] Sales increased from $1.22 billion in 1955 to $1.29 billion in 1956; net income grew from $46.1 million to $46.7

million.[64] At this same time, company officers and directors decided to expand their advertising of private label brands to better compete with nationally advertised brand merchandise. Since the 1930s, the three nationwide chains had advertised only in local newspapers and on radio stations. In 1956, however, for the first time since the 1920s, Sears, Penney and Montgomery Ward resumed advertising in national magazines. Television was also being studied as another means of reaching customers.[65]

By the mid-1950s, Penney himself had already been featured in popular magazines such as *Life* and *Readers Digest*. School children across the country read about him in *Scholastic* magazine. In fact, Penney was the company's pioneer in national mass media publicity. Appropriately, in January 1956, the company placed its first national media advertisement in *Life* magazine, whose millions of readers were familiar with Penney's first store in Kemmerer and his recent birthday. Penney also appeared on the national network television program "Masquerade Party" on November 10, 1956, and he and Caroline were interviewed on Edward R. Morrow's "Person to Person" program on May 31, 1957. Over eight million households watched "Person to Person" in 1957 and 1958. For "Masquerade Party," a quiz show, Penney was disguised as the Prisoner of Zenda with manacles and a ball and chain; he was dressed in a ruffled shirt and baggy pants. However, it is not known if the panelists correctly identified their celebrity guest as the founder of a nationwide chain of stores. The influence of television on consumers was seen in another mid-1950s TV appearance made by Penney and Caroline. Caroline told the interviewer how she had convinced a banker she met at a dinner party of the merits of the company's $2.98 men's shirts. The banker told her, "What's good enough for Mr. Penney is good enough for me," and he went out the next day and bought six of the shirts. The day after the television program was broadcast, stores across the country reported they were soon sold out of this item.[66]

In early 1956 Penney's circle of influence as a Christian layman and businessman widened considerably. He and Caroline visited the Far East for several months. They enjoyed staying with Carol and her family in New Delhi, India, and with Kimball, who had recently moved to Taiwan. Carol's husband, David Guyer, was an Assistant Liaison Officer for the United Nations Technical Assistance Board.

As a director and representative of the Laymen's Movement for a Christian World, Penney also had a full schedule of speaking engagements in India, Siam, Japan and Korea. His topic was the "Application of Christian Principles in Business," which emphasized using the Golden Rule tenet in business.[67]

After he returned, Penney resumed working full time at the company's Central Office in Manhattan where he had an office on the 18th floor. He and Caroline had recently purchased a cooperative apartment at 888 Park Avenue in Manhattan and he travelled to and from work by bus. He arrived at 8:30 and left at 4:30, unless he was out of town on company business. Penney's business trip to Tucson, Arizona for a store opening in September 1957 was a good example of his activities. After he and Caroline arrived by airplane in Tucson, they were expected to relax in the hotel suite until attending a banquet that evening to celebrate Penney's 82nd birthday. While Caroline, aptly described as "a small, sparkly woman," waited in the hotel room, however, Penney was flown by helicopter over the city to the new company store building. The next morning, after the ribbon cutting ceremony at the store, Penney stood throughout the day greeting customers and old friends.[68]

The company had become more successful because it was opening more stores in suburban shopping centers and remodeling and enlarging other stores. But its success led to a major crossroads in its history. In early fall 1957, the Board of Directors decided to change the company's most fundamental policy. A brief announcement appeared in *Business Week* in mid-September 1957 under the title "J.C. Penney Plans to Try Out Consumer Credit in a Few Stores." It said in early 1958 consumer credit would be used in a few stores on an "experimental basis."[69]

The company's observations of its market, its customers and its competitors had finally convinced officials and most directors that credit sales were necessary for continued success in the new environment. The decision was made the same year that sales and earnings were the highest in the company's history. With a record $1.3 billion in sales and $49.4 million net income, the Penney company had surpassed Montgomery Ward in sales by a small margin, and in income by a large margin. In 1956, Montgomery Ward had sales of $1.07 billion and net income of $29.7 million, but

Sears, Roebuck and Co. had moved even further ahead of its competitors with sales of $3.6 billion and net income of $161 million.[70]

The historic decision to test credit sales, made just before Penney travelled to Tucson, signalled the end of an era in American retailing. Penney's reaction to the change was very predictable: he firmly opposed it, but he accepted it as the decision of the people responsible for running the company.[71] Under the leadership of William M. Batten, the "King of the Soft Goods" aimed to become a new type of company to better serve its customers.

NOTES

1.   "Penney Sales at Record," *New York Times,* January 13, 1936, p. 24, col. 4; "J.C. Penney's Sales and Earnings in '57 Highest in Company's 56 Year History," *New York Times,* February 18, 1958, p. 41, col. 3; *Annual Report 1935,* p. 4; Beasley, *Main Street Merchant,* p. 222.

2.   *Annual Report 1946,* p. 3, "New or Additional Merchandise Lines."

3.   *Annual Report 1940,* p. 14; "Penney's: King of The Soft Goods," *Fortune,* September 1950, pp. 101, 127; *Annual Report 1953,* pp. 6-7.

4.   "Best Net Since '29 for Sears, Roebuck," *New York Times,* March 26, 1936, p. 41, col. 1.; "Montgomery Ward Clears $13,527,310," *New York Times,* March 19, 1936, p. 46, col. 1.

5.   Emmet and Jeuck, *Catalogues and Counters,* pp. 505-19. Ch. 27, "Easy Payments and Modern Homes" compares the credit plans offered by Sears and Wards and describes the growth of credit sales at Sears.

6.   *Annual Report 1941* p. 1.

7.   Ibid., pp. 1, 15.

8.   Ibid., p. 1; "The Homely Philosophy of the Man With a Thousand Partners, J.C. Penney" (New York: J.C. Penney Company, c. 1941): 20. The series of one-page articles in the 25-page booklet were based on radio talks that Penney had given every week for over a year. It is not clear exactly when these radio talks were given, and no other reference was found to Penney giving radio talks after the 1920s.

9.   Interview with William M. Batten, October 29, 1986.

10.   "Penney Stock Sale Approved," *New York Times,* November 21, 1936, p. 27, col. 4. The sale of 150,000 shares of the company's common stock to store managers, buyers and executives was voted and approved by stockholders. The shares were to be sold for cash at an unspecified below market price, and not more than 75,000 shares were to be sold in any one year.; *Annual Report 1943,* p. 3; Beasley, *Main Street Merchant,* pp. 118-119, 143-144.

11.   Interview with Carol Penney Guyer on February 28, 1986, and Interview with Mary Frances Penney Wagley on December 31, 1986. Interviews are hereafter referred to as Interviews with Penney Daughters.

12.   "Files $80,000 [sic] Bank Suit," *New York Times,* June 2, 1936, p. 41, col. 1. Note that the amount should have been $880,000; "Penney is Ordered to Meet Bank Loss," *New York Times,* February 6, 1941, p. 23, col. 4; "$2,424,300 Judgment is Entered," *New York Times,* January 31, 1942, p. 25, col. 6; "Bank Judgment Reduced," *New York Times,* March 20, 1943, p. 30, col. 3.

13.   Interviews with Penney Daughters.

14.   Ibid.

15.   "J.C. Penney Jr.," *New York Times,* June 8, 1938, p. 23, col. 2., obituary.

16.   Interview with William M. Batten, July 8, 1986.

17.   "J.C. Penney Talk on His Early Life . . . ," *Kemmerer Gazette,* May 3, 1940; "J.C. Penney was Kemmerer's Guest," *Kemmerer Gazette,* May 7, 1943.

18.   "T.M. Callahan Dies in Reno Hospital," *Longmont Times Call,* December 21, 1940, p. 1.

19. "Thrift Policies Reaffirmed on 40th Birthday of Penney Chain," *Wyoming State Tribune*, April 8, 1942.

20. *Annual Report* 1941, pp. 1, 3; *Annual Report* 1943, p. 4.

21. *Encyclopedia of American History*, pp. 380-81; *Annual Report* 1942, pp. 2-3; *Annual Report* 1943, p. 2; *Annual Report* 1944, pp. 2, 4.

22. *Annual Report* 1942, p. 4; *Annual Report* 1944, p. 3; Beasley, *Main Street Merchant*, pp. 144-45, Sams' speech; *Penney and Allied Families*, p. 84, Penney's speech.

23. Loris Gordon and Alan Gordon, *American Chronicle, Six Decades in American Life 1920-1980* (New York: Atheneum, 1987), pp. 219, 237; *Annual Report* 1943, p. 3; *Annual Report* 1942, pp. 2, 12.

24. *Annual Report* 1942, p. 5; *Annual Report* 1945, p. 5; Note that the *Annual Report* 1942 called it a "Thrift and Savings Plan."

25. *Annual Report* 1942, p. 9; *Annual Report* 1943, p. 1; *Annual Report* 1944, p. 1; *Annual Report* 1945, p. 9. Federal Income, Surtax and Excess Profit Taxes for 1942 were approximately $35 million, and approximately $43 million for 1945.

26. *Annual Reports* for 1941-1946, 1950, 1953, 1954, 1956, 1957, 1968, balance sheets and discussion of results. In 1957, the company did not even have to borrow money temporarily from outside sources because its cash position was so strong.

27. Interview and correspondence with Maurice J. Wright, August and September 1978; "Day by Day," by C. Watt Brandon, *Kemmerer Gazette*, May 4, 1945.

28. Interviews with Penney Daughters.

29. *Current Biography* (1947), p. 509, s.v. "James Cash Penney"; *Penney and Allied Families*, pp. 70, 78. Note: there is a discrepancy in sources concerning the *Current Biography* reference to Penney donating $250,000 in 1946 to Memorial Home Community as part of their $1 million fund raising effort. Histories of Memorial Home Community did not mention this contribution. However, Penney was donating smaller sums of money to Christian Herald Association, which owned Memorial Home Community, and directly to Memorial Home Community from the 1940s through the 1960s.

30. Beasley, *Main Street Merchant*, pp. 145-147; *Annual Report* 1947, pp. 2-3.

31. John A. Barr, Chairman and President, "Montgomery Ward & Co. Today," Text of Address before The Bond Club of Chicago, November 2, 1956, p. 8; Batten Interview, October 29, 1986.

32. *Annual Report* 1946, p. 3.

33. Ibid., p. 2; *Annual Report* 1945, p. 4.; *American Chronicle*, p. 264.

34. Beasley, *Main Street Merchant*, p. 169, 213.

35. Batten Interview, October 29, 1986.

36. *Annual Reports* 1946 to 1950, sales, profits and dividend figures; *JCPenney, An American Legacy*, p. 19; *Annual Report* 1953, p. 3, "Suburban Stores and Simplified Selling."

37. *Encyclopedia of American History*, p. 354; Beasley, *Main Street Merchant*, pp. 239-242.

38. Penney, *Fifty Years*, p. 214-215;

39. *Lines of A Layman*, Foreword by Daniel A. Poling; *Fortune*, September 1950, p. 102; J.C. Penney, "Faith Gave Me A New Start At 56," reprint from *Journal of Living*, November 1952, p. 4.

40. *Penney and Allied Families*, pp. 81-82.

41. "Earl C. Sams Dies; Store Chain Head," *New York Times*, July 24, 1950, p. 17, col. 1; Batten Interview, July 8, 1986. Sams, who was survived by his wife Lula and daughters Gladys and Camile, was buried at Beechwood Cemetery in New Rochelle, N.Y., after funeral services at North Avenue Presbyterian Church in New Rochelle.

42. Ibid.

43. "Penney's: King of The Soft Goods," *Fortune*, September 1950, p. 101.

44. Ibid., p. 104; *American Chronicle*, p. 284.

45. "Penney's: King of The Soft Goods," p. 102. The chart comparing sales among the five largest nonfood retailers in America showed that Penney's had climbed from fourth place to third place between 1932 and 1950, overtaking Woolworths. However, Woolworths was a variety store chain and not as direct a competitor to Penney's as were Sears or Montgomery Ward.

46. Ibid., p. 101.

47. "Salesman Penney Sells Again," *Life*, May 14, 1951, pp. 51-56; "Like a Land Rush, Shoppers Say at Opening of Store," *The Indianapolis News*, February 22, 1951.

48. *Pay Day*, April 1952, pp. 10, 12. Sales were $1,035,201,519.

49. Ibid., p. 10.

50. "J.C. Penney Returns to the Town Where He Laid the Ground Work for His Vast Merchandising Empire Fifty Years Ago," *Kemmerer Gazette*, April 4, 1952.

51. *Penney and Allied Families*, pp. 74-76; "J.C. Penney Gives Famed Cattle Herd to U. of Missouri," *Torrington Telegram* (Wyoming), June 19, 1952; Batten Interview, July 8, 1986.

52. *Annual Report* 1953, pp. 1-2; *Annual Report* 1950, p. 1.

53. *Annual Report* 1953, pp. 1-2; *Annual Report* 1954, p. 1.

54. *Annual Report* 1954, p. 2.

55. Ibid., pp. 1-4.

56. Ibid., pp. 16-17; *Annual Report* 1942, pp. 16-17.

57. "Warehouses Out," *Business Week*, April 10, 1954, p. 133; "Special 75th Anniversary Edition," *Penney News*, March/April 1977, pp. 12-13.

58. Certificate of Incorporation of James C. Penney Foundation, Inc., Minutes of the Board of Directors of the James C. Penney Foundation, Inc., New York, N.Y. Hereafter referred to as Minutes, James C. Penney Foundation, Inc.

59. Minutes, James C. Penney Foundation, Inc., January 3, 1956, List of Contributions to Charitable Organizations. The list contained the following organizations and respective donations: New York City Y.M.C.A. For World Service, $50; National Council of the Churches of Christ in the U.S.A., $500; The Laymen's Movement for A Christian World, Inc., $500; Bertha A. Penney Memorial Methodist Church, $250; Methodist Church, Hamilton, Missouri, $250; International Society of Christian Endeavor, $25; Broadway Temple, Washington Heights Methodist Church, $200; Reorganized School District #R-2 of Caldwell County, Hamilton, Mo., $25,000; The National Foundation for Infantile Paralysis, $100; The White Plains Hospital Association, $100; Westchester Children's Association, Inc., $25; Allied Youth, Inc., $500; America's Future, $25; Freedom's Foundation, Inc., Valley Forge, Pa., $100; United Jewish Appeal of Greater New York, $100; Total, $27,725.

60. *Penney and Allied Families*, pp. 78-79.

61.   "A Party for Penney, Merchant Celebrates A Life By Golden Rule," *Life*, October 3, 1955, pp. 146-47.

62.   "500 Honor Penney on 80th Birthday," *New York Times*, September 18, 1955, p. 72, col. 1; "Penney, 80, Honored at 2 Celebrations," *New York Times*, September 17, 1955, p. 17, col. 8; "At 80, J.C. Penney Has Topped Alger," *New York Times*, September 16, 1955, p. 16, col. 1, and "James Cash Penney At 80," *New York Times*, September 16, 1955, p. 22, cols. 2-3, Editorial.

63.   "Back on the Upward Beam," *Business Week*, October 27, 1956, p. 196. *Business Week* prepared a report called the Composite of Regional Income Indexes, based on Federal Reserve District reports.

64.   *Annual Report* 1956, pp. 9, 14.

65.   "Chains Try Out National Media," *Business Week*, November 10, 1956, pp. 51-52. The article stated, "Consumer tastes, at all counts, are constantly being upgraded. The mail order houses and retail chains that have sold largely on price have recognized this for some time in the quality of goods they are offering. Now they figure that they must—through the prestige of being seen alongside top brand merchandise in national magazines—educate the public that shopping at, say, Penney's and buying Penney brands (at extremely competitive prices) is not basement store shopping."

66.   Ibid.; information courtesy of J.C. Penney Archives, CBS Audience Services and ABC Programming Information; Joseph E. Persico, *Edward R. Morrow, An American Original* (New York: McGraw-Hill Publishing Co., 1988), p. 350; "Mrs. Penney Loves Tucson Welcome," *Tucson Star*, September 1957, news clipping, Penney Family Files.

67.   "Penney Urges Revival of Self-Sufficiency," *Gazette* [Arizona], September 20, 1957, located in Penney Family Files; J.C. Penney, *Lines of A Layman*, Foreword by Daniel A. Poling.

68.   "Mrs. Penney Loves Tucson," Penney Family News Clippings File; "Penney Urges Revival of Self-Sufficiency," Penney Family File.

69.   "J.C. Penney Plans to Try Out Consumer Credit in a Few Stores," *Business Week*, September 14, 1957, p. 53.

70.   *Annual Report* 1957, p. 4; "J.C. Penney's Sales and Earnings in '57 Highest in Company's 56 Year History," *New York Times*, February 18, 1958, p. 41, col. 3; "Ward's Sales Up; Profit Off 17.2%," *New York Times*, March 25, 1958, p. 45, col. 7; "Sears' Sales Up; Net Falls 2.28%," *New York Times*, p. 37.

71.   Batten Interview, July 8, 1986.

MAIN STREET MERCHANT
TO SHOPPING MALL ANCHOR

The J.C. Penney Company was the last of the large nationwide retailers to offer credit. Selling for cash had been a fundamental policy of the company since its founding in 1902 and could be traced back to the Callahans' Golden Rule Store in Longmont. However, credit sales were the cornerstone of the new type of company Batten proposed in a memorandum he presented to Hughes and the Board of Directors in early 1957.

To help make this important decision, however, the company commissioned a comprehensive study on credit by the management consulting department of their accounting firm, Peat, Marwick, Mitchell & Co. A Peat, Marwick partner, Kenneth S. Axelson, was in charge of preparing the massive report that concluded the company should offer credit to its customers.[1] Although company officers agreed with its conclusions, the final decision required approval by the Board of Directors. Batten, a director since 1955, presided over the meeting when the historic decision was made to proceed with credit. He recalled Penney's exact words.

> This was a critical Board Meeting. I was at the head of the table, Mr. Hughes was on my left and Mr. Penney was on my right side. I told the Board Members because of the seriousness of the question involved, I wanted each member to speak. We wanted to hear each person's view even if they repeated what another member said. I said we will start on my left with Mr. Hughes and proceed around the table. I wanted Mr. Penney to have the benefit of all the other views. Mr. Hughes said he had reservations; he was not enthusiastic, but being realistic; on balance he said it was the right course of action to offer charge accounts. Every person around the table said the same thing in essence. They all had some reservations, but said it was necessary. By the time we came to Mr. Penney, the views were unanimous.

Now, I said to Mr. Penney, we want to hear from you. Mr. Penney said, "I really appreciated the opportunity to hear your views, the candor and the intensity with which you have spoken, but I have not heard anything new here today. All the arguments you have given I have heard before. They did not persuade me then and they do not persuade me now. I am still as opposed to credit as I ever was. It will increase our sales and our profits, I agree with that. My concern is not that. It has to do with something else. We all know there are times when sales and profits are hard to get and this puts pressure on management. It will come again. Without intending to do so you will get very aggressive in your selling, and you will end up encouraging people to buy things they can not afford and should not buy. By offering credit we encourage them to overbuy. With me, it is a moral issue of getting people in financial trouble."

Mr. Penney then turned to me and said, "The decision is very easy. You have to go into credit. You have no choice. I have another conviction and that is the people who are responsible have to follow their convictions. It is very clear you all believe in this very much. Therefore, you must do it." After Mr. Penney finished, we took the vote. Mr. Penney was the only Director to vote "No."[2]

In April 1958, Batten became the company's President and Chief Executive Officer; he was the fourth President in its 56-year history. Hughes, who had recommended that Batten succeed him, was Chairman of the Board until 1964. Penney remained on the Board as a director and was described in news articles as the company founder, former chairman and a director. His continuing work on the company's behalf helped transform the soft goods chain into the present-day company. Penney had a full schedule of store openings and company conventions to attend. He also commented publicly on the company's progress and was featured in news magazine stories with Batten.

However, Penney's daughters and Batten agreed Penney never changed his views about credit sales, and frankly preferred "straight cash dealings" all his life.[3] When the dramatic change occurred, though, Penney used his prestige and reputation to help the company explain the credit plan to its nearly 50 million customers and approximately 35,000 stockholders. The new policy naturally caused a great amount of comment inside and outside the company. Stockholders were reminded in early 1958 that the use of credit was only a test in a small group of stores. No final decision would be made until the test results were analyzed.[4] To reassure the company's long time cash customers, Batten publicly stated in June 1958 that credit was being offered as a "customer convenience but the traditional mark-up policy will be retained."[5]

Penney was equally concerned about loyal customers' reaction as the test was expanded to 144 more stores in fall 1959. Since its founding, company advertisements had stated customers did not pay for extra expenses caused by items such as bad debts from credit sales, delivery costs or expensive store furnishings. In 1960, before travelling to Kemmerer to celebrate his 85th birthday and to cut the ribbon at the newly remodeled "Mother Store," Penney's forthright views on credit appeared in news articles. He said, "Prices to cash customers will not be raised to carry the credit load. Those who want the privilege of buying on credit must pay for it."[6]

In fact, increasing numbers of Americans were willing to pay for the privilege of buying on credit. Results from the "test" stores satisfied company officers and directors, but it was not until 1962 that nationwide credit facilities were operating. Although it was the last major retailer to offer a company credit card, its record keeping system became a retailing industry "first." A new electronic data processing system developed by IBM meant thousands of accounts could be handled efficiently and two customer statements could be issued every second.[7] This credit system created in 1961 was a forerunner of the company's pioneering use of electronic data systems in its mail order catalog system, buying offices, distribution system, payroll and sales record keeping. To continue improving company communications, the company eventually established a satellite communications network system in 1982.[8] Computer systems and satellite communications were exactly what Batten intended the new company to have. He believed the Penney company's survival in the second half of the twentieth century depended on its "ability to recognize, and accept, the things our customers expect us to change—and the things our customers expect us never to change."[9] Trying to meet the "ever-changing demands of the consumer market" was Batten's goal.

In 1958, though, Batten faced a tremendous challenge to mobilize the resources of the far-flung chain, one of America's largest corporations with over 50,000 associates. He had to convince associates and managers, many whose entire careers had been spent with the company, as well as loyal customers, stockholders, financial analysts and bankers, of the soundness and feasibility of his plans. Batten said:

> We have to keep in mind that the J.C. Penney Company was a very successful company. It was not a turnaround situation I was inheriting. It is often more difficult to make changes in a very successful company than in one not doing so well. When you are successful there are hard facts, operating results, that people can point to. They ask, "Why change a winning combination? 'If it ain't broke, some say, why fix it?'" This creates a major attitudinal problem. Since attitude determines behavior, the first thing you have to deal with is attitude. In order to deal with attitude, you have to have something specific, a plan that can be examined, scrutinized, evaluated, criticized. You can not ask people to rally around a general idea. The first step was to develop a plan for the future and communicate it effectively to all the people who are going to have to implement it to get their commitment to it.[10]

While Batten prepared the all important "Strategic Plan" for the company's future, the company's origins in a remote western mining town were not forgotten. To help celebrate the company's 58th anniversary, the "Mother Store" in Kemmerer was completely remodeled. The grand opening was held on September 29, 1960. Penney and company officials began the celebration with breakfast at Hotel Kemmerer across the street from the store. Penney gave a public address from the bandstand in Triangle Park, and everyone, including several hundred local residents, walked to the store for the ribbon cutting ceremony. Penney stood and greeted customers and old friends for several hours.

The "hometown store" image seen in the 1960 Kemmerer ceremony was an important part of the company's otherwise sophisticated modern retailing system. This combination of traditional ideas and modern practices paralleled Penney's life in many ways. In 1960 the majority of company stores were still in small to medium size towns; store managers were leaders of local civic and business organizations; they greeted customers by name and worked side by side with associates. They were the final judges on merchandise selection and pricing. Stores were closed every Sunday, but the manager and several assistants were often inside working hard. Behind each store, however, was an increasingly efficient distribution system centered in Manhattan; improved operations and communications facilities, using electronic data systems, were in the planning stages.

In 1960 Penney was happiest visiting Kemmerer and greeting customers in stores across the country, or else working outdoors dressed in overalls on one of his Caldwell County farms. He continued to check sales figures in the Hamilton store and teach sales clerks how to sell merchandise and wrap packages. In Manhattan, though, he was a modern executive, dressed in a company private label brand dark blue suit, white shirt and bow tie. Several secretaries worked full time handling his correspondence and preparing schedules for Penney's speeches and trips to conventions and store openings. During the previous year he attended 59 store opening ceremonies in 24 states and travelled on company business almost 200 days covering over 60,000 miles. Penney also had delivered speeches to over 100 organizations, and appeared on 27 radio and television programs.[11]

In 1960, Penney's book *View from the Ninth Decade* was published. He dedicated the book to Caroline. As usual, Penney did not want to receive any special treatment from the company even though he was now 85 years old.

Batten explained:

> I had to use a subterfuge to get him to use a car. He was taking a bus to work on 34th Street from his apartment on Park Avenue. I was CEO then and knew Mr. Penney would not accept a car, but I was concerned about the crowded buses and if something should happen to him. However, we needed a car for some other uses—not for executives to ride in, but rather to meet and take people to airports, etc.
>
> I said to Mr. Penney, "We have a need for a car for Company use, so we are going to buy a car. We might as well pick you up in the morning and take you home at night." Mr. Penney said, "Are you buying this car for me?" Mr. Batten said, "I wouldn't buy a car just for you to ride in because I know you wouldn't accept it. But there is no point in your not using it. We are not incurring any extra expense because one of the guards who works here will pick you up and take you home." Mr. Penney agreed, but only because he was assured it was not a special car for him. It was either an Oldsmobile or a small Buick.[12]

Stories about Penney's frugality were almost legendary. This was partly because the examples contrasted so well with his increasing income. In 1958 Penney's income, which came mostly from dividend payments, was about $595,000 before income taxes and expenses. His net worth was approximately $1.7 million, according to a balance sheet statement prepared by his accountant. But according to this statement Penney only owned 2,666 shares of common stock of the company. Other stockholdings included 171,000 shares of Foremost Dairies, Inc. common stock, and 13,800 shares of Sterling Industries, Inc. common stock. By 1965, however, Penney reportedly owned 258,018 shares of the company's common stock, or one percent of the outstanding shares.[13] Between 1958 and 1965 Penney evidently made large purchases of company stock, or else the stockholdings reported in 1965 included amounts owned by other family members, or held in a family trust, while the 1958 statement did not. No matter what its source, his income was sufficient to pay $160,000 in 1958 for a waterfront estate overlooking Long Island Sound. He bought the fifteen-room mansion in Greens Farms, Connecticut at Caroline's request. He believed the property was overpriced but Penney could not refuse Caroline anything she really wanted.[14]

Caroline Penney's life was dedicated to taking care of her husband and children. In 1932 when several banks had sold the company stock Penney used as collateral for his philanthropic projects, she went on her own to the Board of Directors and asked the company to help Penney by lending him money. The directors would only agree to pay Penney a salary; some directors believed Penney had caused his own financial problems.[15]

During the 1930s and 1940s, Caroline was busy raising their two daughters. In the 1950s she began appearing more often with Penney at store openings and conventions and on television programs. She described her role to reporters as "I keep the home fires burning."[16] But Caroline, a director of the James C. Penney Foundation since its founding in 1954, did much more. She was actively involved in organizations that helped women and children. By the mid-1950s she was a member of the board of the Y.W.C.A. of New York and was active in the American Mothers Committee and Save the Children Federation. In 1958 on her recommendation the James C. Penney Foundation gave $10,000 to the Y.W.C.A. Building Fund. Earlier, she had also assisted in establishing the Meditation Room at the United Nations headquarters in Manhattan. In the mid-1960s, Caroline was an active member of the board of the World Service Committee of the National Board of the Y.W.C.A. and was a member of the Women's Committee of the Boy Scouts of America. As a life member of the Metropolitan Museum of Art and a patron of the Metropolitan Opera and Opera Guild, she increased her husband's interest in art and music.

Penney's life in his eighties had many facets to it. Through his daughters' interests he received first-hand reports of the social changes in the 1960s. Carol, who graduated from Stanford University in 1951 and had been elected to Phi Beta Kappa, had returned with her family to America and lived nearby. She participated in civil rights volunteer work in Mississippi in the mid-1960s, even though she had six young children. Mary Frances, who had received a doctorate degree in chemistry from St. Hilda's College, Oxford University in 1950, was balancing a career as headmistress of St. Paul's Episcopal School in Baltimore with raising her three children. Her husband, Dr. Philip Wagley, was a physician and professor at Johns Hopkins Hospital and Medical School.[17] Penney was proud that his daughters were continuing the family's tradition of community service.

Penney's travels to all sections of the country and discussions with his daughters kept him informed about social and economic changes in the 1960s. At this same time, the company was preparing its response to consumers' new needs. While the credit plan was expanding to nationwide coverage, Batten and his executive assistant Oakley S. Evans worked on refining a "Strategic Plan." They assessed the reasons for the company's great success and concluded, "Our basic reason for growth in the past was that the Company had targeted the right market and offered great values. It was very much in tune with working people's needs and work habits like thrift. That, and its basic policies, were the reason for the Company's success."[18] When they looked at the future, however, they saw a population shift to the suburbs; more affluent customers, more women working, less time for shopping, more traffic, and a society turning from "blue collar" to "white collar," where suits, dresses and sport clothes were more important.

Since the world was changing the company was in danger of being more in tune with the past than with the future. Batten said, "If we had only customers paying cash for soft goods in a store, we had to lose them to a competitor if they wanted credit, more selection, or to buy from a catalog. Once they go to a competitor, they may stay with them."[19] The Strategic Plan had two objectives, one defensive, one offensive. The company wanted to protect the customer base it already had in its 1,200 smaller stores by adding catalog sales to give customers access to additional merchandise lines. The company also wanted to expand its customer base by offering additional merchandise lines in new full-line department stores.

The company's goal was to turn itself into a general merchandiser selling everything families needed in soft goods and hard goods and providing many new services, including automotive service centers. Lee S. Moore, company sales manager, told a meeting of the Newspaper Advertising Executives Association in February 1963 that the company had a single goal, "completeness." It was preparing to sell major appliances made by General Electric Company's Hotpoint Division under the company private label; that fall, Goodyear Tire & Rubber Company tires, batteries and automobile accessories, also under a private label, would be ready for customers. The same *Business Week* article describing Moore's remarks noted that furniture, hardware, sporting goods, beauty salons and photographic studios would soon be in the company's full-line stores.[20] From the first, fashion was an important component of the Strategic Plan. In 1958, Batten had said the company would put more emphasis on developing "style lines" of merchandise because "that is where a very large and growing slice of our business is coming from."[21]

Overall the main elements the Strategic Plan developed in detail between 1958 and 1961 included having a mixture of small and large stores, with emphasis on developing new large full line stores in shopping centers, and entering new businesses, specifically discount stores, specialty stores, mail order catalog, specialty catalogs, cafeterias, financial services, and selected international markets.[22] However, implementing the Strategic Plan is another story with many different elements. Only the highlights of the Strategic Plan and some examples of how it transformed the company have been presented here.

The new merchandise lines being offered by the company required much larger stores, and real estate developers soon saw the full-line company stores as attractive "anchors" for large regional malls they were planning.[23] The company store at King of Prussia in Pennsylvania, which opened in August 1963, was the company's first newly designed full line department store. But the Audubon Store near Camden, New Jersey, had in fact preceded it by six months. Store #1473 at Black Horse Pike Shopping Center in Audubon, New Jersey was originally opened in November 1961. After being enlarged to 142,000 square feet and remodeled to handle new merchandise lines, in March 1963 it became the first operating full line store in the company's history.[24] Under the leadership of store manager Howard M. Evans, who had joined the company in 1940, Audubon became the most profitable store in the entire company in 1967 and 1968. Its success gave company leaders confidence in their new direction.

Evans exemplified the best management traditions of the company. He proved that management methods used to build morale and productivity in smaller stores could succeed in much larger settings. Evans, who was promoted to a Central Office executive position in 1969 and retired in 1982, said of his long career with the company:

> The highlight of my career had to be the almost ten years I spent at Audubon. I am very proud of the people we had there. Many skilled sales associates and senior sales associates provided stability for the departments and also helped train management associates. Many people who left Audubon have had successful careers. Certainly, Dolores Jones and Dottie Neiman were forerunners of women in management. Managing a large store like Audubon with its almost 600 people was not that much different from running a smaller store. Planning, organizing and executing are the important factors—not size. However, there is one more factor I've always considered when managing a store: I wanted to make sure everybody enjoyed coming to work.[25]

However, Evans knew from experience in earlier stores that having "a merchandise assortment that will satisfy the customer" was the other factor in managing a successful store. There could be "no substitute for customer satisfaction either in merchandise assortment or in service." He believed the "customer's entire shopping experience should be an enjoyable one."[26] The Audubon store received all the new merchandise lines, from the first paint and hardware center, to the most modern apparel for women. The Women's Fashion Department, managed by Dolores Jones, had dramatic display cases showing London designer Mary Quant's exclusive fashions for the company. In December 1966, Penney visited the Audubon store to personally congratulate Evans and his team of associates on their success.

By 1967, fashion merchandise lines like Mary Quant were considered the "draw" that brought more teenagers and their mothers to shop in company stores.[27] Once in the store, women also purchased the traditional staple items for their family, learned about the new merchandise lines, and used the automobile service centers. The company was depending on its reputation for quality and good prices to sell the newer items. But many more changes had occurred between 1961 and 1967, as the company implemented more of its Strategic Plan.

A major part of the Strategic Plan was to have a mail order catalog business to better compete with Sears and Montgomery Ward. In 1962 the company entered the mail order catalog business by purchasing a small computerized catalog company named General Merchandise Company located in Milwaukee, Wisconsin. The first company catalog appeared in fall 1963. By 1971 the catalog operations were profitable and in 1991 catalog sales totalled $3 billion of the company's total $16.2 billion sales. More than 10 million customers received the two general catalogs in 1991; 50 smaller specialty catalogs were also circulated.[28]

In 1964 Batten was named Chairman of the Board and continued as Chief Executive Officer. Ray Jordan became President; Hughes stayed as a director as did Penney. Penney and the Central Office moved to a 45-story new headquarters building at 1301 Avenue of the Americas in 1964.[29] In 1964, Penney had just returned from a trip to New Zealand and Australia, and he was looking forward to celebrating his 90th birthday at Greens Farms next year with his family. He told everyone he wanted to live to be 100 years old. He was still travelling 50,000 miles a year across the country to attend company conventions, store openings and also H.C.S.C. Club events. The H.C.S.C. Club, Inc., was an association of retired company management associates, and its members, all stockholders, were eager to visit with Penney and Caroline. After 1961 Penney was often accompanied on trips by Clifford D. Anderson who was the manager of the company's Educational and Consumer Relations department. Even though Penney's eyesight was failing, Penney continued to travel on the company's behalf as long as he was able.

Anderson witnessed the tremendous interest Penney had in young people and how, in turn, the young members of 4-H and DECA (Distributive Education Clubs of America) saw Penney as their hero and a "living legend." Penney was always invited to their youth conventions to give speeches. One DECA convention held in Houston, Texas in the mid-1960s stands out as an example of Penney's dedication. Because of airplane trouble in New York City, Penney had to wait several hours on the plane. When he finally arrived at the banquet hall, he told the group he had seriously considered canceling the trip and returning to the city, but "standing here and being with you, looking out at you young people, it would have been the greatest mistake of my life." Penney had received a standing ovation when he arrived at the banquet, which incidentally had been sponsored by Sears, Roebuck and Company.[30]

In 1965 when he was 90, Penney and Caroline enjoyed attending company conventions held in Colorado Springs, St. Louis, Pittsburgh, Dallas, San Francisco and New York. At his office in New York, Penney's executive secretary E. Virginia Mowry coordinated scheduling and oversaw the voluminous correspondence that arrived from retirees, associates, and the general public. Businessmen from foreign countries also came to see Penney. When he was not travelling or in his office, Penney enjoyed visits with his grandchildren who lived nearby, attended performances at the Metropolitan Opera with Caroline and guests, and took weekend trips to Greens Farms. Winter vacations were spent at Camelback Inn or the Arizona Biltmore in Phoenix. While in Arizona, Penney and Caroline visited many stores in the Phoenix area. Over the next several years, Penney maintained a similar schedule.[31]

The next two years, 1967 and 1968, were important years for the company as the Audubon store proved how profitable its new full line stores were. By the end of 1968 the company had 176 full line stores in operation, and 1,476 soft line stores. Total company sales were $3.4 billion; of this, credit sales were 35.5 percent. At its 176 full line stores, sales reached $1 billion for the first time while sales at its more numerous soft line stores were just over $2 billion.[32] In 1968 the company's future path seemed clear. Batten remained Chairman until 1974, and Cecil L. Wright was President from 1968 to 1972. With additional full line stores opening every year, sales and profits would increase rapidly. By the end of 1968, the company had become an accepted "anchor" store that developers wanted in their new regional malls to attract other merchants. To provide expansion funds, instead of using a revolving credit line, the company issued $125 million of 25-year convertible subordinated debentures.[33] The category of long term debt was now added to its balance sheet as the company went from being not leveraged before 1968 to being highly leveraged by the end of the 1970s.[34]

By 1977, ten years later, company sales had increased to $9.3 billion; its 460 full line stores accounted for $5.5 billion of this amount, while 1,226 soft line stores sold $2.24 billion of goods. Catalog sales were $1 billion, and its Belgium stores, Treasury discount stores, and Thrift Drug sales accounted for the remainder. In 1977, long term debt was $415 million. There were 83,000 stockholders, and 193,000 associates.[35] Great progress in sales had been made but net income of $295 million in 1977 was 3.1 percent of sales. This figure had been 3.3 percent in 1968, but had averaged about 2.7 percent during the ten-year interval. Net income as percent of sales had been significantly higher in previous decades, as high as 6 percent in the 1930s.[36] The search for profitability as sales increased motivated company leaders to later modify the initial Strategic Plan in the mid-1970s.

Penney hoped to live to the mid-1970s; his 100th birthday would be on September 16, 1975. At age 93 he continued to be actively interested in the company's progress, and he was greatly admired for his work by businessmen who voted him one of the "three greatest living American businessmen" in 1967.[37] About this time, Anderson brought together the National 4-H Foundation, the Penney company and the Penney family to jointly contribute to completely refurbishing the National 4-H Center headquarters in Chevy Chase, Maryland. The "J.C. Penney Hall" was dedicated in 1977. Besides offices, it contains a chapel dedicated to Penney by his family, a library with memorabilia of Penney, and a large mural in the entrance hallway by the artist Dean Fausett portraying Penney and his many interests.[38] Unfortunately, Penney did not live to see the new building.

Penney was still coming to his office three days a week when he was 95, but on December 26, 1970 he fell in his apartment. He was in the hospital recuperating from a fractured hip when he had a heart attack and died on February 12, 1971. It was a sad occasion for thousands of people inside and outside the company in addition to Caroline, his children and grandchildren. Penney's funeral was held at St. James Episcopal Church in Manhattan and he was buried at Woodlawn Cemetery in the Bronx. The funeral service was attended by 1,500 people who came from all over the country. Thousands of condolence messages were received, including telegrams from President Richard Nixon, and from government and business officials in America and from around the world. The Reverend Norman Vincent Peale gave the eulogy on the young man from Missouri, the son of a Populist politician and descendant of preachers, who grew up to become one of America's greatest merchants. The young boy who could not afford to attend college in 1893 had received 17 honorary degrees from colleges and universities by the time he died, as well as the highest awards given by the retailing and business community. What impressed Penney's admirers almost as much as his achievements was his optimistic personality, summed up once by Caroline simply as "he loved life and he thought young."[39]

Penney's estate was in excess of $25 million. Caroline and family members were the main beneficiaries. Trust funds were established for several relatives; Penney's philanthropies, colleges and universities that awarded him honorary degrees also received bequests from his estate.

NOTES

1. Batten Interview, July 8, 1986, p. 27.
2. Ibid., pp. 28-29.
3. Ibid., p. 27; Interviews with Penney Daughters.
4. *Annual Report* 1957, p. 5.
5. "Penney to Stress Style More," *New York Times*, June 3, 1958, p. 45, col. 2; Batten was pleased when a California Department of Consumer Affairs study made some time later compared credit plans and rated the company's plan as the fairest one. Interest was not charged until after the first 30 days, and then customers paid interest only on the balance due and not, as was customary at this time, on the full purchase price. Batten Interview, October 29, 1986, pp. 15-16.
6. "James Cash Penney Founder-Director J.C. Penney Co., 85 Years Old and Still Going Strong," *Kemmerer Gazette*, September 22, 1960; "First 'Outsider' on Penney Board," *New York Times*, May 27, 1959, p. 47, col. 2.
7. "Pittsburgh Credit Office Gets New IBM Data System," *Penney News*, September 1961. (*Penney News* was the successor to *Pay Day*, the company's in-house monthly newspaper.)
8. "Eighty Years of Service To America," *JCPenney Today*, Special Commemorative Edition, Summer 1982. (*JCPenney Today* was the successor to *Penney News*.)
9. William M. Batten, *The Penney Idea, Foundation for the Continuing Growth of the J.C. Penney Company* (New York: The Newcomen Society in North America, 1967), p. 18.
10. Batten Interview, October 29, 1986, pp. 15-16.
11. "James Cash Penney Founder-Director."
12. Batten Interview, July 8, 1986, p. 23.
13. J.C. Penney Balance Sheet at December 31, 1958, James C. Penney Foundation files; "Changes for a Penney," *Time*, May 28, 1965, pp. 95-96.
14. Batten Interview, July 8, 1986, pp. 23-24; "Penney Buys Westport Estate," *New York Times*, June 27, 1958, p. 14, col. 5.
15. Interviews with Penney Daughters.
16. "Mrs. Penney Loves Tucson Welcome."
17. Ibid.; *Penney and Allied Families*, pp. 87-89; Interviews with Penney Daughters.
18. Batten Interview, July 8, 1986, pp. 32-33.
19. Ibid.
20. "Penney Goes for 'Completeness,'" *Business Week*, February 2, 1963, p. 44.
21. "Penney to Stress Style More," p. 45, col. 2.
22. Batten Interview, July 8, 1986, pp. 35-36.
23. Ibid., pp. 32-33; John McDonald, "How They Minted the New Penney," *Fortune*, July 1967, p. 112.
24. "Howard Evans Living the Penney Idea," *JCPenney Today*, Special Edition, November 1982, pp. 22-23.
25. Ibid., p. 26.

26. Ibid.

27. "How They Minted the New Penney," p. 113.

28. *JCPenney, An American Legacy. A 90th Anniversary History* (J.C. Penney Co., Inc., 1992), pp. 25, 29.

29. J.C. Penney Milestones (J.C. Penney Co., Inc.), p. 4.

30. Interview with Clifford D. Anderson, March 12, 1986.

31. "J.C. Penney Views Life—Hopes to Be One Hundred," *The Arizonian,* April 11, 1968, news clipping, Penney Family Files.

32. *Annual Report* 1977, pp. 30-31.

33. *Annual Report* 1968, p. 6.

34. Ibid., p. 13; J.C. Penney Annual Management Meeting 1979, p. 27. The company's debt to equity ratio was 1.36 in 1979, and the company had more debt in relation to total capitalization than other retailers, according to Kenneth S. Axelson, the company's Director of Finance and Public Affairs.

35. *Annual Report* 1977, p. 30.

36. Ibid., pp. 30-31; *Annual Reports* 1935-1957. In 1936 net income as percent of sales was 6.64; in 1941, it was 4.53; in 1954, it was 3.94; in 1957 it was 3.8.

37. "Top Businessmen—As Voted by 500 Leaders," *U.S. News & World Report,* July 17, 1967, p. 67.

38. Anderson Interview.

39. "The Last of the Merchant Princes Is Dead," *Penney News,* Special Edition, March 1971; "Mrs. Penney Minding Store," *Sun-Sentinel* [Palm Beach, Fla.], March 7, 1975, news clipping, Penney Family Files.

RETURN TO KEMMERER: AN EPILOGUE

The company James Cash Penney founded in 1902 had changed in many respects by the time he died in 1971. From a small outpost of the 1890s Golden Rule Store chain, the Kemmerer store had become the "Mother Store" of one of the largest corporations in America. In 1971 there were 162,000 associates, 270 full line stores in shopping malls, over 1,300 soft line stores, and sales of $4.8 billion. Credit sales were an accepted way of doing business.[1]

The principles of The Penney Idea, the Golden Rule and the H.C.S.C. motto that inspired the small group of western entrepreneurs in the first quarter of the twentieth century, however, were the same ideals that motivated new company leaders in the last quarter of the twentieth century. In the mid-1960s, Batten had said The Penney Idea was the foundation for the continuing growth of the company. Under Chairman of the Board Donald V. Seibert from 1974 to 1983 and Chairman of the Board William R. Howell from 1983 to the present, the company undertook more studies to meet the "ever-changing demands of the consumer market," and many changes resulted.[2] Under Howell's leadership, the company has been transformed from a general merchandiser into a national department store that has more space in shopping malls in the 1990s than any other retailer, almost 85 million square feet. In 1990, the company's sales were $16.4 billion and net income was $577 million, making it the nation's fourth largest mass merchandiser.[3] An historic event occurred two years earlier in 1988 when the company moved its headquarters to Dallas, Texas from New York City, where it had been located since 1914. The new headquarters building located in Plano, a suburb of Dallas, will open in spring 1993.

The company's heritage from Penney is seen in its commitment to offer the best possible values on merchandise, having outstanding store personnel, sharing profits with almost 100,000 associates, and serving local communities through charitable contributions and community involvement.

To celebrate its 90th anniversary, the company's annual meeting of stockholders was held in Kemmerer, now a town of 3,020 residents, in May 1992. Howell told the audience of several hundred people who came from across the country:

> We have returned to Kemmerer to honor and commemorate our founder, James Cash Penney. It was in this community that Mr. Penney established his first store and adopted the four principles on which our company was founded: honor, confidence, service, and cooperation.
>
> We have come here to renew that sense of vigor and freshness Mr. Penney displayed in every aspect of his life and to be in touch with our roots in a very real way. We know we will leave here inspired with a fresh sense of determination to take our company in the next century at least as far as we've come since Mr. Penney opened for business in 1902.[4]

Certainly memories of Penney greeting customers and standing behind the counter in the "Mother Store" even when he was 85 years old, remain strong in southwestern Wyoming. In 1978 the wood frame cottage where Penney, Berta, Roswell and J.C., Jr. lived from 1903 to 1909 and the nearby site of his second store were designated a National Historic Landmark district. In 1982, after a combined effort by town and state officials, the company, Penney's family, H.C.S.C. Club members and many friends, the restored and refurbished home was officially dedicated and opened to the public as a museum and tribute to Penney's retailing roots in Wyoming. In Missouri, the town of Hamilton had undertaken a similar cooperative effort and built the modern J.C. Penney Memorial Library and Museum to honor their native son. The dedication ceremony was held on April 11, 1976.[5] However, an event that symbolized the changes brought by modern highways and shopping malls was the 1981 closing of store #500 in Hamilton, now a town of 1,700 residents.[6]

Penney's great interest in the company's progress was maintained by Caroline who enjoyed participating in the company's 75th and 80th anniversary celebrations, and attended many holiday events at the Central Office in Manhattan. She represented the family at the dedication ceremonies in Hamilton in 1976, in Chevy Chase, Maryland in 1977 for the National 4-H Center's "J.C. Penney

Hall," and in Kemmerer in 1982. Caroline was president of the family foundation from 1971 to 1979 when she turned control over to her daughters. However, she regularly attended H.C.S.C. conventions until she was 88 years old in 1984. When Caroline died on March 17, 1992, it was the end of an era. She was the last direct link to her husband's work on the company's behalf.

Today in the 1990s, the company he founded continues Penney's goal of providing good service to the public and Penney's children and grandchildren are carrying forward the family tradition of helping improve other people's lives through the family foundation and their careers. James Cash Penney, the Golden Rule Merchant, certainly fulfilled his father's prediction that "Jim will make it, I like the way he has started out."

NOTES

1.   *Annual Report* 1977, p. 31. Ten Year Financial Summary.

2.   Batten, *Penney Idea*, p. 18.

3.   *JCPenney, An American Legacy*, p. 29; *Annual Report* 1991, p. 32.

4.   "JCPenney Returns to Its Roots for Annual Meeting," PR Newswire, May 14, 1992.

5.   "The J.C. Penney Homestead," *JCPenney Today*, Special Commemorative Edition, Summer 1982; "Dedication of the J.C. Penney Memorial Library and Museum," *Advocate-Hamilton*, Mo., April 7, 1976, section B.

6.   David P. Garino, "Town to Lose Favorite Son's Favorite Store," *Wall Street Journal*, May 28, 1981, p. 27. Since 1981, Hamilton residents established a J.C. Penney Park in town; the cottage where Penney was born was recently relocated to this park, said Dennis Cox, managing editor of *The Hamilton-Advocate*. Cox said Hamilton hopes to have a J.C. Penney Co. catalog store sometime in the future.

SELECTED BIBLIOGRAPHY

Section I. Selected Manuscript Collections

J.C. Penney Company Historical File. J.C. Penney Company Central Office, New York City. Referred to as PHF in chapters one to eleven, which were completed in 1980. In 1992 the collection described below is known as the JCPenney Archives and is filed in boxes at the headquarters offices of the J.C. Penney Company, Inc., Plano, Texas.

This extensive collection of personal and business records, which originally filled 23 file drawers and cabinets, was the major source of material for the biography. In addition to letters and business artifacts, photographs and Company publications are also catalogued. While not complete in every respect, it is the major source on J.C. Penney and the Company he founded. Materials range in time from Penney's ancestors to recent Company activities.

Eben Fine Collection. Western Historical Collections, University of Colorado at Boulder.

This was useful for descriptions of northwest central Missouri in the 1870s and 1880s.

L.H. Guldman Papers. Western Historical Collections, University of Colorado at Boulder.

An important source for the history of dry goods retailing in Denver. L.H. Guldman was owner of the Golden Eagle Department Store which operated in Denver from the 1880s to the 1930s.

The Western History Research Center of The University of Wyoming.

The Center's Wyoming Clipping File contains numerous articles on J.C. Penney's visits to Kemmerer.

*Section II. Selected J.C. Penney Company
Publications and Records*

Annual Reports. J.C. Penney Company, Inc.

Batten, William M. *The Penney Idea. Foundation for the Continuing Growth of The J.C. Penney Company*. New York: The Newcomen Society in North America, 1967. Pp. 24.

Bushnell, George H. *The Building of a Merchant*. New York: J.C. Penney Co., 1924.

Bushnell, George H. *The Creative Process in Business. Address Delivered at the April and May 1923 Conventions of the J.C. Penney Company*. New York: Clark & Fritts, c. 1923.

Bushnell, George H. *Fundamentals in the Development of Our Organization*. New York: J.C. Penney Co., 1921.

Business Training Course. Vols. I & II. Lessons One to Seventeen. New York: J.C. Penney Co., 1921.

Day, Lew V. *The Manager: His Duties and Responsibilities*. New York: J.C. Penney Co., 1920.

The Dynamo. New York: J.C. Penney Co., April 1917-April 1932. Vols. I-XVI. Note: Only the April 1932 issue of Vol. XVI was published.

"Eighty Years of Service to America. A JCPenney Celebration." *JCPenney Today*. Special Commemorative Edition. Summer 1982.

Evans, Howard. "Living the Penney Idea." *JCPenney Today.* Special Edition. November 1982.

"James Cash Penney, September 16, 1975 - February 12, 1971." *Penney News.* Special Edition. March 1971.

JCPenney Annual Management Meeting 1979. "The Professional Merchant." New York: J.C. Penney Co., c. 1980.

JCPenney, An American Legacy. A 90th Anniversary Issue. New York: J.C. Penney Co., 1992.

Mark-Up and Turnover. New York: J.C. Penney Co., September 1924.

Minutes of the Meetings of the Board of Directors of the J.C. Penney Company. Vols. I & II, Utah Corporation, 1913-1925. Vols. I-III, Delaware Corporation, 1925-c. 1933. Legal Department, J.C. Penney Co.

Penney News Special 75th Anniversary Edition. March-April 1977.

Sams, Earl C. *Reciprocity in the Business Organization.* New York: Madison Square Press, 1922. Pp. 60.

Sams, Earl C. *What Is the Chain Store's Responsibility to Its Community?* New York: J.C. Penney Co., 1929.

Sams, Earl C. *Yesterday, To-day and To-morrow. Address Delivered at the Dallas and Tulsa Sessions of the Spring Convention, 1929.* New York: J.C. Penney Co., 1929.

Store Meeting Manual for 1927. New York: J.C. Penney Co., 1927.

"W.M. Batten, Architect of the New JCPenney Company." *Penney News.* Special Edition. October 1, 1974.

Section III. Selected State and Federal Records

Federal Census Records, 1840-1900: Colorado, Illinois, Kentucky, Missouri and Wyoming. National Archives, Washington, D.C.

Incorporation Records, 1902, 1904, 1911. Wyoming State Archives.

Index to Compiled Service Records of Confederate Soldiers who served in organizations from Missouri. National Archives, Washington, D.C.

Pension Records for Union Service. National Archives, Washington, D.C.

Recorder of Deeds Offices: Boulder, Colo.; Kingston, Mo.; Peoria, Ill.; Salt Lake City, Utah; Evanston, Wyo.

Register of Deaths, Salt Lake County, Utah. Mormon Genealogical Library, Salt Lake City, Utah.

Revolutionary War Pension Records. National Archives, Washington, D.C.

Section IV. Selected Interviews
and Correspondence

Anderson, Clifford D. rEx.* New York, N.Y. Interview, March 1986.

Batten, William M. rEx. New York, N.Y. Interviews, July and October 1986.

Burns, Harry J. rPM. Englewood, Colo. Interview, September 1978.

Crayne, Vern. rPM. Lakewood, Colo. Interview, September 1978.

---

* Note: rPM indicates retired J.C. Penney Co. store managers, and rEx indicates retired J.C. Penney Co. executive.

Estes, Mrs. Donald J. Longmont, Colo. Correspondence, 1977-78.

Faulkner, Earl D. rPM. Estes Park, Colo. Interview, September 1978.

Ferguson, Charles. rPM. Englewood, Colo. Interview, September 1978.

Foote, Donald F. rPM. Loveland, Colo. Correspondence and Interview, 1977-78.

Fox, Mrs. Ina Ramsay. Montecito, Calif. Taped Answers to Questionnaire, January 1978.

Gross, Harold G. rPM. Denver, Colo. Interview, September 1978.

Guyer, Carol Penney. New York, N.Y. Interview, February 1986.

Hagen, Paul P. Executive Director, Penney Retirement Community, Penney Farms, Fla. Interview, April 1979.

Hayden, Thomas. Chillicothe, Ill. Interview, August 1979.

Hood, John, and Hood, Emmett. New York, N.Y. Interviews, June 1979.

Jenkins, Ray M. rPM, rEx. Denver, Colo. Interview, September 1978.

McDonough, Mrs. Frank. Longmont, Colo. Correspondence, 1977-78.

Miller, Mrs. George D. Los Angeles, Calif. Correspondence, 1977-79.

Morgan, Phil. rPM. Loveland, Colo. Interview, September 1978.

Murphy, Paul. rPM. Chillicothe, Ill. Interview, August 1979.

Orr, Colonel Leonard. Hamilton, Mo. Correspondence, 1978.

Overstreet, Mrs. Marguerite E. Hamilton, Mo. Interview, 1978.

Owens, Mrs. Mary A. Humansville, Mo. Interview and Correspondence, 1978-80.

Peak, Mrs. A.B. Salt Lake City, Utah. Correspondence and Interview, 1977-78.

Penney, R.E. rPM. Modesto, Calif. Telephone Interviews, 1977-78.

Saltzman, Sylvia. Librarian, The Field Library, Inc. Peekskill, N.Y. Correspondence, March 1978.

Schmidt, Ted. rPM. Ogden, Utah. Interview, September 1978.

Vaughan, Mrs. Nelson M. Alumni Secretary, The Hill School, Pottstown, Pa. Correspondence, 1978.

Wagley, Mary Frances Penney. Baltimore, Md. Interview, December 1986.

Wright, Maurice J. rPM, rEx. Salt Lake City, Utah. Interview, September 1978.

*Section V. Selected Books and Articles
by and about J.C. Penney*

Albus, Harry J. *Mr. Penney, The Life of J.C. Penney in Story Form.* Grand Rapids: William B. Eerdsmans, 1961.

Barmash, Isadore. "J.C. Penney, Founder of Chain Stores, Dies at 95." *The New York Times* Biographical Edition, 18 February 1971, 389-91.

Beasley, Norman. *Main Street Merchant. The Story of the J.C. Penney Company.* New York, Toronto: Whittlesey House, McGraw-Hill, 1948.

Booth, Bertha. "Brief Sketch of the Life of J.C. Penney." *Hamilton-Advocate-Hamiltonian* (Hamilton, Mo.), 7 April 1938, and ff. In three parts.

"Common Stocks Undervalued on Earnings and Prospects." *The Magazine of Wall Street*, July 17, 1937, 422-24.

"Democratic Head of Great Chain Store Organization Supports Hoover." *Manufacturers Record* (Baltimore) 27 September 1928, 51.

Dickinson, Roy. "Penney's Plan." *Good Housekeeping* 71 (October 1920): 55, 85-90.

Dorsey, C.P. "Missourians Abroad—No. 15, James Cash Penney," *Missouri Historical Review* 21 (July 1927): 545-61.

Gates, Ward. "Marchandising Companies Stimulated by Wave of Public Buying." *The Magazine of Wall Street*, December 7, 1935, 212-13, 230.

"How a Chain of Stores Is Run—Buy and Sell for Cash, Have No Deliveries, and Do a Business of Millions Yearly." *New York Times*, 1 February 1914, Sec. 8, p. 10.

Hunter, Pat. "Mrs. J.C. Penney Leads Full Life." *The Sunday Star-Bulletin & Advertiser* (Honolulu), February 11, 1968.

J.C. Penney Memorial Library and Museum Hamilton, Missouri, Honoring the 100th Anniversary of a Native Son—September 16, 1975. Privately printed, 1975. Pp. 12.

"J.C. Penney: Getting More from the Same Space." *Business Week*, August 18, 1975, 80-88.

"J.C. Penney's Fashion Gamble." *Business Week*, January 16, 1978, 66-74.

"James C. Penney, Who Runs Seventy Stores." *System. The Magazine of Business* 25 (June 1914): 637-40.

McDonald, John. "How They Minted the New Penney." *Fortune*, July 1967.

"The Memo that Moved a Mountain." *Business Week*, December 12, 1964, 69-74.

Miller, Jane. "New York Woman Researches Local J.C. Penney History." *The Chillicothe Bulletin*, 23 August 1979, 2.

Penney and Allied Families, Genealogical and Biographical. New York: National Americana Publications, 1963.

Penney, J.C. "The Bible in Business." *The Saturday Evening Post*, 22 September 1928, 105.

Penney, J.C. *Fifty Years with the Golden Rule.* New York: Harper & Brothers, 1950.

Penney, J.C. "It Is One Thing to Desire—and Another to Determine." *The American Magazine* 88 (August 1919): 51, 95-100.

Penney, J.C. *J.C. Penney, The Man with a Thousand Partners. An Autobiography of J.C. Penney as Told to Robert W. Bruere.* New York: Harper & Brothers, 1931.

Penney, J.C. *Lines of a Layman.* Great Neck, New York: Channel Press, 1956.

Penney, J.C. *View from the Ninth Decade. Jottings from a Merchant's Daybook.* New York: Thomas Nelson & Sons, 1960.

"Penney's, King of the Soft Goods." *Fortune*, September 1950.

Poling, Daniel A. "James Cash Penney—A Personality." *Christian Herald*, 23 August 1927, 3.

Poling, Daniel A. "President J.C. Penney!" *Christian Herald*, 7 January 1928.

Plumb, Beatrice. *J.C. Penney, Merchant Prince. A Biography of a Man Who Built a Business Empire Based on the Golden Rule.* Minneapolis: T.S. Denison, 1963.

Saunders, John Monk. "The Man with a Thousand Partners." *The American Magazine* 98 (October 1924): 19, 171-77.

Section VI. Selected Books and Pamphlets

Ballenger, Kenneth. *Miami Millions. The Dance of the Dollars in the Great Florida Land Boom of 1925.* Miami: Franklin Press, 1936.

Barrett, Glen. *Kemmerer, Wyoming, The Founding of an Independent Coal Town, 1897-1902.* Kemmerer, Wyo.: Quealy Services, 1972.

Blakey, Arch Frederic. *Parade of Memories. A History of Clay County, Florida.* Jacksonville, Fla.: Clay County Board of County Commissioners, 1976.

Boorstin, Daniel J. *The Americans: The Democratic Experience.* New York: Random House, 1973.

Boyd, Jesse L. *A History of Baptists in America Prior to 1845.* New York: American Press, 1957.

Buck, Solon Justus. *The Granger Movement.* Cambridge: Harvard University Press, 1913.

Chandler, Aldred D., Jr. *Strategy and Structure, Chapters in the History of American Industrial Enterprise.* Cambridge: MIT Press, 1969.

Cochran, Thomas C. *American Business in the Twentieth Century.* Cambridge: Harvard University Press, 1972.

Commager, Henry Steele. *The American Mind. An Interpretation of American Thought and Character Since the 1880s.* New Haven: Yale University Press, 1950.

Cooper, Arthur. *Visitors' Pocket Guide to Denver*. Denver: A.J. Ludditt, 1896.

Darby, William Dermot. *Story of the Chain Store*. New York: Dry Goods Economist, 1928.

Emmet, Boris, and Jeuck, John E. *Catalogues and Counters. A History of Sears, Roebuck and Company*. Chicago: University of Chicago Press, 1951.

Greene, Theodore P. *America's Heroes, The Changing Models of Success in American Magazines*. New York: Oxford University Press, 1970.

Hacker, Louis. *The World of Andrew Carnegie 1865-1901*. Philadelphia: J.B. Lippincott 1968.

Hannibal & St. Joseph Railroad. *600,000 Acres of Hannibal & St. Joseph Railroad Lands in North Missouri*. Hannibal, Mo.: Hannibal & St. Joseph RR Office, 1860.

Hansen, Harry, ed. *Colorado. A Guide to the Highest State*. New York: Hastings House, 1970 ed.

Hicks, John D. *The Populist Revolt*. University of Nebraska Press, 1961 ed.

Historical Statistics of the United States, Colonial Times to 1957. Washington, D.C.: U.S. Department of Commerce, Bureau of the Census, 1960.

History of Caldwell and Livingston Counties, Missouri. National Historical Co., 1886.

History of Hickory, Polk, Cedar, Dade and Barton Counties, Missouri. Chicago: Goodspeed Publishing, 1889.

Hofstadter, Richard. *The Age of Reform. From Bryan to F.D.R.*. New York: Vintage Books, Random House, 1955.

Hughes, Jonathan. *The Vital Few, American Economic Progress and Its Protagonists.* London: Oxford University Press, 1965, 1973.

Hugus, J.W. and Company. *Souvenir History 1908.* Denver: Press of the Smith-Brooks Company, c. 1908.

Humansville, Missouri 1872-1972, Centennial. Humansville-Lincoln-Cole-Camp, Mo.: Williams Press, c. 1973.

Jackson, Kenneth T. *Crabgrass Frontier. The Suburbanization of the United States.* New York: Oxford University Press, 1985.

James, Gorton. *Profit Sharing and Stock Ownership for Employees.* New York: Harper & Brothers 1926. Note: On page 129 James describes the J.C. Penney Company plan as a unique attempt to win back the strong personal incentive of the partnership while combining it with the economics of the large organization and the marketing advantages of the chain stores.

Jehring, J.C. *Profit Sharing, The Capitalist Challenge.* Evanston, Ill.: Profit Sharing Research Foundation, 1956.

Jennings, Eugene E. *An Anatomy of Leadership.* New York, etc.: McGraw-Hill, 1972; 1st pub. 1960.

Jillson, William Rouse. *Old Kentucky Entries and Deeds—Jefferson Entries.* Louisville, Ky.: Filson Club Club Publications: No. 34, 1926, reprint ed., Baltimore: Genealogical Publishing, 1978.

Jillson, William Rouse. *A Transylvania Trilogy.* Frankfort, Ky.: Kentucky State Historical Society, 1932.

Kidwell, Claudia B., and Christman, Margaret C. *Suiting Everyone: The Democratization of Clothing in America.* Washington, D.C.: The Smithsonian Institution, National Museum of History and Technology, 1974.

Kowinski, William Severini. *The Malling of America. An Inside Look at the Great Consumer Paradise.* New York: William Morrow, 1985.

Lebhar, Godfrey M. *Chain Stores in America 1859-1950*. New York: Chain Store Publishing Corp., 1952.

Levinson, Daniel J. *The Seasons of a Man's Life*. New York: Ballantine Books, 1978.

Life More Abundant. The Story of a Retirement Community at Penney Farms, Florida. Penney Farms, Fla.: Penney Retirement Community Association, 1973.

McKee, Lewis W., and Bond, Lydia K. *A History of Anderson County 1780-1936*. Frankfort, Ky.: Roberts Publishing, c. 1936.

McNeil, D.S. *The Story of Humansville*. Humansville, Mo.: Star-Leader Print, 1934.

March, David D. *The History of Missouri*. Vol. 1. New York: Lewis Historical Publishing Co., 1967.

Martin, Albro. *Enterprise Denied. Origis of the Decline of American Railroads, 1897-1917*. New York: Columbia University Press, 1971.

Metzger, B.L. *Profit Sharing in Perspective, In American Medium Sized and Small Business*. Evanston, Ill.: Profit Sharing Research Foundation, 1966.

Morris, Richard B., ed. *Encyclopedia of American History*. New York: Harper & Row, 1956.

Nichols, John P. *Skyline Queen and The Merchant Prince. The Woolworth Story*. New York: Trident Press, 1973.

Owens, Mrs. Mary A. *My Town*. Lincoln, Mo.: Williams Press, 1976.

Owens, Richard N. *Owens on Business Organization and Combination*. Rev. ed. New York: Prentice-Hall, 1940.

Parker, Nathan H. *Missouri As It Is in 1867*. Philadelphia: J.B. Lippincott, 1867.

Paxton, W.M. *Annals of Platte County, Missouri.* Kansas City: Hudson-Kimberly, 1897.

Paxton, W.M. *The Paxtons, We Are One!* Platte City, Mo.: Landmark Print., 1903.

Philipsborn, The Outer Garment House—Chicago, Fall and Winter 1917-1918. Chicago: Philipsborn, 1917.

Porter, Glenn. *The Rise of Big Business, 1860-1910.* New York: Thomas Y. Crowell, 1973.

Rader, Perry S. *Civil Government and History of Missouri.* Columbia, Mo.: E.W. Stephens, 1898.

Ray, Joseph. *Practical Arithmetic by Induction and Analysis.* Cincinnati: Sargent, Wilson & Hinkle; New York: Clark & Maynard, 1857.

Redford, Polly. *Billion Dollar Sandbar.* New York: E.P. Dutton, 1970.

Report of the Directors of the Hannibal & St. Joseph Railroad Co.. New York: John Polhemus Printer, 1878.

The Resources and Attractions of Colorado for the Home Seeker, Capitalist and Tourist. St. Louis: Woodward & Tiernan, 1893.

Rodgers, Daniel T. *The Work Ethic in Industrial America 1850-1920.* Chicago: University of Chicago Press, 1974, 1978.

Royse, Noble Kilby. *A Manual of American Literature Designed for the Use of Schools of Advanced Grades.* Rev. ed. Philadelphia: Cowperthwait, c. 1883.

Rules and Regulations and Course of Study of the Hamilton Public Schools 1892-93, By Order of the Board of Education. Hamilton, Mo.: Advocate Book and Job Print., 1892.

St. Vrain Valley Historical Association. *They Came to Stay, Longmont, Colorado 1858-1920*. Centennial Edition. Longmont, Colo.: Longmont Printing Company, 6/1/1971.

Scott, Sharon. *Chillicothe, The Way We Grew*. Chillicothe, Ill.: Chillicothe Historical Society, c. 1978.

Scull, Penrose. *From Peddlers to Merchant Princes, A History of Selling in America*. Chicago: Follett, 1967.

Semple, Robert B. *A History of the Rise and Progress of the Baptists in Virginia*. Richmond, Va.: John O'Lynch, 1810.

Shely, Forest Wyatt. *This Is Goshen, 1812-1962*. Lawrenceburg, Ky.: By the Author, 1964.

Spencer, J.H. *A History of Kentucky Baptists from 1769 to 1885*. 2 vols. Cincinnati, 1886.

Steele, Joel Dorman. *A Brief History of the United States*. New York: A.S. Barnes, 1885.

Steen, Herman. *The O.W. Fisher Heritage*. Seattle: Frank McCaffrey 1961.

Stone, Elizabeth Arnold. *Uinta County, Its Place in History*. Laramie Printing Co., 1924.

Sweet, William Warren. *Religion on the American Frontier. The Baptists, 1783-1830. A Collection of Source Material*. New York: Cooper Square, 1964.

Townsend, Calvin. *A Shorter Course in Civil Government*. New York: American Book Co., 1892.

Wyllie, Irvin G. *The Self-Made Man in America. The Myth of Rags to Riches*. New York: Free Press, 1954.

Wyoming. A Guide to Its History, Highways and People. American Guide Series. New York: Oxford University Press, 1941.

Zion Cooperative Mercantile Institution. *ZCMI, America's First Department Store: The One Hundredth Year 1868-1968.* Salt Lake City: ZCMI, 1968.

Section VII. Selected Periodicals and Newspapers

The Anderson News (Lawrenceburg, Ky.), 31 May 1962, 8 August, 1 September, 3 November 1977.

Boulder Daily Camera (Boulder, Colo.), 1891-1893.

Bradstreet's Commercial Reports (New York), 1878-1915.

Chain Store Age (New York), 1925-1930.

Chillicothe Bulletin (Chillicothe, Ill.), 1878-1893, 27 December 1940.

Clevenger, Homer. "The Farmers' Alliance in Missouri. *Missouri Historical Review* 30 (October 1944): 24-44.

Colorado Prospector (Denver), *Historical Highlights from Early Day Newspapers.* Vol. 5, No. 8.

Denver Dry Goods Company. Spring and Summer 1903 Catalogue.

Deseret Evening News (Salt Lake City, Utah), 1909-1911.

Dry Goods Chronicle and Fancy Goods Review (New York), March 1893, February 1898.

Dun, Barlow & Co. *The Mercantile Agency Reference Book (New York),* 1873.

Dun, R.G. & Company. *The Mercantile Agency Reference Book (New York)*, 1878-1915.

Farmers' Advocate (Hamilton, Mo.), 1890-1897.

Gates, Paul W. "The Railroads of Missouri, 1850-1870." *Missouri Historical Review* 26 (January 1932): 126-41.

Hamilton News-Graphic (Hamilton, Mo.), 1886-1897.

The Hamiltonian (Hamilton, Mo.), 1878-1897.

Herald, Morrell. "Business Thought in the Twenties: Social Responsibility." *American Quarterly* 13 (1961): 126-39.

Johnson, Crosby. "History of Caldwell." *An Illustrated Historical Atlas of Caldwell County, Missouri*. Philadelphia: Edwards Brothers, 1876: 10.

The Kemmerer Camera (Kemmerer, Colo.), 1902-1909.

Longmont Ledger (Longmont, Colo.), 1889-1905.

Miami (Fla.) Herald. December 1924; June to December 1930.

The Weekly Pocatello Tribune (Pocatello, Id.), 1900-1902.

Ressequie, Harry E. "Alexander Turney Stewart and the Development of the Department Store, 1823-1876." *Business History Review* 39 (1965): 301-22.

Sears, Roebuck & Co. *1908 Catalogue No. 117, The Great Price Maker*. Reprint Edition. Edited by J.J. Shroeder, Jr. Northfield, Ill.: DBI Books, c. 1969.

Signs of the Times (Mt. Vernon and Middletown, NY), 1832-1890.

Trow's General Directory of the Boroughs of Manhattan and Bronx City of New York, 1910-1920.

INDEX